BUDDY BITES THE BULLET!

BUDDY BITES THE BULLET!

VOL. VI
THE COMPLETE
BUDDY BRADLEY
STORIES FROM
HATE!

BY
PETER BAGGE

FANTAGRAPHICS BOOKS

7563 Lake City Way NE
Seattle, WA 98115

Editorial Co-Ordinbation by Kim Thompson
Design and Art Direction by Ryan Frederiksen
Inking by Jim Blanchard
Coloring by Joanne Bagge
Computer Coloring by Jeff Johnson and Rhea Patton
Cover Colors by Joanne Bagge and Rhea Patton
Published by Gary Groth and Kim Thompson

The material in this collection originally appeared in Hate #22, 26-30.

First Fantagraphics Books edition: March, 2001
Printed in Canada

ISBN 1-56097-415-X

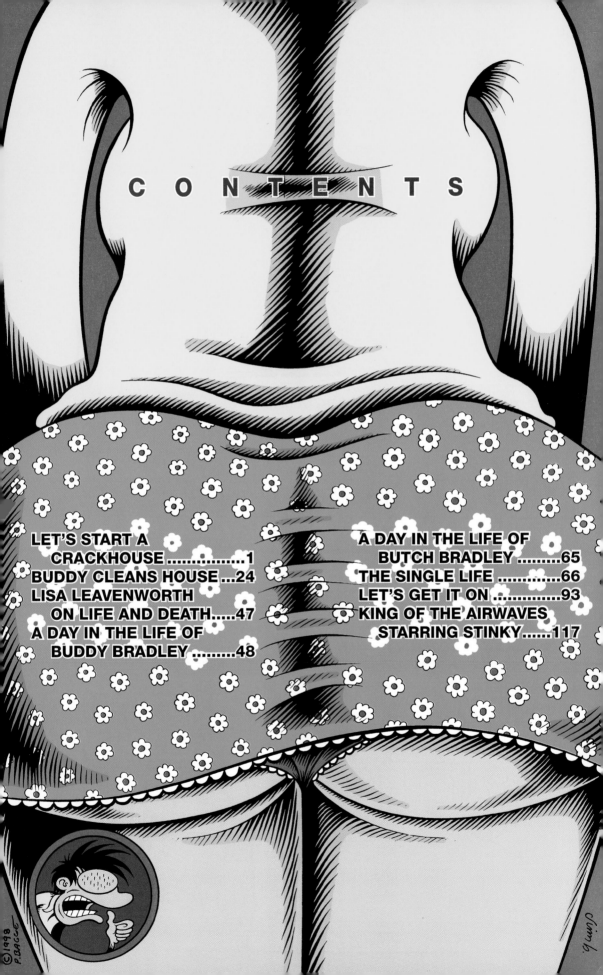

C O N T E N T S

© 1998
P. BAGGE

MEET THE CAST OF HATE:

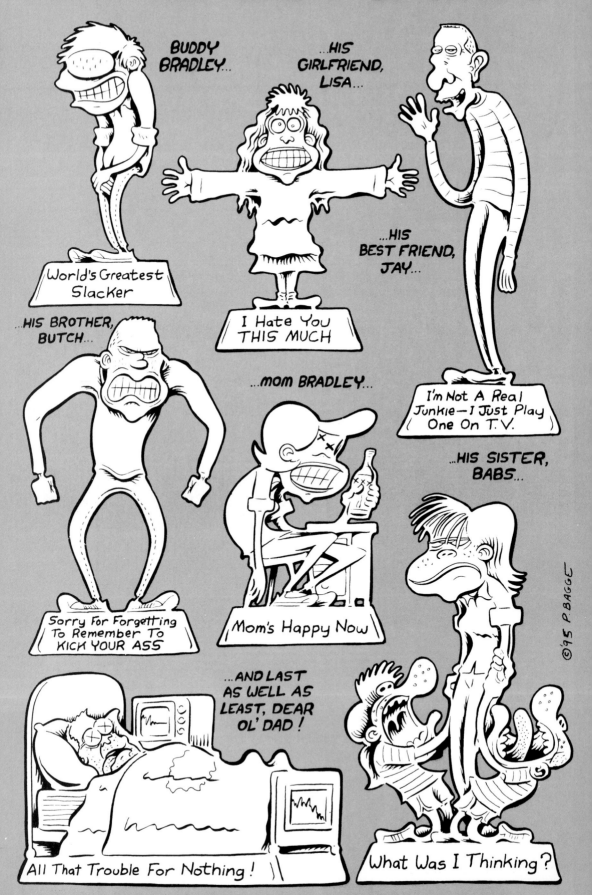

BUDDY BRADLEY...

World's Greatest Slacker

...HIS GIRLFRIEND, LISA...

I Hate You THIS MUCH

...HIS BEST FRIEND, JAY...

I'm Not A Real Junkie—I Just Play One On T.V.

...HIS BROTHER, BUTCH...

Sorry For Forgetting To Remember To KICK YOUR ASS

...MOM BRADLEY...

Mom's Happy Now

...HIS SISTER, BABS...

...AND LAST AS WELL AS LEAST, DEAR OL' DAD !

All That Trouble For Nothing !

What Was I Thinking?

©'95 P.BAGGE

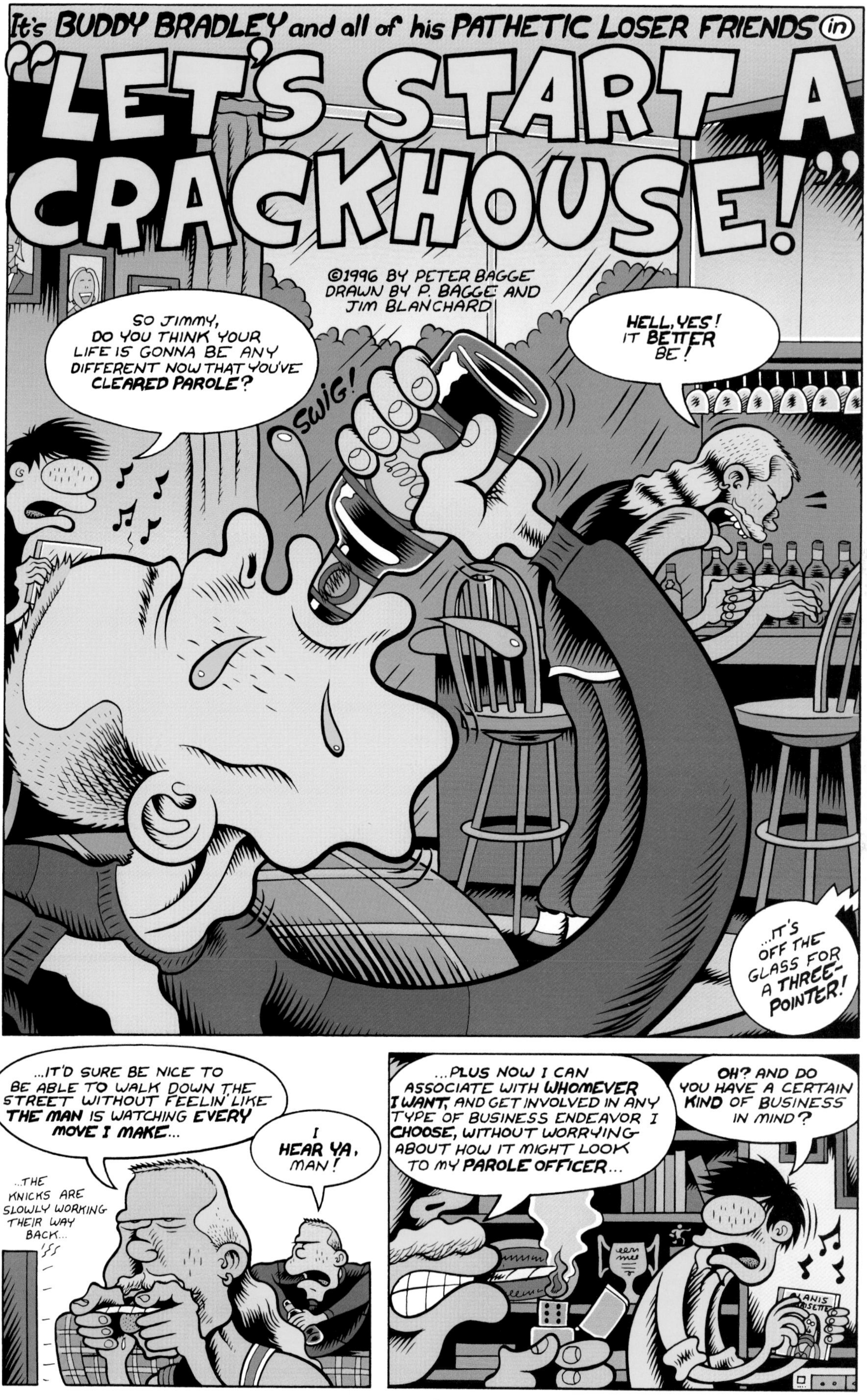
It's BUDDY BRADLEY and all of his PATHETIC LOSER FRIENDS in
"LET'S START A CRACKHOUSE!"
©1996 BY PETER BAGGE
DRAWN BY P. BAGGE AND JIM BLANCHARD
SO JIMMY, DO YOU THINK YOUR LIFE IS GONNA BE ANY DIFFERENT NOW THAT YOU'VE CLEARED PAROLE?
SWIG!
HELL, YES! IT BETTER BE!
...IT'S OFF THE GLASS FOR A THREE-POINTER!
...IT'D SURE BE NICE TO BE ABLE TO WALK DOWN THE STREET WITHOUT FEELIN' LIKE THE MAN IS WATCHING EVERY MOVE I MAKE...
I HEAR YA, MAN!
...THE KNICKS ARE SLOWLY WORKING THEIR WAY BACK...
...PLUS NOW I CAN ASSOCIATE WITH WHOMEVER I WANT, AND GET INVOLVED IN ANY TYPE OF BUSINESS ENDEAVOR I CHOOSE, WITHOUT WORRYING ABOUT HOW IT MIGHT LOOK TO MY PAROLE OFFICER...
OH? AND DO YOU HAVE A CERTAIN KIND OF BUSINESS IN MIND?

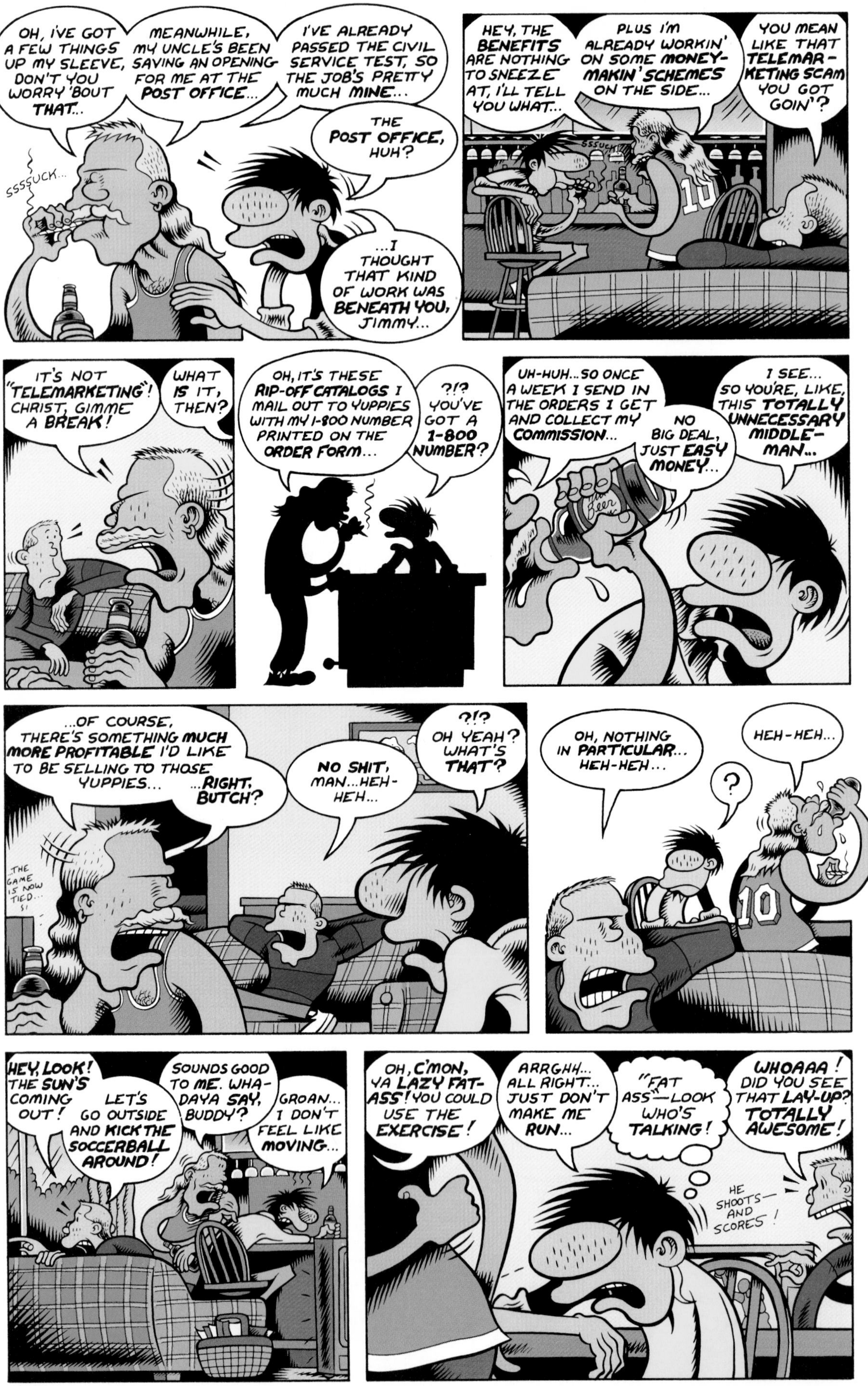
OH, I'VE GOT A FEW THINGS UP MY SLEEVE, DON'T YOU WORRY 'BOUT THAT...
MEANWHILE, MY UNCLE'S BEEN SAVING AN OPENING FOR ME AT THE POST OFFICE...
I'VE ALREADY PASSED THE CIVIL SERVICE TEST, SO THE JOB'S PRETTY MUCH MINE...
SSSSUCK...
THE POST OFFICE, HUH?
...I THOUGHT THAT KIND OF WORK WAS BENEATH YOU, JIMMY...
HEY, THE BENEFITS ARE NOTHING TO SNEEZE AT, I'LL TELL YOU WHAT...
PLUS I'M ALREADY WORKIN' ON SOME MONEY-MAKIN' SCHEMES ON THE SIDE...
YOU MEAN LIKE THAT TELEMARKETING SCAM YOU GOT GOIN'?
SSSUCK
IT'S NOT "TELEMARKETING"! CHRIST, GIMME A BREAK!
WHAT IS IT, THEN?
OH, IT'S THESE RIP-OFF CATALOGS I MAIL OUT TO YUPPIES WITH MY 1-800 NUMBER PRINTED ON THE ORDER FORM...
?!? YOU'VE GOT A 1-800 NUMBER?
UH-HUH... SO ONCE A WEEK I SEND IN THE ORDERS I GET AND COLLECT MY COMMISSION...
NO BIG DEAL, JUST EASY MONEY...
I SEE... SO YOU'RE, LIKE, THIS TOTALLY UNNECESSARY MIDDLE-MAN...
...OF COURSE, THERE'S SOMETHING MUCH MORE PROFITABLE I'D LIKE TO BE SELLING TO THOSE YUPPIES... ...RIGHT, BUTCH?
NO SHIT, MAN... HEH-HEH...
?!? OH YEAH? WHAT'S THAT?
...THE GAME IS NOW TIED...
OH, NOTHING IN PARTICULAR... HEH-HEH...
HEH-HEH...
?
HEY, LOOK! THE SUN'S COMING OUT!
LET'S GO OUTSIDE AND KICK THE SOCCERBALL AROUND!
SOUNDS GOOD TO ME. WHA-DAYA SAY, BUDDY?
GROAN... I DON'T FEEL LIKE MOVING...
OH, C'MON, YA LAZY FAT-ASS! YOU COULD USE THE EXERCISE!
ARRGHH... ALL RIGHT... JUST DON'T MAKE ME RUN...
"FAT ASS"—LOOK WHO'S TALKING!
WHOAAA! DID YOU SEE THAT LAY-UP? TOTALLY AWESOME!
HE SHOOTS—AND SCORES!

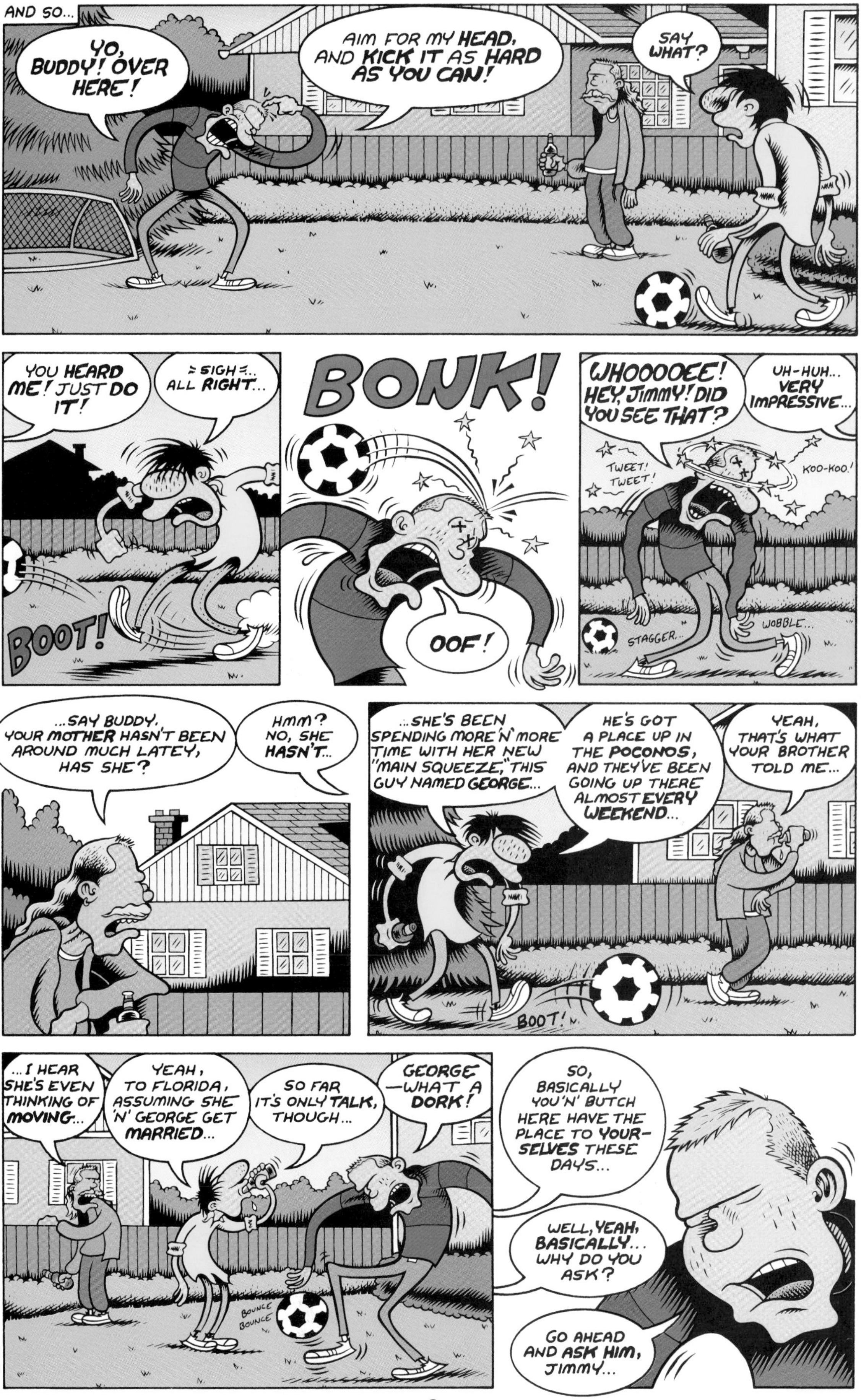
AND SO...
YO, BUDDY! OVER HERE!
AIM FOR MY HEAD, AND KICK IT AS HARD AS YOU CAN!
SAY WHAT?
YOU HEARD ME! JUST DO IT!
≥SIGH≤.. ALL RIGHT...
BOOT!
BONK!
OOF!
WHOOOOEE! HEY, JIMMY! DID YOU SEE THAT?
UH-HUH... VERY IMPRESSIVE...
TWEET! TWEET!
KOO-KOO!
STAGGER...
WOBBLE...
...SAY BUDDY, YOUR MOTHER HASN'T BEEN AROUND MUCH LATEY, HAS SHE?
HMM? NO, SHE HASN'T...
...SHE'S BEEN SPENDING MORE 'N' MORE TIME WITH HER NEW "MAIN SQUEEZE," THIS GUY NAMED GEORGE...
HE'S GOT A PLACE UP IN THE POCONOS, AND THEY'VE BEEN GOING UP THERE ALMOST EVERY WEEKEND...
YEAH, THAT'S WHAT YOUR BROTHER TOLD ME...
BOOT!
...I HEAR SHE'S EVEN THINKING OF MOVING...
YEAH, TO FLORIDA, ASSUMING SHE 'N' GEORGE GET MARRIED...
SO FAR IT'S ONLY TALK, THOUGH...
GEORGE —WHAT A DORK!
BOUNCE BOUNCE
SO, BASICALLY YOU 'N' BUTCH HERE HAVE THE PLACE TO YOURSELVES THESE DAYS...
WELL, YEAH, BASICALLY... WHY DO YOU ASK?
GO AHEAD AND ASK HIM, JIMMY...

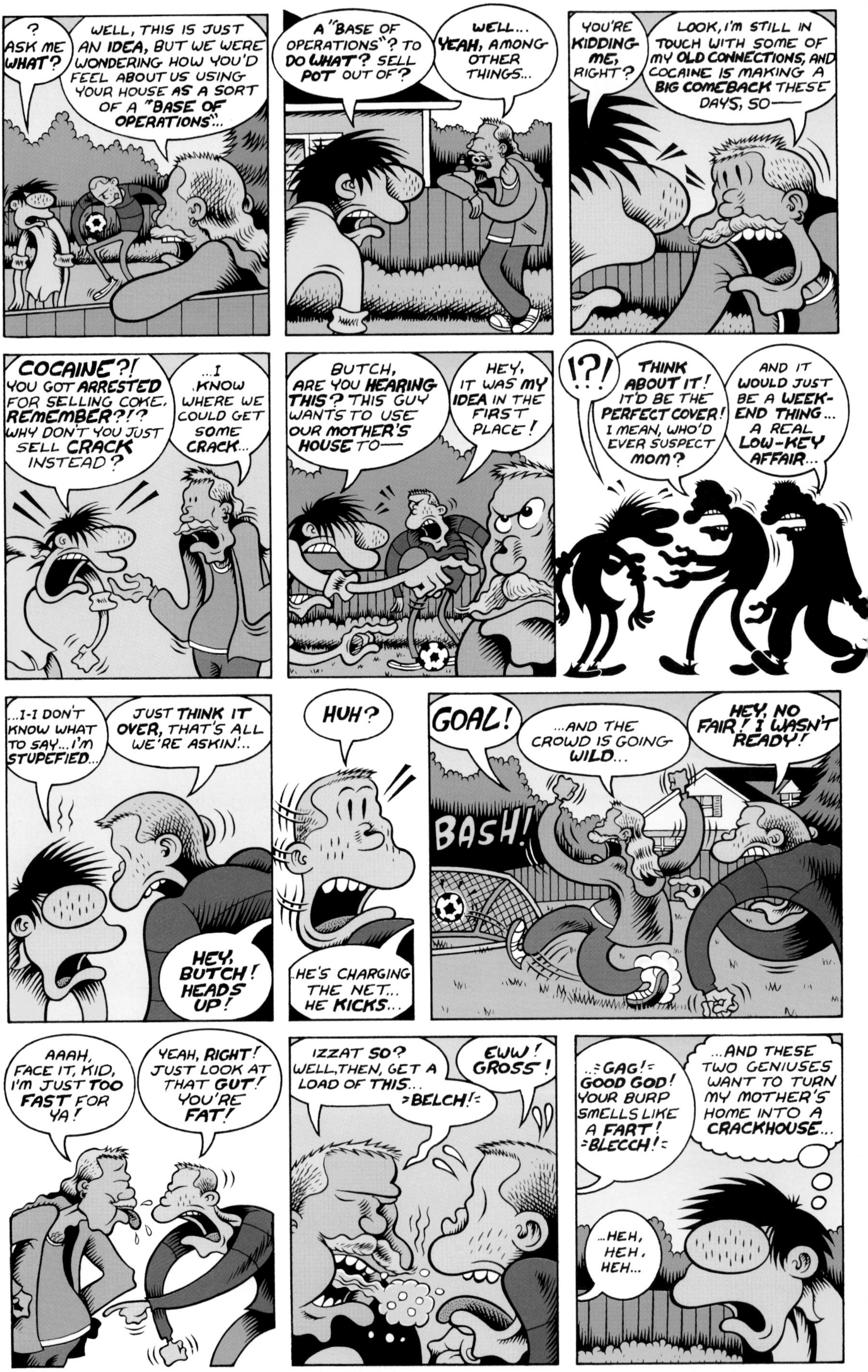
?
ASK ME WHAT?
WELL, THIS IS JUST AN IDEA, BUT WE WERE WONDERING HOW YOU'D FEEL ABOUT US USING YOUR HOUSE AS A SORT OF A "BASE OF OPERATIONS"...
A "BASE OF OPERATIONS"? TO DO WHAT? SELL POT OUT OF?
WELL... YEAH, AMONG OTHER THINGS...
YOU'RE KIDDING ME, RIGHT?
LOOK, I'M STILL IN TOUCH WITH SOME OF MY OLD CONNECTIONS, AND COCAINE IS MAKING A BIG COMEBACK THESE DAYS, SO—
COCAINE?! YOU GOT ARRESTED FOR SELLING COKE, REMEMBER?!? WHY DON'T YOU JUST SELL CRACK INSTEAD?
...I KNOW WHERE WE COULD GET SOME CRACK...
BUTCH, ARE YOU HEARING THIS? THIS GUY WANTS TO USE OUR MOTHER'S HOUSE TO—
HEY, IT WAS MY IDEA IN THE FIRST PLACE!
!?!
THINK ABOUT IT! IT'D BE THE PERFECT COVER! I MEAN, WHO'D EVER SUSPECT MOM?
AND IT WOULD JUST BE A WEEK-END THING... A REAL LOW-KEY AFFAIR...
...I-I DON'T KNOW WHAT TO SAY... I'M STUPEFIED...
JUST THINK IT OVER, THAT'S ALL WE'RE ASKIN'...
HEY, BUTCH! HEADS UP!
HUH?
..HE'S CHARGING THE NET... HE KICKS...
GOAL!
BASH!
...AND THE CROWD IS GOING WILD...
HEY, NO FAIR! I WASN'T READY!
AAAH, FACE IT, KID, I'M JUST TOO FAST FOR YA!
YEAH, RIGHT! JUST LOOK AT THAT GUT! YOU'RE FAT!
IZZAT SO? WELL, THEN, GET A LOAD OF THIS...
=BELCH!=
EWW! GROSS!
=GAG!= GOOD GOD! YOUR BURP SMELLS LIKE A FART! =BLECCH!=
...AND THESE TWO GENIUSES WANT TO TURN MY MOTHER'S HOME INTO A CRACKHOUSE...
...HEH, HEH, HEH...

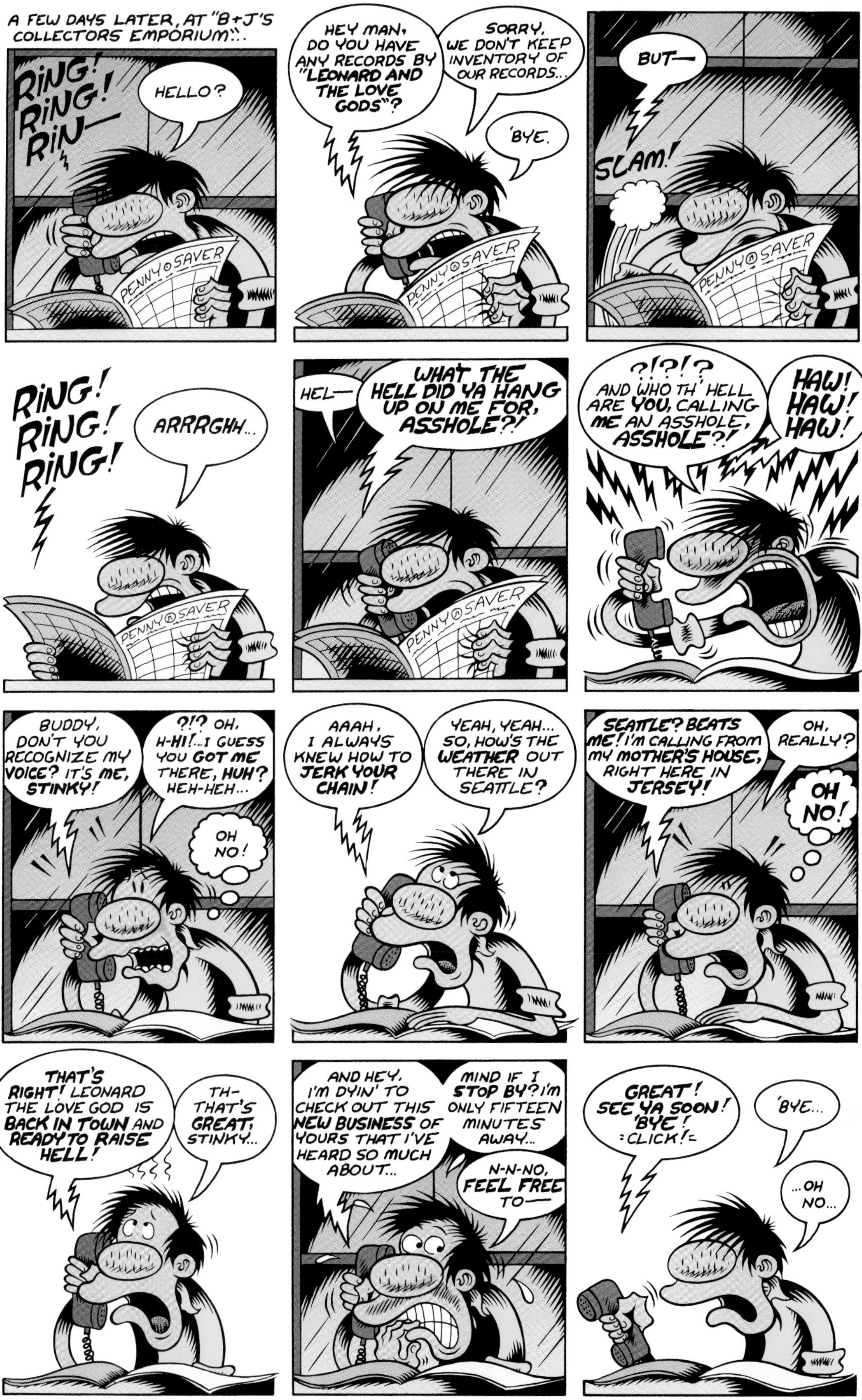

A FEW DAYS LATER, AT "B+J'S COLLECTORS EMPORIUM"...
RING! RING! RIN—
HELLO?
HEY MAN, DO YOU HAVE ANY RECORDS BY "LEONARD AND THE LOVE GODS"?
SORRY, WE DON'T KEEP INVENTORY OF OUR RECORDS...
'BYE.
PENNY SAVER
BUT—
SLAM!
RING! RING! RING!
ARRRGHH...
HEL—
WHAT THE HELL DID YA HANG UP ON ME FOR, ASSHOLE?!
?!?!?
AND WHO TH' HELL ARE YOU, CALLING ME AN ASSHOLE, ASSHOLE?!
HAW! HAW! HAW!
BUDDY, DON'T YOU RECOGNIZE MY VOICE? IT'S ME, STINKY!
?!? OH, H-HI!...I GUESS YOU GOT ME THERE, HUH? HEH-HEH...
OH NO!
AAAH, I ALWAYS KNEW HOW TO JERK YOUR CHAIN!
YEAH, YEAH... SO, HOW'S THE WEATHER OUT THERE IN SEATTLE?
SEATTLE? BEATS ME! I'M CALLING FROM MY MOTHER'S HOUSE, RIGHT HERE IN JERSEY!
OH, REALLY?
OH NO!
THAT'S RIGHT! LEONARD THE LOVE GOD IS BACK IN TOWN AND READY TO RAISE HELL!
TH-THAT'S GREAT, STINKY...
AND HEY, I'M DYIN' TO CHECK OUT THIS NEW BUSINESS OF YOURS THAT I'VE HEARD SO MUCH ABOUT...
MIND IF I STOP BY? I'M ONLY FIFTEEN MINUTES AWAY...
N-N-NO, FEEL FREE TO—
GREAT! SEE YA SOON! 'BYE! =CLICK!=
'BYE...
...OH NO...

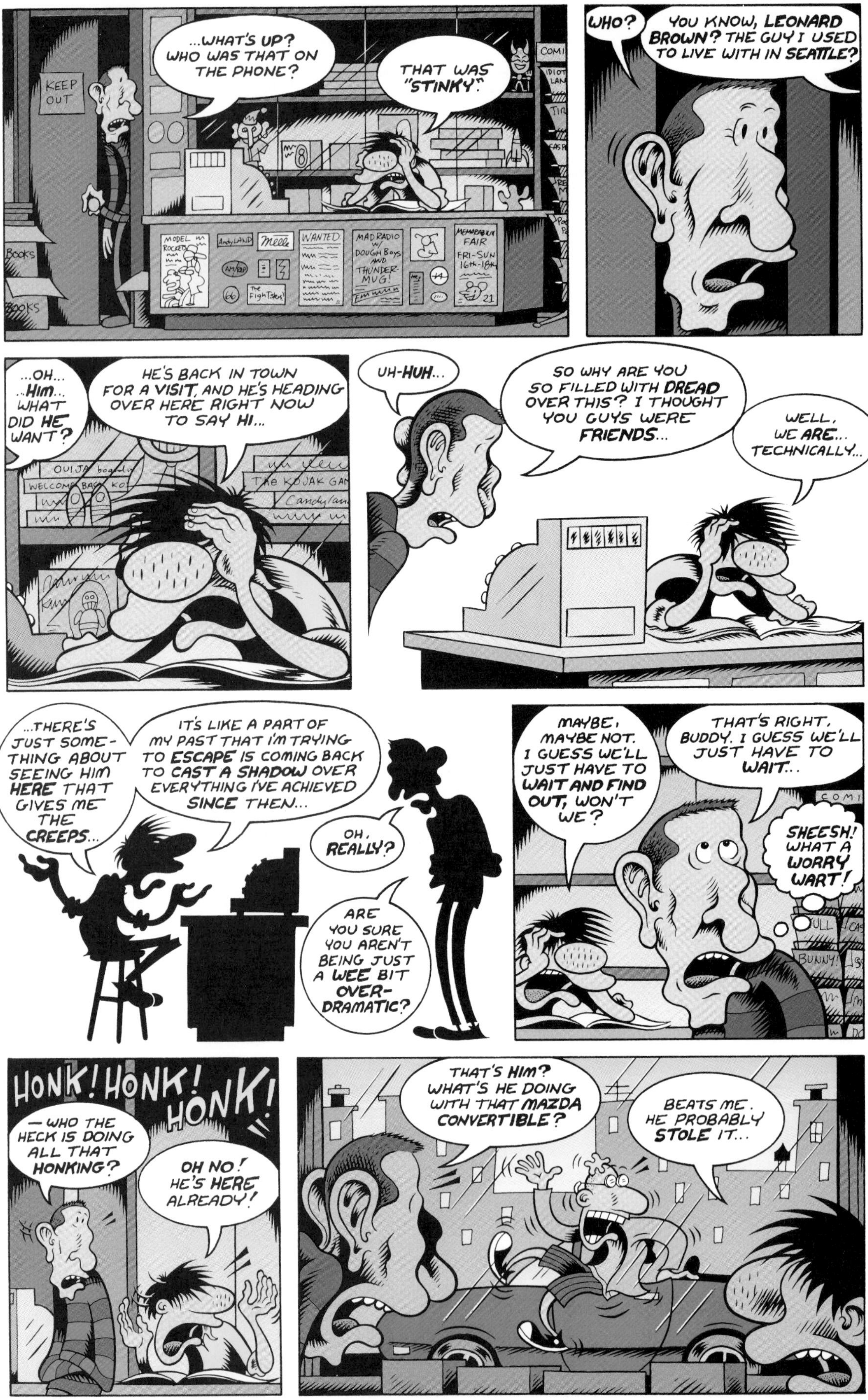

KEEP OUT
...WHAT'S UP? WHO WAS THAT ON THE PHONE?
THAT WAS "STINKY".
BOOKS
BOOKS
WANTED
MAD RADIO W/ DOUGH BOYS AND THUNDER-MUG!
MEMORABILIA FAIR FRI-SUN 16th-18th
WHO?
YOU KNOW, LEONARD BROWN? THE GUY I USED TO LIVE WITH IN SEATTLE?
...OH... ..HIM... WHAT DID HE WANT?
HE'S BACK IN TOWN FOR A VISIT, AND HE'S HEADING OVER HERE RIGHT NOW TO SAY HI...
UH-HUH...
SO WHY ARE YOU SO FILLED WITH DREAD OVER THIS? I THOUGHT YOU GUYS WERE FRIENDS...
WELL, WE ARE... TECHNICALLY...
...THERE'S JUST SOME-THING ABOUT SEEING HIM HERE THAT GIVES ME THE CREEPS...
IT'S LIKE A PART OF MY PAST THAT I'M TRYING TO ESCAPE IS COMING BACK TO CAST A SHADOW OVER EVERYTHING I'VE ACHIEVED SINCE THEN...
OH, REALLY?
ARE YOU SURE YOU AREN'T BEING JUST A WEE BIT OVER-DRAMATIC?
MAYBE, MAYBE NOT. I GUESS WE'LL JUST HAVE TO WAIT AND FIND OUT, WON'T WE?
THAT'S RIGHT, BUDDY. I GUESS WE'LL JUST HAVE TO WAIT...
SHEESH! WHAT A WORRY WART!
HONK! HONK! HONK!
—WHO THE HECK IS DOING ALL THAT HONKING?
OH NO! HE'S HERE ALREADY!
THAT'S HIM? WHAT'S HE DOING WITH THAT MAZDA CONVERTIBLE?
BEATS ME. HE PROBABLY STOLE IT...

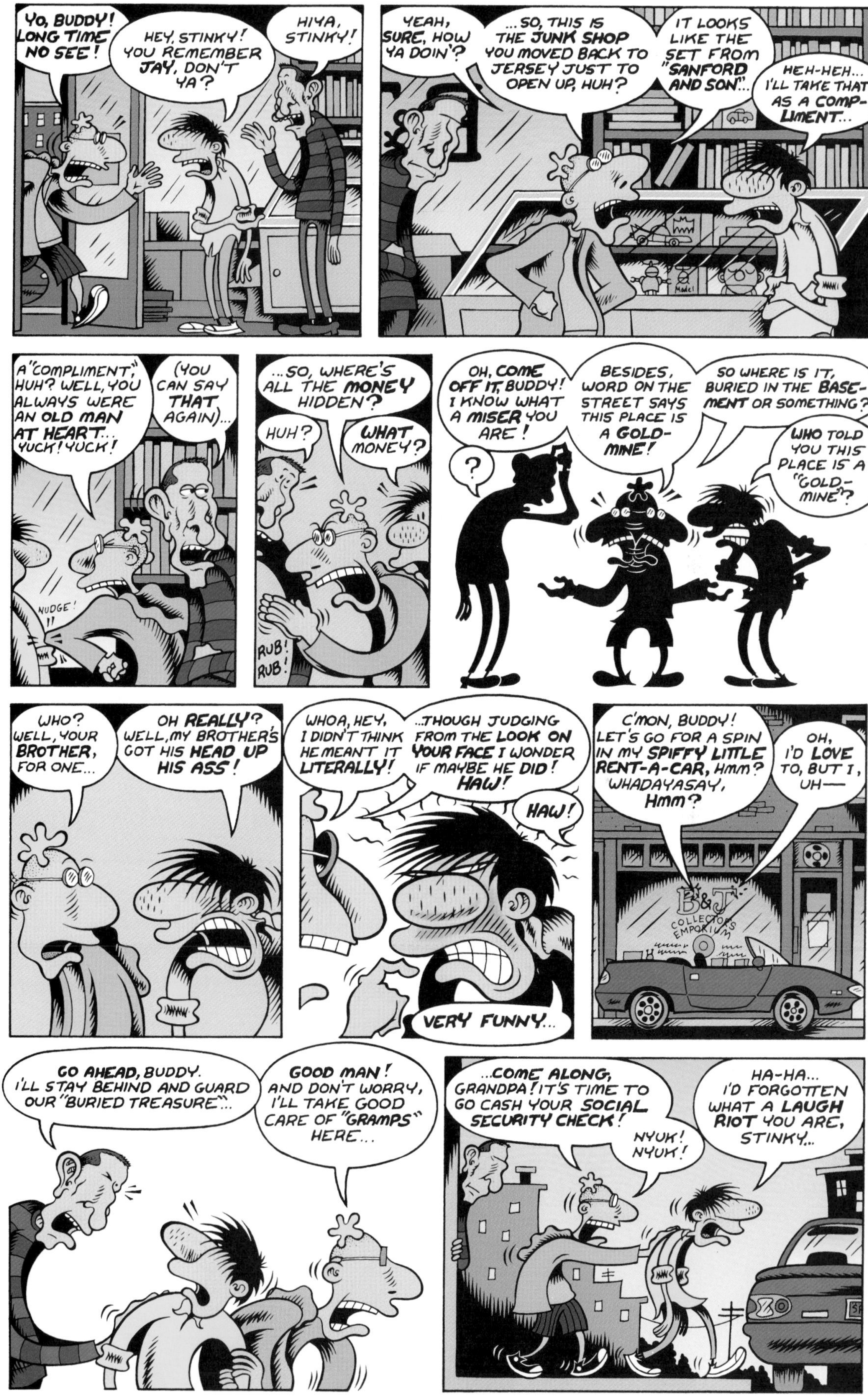
YO, BUDDY! LONG TIME NO SEE!
HEY, STINKY! YOU REMEMBER JAY, DON'T YA?
HIYA, STINKY!
YEAH, SURE, HOW YA DOIN'?
...SO, THIS IS THE JUNK SHOP YOU MOVED BACK TO JERSEY JUST TO OPEN UP, HUH?
IT LOOKS LIKE THE SET FROM "SANFORD AND SON"...
HEH-HEH... I'LL TAKE THAT AS A COMPLIMENT...
A "COMPLIMENT," HUH? WELL, YOU ALWAYS WERE AN OLD MAN AT HEART... YUCK! YUCK!
(YOU CAN SAY THAT AGAIN)...
NUDGE!
...SO, WHERE'S ALL THE MONEY HIDDEN?
HUH?
WHAT MONEY?
RUB! RUB!
OH, COME OFF IT, BUDDY! I KNOW WHAT A MISER YOU ARE!
?
BESIDES, WORD ON THE STREET SAYS THIS PLACE IS A GOLDMINE!
SO WHERE IS IT, BURIED IN THE BASEMENT OR SOMETHING?
WHO TOLD YOU THIS PLACE IS A "GOLDMINE"?
WHO? WELL, YOUR BROTHER, FOR ONE...
OH REALLY? WELL, MY BROTHER'S GOT HIS HEAD UP HIS ASS!
WHOA, HEY, I DIDN'T THINK HE MEANT IT LITERALLY!
...THOUGH JUDGING FROM THE LOOK ON YOUR FACE I WONDER IF MAYBE HE DID! HAW!
HAW!
VERY FUNNY...
C'MON, BUDDY! LET'S GO FOR A SPIN IN MY SPIFFY LITTLE RENT-A-CAR, HMM? WHADAYASAY, HMM?
OH, I'D LOVE TO, BUT I, UH—
B&J COLLECTORS EMPORIUM
GO AHEAD, BUDDY. I'LL STAY BEHIND AND GUARD OUR "BURIED TREASURE"...
GOOD MAN! AND DON'T WORRY, I'LL TAKE GOOD CARE OF "GRAMPS" HERE...
...COME ALONG, GRANDPA! IT'S TIME TO GO CASH YOUR SOCIAL SECURITY CHECK!
NYUK! NYUK!
HA-HA... I'D FORGOTTEN WHAT A LAUGH RIOT YOU ARE, STINKY...

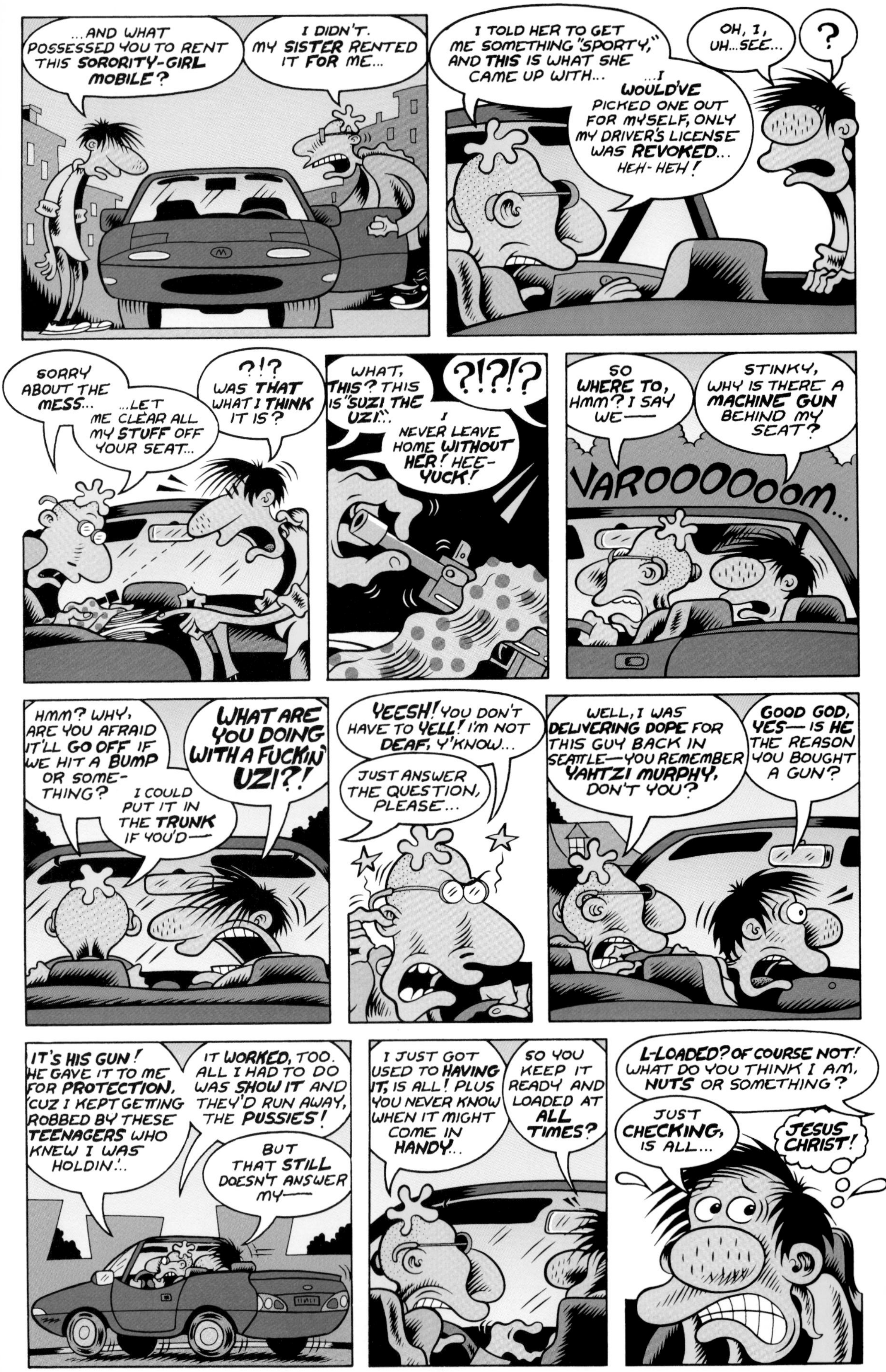
...AND WHAT POSSESSED YOU TO RENT THIS SORORITY-GIRL MOBILE?
I DIDN'T. MY SISTER RENTED IT FOR ME...
I TOLD HER TO GET ME SOMETHING "SPORTY," AND THIS IS WHAT SHE CAME UP WITH...
...I WOULD'VE PICKED ONE OUT FOR MYSELF, ONLY MY DRIVER'S LICENSE WAS REVOKED... HEH-HEH!
OH, I, UH...SEE...
?
SORRY ABOUT THE MESS...
...LET ME CLEAR ALL MY STUFF OFF YOUR SEAT...
?!? WAS THAT WHAT I THINK IT IS?
WHAT, THIS? THIS IS "SUZI THE UZI"...
?!?!?
I NEVER LEAVE HOME WITHOUT HER! HEE-YUCK!
SO WHERE TO, HMM? I SAY WE—
STINKY, WHY IS THERE A MACHINE GUN BEHIND MY SEAT?
VAROOOOOom...
HMM? WHY, ARE YOU AFRAID IT'LL GO OFF IF WE HIT A BUMP OR SOMETHING?
I COULD PUT IT IN THE TRUNK IF YOU'D—
WHAT ARE YOU DOING WITH A FUCKIN' UZI?!
YEESH! YOU DON'T HAVE TO YELL! I'M NOT DEAF, Y'KNOW...
JUST ANSWER THE QUESTION, PLEASE...
WELL, I WAS DELIVERING DOPE FOR THIS GUY BACK IN SEATTLE—YOU REMEMBER YAHTZI MURPHY, DON'T YOU?
GOOD GOD, YES—IS HE THE REASON YOU BOUGHT A GUN?
IT'S HIS GUN! HE GAVE IT TO ME FOR PROTECTION, 'CUZ I KEPT GETTING ROBBED BY THESE TEENAGERS WHO KNEW I WAS HOLDIN'...
IT WORKED, TOO. ALL I HAD TO DO WAS SHOW IT AND THEY'D RUN AWAY, THE PUSSIES!
BUT THAT STILL DOESN'T ANSWER MY—
I JUST GOT USED TO HAVING IT, IS ALL! PLUS YOU NEVER KNOW WHEN IT MIGHT COME IN HANDY...
SO YOU KEEP IT READY AND LOADED AT ALL TIMES?
L-LOADED? OF COURSE NOT! WHAT DO YOU THINK I AM, NUTS OR SOMETHING?
JUST CHECKING, IS ALL...
JESUS CHRIST!

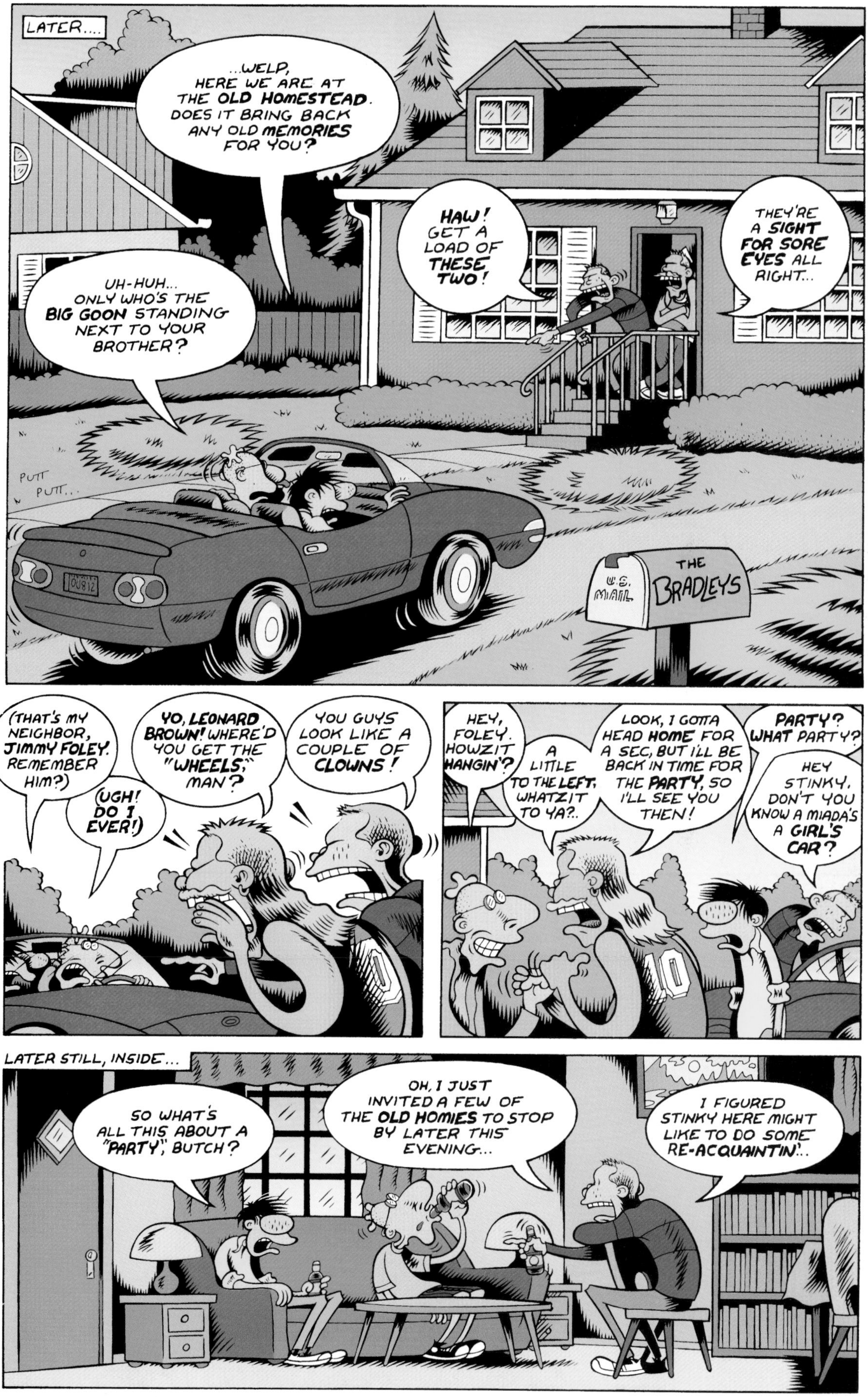
LATER....
...WELP, HERE WE ARE AT THE OLD HOMESTEAD. DOES IT BRING BACK ANY OLD MEMORIES FOR YOU?
UH-HUH... ONLY WHO'S THE BIG GOON STANDING NEXT TO YOUR BROTHER?
HAW! GET A LOAD OF THESE TWO!
THEY'RE A SIGHT FOR SORE EYES ALL RIGHT...
PUTT PUTT...
U.S. MAIL
THE BRADLEYS
(THAT'S MY NEIGHBOR, JIMMY FOLEY. REMEMBER HIM?)
(UGH! DO I EVER!)
YO, LEONARD BROWN! WHERE'D YOU GET THE "WHEELS," MAN?
YOU GUYS LOOK LIKE A COUPLE OF CLOWNS!
HEY, FOLEY. HOWZIT HANGIN'?
A LITTLE TO THE LEFT. WHATZIT TO YA?..
LOOK, I GOTTA HEAD HOME FOR A SEC, BUT I'LL BE BACK IN TIME FOR THE PARTY, SO I'LL SEE YOU THEN!
PARTY? WHAT PARTY?
HEY STINKY, DON'T YOU KNOW A MIADA'S A GIRL'S CAR?
LATER STILL, INSIDE...
SO WHAT'S ALL THIS ABOUT A "PARTY," BUTCH?
OH, I JUST INVITED A FEW OF THE OLD HOMIES TO STOP BY LATER THIS EVENING...
I FIGURED STINKY HERE MIGHT LIKE TO DO SOME RE-ACQUAINTIN'...

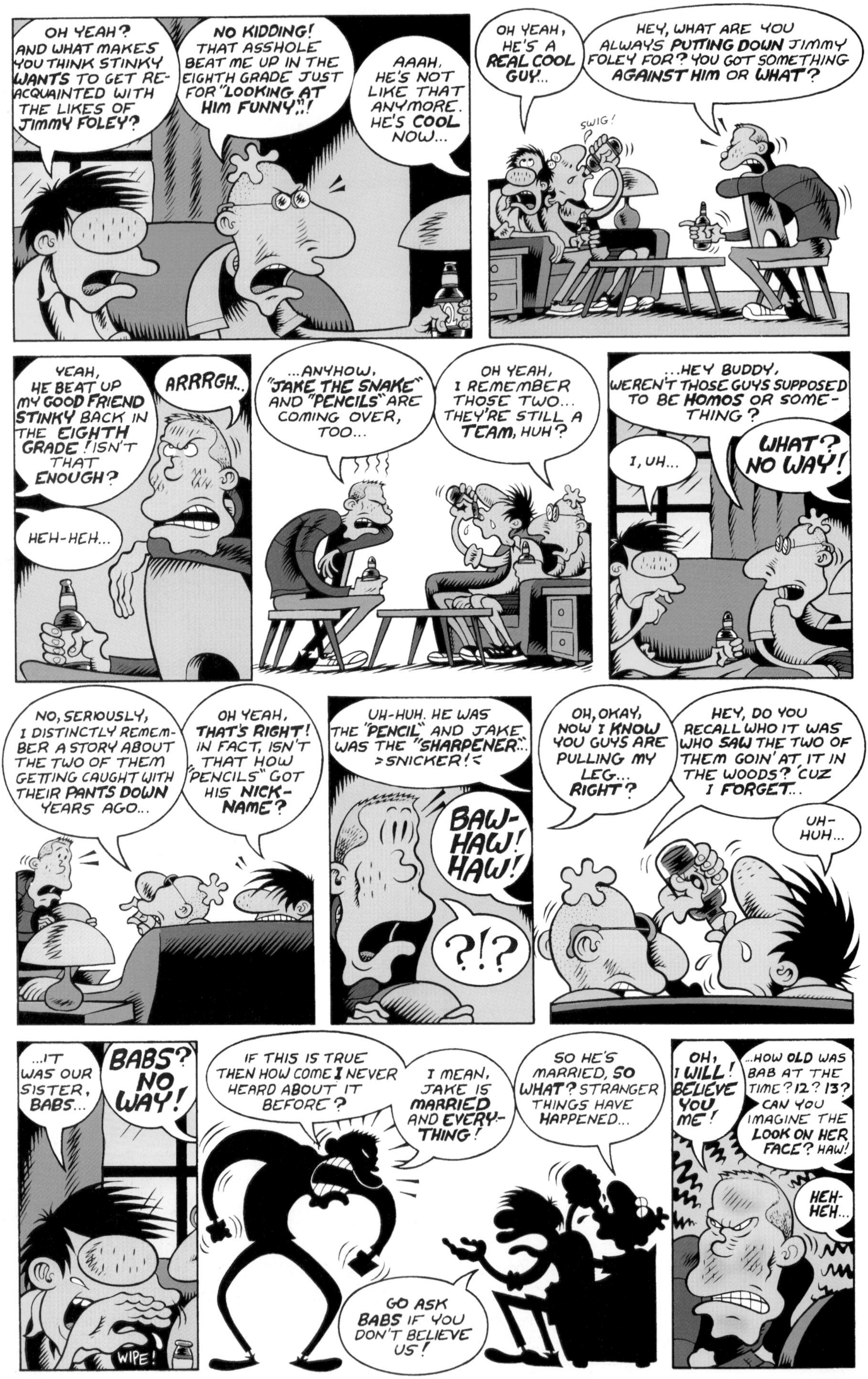
OH YEAH? AND WHAT MAKES YOU THINK STINKY WANTS TO GET RE-ACQUAINTED WITH THE LIKES OF JIMMY FOLEY?
NO KIDDING! THAT ASSHOLE BEAT ME UP IN THE EIGHTH GRADE JUST FOR "LOOKING AT HIM FUNNY"!
AAAH, HE'S NOT LIKE THAT ANYMORE. HE'S COOL NOW...
OH YEAH, HE'S A REAL COOL GUY...
HEY, WHAT ARE YOU ALWAYS PUTTING DOWN JIMMY FOLEY FOR? YOU GOT SOMETHING AGAINST HIM OR WHAT?
SWIG!
YEAH, HE BEAT UP MY GOOD FRIEND STINKY BACK IN THE EIGHTH GRADE! ISN'T THAT ENOUGH?
ARRRGH...
HEH-HEH...
...ANYHOW, "JAKE THE SNAKE" AND "PENCILS" ARE COMING OVER, TOO...
OH YEAH, I REMEMBER THOSE TWO... THEY'RE STILL A TEAM, HUH?
...HEY BUDDY, WEREN'T THOSE GUYS SUPPOSED TO BE HOMOS OR SOME-THING?
I, UH...
WHAT? NO WAY!
NO, SERIOUSLY, I DISTINCTLY REMEM-BER A STORY ABOUT THE TWO OF THEM GETTING CAUGHT WITH THEIR PANTS DOWN YEARS AGO...
OH YEAH, THAT'S RIGHT! IN FACT, ISN'T THAT HOW "PENCILS" GOT HIS NICK-NAME?
UH-HUH. HE WAS THE "PENCIL" AND JAKE WAS THE "SHARPENER"... >SNICKER!<
BAW-HAW! HAW!
?!?
OH, OKAY, NOW I KNOW YOU GUYS ARE PULLING MY LEG... RIGHT?
HEY, DO YOU RECALL WHO IT WAS WHO SAW THE TWO OF THEM GOIN' AT IT IN THE WOODS? 'CUZ I FORGET...
UH-HUH...
...IT WAS OUR SISTER, BABS...
BABS? NO WAY!
WIPE!
IF THIS IS TRUE THEN HOW COME I NEVER HEARD ABOUT IT BEFORE?
I MEAN, JAKE IS MARRIED AND EVERY-THING!
SO HE'S MARRIED, SO WHAT? STRANGER THINGS HAVE HAPPENED...
GO ASK BABS IF YOU DON'T BELIEVE US!
OH, I WILL! BELIEVE YOU ME!
...HOW OLD WAS BAB AT THE TIME? 12? 13? CAN YOU IMAGINE THE LOOK ON HER FACE? HAW!
HEH-HEH...

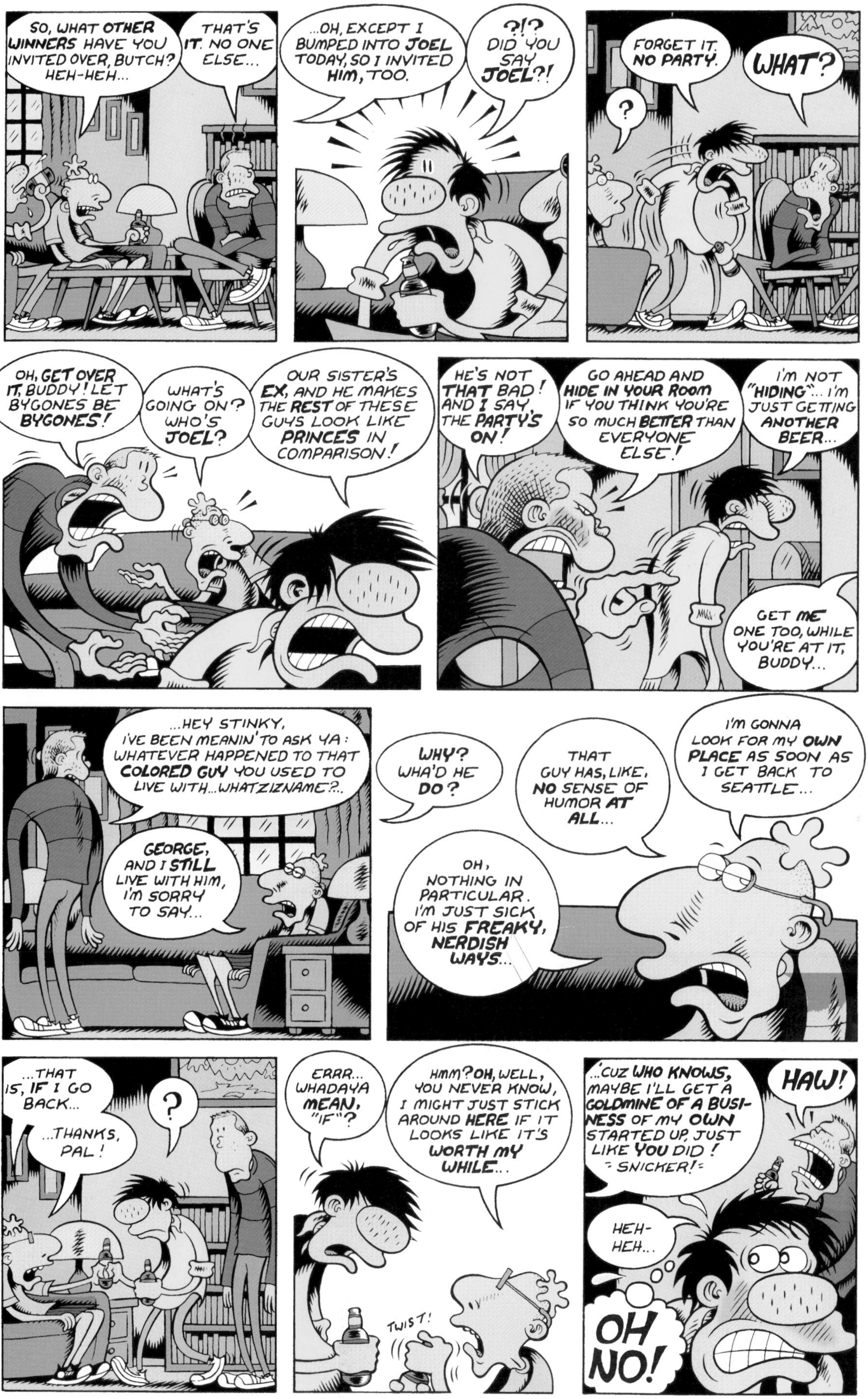
SO, WHAT OTHER WINNERS HAVE YOU INVITED OVER, BUTCH? HEH-HEH...
THAT'S IT. NO ONE ELSE...
...OH, EXCEPT I BUMPED INTO JOEL TODAY, SO I INVITED HIM, TOO.
?!? DID YOU SAY JOEL?!
FORGET IT. NO PARTY.
WHAT?
?
OH, GET OVER IT, BUDDY! LET BYGONES BE BYGONES!
WHAT'S GOING ON? WHO'S JOEL?
OUR SISTER'S EX, AND HE MAKES THE REST OF THESE GUYS LOOK LIKE PRINCES IN COMPARISON!
HE'S NOT THAT BAD! AND I SAY, THE PARTY'S ON!
GO AHEAD AND HIDE IN YOUR ROOM IF YOU THINK YOU'RE SO MUCH BETTER THAN EVERYONE ELSE!
I'M NOT "HIDING"... I'M JUST GETTING ANOTHER BEER...
GET ME ONE TOO, WHILE YOU'RE AT IT, BUDDY...
...HEY STINKY, I'VE BEEN MEANIN' TO ASK YA: WHATEVER HAPPENED TO THAT COLORED GUY YOU USED TO LIVE WITH...WHATZIZNAME?..
GEORGE, AND I STILL LIVE WITH HIM, I'M SORRY TO SAY...
WHY? WHA'D HE DO?
OH, NOTHING IN PARTICULAR. I'M JUST SICK OF HIS FREAKY, NERDISH WAYS...
THAT GUY HAS, LIKE, NO SENSE OF HUMOR AT ALL...
I'M GONNA LOOK FOR MY OWN PLACE AS SOON AS I GET BACK TO SEATTLE...
...THAT IS, IF I GO BACK...
...THANKS, PAL!
?
ERRR... WHADAYA MEAN, "IF"?
HMM? OH, WELL, YOU NEVER KNOW, I MIGHT JUST STICK AROUND HERE IF IT LOOKS LIKE IT'S WORTH MY WHILE...
TWIST!
...'CUZ WHO KNOWS, MAYBE I'LL GET A GOLDMINE OF A BUSINESS OF MY OWN STARTED UP, JUST LIKE YOU DID! =SNICKER!=
HAW!
HEH-HEH...
OH NO!

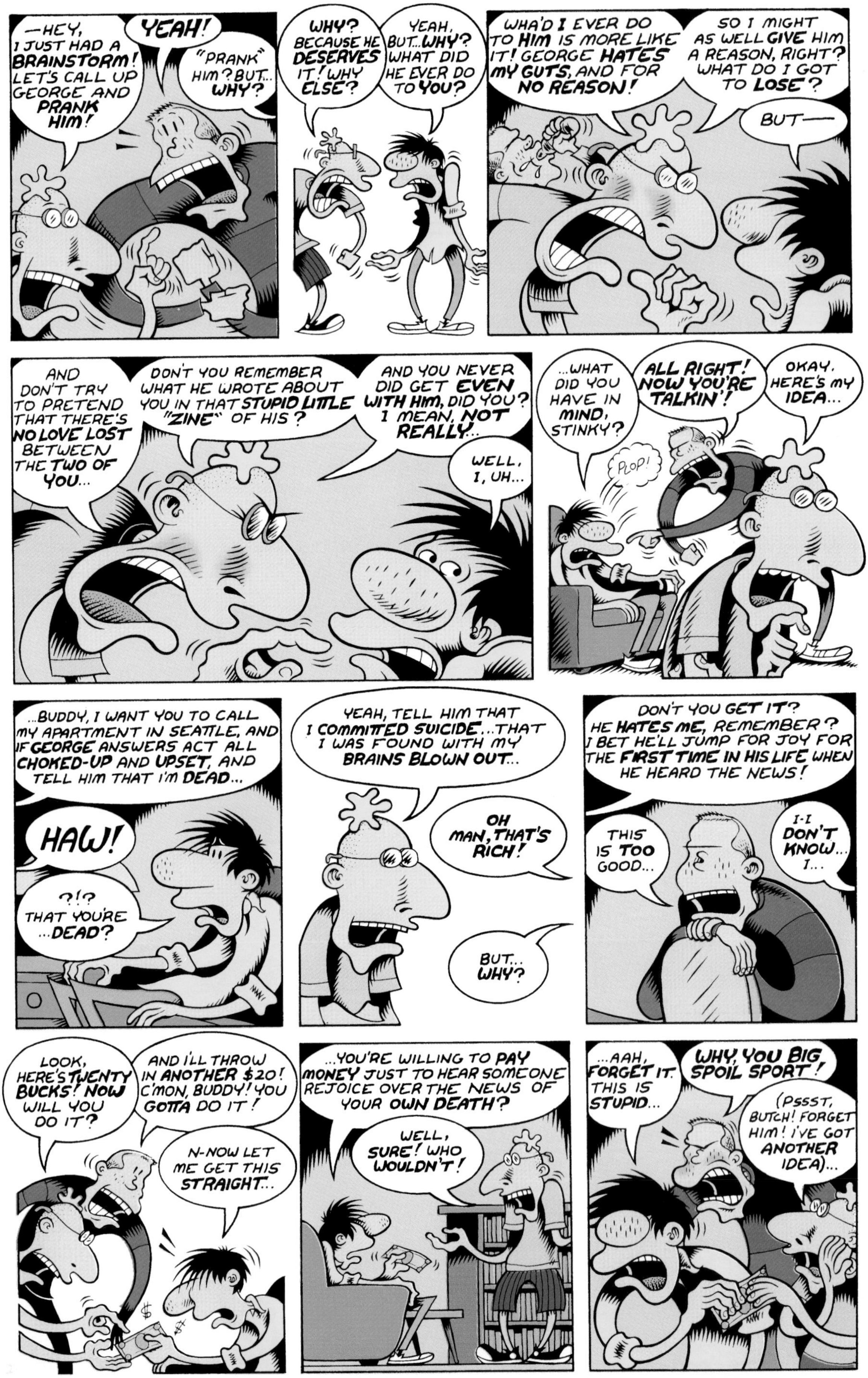
—HEY, I JUST HAD A BRAINSTORM! LET'S CALL UP GEORGE AND PRANK HIM!
YEAH!
"PRANK" HIM? BUT... WHY?
WHY? BECAUSE HE DESERVES IT! WHY ELSE?
YEAH, BUT... WHY? WHAT DID HE EVER DO TO YOU?
WHA'D I EVER DO TO HIM IS MORE LIKE IT! GEORGE HATES MY GUTS, AND FOR NO REASON!
SO I MIGHT AS WELL GIVE HIM A REASON, RIGHT? WHAT DO I GOT TO LOSE?
BUT—
AND DON'T TRY TO PRETEND THAT THERE'S NO LOVE LOST BETWEEN THE TWO OF YOU...
DON'T YOU REMEMBER WHAT HE WROTE ABOUT YOU IN THAT STUPID LITTLE "ZINE" OF HIS?
AND YOU NEVER DID GET EVEN WITH HIM, DID YOU? I MEAN, NOT REALLY...
WELL, I, UH...
...WHAT DID YOU HAVE IN MIND, STINKY?
ALL RIGHT! NOW YOU'RE TALKIN'!
OKAY, HERE'S MY IDEA...
PLOP!
...BUDDY, I WANT YOU TO CALL MY APARTMENT IN SEATTLE, AND IF GEORGE ANSWERS ACT ALL CHOKED-UP AND UPSET, AND TELL HIM THAT I'M DEAD...
HAW!
?!? THAT YOU'RE ...DEAD?
YEAH, TELL HIM THAT I COMMITED SUICIDE... THAT I WAS FOUND WITH MY BRAINS BLOWN OUT...
OH MAN, THAT'S RICH!
BUT... WHY?
DON'T YOU GET IT? HE HATES ME, REMEMBER? I BET HE'LL JUMP FOR JOY FOR THE FIRST TIME IN HIS LIFE WHEN HE HEARD THE NEWS!
THIS IS TOO GOOD...
I-I DON'T KNOW... I...
LOOK, HERE'S TWENTY BUCKS! NOW WILL YOU DO IT?
AND I'LL THROW IN ANOTHER $20! C'MON, BUDDY! YOU GOTTA DO IT!
N-NOW LET ME GET THIS STRAIGHT...
...YOU'RE WILLING TO PAY MONEY JUST TO HEAR SOMEONE REJOICE OVER THE NEWS OF YOUR OWN DEATH?
WELL, SURE! WHO WOULDN'T!
...AAH, FORGET IT. THIS IS STUPID...
WHY, YOU BIG SPOIL SPORT!
(PSSST, BUTCH! FORGET HIM! I'VE GOT ANOTHER IDEA)...

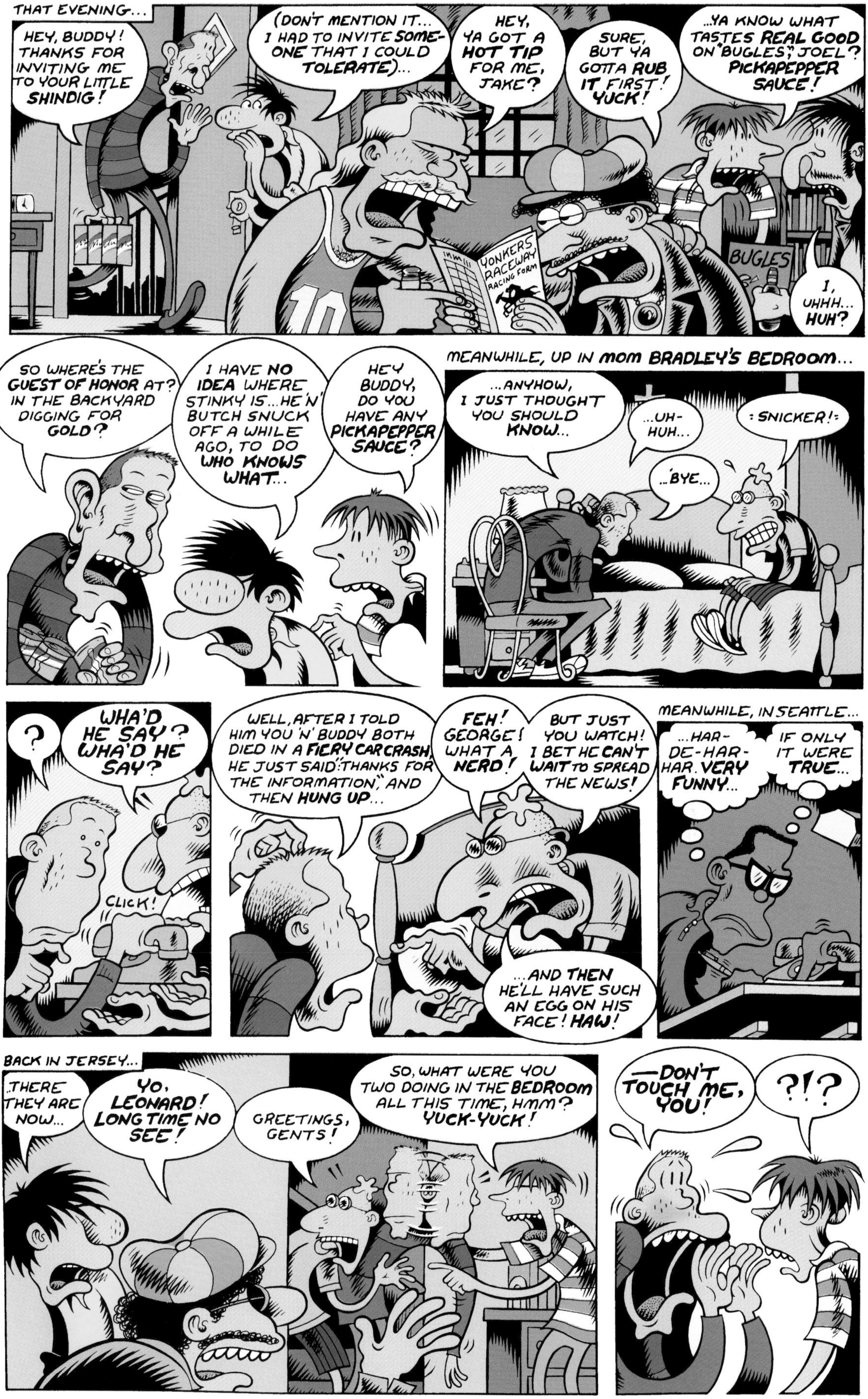
THAT EVENING...
HEY, BUDDY! THANKS FOR INVITING ME TO YOUR LITTLE SHINDIG!
(DON'T MENTION IT... I HAD TO INVITE SOME-ONE THAT I COULD TOLERATE)...
HEY, YA GOT A HOT TIP FOR ME, JAKE?
YONKERS RACEWAY RACING FORM
SURE, BUT YA GOTTA RUB IT FIRST! YUCK!
...YA KNOW WHAT TASTES REAL GOOD ON "BUGLES," JOEL? PICKAPEPPER SAUCE!
BUGLES
I, UHHH... HUH?
SO WHERE'S THE GUEST OF HONOR AT? IN THE BACKYARD DIGGING FOR GOLD?
I HAVE NO IDEA WHERE STINKY IS... HE 'N' BUTCH SNUCK OFF A WHILE AGO, TO DO WHO KNOWS WHAT...
HEY BUDDY, DO YOU HAVE ANY PICKAPEPPER SAUCE?
MEANWHILE, UP IN MOM BRADLEY'S BEDROOM...
...ANYHOW, I JUST THOUGHT YOU SHOULD KNOW...
...UH-HUH...
:SNICKER!:
...BYE...
?
WHA'D HE SAY? WHA'D HE SAY?
CLICK!
WELL, AFTER I TOLD HIM YOU 'N' BUDDY BOTH DIED IN A FIERY CAR CRASH, HE JUST SAID: "THANKS FOR THE INFORMATION," AND THEN HUNG UP...
FEH! GEORGE! WHAT A NERD!
BUT JUST YOU WATCH! I BET HE CAN'T WAIT TO SPREAD THE NEWS!
...AND THEN HE'LL HAVE SUCH AN EGG ON HIS FACE! HAW!
MEANWHILE, IN SEATTLE...
...HAR-DE-HAR-HAR. VERY FUNNY...
IF ONLY IT WERE TRUE...
BACK IN JERSEY...
...THERE THEY ARE NOW...
YO, LEONARD! LONG TIME NO SEE!
GREETINGS, GENTS!
SO, WHAT WERE YOU TWO DOING IN THE BEDROOM ALL THIS TIME, HMM? YUCK-YUCK!
—DON'T TOUCH ME, YOU!
?!?

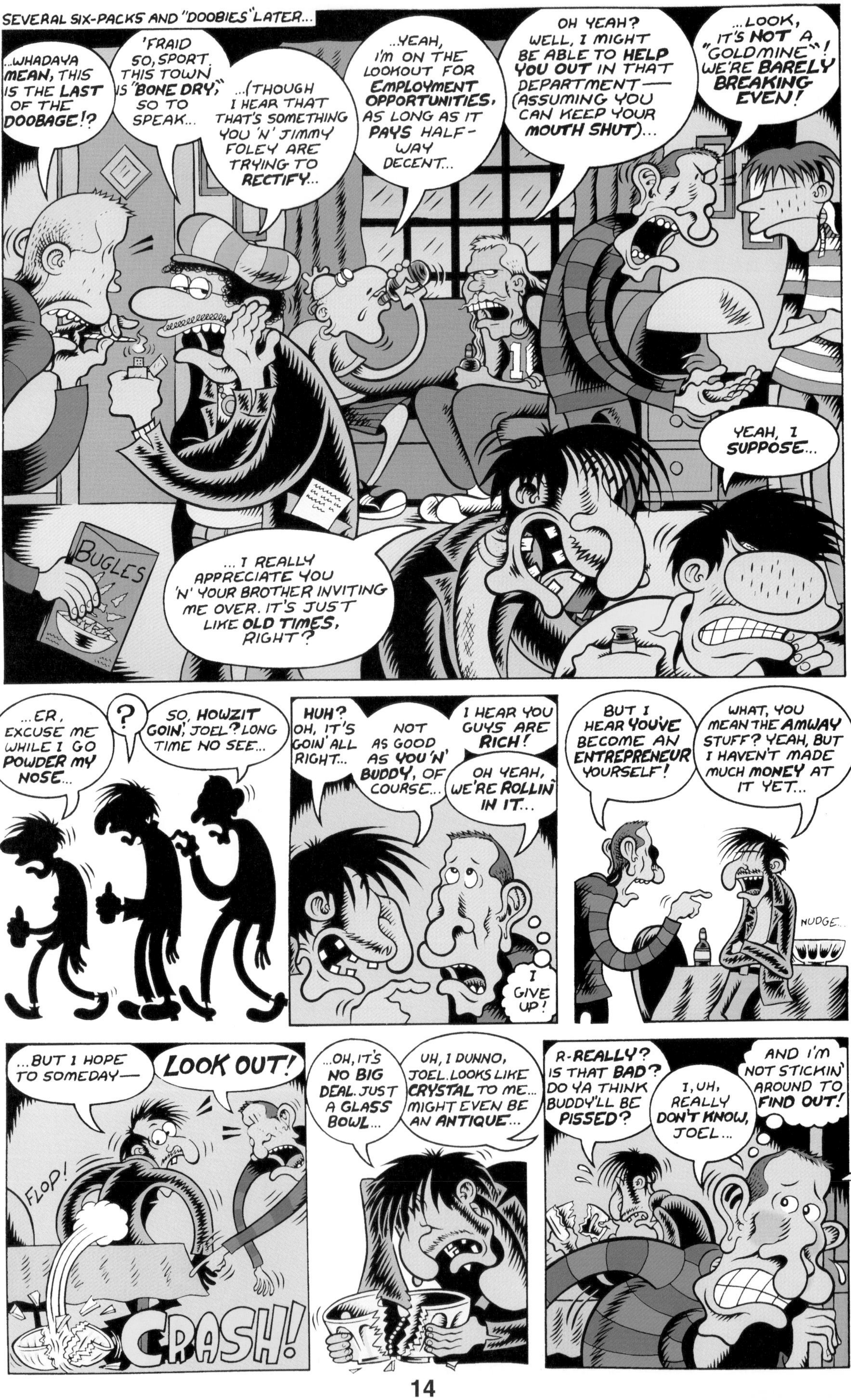
SEVERAL SIX-PACKS AND "DOOBIES" LATER...
...WHADAYA MEAN, THIS IS THE LAST OF THE DOOBAGE!?
'FRAID SO, SPORT. THIS TOWN IS "BONE DRY," SO TO SPEAK...
...(THOUGH I HEAR THAT THAT'S SOMETHING YOU 'N' JIMMY FOLEY ARE TRYING TO RECTIFY...
...YEAH, I'M ON THE LOOKOUT FOR EMPLOYMENT OPPORTUNITIES, AS LONG AS IT PAYS HALF-WAY DECENT...
OH YEAH? WELL, I MIGHT BE ABLE TO HELP YOU OUT IN THAT DEPARTMENT— (ASSUMING YOU CAN KEEP YOUR MOUTH SHUT)...
...LOOK, IT'S NOT A "GOLDMINE"! WE'RE BARELY BREAKING EVEN!
YEAH, I SUPPOSE...
BUGLES
...I REALLY APPRECIATE YOU 'N' YOUR BROTHER INVITING ME OVER. IT'S JUST LIKE OLD TIMES, RIGHT?
...ER, EXCUSE ME WHILE I GO POWDER MY NOSE...
?
SO, HOWZIT GOIN', JOEL? LONG TIME NO SEE...
HUH? OH, IT'S GOIN' ALL RIGHT...
NOT AS GOOD AS YOU 'N' BUDDY, OF COURSE...
I HEAR YOU GUYS ARE RICH!
OH YEAH, WE'RE ROLLIN' IN IT...
I GIVE UP!
BUT I HEAR YOU'VE BECOME AN ENTREPRENEUR YOURSELF!
WHAT, YOU MEAN THE AMWAY STUFF? YEAH, BUT I HAVEN'T MADE MUCH MONEY AT IT YET...
NUDGE...
...BUT I HOPE TO SOMEDAY—
LOOK OUT!
FLOP!
CRASH!
...OH, IT'S NO BIG DEAL. JUST A GLASS BOWL...
UH, I DUNNO, JOEL. LOOKS LIKE CRYSTAL TO ME... MIGHT EVEN BE AN ANTIQUE...
R-REALLY? IS THAT BAD? DO YA THINK BUDDY'LL BE PISSED?
I, UH, REALLY DON'T KNOW, JOEL...
AND I'M NOT STICKIN' AROUND TO FIND OUT!

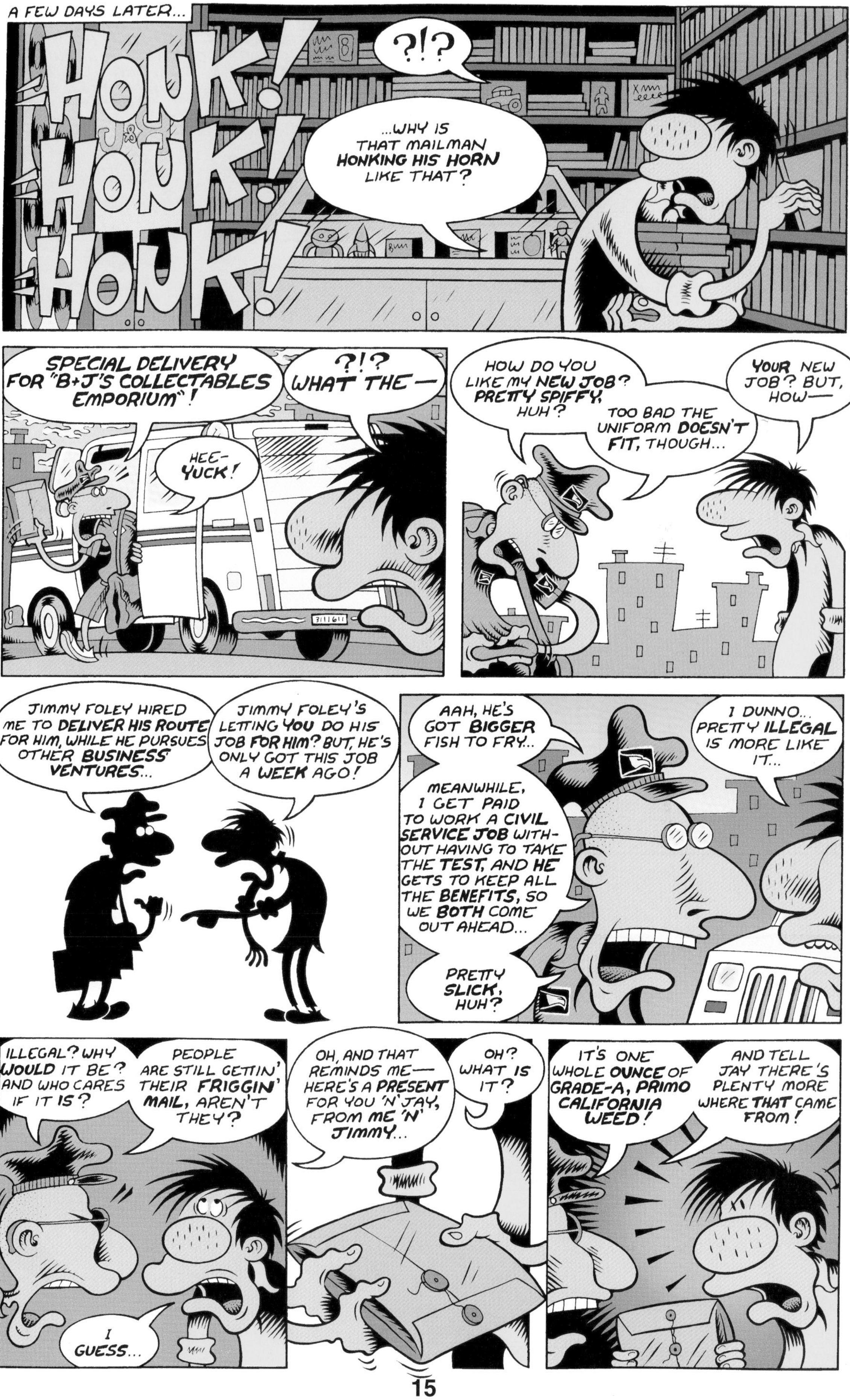
A FEW DAYS LATER...
HONK! HONK! HONK!
?!?
...WHY IS THAT MAILMAN HONKING HIS HORN LIKE THAT?
SPECIAL DELIVERY FOR "B+J'S COLLECTABLES EMPORIUM"!
?!? WHAT THE—
HEE-YUCK!
HOW DO YOU LIKE MY NEW JOB? PRETTY SPIFFY, HUH?
TOO BAD THE UNIFORM DOESN'T FIT, THOUGH...
YOUR NEW JOB? BUT, HOW—
JIMMY FOLEY HIRED ME TO DELIVER HIS ROUTE FOR HIM, WHILE HE PURSUES OTHER BUSINESS VENTURES...
JIMMY FOLEY'S LETTING YOU DO HIS JOB FOR HIM? BUT, HE'S ONLY GOT THIS JOB A WEEK AGO!
AAH, HE'S GOT BIGGER FISH TO FRY...
MEANWHILE, I GET PAID TO WORK A CIVIL SERVICE JOB WITHOUT HAVING TO TAKE THE TEST, AND HE GETS TO KEEP ALL THE BENEFITS, SO WE BOTH COME OUT AHEAD...
PRETTY SLICK, HUH?
I DUNNO... PRETTY ILLEGAL IS MORE LIKE IT...
ILLEGAL? WHY WOULD IT BE? AND WHO CARES IF IT IS?
PEOPLE ARE STILL GETTIN' THEIR FRIGGIN' MAIL, AREN'T THEY?
I GUESS...
OH, AND THAT REMINDS ME— HERE'S A PRESENT FOR YOU 'N' JAY, FROM ME 'N' JIMMY...
OH? WHAT IS IT?
IT'S ONE WHOLE OUNCE OF GRADE-A, PRIMO CALIFORNIA WEED!
AND TELL JAY THERE'S PLENTY MORE WHERE THAT CAME FROM!

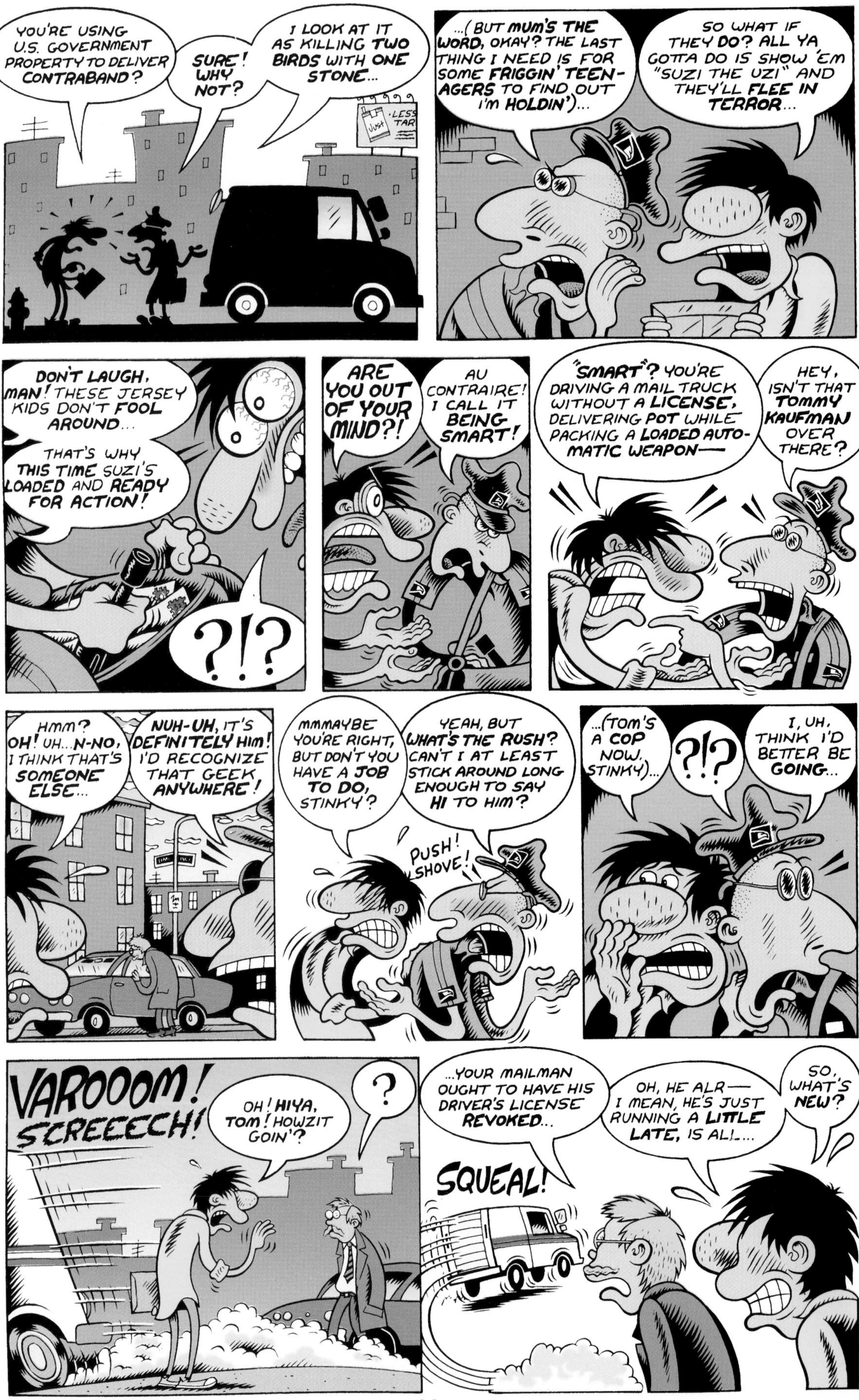
YOU'RE USING U.S. GOVERNMENT PROPERTY TO DELIVER CONTRABAND?
SURE! WHY NOT?
I LOOK AT IT AS KILLING TWO BIRDS WITH ONE STONE...
...(BUT MUM'S THE WORD, OKAY? THE LAST THING I NEED IS FOR SOME FRIGGIN' TEEN-AGERS TO FIND OUT I'M HOLDIN')...
SO WHAT IF THEY DO? ALL YA GOTTA DO IS SHOW 'EM "SUZI THE UZI" AND THEY'LL FLEE IN TERROR...
DON'T LAUGH, MAN! THESE JERSEY KIDS DON'T FOOL AROUND...
THAT'S WHY THIS TIME SUZI'S LOADED AND READY FOR ACTION!
?!?
ARE YOU OUT OF YOUR MIND?!
AU CONTRAIRE! I CALL IT BEING SMART!
"SMART"? YOU'RE DRIVING A MAIL TRUCK WITHOUT A LICENSE, DELIVERING POT WHILE PACKING A LOADED AUTO-MATIC WEAPON—
HEY, ISN'T THAT TOMMY KAUFMAN OVER THERE?
HMM? OH! UH... N-NO, I THINK THAT'S SOMEONE ELSE...
NUH-UH, IT'S DEFINITELY HIM! I'D RECOGNIZE THAT GEEK ANYWHERE!
MMMAYBE YOU'RE RIGHT, BUT DON'T YOU HAVE A JOB TO DO, STINKY?
YEAH, BUT WHAT'S THE RUSH? CAN'T I AT LEAST STICK AROUND LONG ENOUGH TO SAY HI TO HIM?
PUSH! SHOVE!
...(TOM'S A COP NOW, STINKY)...
?!?
I, UH, THINK I'D BETTER BE GOING...
VAROOOM! SCREEECH!
OH! HIYA, TOM! HOWZIT GOIN'?
?
...YOUR MAILMAN OUGHT TO HAVE HIS DRIVER'S LICENSE REVOKED...
SQUEAL!
OH, HE ALR— I MEAN, HE'S JUST RUNNING A LITTLE LATE, IS ALL...
SO, WHAT'S NEW?

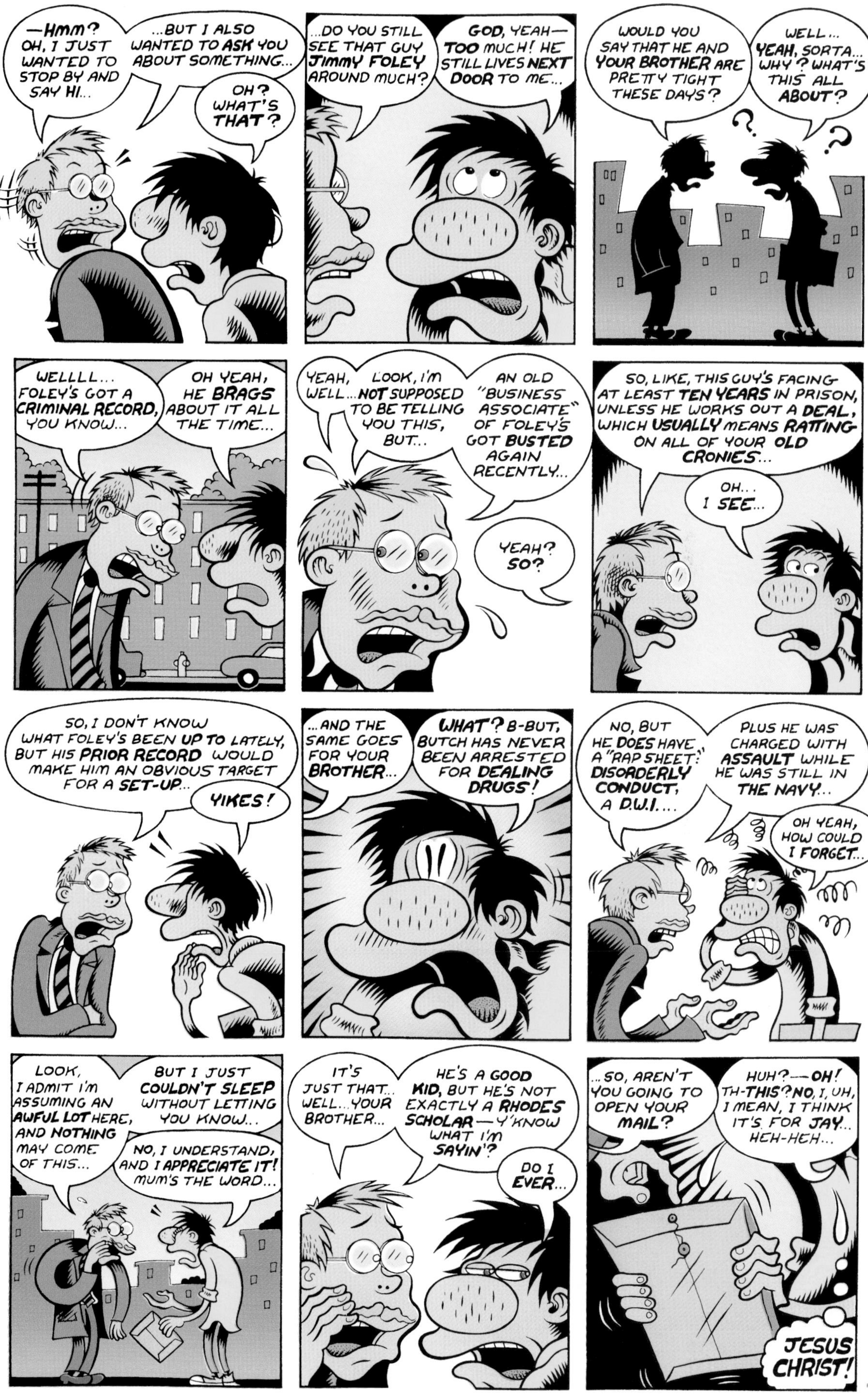
—HMM? OH, I JUST WANTED TO STOP BY AND SAY HI...
...BUT I ALSO WANTED TO ASK YOU ABOUT SOMETHING...
OH? WHAT'S THAT?
...DO YOU STILL SEE THAT GUY JIMMY FOLEY AROUND MUCH?
GOD, YEAH— TOO MUCH! HE STILL LIVES NEXT DOOR TO ME...
WOULD YOU SAY THAT HE AND YOUR BROTHER ARE PRETTY TIGHT THESE DAYS?
WELL... YEAH, SORTA... WHY? WHAT'S THIS ALL ABOUT?
WELLLL... FOLEY'S GOT A CRIMINAL RECORD, YOU KNOW...
OH YEAH, HE BRAGS ABOUT IT ALL THE TIME...
YEAH, WELL...
LOOK, I'M NOT SUPPOSED TO BE TELLING YOU THIS, BUT...
AN OLD "BUSINESS ASSOCIATE" OF FOLEY'S GOT BUSTED AGAIN RECENTLY...
YEAH? SO?
SO, LIKE, THIS GUY'S FACING AT LEAST TEN YEARS IN PRISON, UNLESS HE WORKS OUT A DEAL, WHICH USUALLY MEANS RATTING ON ALL OF YOUR OLD CRONIES...
OH... I SEE...
SO, I DON'T KNOW WHAT FOLEY'S BEEN UP TO LATELY, BUT HIS PRIOR RECORD WOULD MAKE HIM AN OBVIOUS TARGET FOR A SET-UP...
YIKES!
...AND THE SAME GOES FOR YOUR BROTHER...
WHAT? B-BUT, BUTCH HAS NEVER BEEN ARRESTED FOR DEALING DRUGS!
NO, BUT HE DOES HAVE A "RAP SHEET": DISORDERLY CONDUCT, A D.W.I. ...
PLUS HE WAS CHARGED WITH ASSAULT WHILE HE WAS STILL IN THE NAVY...
OH YEAH, HOW COULD I FORGET...
LOOK, I ADMIT I'M ASSUMING AN AWFUL LOT HERE, AND NOTHING MAY COME OF THIS...
BUT I JUST COULDN'T SLEEP WITHOUT LETTING YOU KNOW...
NO, I UNDERSTAND, AND I APPRECIATE IT! MUM'S THE WORD...
IT'S JUST THAT... WELL... YOUR BROTHER...
HE'S A GOOD KID, BUT HE'S NOT EXACTLY A RHODES SCHOLAR — Y'KNOW WHAT I'M SAYIN'?
DO I EVER...
...SO, AREN'T YOU GOING TO OPEN YOUR MAIL?
HUH?—OH! TH-THIS? NO, I, UH, I MEAN, I THINK IT'S FOR JAY... HEH-HEH...
JESUS CHRIST!

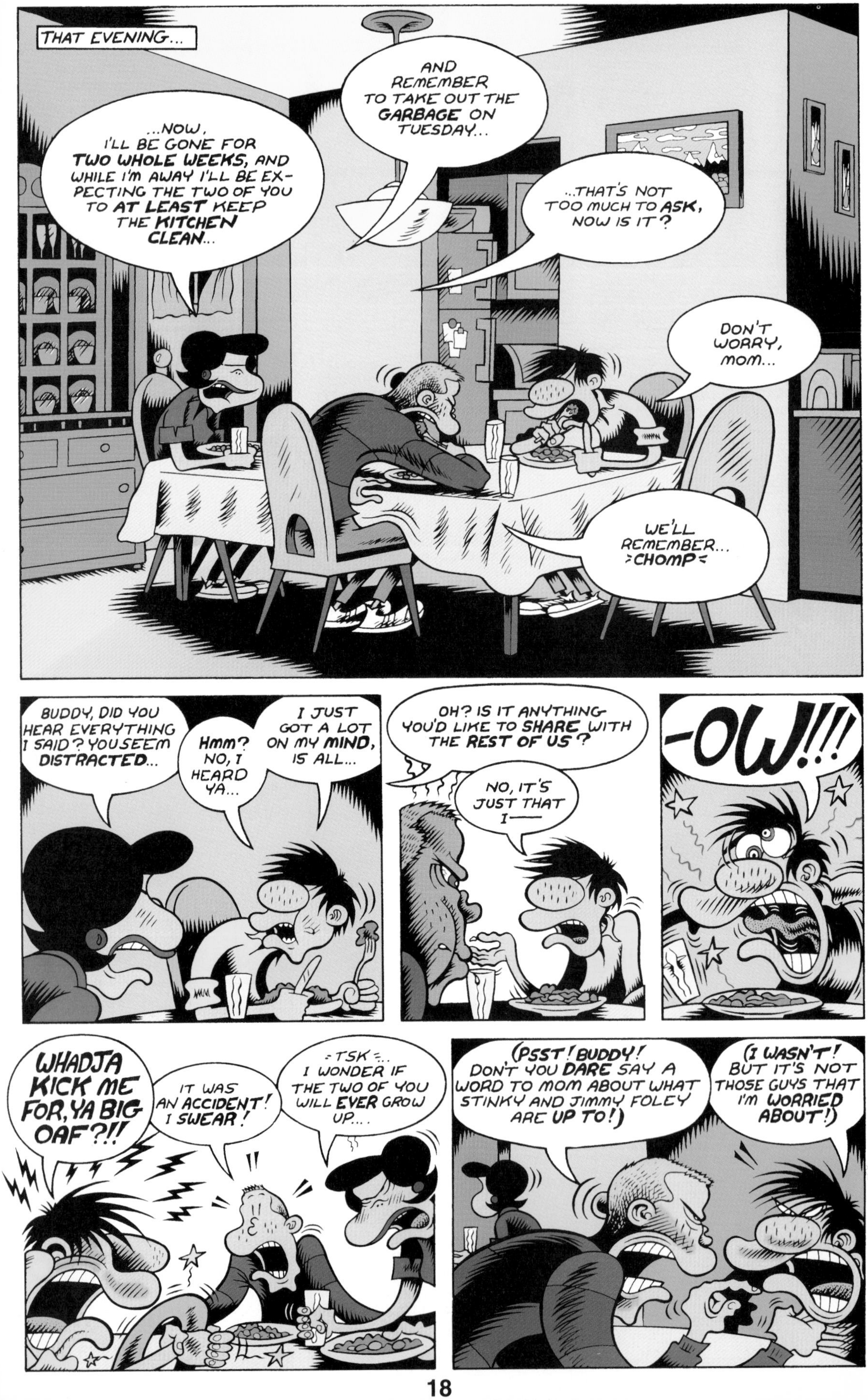
THAT EVENING...
...NOW, I'LL BE GONE FOR TWO WHOLE WEEKS, AND WHILE I'M AWAY I'LL BE EXPECTING THE TWO OF YOU TO AT LEAST KEEP THE KITCHEN CLEAN...
AND REMEMBER TO TAKE OUT THE GARBAGE ON TUESDAY...
...THAT'S NOT TOO MUCH TO ASK, NOW IS IT?
DON'T WORRY, MOM...
WE'LL REMEMBER... CHOMP
BUDDY, DID YOU HEAR EVERYTHING I SAID? YOU SEEM DISTRACTED...
Hmm? NO, I HEARD YA...
I JUST GOT A LOT ON MY MIND, IS ALL...
OH? IS IT ANYTHING YOU'D LIKE TO SHARE WITH THE REST OF US?
NO, IT'S JUST THAT I—
-OW!!!
WHADJA KICK ME FOR, YA BIG OAF?!!
IT WAS AN ACCIDENT! I SWEAR!
TSK... I WONDER IF THE TWO OF YOU WILL EVER GROW UP....
(PSST! BUDDY! DON'T YOU DARE SAY A WORD TO MOM ABOUT WHAT STINKY AND JIMMY FOLEY ARE UP TO!)
(I WASN'T! BUT IT'S NOT THOSE GUYS THAT I'M WORRIED ABOUT!)

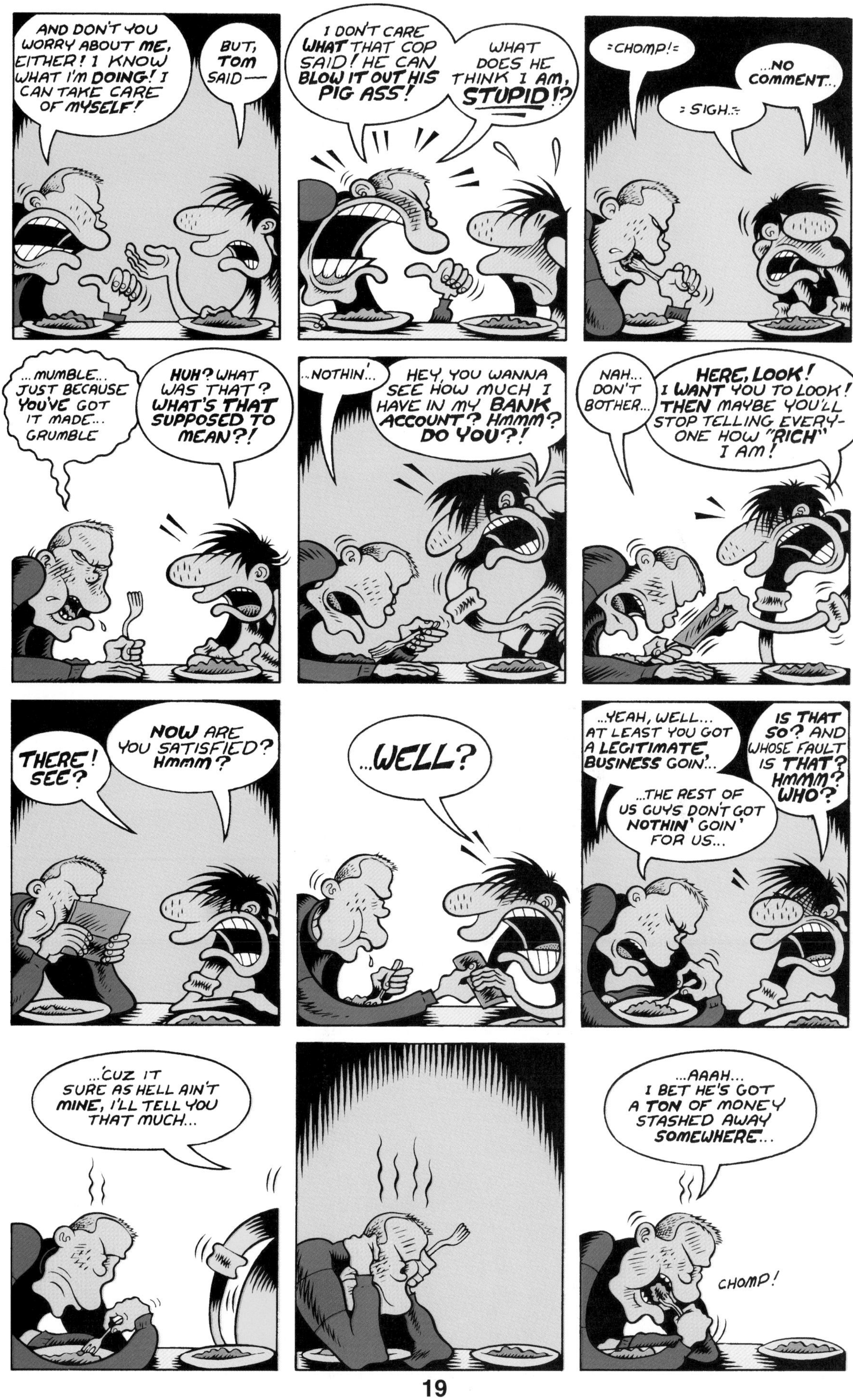
AND DON'T YOU WORRY ABOUT ME, EITHER! I KNOW WHAT I'M DOING! I CAN TAKE CARE OF MYSELF!
BUT, TOM SAID—
I DON'T CARE WHAT THAT COP SAID! HE CAN BLOW IT OUT HIS PIG ASS!
WHAT DOES HE THINK I AM, STUPID!?
=CHOMP!=
...NO COMMENT...
=SIGH.=
...MUMBLE... JUST BECAUSE YOU'VE GOT IT MADE... GRUMBLE
HUH? WHAT WAS THAT? WHAT'S THAT SUPPOSED TO MEAN?!
...NOTHIN'...
HEY, YOU WANNA SEE HOW MUCH I HAVE IN MY BANK ACCOUNT? HMMM? DO YOU?!
NAH... DON'T BOTHER...
HERE, LOOK! I WANT YOU TO LOOK! THEN MAYBE YOU'LL STOP TELLING EVERYONE HOW "RICH" I AM!
THERE! SEE?
NOW ARE YOU SATISFIED? HMMM?
...WELL?
...YEAH, WELL... AT LEAST YOU GOT A LEGITIMATE BUSINESS GOIN'...
...THE REST OF US GUYS DON'T GOT NOTHIN' GOIN' FOR US...
IS THAT SO? AND WHOSE FAULT IS THAT? HMMM? WHO?
...'CUZ IT SURE AS HELL AIN'T MINE, I'LL TELL YOU THAT MUCH...
...AAAH... I BET HE'S GOT A TON OF MONEY STASHED AWAY SOMEWHERE...
CHOMP!

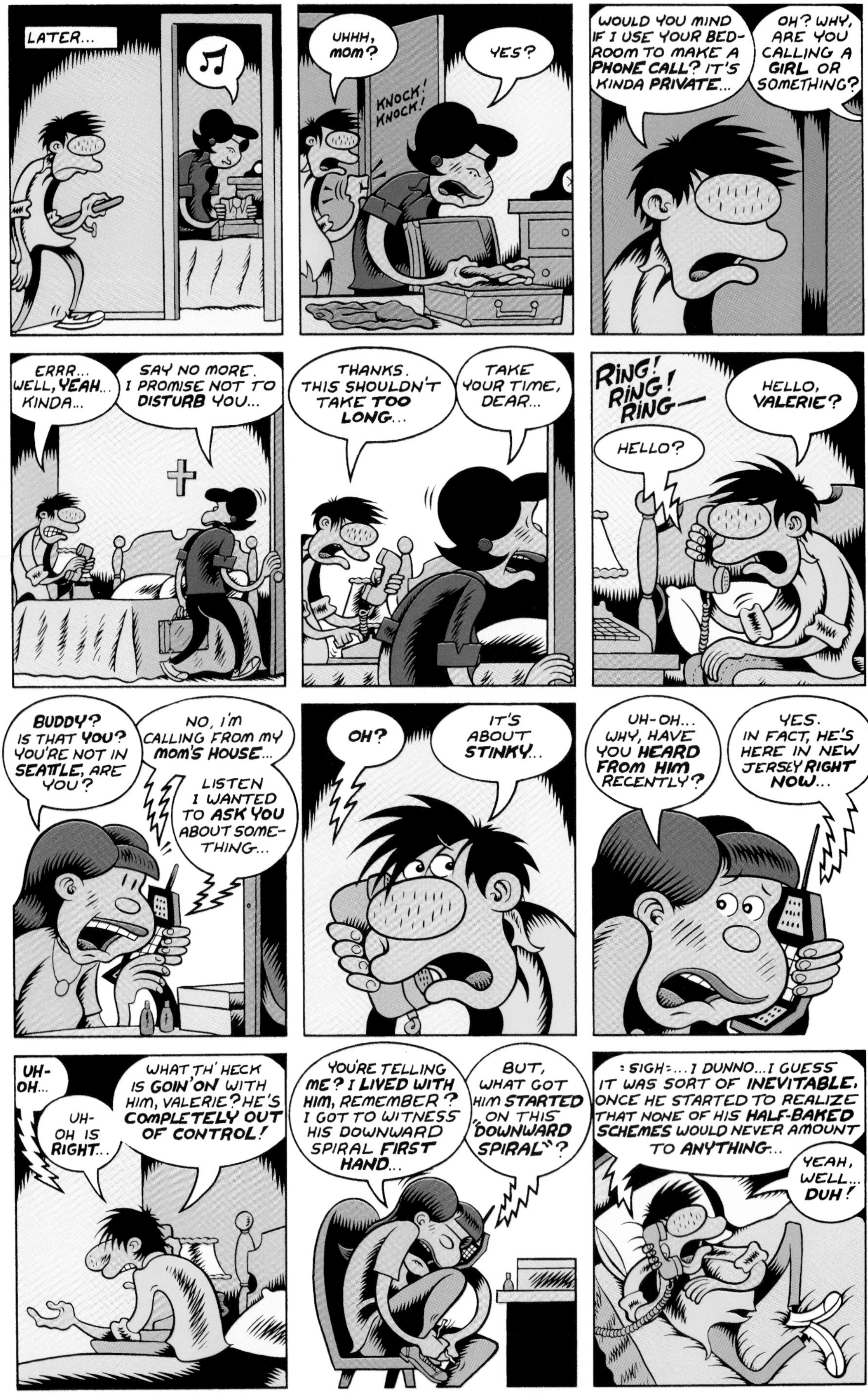
LATER...
♫
UHHH, MOM?
KNOCK! KNOCK!
YES?
WOULD YOU MIND IF I USE YOUR BED-ROOM TO MAKE A PHONE CALL? IT'S KINDA PRIVATE...
OH? WHY, ARE YOU CALLING A GIRL OR SOMETHING?
ERRR... WELL, YEAH... KINDA...
SAY NO MORE. I PROMISE NOT TO DISTURB YOU...
THANKS. THIS SHOULDN'T TAKE TOO LONG...
TAKE YOUR TIME, DEAR...
RING! RING! RING—
HELLO?
HELLO, VALERIE?
BUDDY? IS THAT YOU? YOU'RE NOT IN SEATTLE, ARE YOU?
NO, I'M CALLING FROM MY MOM'S HOUSE...
LISTEN I WANTED TO ASK YOU ABOUT SOME-THING...
OH?
IT'S ABOUT STINKY...
UH-OH... WHY, HAVE YOU HEARD FROM HIM RECENTLY?
YES. IN FACT, HE'S HERE IN NEW JERSEY RIGHT NOW...
UH-OH...
UH-OH IS RIGHT...
WHAT TH' HECK IS GOIN' ON WITH HIM, VALERIE? HE'S COMPLETELY OUT OF CONTROL!
YOU'RE TELLING ME? I LIVED WITH HIM, REMEMBER? I GOT TO WITNESS HIS DOWNWARD SPIRAL FIRST HAND...
BUT, WHAT GOT HIM STARTED ON THIS "DOWNWARD SPIRAL"?
:SIGH:... I DUNNO... I GUESS IT WAS SORT OF INEVITABLE, ONCE HE STARTED TO REALIZE THAT NONE OF HIS HALF-BAKED SCHEMES WOULD NEVER AMOUNT TO ANYTHING...
YEAH, WELL... DUH!

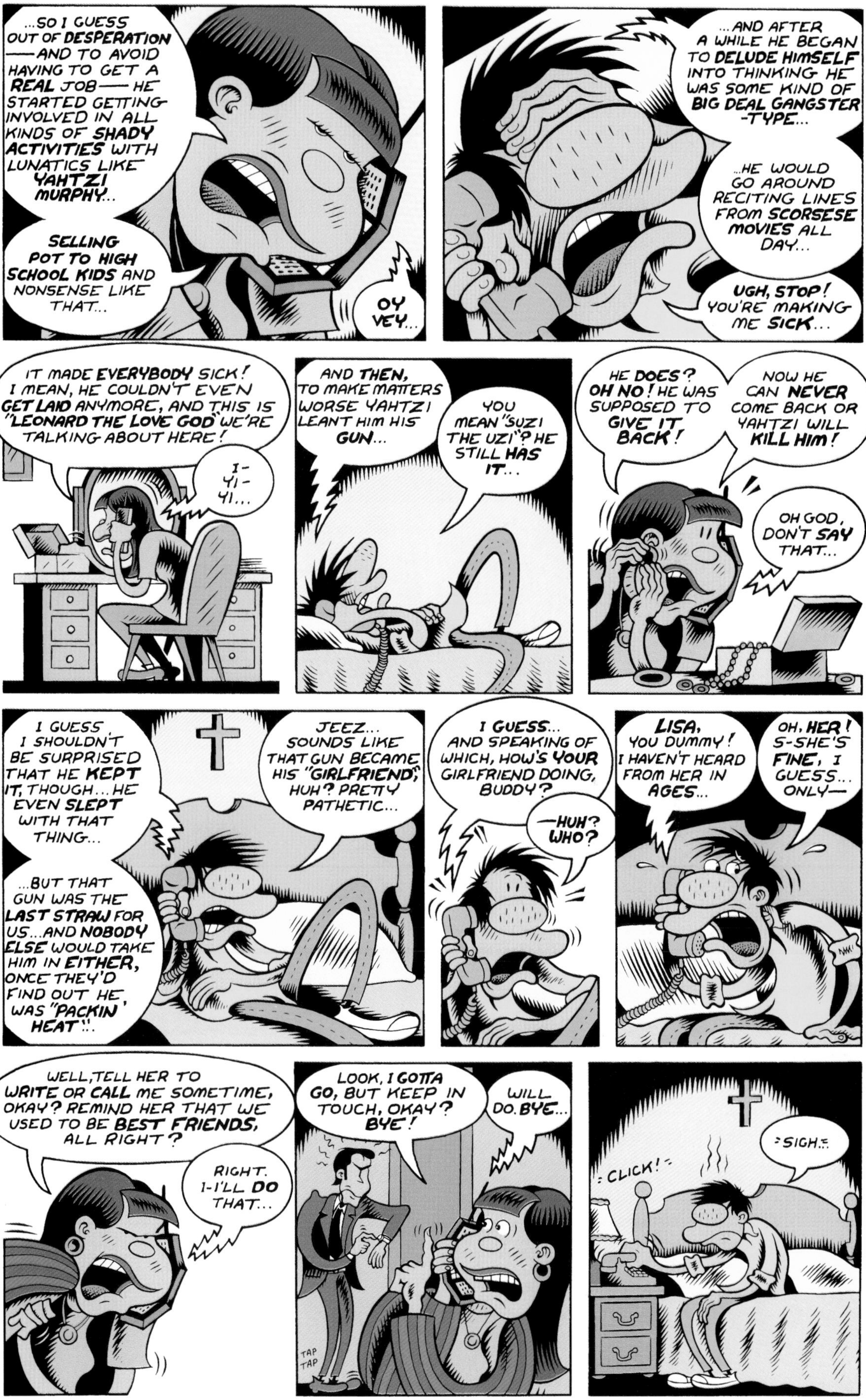
...SO I GUESS OUT OF DESPERATION —AND TO AVOID HAVING TO GET A REAL JOB— HE STARTED GETTING INVOLVED IN ALL KINDS OF SHADY ACTIVITIES WITH LUNATICS LIKE YAHTZI MURPHY...
SELLING POT TO HIGH SCHOOL KIDS AND NONSENSE LIKE THAT...
OY VEY...
...AND AFTER A WHILE HE BEGAN TO DELUDE HIMSELF INTO THINKING HE WAS SOME KIND OF BIG DEAL GANGSTER -TYPE...
...HE WOULD GO AROUND RECITING LINES FROM SCORSESE MOVIES ALL DAY...
UGH, STOP! YOU'RE MAKING ME SICK...
IT MADE EVERYBODY SICK! I MEAN, HE COULDN'T EVEN GET LAID ANYMORE, AND THIS IS "LEONARD THE LOVE GOD" WE'RE TALKING ABOUT HERE!
I- YI- YI...
AND THEN, TO MAKE MATTERS WORSE YAHTZI LEANT HIM HIS GUN...
YOU MEAN "SUZI THE UZI"? HE STILL HAS IT...
HE DOES? OH NO! HE WAS SUPPOSED TO GIVE IT BACK!
NOW HE CAN NEVER COME BACK OR YAHTZI WILL KILL HIM!
OH GOD, DON'T SAY THAT...
I GUESS I SHOULDN'T BE SURPRISED THAT HE KEPT IT, THOUGH... HE EVEN SLEPT WITH THAT THING...
...BUT THAT GUN WAS THE LAST STRAW FOR US... AND NOBODY ELSE WOULD TAKE HIM IN EITHER, ONCE THEY'D FIND OUT HE WAS "PACKIN' HEAT"!...
JEEZ... SOUNDS LIKE THAT GUN BECAME HIS "GIRLFRIEND," HUH? PRETTY PATHETIC...
I GUESS... AND SPEAKING OF WHICH, HOW'S YOUR GIRLFRIEND DOING, BUDDY?
—HUH? WHO?
LISA, YOU DUMMY! I HAVEN'T HEARD FROM HER IN AGES...
OH, HER! S-SHE'S FINE, I GUESS... ONLY—
WELL, TELL HER TO WRITE OR CALL ME SOMETIME, OKAY? REMIND HER THAT WE USED TO BE BEST FRIENDS, ALL RIGHT?
RIGHT. I-I'LL DO THAT...
LOOK, I GOTTA GO, BUT KEEP IN TOUCH, OKAY? BYE!
WILL DO. BYE...
TAP TAP
CLICK!
SIGH.

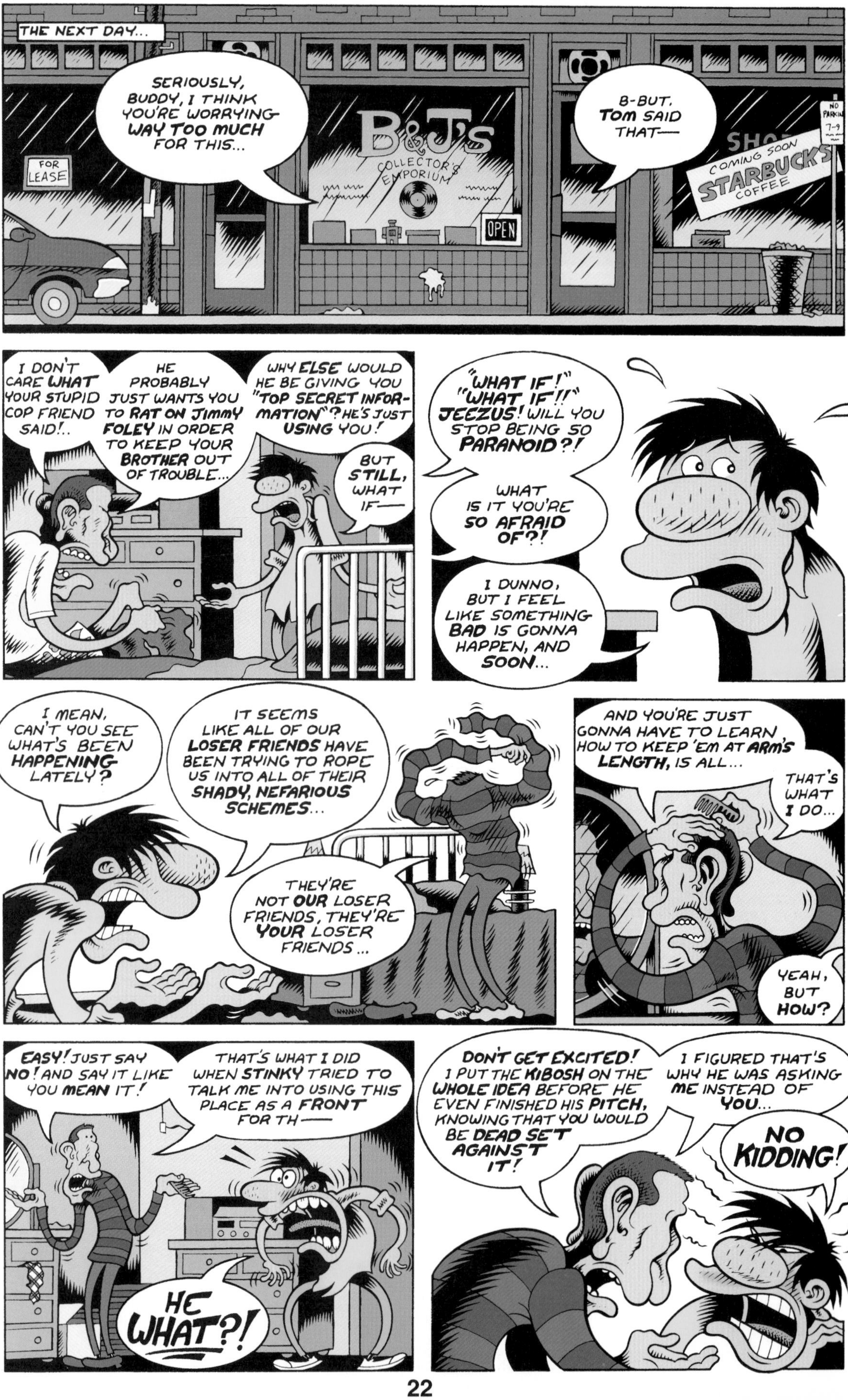
THE NEXT DAY...
SERIOUSLY, BUDDY, I THINK YOU'RE WORRYING WAY TOO MUCH FOR THIS...
B&J'S COLLECTOR'S EMPORIUM
FOR LEASE
OPEN
B-BUT, TOM SAID THAT—
COMING SOON STARBUCKS COFFEE
I DON'T CARE WHAT YOUR STUPID COP FRIEND SAID!..
HE PROBABLY JUST WANTS YOU TO RAT ON JIMMY FOLEY IN ORDER TO KEEP YOUR BROTHER OUT OF TROUBLE...
WHY ELSE WOULD HE BE GIVING YOU "TOP SECRET INFORMATION"? HE'S JUST USING YOU!
BUT STILL, WHAT IF—
"WHAT IF!" "WHAT IF!!" JEEZUS! WILL YOU STOP BEING SO PARANOID?!
WHAT IS IT YOU'RE SO AFRAID OF?!
I DUNNO, BUT I FEEL LIKE SOMETHING BAD IS GONNA HAPPEN, AND SOON...
I MEAN, CAN'T YOU SEE WHAT'S BEEN HAPPENING LATELY?
IT SEEMS LIKE ALL OF OUR LOSER FRIENDS HAVE BEEN TRYING TO ROPE US INTO ALL OF THEIR SHADY, NEFARIOUS SCHEMES...
THEY'RE NOT OUR LOSER FRIENDS, THEY'RE YOUR LOSER FRIENDS...
AND YOU'RE JUST GONNA HAVE TO LEARN HOW TO KEEP 'EM AT ARM'S LENGTH, IS ALL...
THAT'S WHAT I DO...
YEAH, BUT HOW?
EASY! JUST SAY NO! AND SAY IT LIKE YOU MEAN IT!
THAT'S WHAT I DID WHEN STINKY TRIED TO TALK ME INTO USING THIS PLACE AS A FRONT FOR TH—
HE WHAT?!
DON'T GET EXCITED! I PUT THE KIBOSH ON THE WHOLE IDEA BEFORE HE EVEN FINISHED HIS PITCH, KNOWING THAT YOU WOULD BE DEAD SET AGAINST IT!
I FIGURED THAT'S WHY HE WAS ASKING ME INSTEAD OF YOU...
NO KIDDING!

...BUT ARE YOU INSINUATING THAT IF IT WAS TOTALLY UP TO YOU, THAT YOU WOULD'VE GONE ALONG WITH HIS IDEA?

OH, WELL, I DUNNO...I, UH...

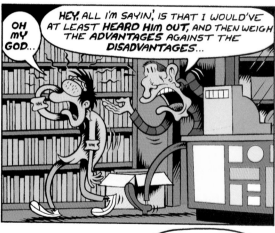

OH MY GOD...

HEY, ALL I'M SAYIN', IS THAT I WOULD'VE AT LEAST *HEARD HIM OUT*, AND THEN WEIGH THE *ADVANTAGES* AGAINST THE *DISADVANTAGES*...

"ADVANTAGES"? *WHAT* ADVANTAGES?

MONEY! WHADAYA THINK?!

SIGH... LOOK, BUDDY, ALL YOUR "LOSER FRIENDS" ARE TRYING TO DO IS FIGURE OUT A WAY TO AVOID HAVING TO *WORK FOR A LIVING* FOR THE *REST OF THEIR LIVES*...

THEY'LL PROBABLY *FAIL*, BUT YA GOTTA GIVE 'EM CREDIT FOR *TRYING*...

SO CUT 'EM A LITTLE *SLACK*, WILL YA?

HMMM...

YEAH, PERHAPS YOU'RE RIGHT...MAYBE I AM BEING A LITTLE *TOO UPTIGHT*...

A "LITTLE"?

BUT I STILL DON'T TRUST *ANY* OF THEM, ESPECIALLY *STINKY*. THAT GUY—

WHOA, SPEAK OF THE *DEVIL*...

OH NO, *NOT* AGAIN...

AND HE LOOKS PRETTY IRATE OVER SOMETHING...

SLAM!

WHAT'S THE MATTER, STINKY? DID YOU GET *HELD UP* BY A BUNCH OF *TEENAGERS* AGAIN?

THAT AIN'T THE *HALF* OF IT...

...THOSE LITTLE FUCKERS STOLE *SUZI!*

?!?

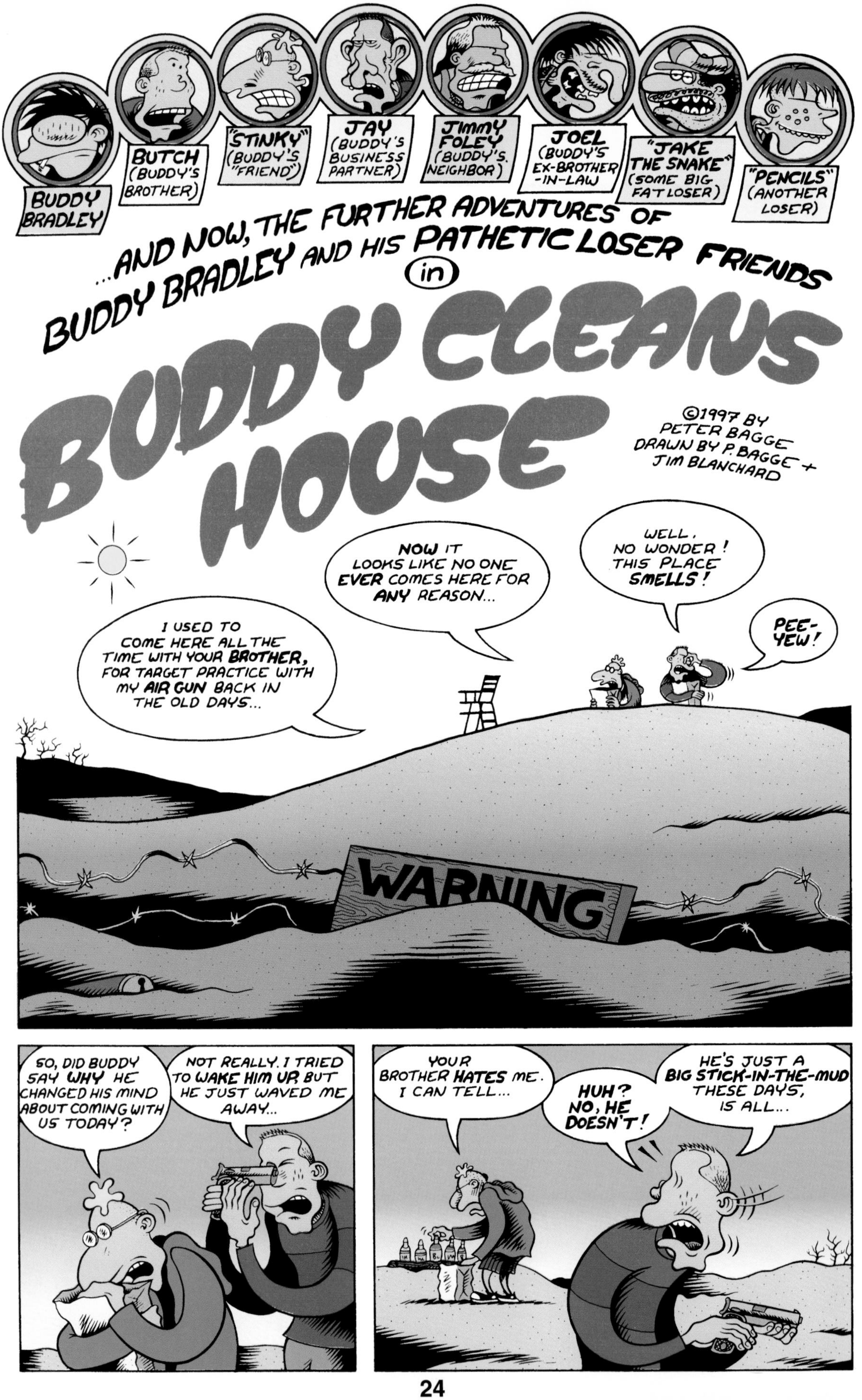

BUDDY BRADLEY
BUTCH (BUDDY'S BROTHER)
"STINKY" (BUDDY'S "FRIEND")
JAY (BUDDY'S BUSINESS PARTNER)
JIMMY FOLEY (BUDDY'S NEIGHBOR)
JOEL (BUDDY'S EX-BROTHER-IN-LAW
"JAKE THE SNAKE" (SOME BIG FAT LOSER)
"PENCILS" (ANOTHER LOSER)
...AND NOW, THE FURTHER ADVENTURES OF BUDDY BRADLEY AND HIS PATHETIC LOSER FRIENDS in
BUDDY CLEANS HOUSE
©1997 BY PETER BAGGE DRAWN BY P. BAGGE + JIM BLANCHARD
I USED TO COME HERE ALL THE TIME WITH YOUR BROTHER, FOR TARGET PRACTICE WITH MY AIR GUN BACK IN THE OLD DAYS...
NOW IT LOOKS LIKE NO ONE EVER COMES HERE FOR ANY REASON...
WELL, NO WONDER! THIS PLACE SMELLS!
PEE-YEW!
WARNING
SO, DID BUDDY SAY WHY HE CHANGED HIS MIND ABOUT COMING WITH US TODAY?
NOT REALLY. I TRIED TO WAKE HIM UP, BUT HE JUST WAVED ME AWAY...
YOUR BROTHER HATES ME. I CAN TELL...
HUH? NO, HE DOESN'T!
HE'S JUST A BIG STICK-IN-THE-MUD THESE DAYS, IS ALL...

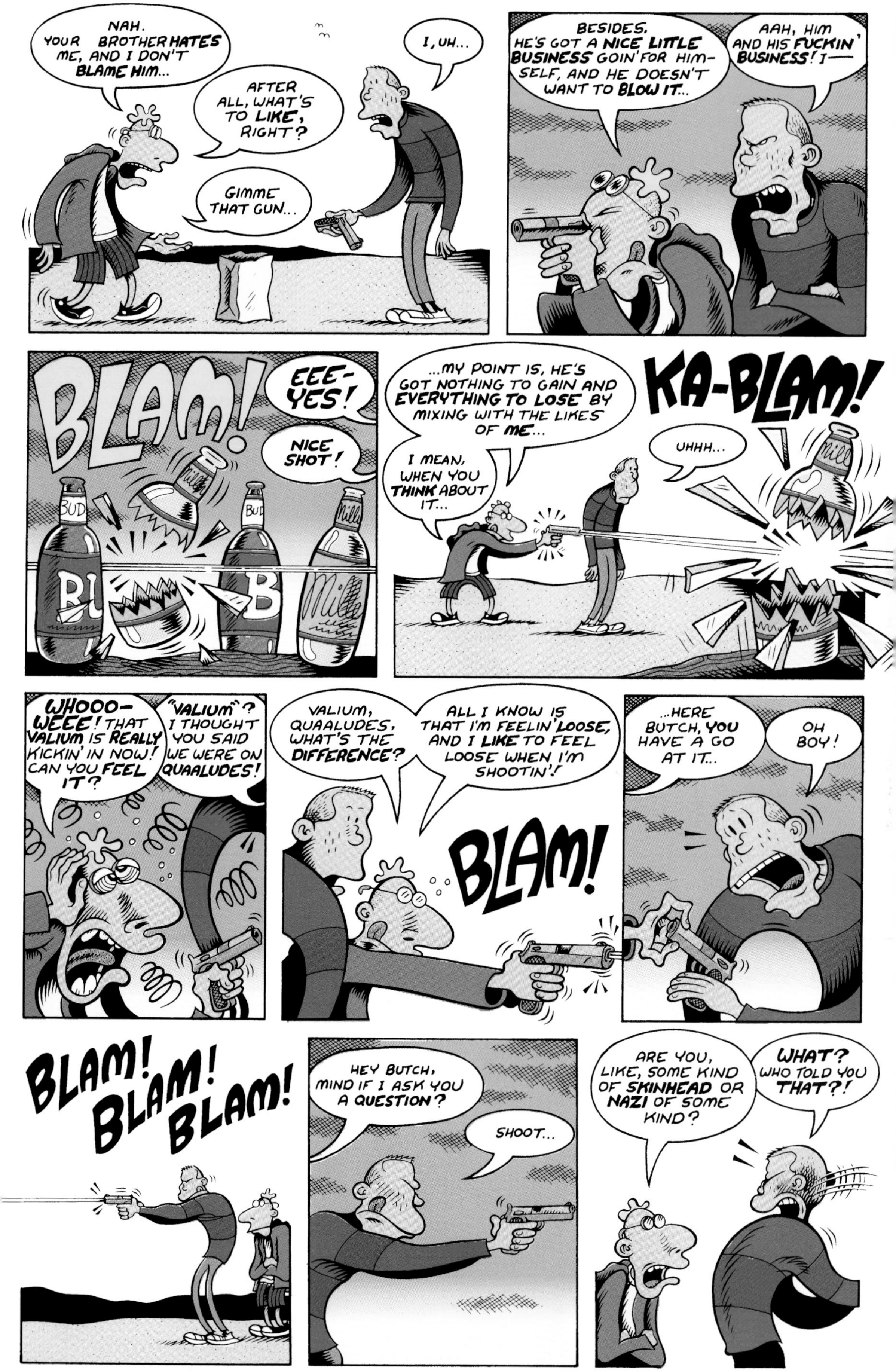
NAH. YOUR BROTHER HATES ME, AND I DON'T BLAME HIM...
AFTER ALL, WHAT'S TO LIKE, RIGHT?
I, UH...
GIMME THAT GUN...
BESIDES, HE'S GOT A NICE LITTLE BUSINESS GOIN' FOR HIMSELF, AND HE DOESN'T WANT TO BLOW IT...
AAH, HIM AND HIS FUCKIN' BUSINESS! I—
BLAM!
EEE-YES!
NICE SHOT!
BUD
BUD
...MY POINT IS, HE'S GOT NOTHING TO GAIN AND EVERYTHING TO LOSE BY MIXING WITH THE LIKES OF ME...
I MEAN, WHEN YOU THINK ABOUT IT...
KA-BLAM!
UHHH...
WHOOO-WEEE! THAT VALIUM IS REALLY KICKIN' IN NOW! CAN YOU FEEL IT?
"VALIUM"? I THOUGHT YOU SAID WE WERE ON QUAALUDES!
VALIUM, QUAALUDES, WHAT'S THE DIFFERENCE?
ALL I KNOW IS THAT I'M FEELIN' LOOSE, AND I LIKE TO FEEL LOOSE WHEN I'M SHOOTIN'!
BLAM!
...HERE BUTCH, YOU HAVE A GO AT IT...
OH BOY!
BLAM! BLAM! BLAM!
HEY BUTCH, MIND IF I ASK YOU A QUESTION?
SHOOT...
ARE YOU, LIKE, SOME KIND OF SKINHEAD OR NAZI OF SOME KIND?
WHAT? WHO TOLD YOU THAT?!

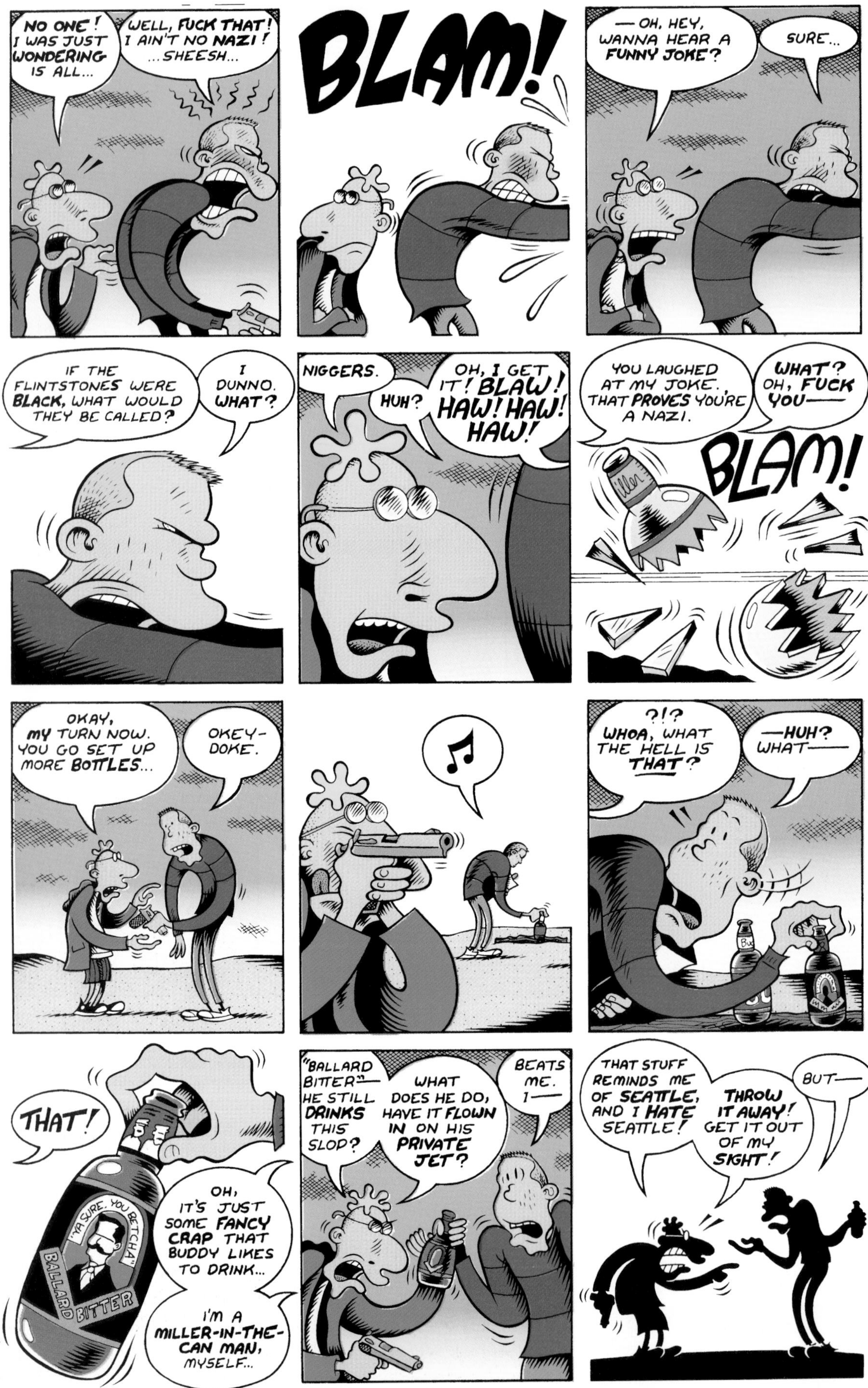
NO ONE! I WAS JUST WONDERING IS ALL...
WELL, FUCK THAT! I AIN'T NO NAZI! ...SHEESH...
BLAM!
—OH, HEY, WANNA HEAR A FUNNY JOKE?
SURE...
IF THE FLINTSTONES WERE BLACK, WHAT WOULD THEY BE CALLED?
I DUNNO. WHAT?
NIGGERS.
HUH?
OH, I GET IT! BLAW! HAW! HAW! HAW!
YOU LAUGHED AT MY JOKE. THAT PROVES YOU'RE A NAZI.
WHAT? OH, FUCK YOU——
BLAM!
OKAY, MY TURN NOW. YOU GO SET UP MORE BOTTLES...
OKEY-DOKE.
?!? WHOA, WHAT THE HELL IS THAT?
—HUH? WHAT——
THAT!
"YA SURE, YOU BETCHA"
BALLARD BITTER
OH, IT'S JUST SOME FANCY CRAP THAT BUDDY LIKES TO DRINK...
I'M A MILLER-IN-THE-CAN MAN, MYSELF...
"BALLARD BITTER"— HE STILL DRINKS THIS SLOP?
WHAT DOES HE DO, HAVE IT FLOWN IN ON HIS PRIVATE JET?
BEATS ME. I—
THAT STUFF REMINDS ME OF SEATTLE, AND I HATE SEATTLE!
THROW IT AWAY! GET IT OUT OF MY SIGHT!
BUT—

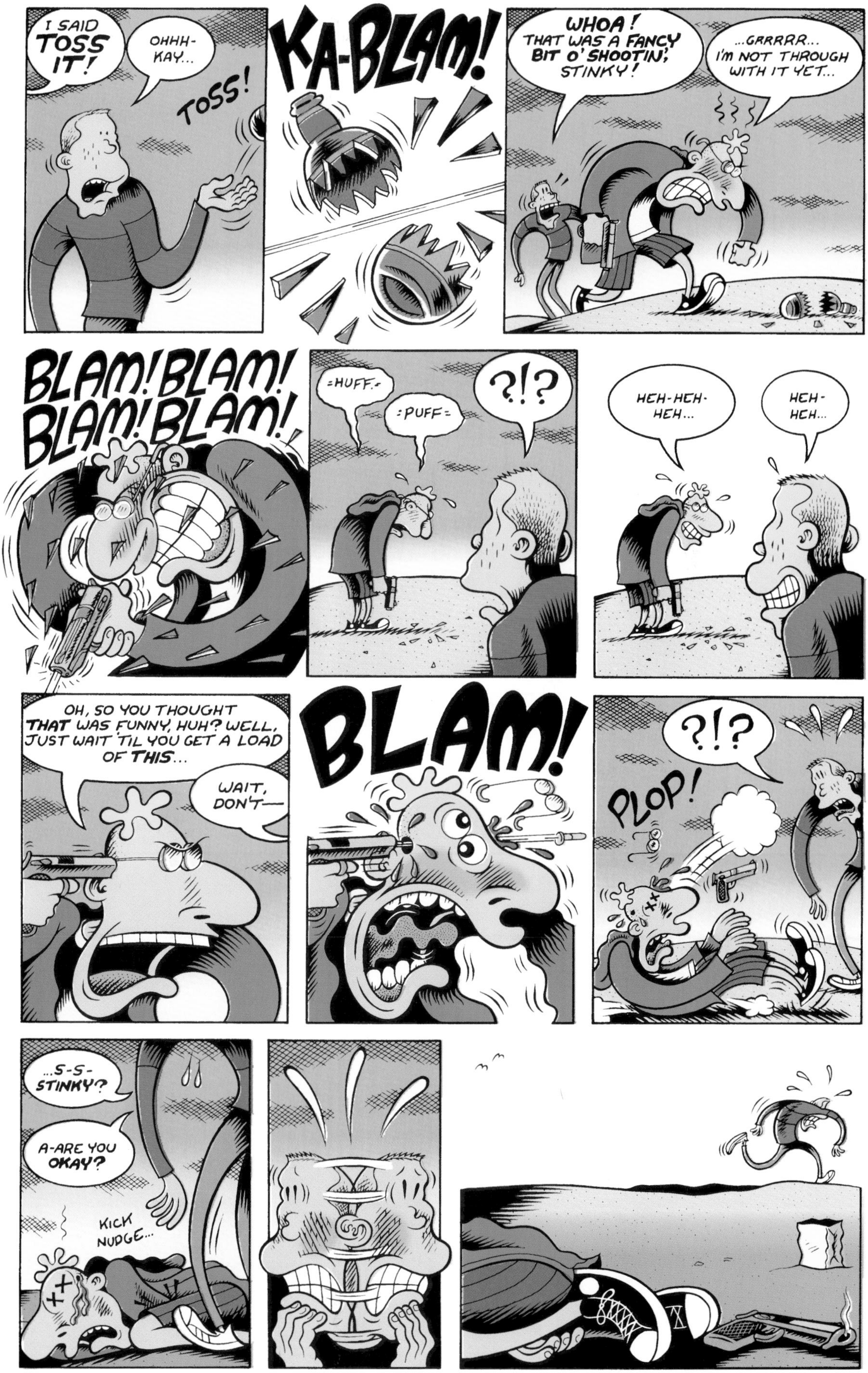
I SAID TOSS IT!
OHHH-KAY...
TOSS!
KA-BLAM!
WHOA! THAT WAS A FANCY BIT O' SHOOTIN', STINKY!
...GRRRRR... I'M NOT THROUGH WITH IT YET...
BLAM! BLAM! BLAM! BLAM!
HUFF
PUFF
?!?
HEH-HEH-HEH...
HEH-HEH...
OH, SO YOU THOUGHT THAT WAS FUNNY, HUH? WELL, JUST WAIT 'TIL YOU GET A LOAD OF THIS...
WAIT, DON'T—
BLAM!
?!?
PLOP!
...S-S-STINKY?
A-ARE YOU OKAY?
KICK NUDGE...

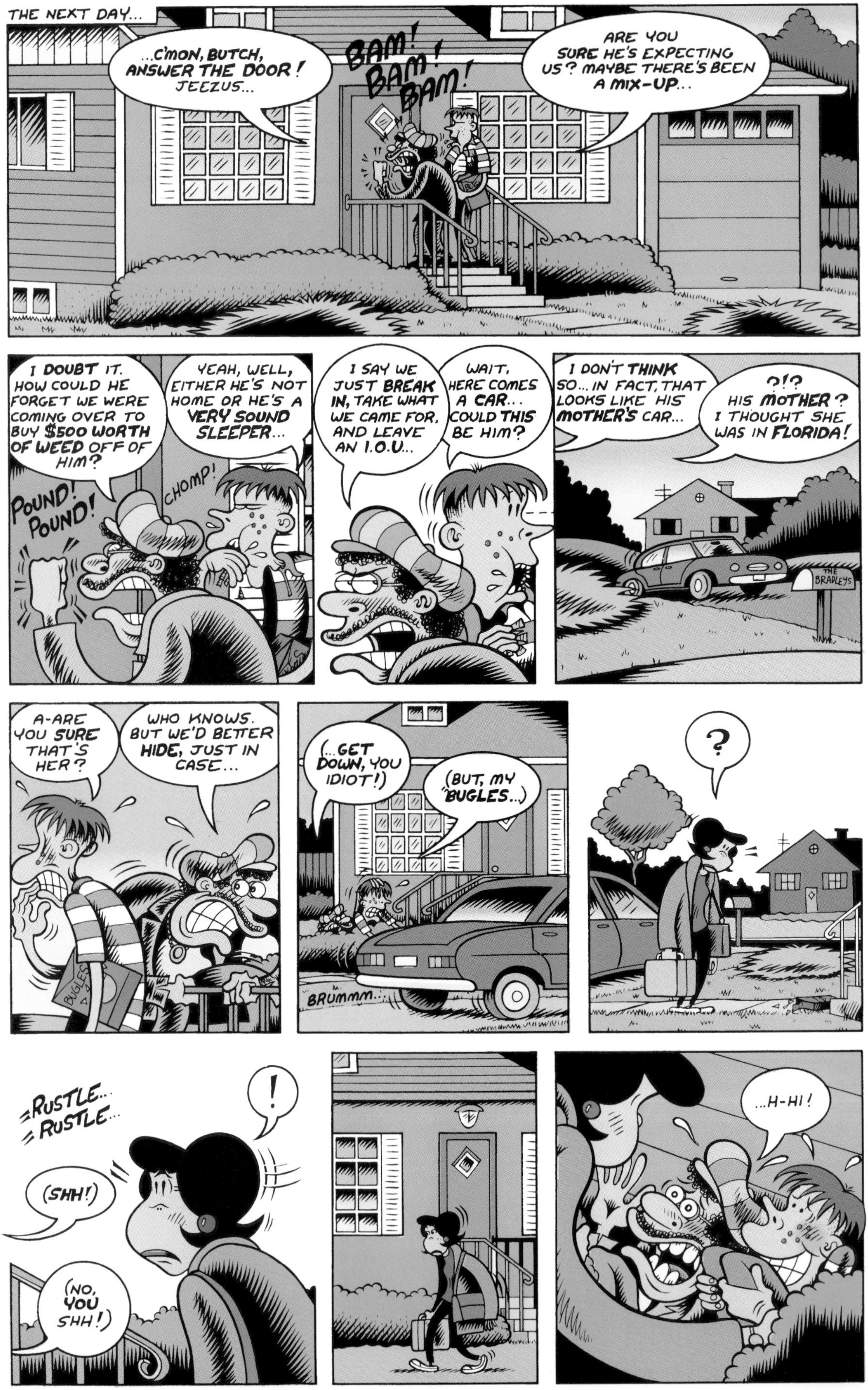
THE NEXT DAY...
...C'MON, BUTCH, ANSWER THE DOOR! JEEZUS...
BAM! BAM! BAM!
ARE YOU SURE HE'S EXPECTING US? MAYBE THERE'S BEEN A MIX-UP...
I DOUBT IT. HOW COULD HE FORGET WE WERE COMING OVER TO BUY $500 WORTH OF WEED OFF OF HIM?
YEAH, WELL, EITHER HE'S NOT HOME OR HE'S A VERY SOUND SLEEPER...
POUND! POUND!
CHOMP!
I SAY WE JUST BREAK IN, TAKE WHAT WE CAME FOR, AND LEAVE AN I.O.U...
WAIT, HERE COMES A CAR... COULD THIS BE HIM?
I DON'T THINK SO... IN FACT, THAT LOOKS LIKE HIS MOTHER'S CAR...
?!? HIS MOTHER? I THOUGHT SHE WAS IN FLORIDA!
THE BRADLEYS
A-ARE YOU SURE THAT'S HER?
WHO KNOWS. BUT WE'D BETTER HIDE, JUST IN CASE...
BUGLES
(...GET DOWN, YOU IDIOT!)
(BUT, MY "BUGLES...)
BRUMMM...
?
RUSTLE... RUSTLE...
!
(SHH!)
(NO, YOU SHH!)
...H-HI!

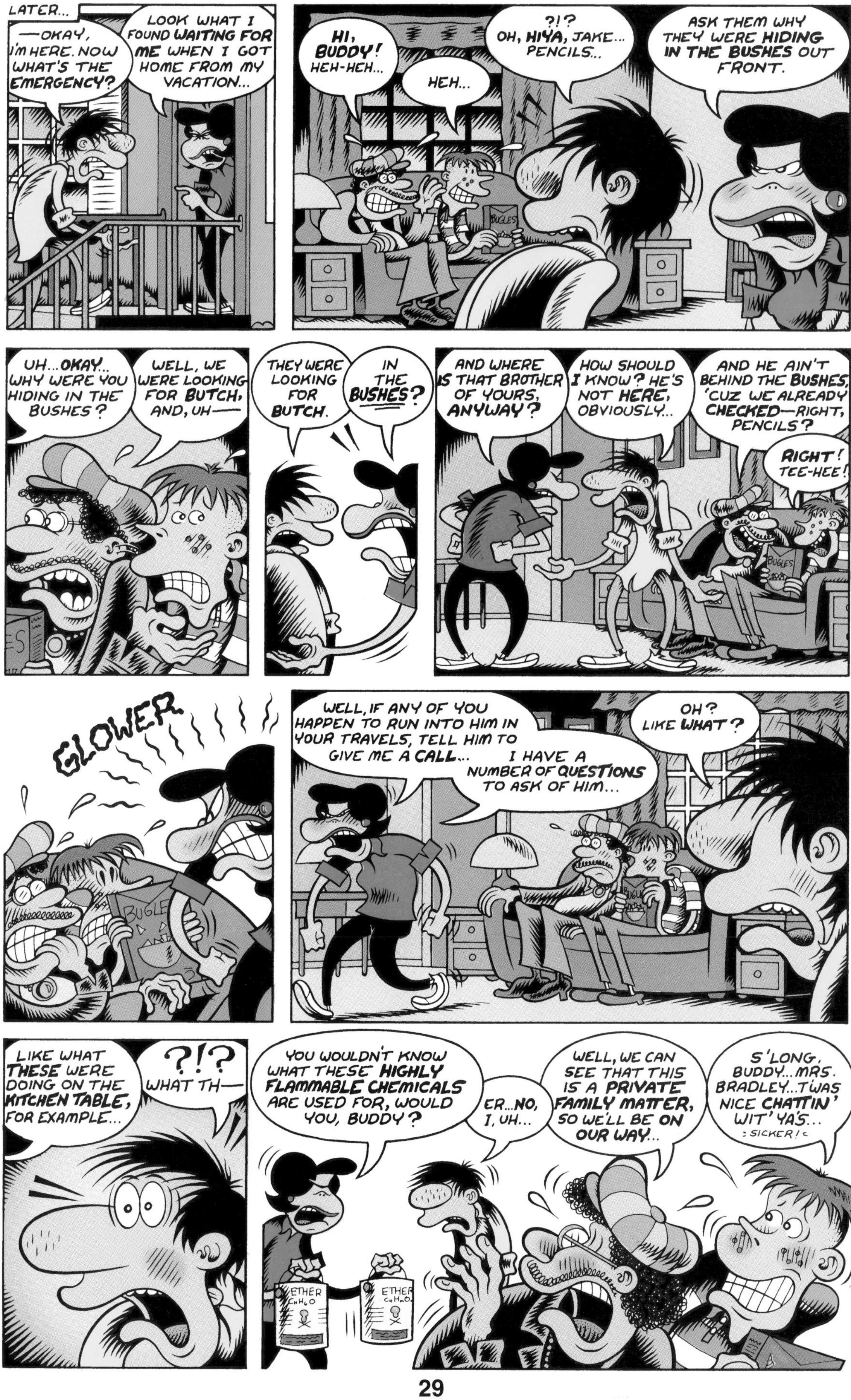
LATER...
—OKAY, I'M HERE. NOW WHAT'S THE EMERGENCY?
LOOK WHAT I FOUND WAITING FOR ME WHEN I GOT HOME FROM MY VACATION...
HI, BUDDY! HEH-HEH...
HEH...
?!? OH, HIYA, JAKE... PENCILS...
ASK THEM WHY THEY WERE HIDING IN THE BUSHES OUT FRONT.
BUGLES
UH...OKAY... WHY WERE YOU HIDING IN THE BUSHES?
WELL, WE WERE LOOKING FOR BUTCH, AND, UH—
THEY WERE LOOKING FOR BUTCH.
IN THE BUSHES?
AND WHERE IS THAT BROTHER OF YOURS, ANYWAY?
HOW SHOULD I KNOW? HE'S NOT HERE, OBVIOUSLY...
AND HE AIN'T BEHIND THE BUSHES, 'CUZ WE ALREADY CHECKED—RIGHT, PENCILS?
RIGHT! TEE-HEE!
BUGLES
GLOWER
BUGLE
WELL, IF ANY OF YOU HAPPEN TO RUN INTO HIM IN YOUR TRAVELS, TELL HIM TO GIVE ME A CALL...
I HAVE A NUMBER OF QUESTIONS TO ASK OF HIM...
OH? LIKE WHAT?
LIKE WHAT THESE WERE DOING ON THE KITCHEN TABLE, FOR EXAMPLE...
?!? WHAT TH—
YOU WOULDN'T KNOW WHAT THESE HIGHLY FLAMMABLE CHEMICALS ARE USED FOR, WOULD YOU, BUDDY?
ER...NO, I, UH...
WELL, WE CAN SEE THAT THIS IS A PRIVATE FAMILY MATTER, SO WE'LL BE ON OUR WAY...
S'LONG, BUDDY...MRS. BRADLEY...T'WAS NICE CHATTIN' WIT' YA'S...
SICKER!
ETHER
ETHER

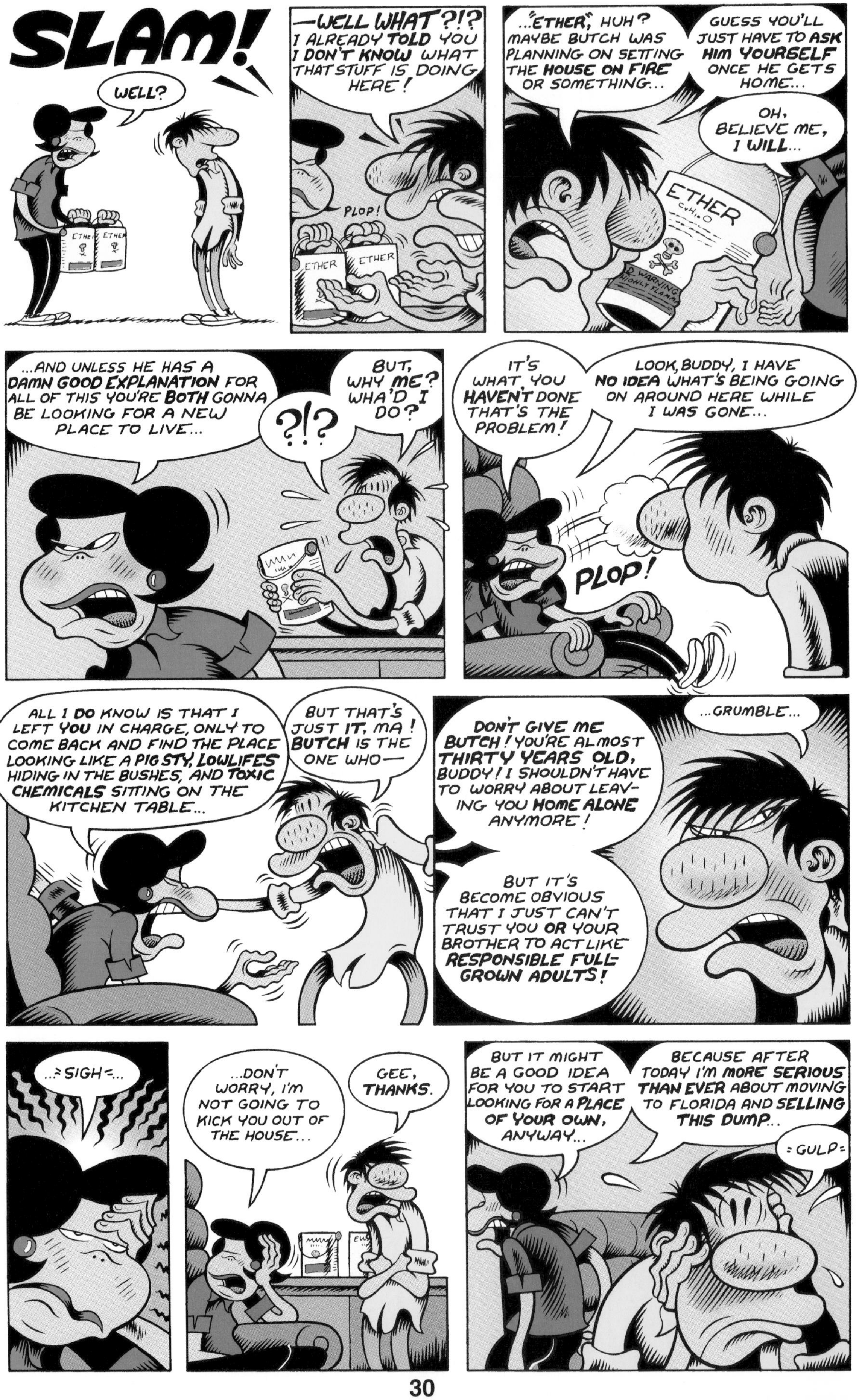
SLAM!
WELL?
ETHER ETHER
—WELL WHAT?!? I ALREADY TOLD YOU I DON'T KNOW WHAT THAT STUFF IS DOING HERE!
PLOP!
ETHER ETHER
..."ETHER," HUH? MAYBE BUTCH WAS PLANNING ON SETTING THE HOUSE ON FIRE OR SOMETHING...
GUESS YOU'LL JUST HAVE TO ASK HIM YOURSELF ONCE HE GETS HOME...
OH, BELIEVE ME, I WILL...
ETHER
WARNING HIGHLY FLAMM
...AND UNLESS HE HAS A DAMN GOOD EXPLANATION FOR ALL OF THIS YOU'RE BOTH GONNA BE LOOKING FOR A NEW PLACE TO LIVE...
?!?
BUT, WHY ME? WHA'D I DO?
IT'S WHAT YOU HAVEN'T DONE THAT'S THE PROBLEM!
LOOK, BUDDY, I HAVE NO IDEA WHAT'S BEING GOING ON AROUND HERE WHILE I WAS GONE...
PLOP!
ALL I DO KNOW IS THAT I LEFT YOU IN CHARGE, ONLY TO COME BACK AND FIND THE PLACE LOOKING LIKE A PIG STY, LOWLIFES HIDING IN THE BUSHES, AND TOXIC CHEMICALS SITTING ON THE KITCHEN TABLE...
BUT THAT'S JUST IT, MA! BUTCH IS THE ONE WHO—
DON'T GIVE ME BUTCH! YOU'RE ALMOST THIRTY YEARS OLD, BUDDY! I SHOULDN'T HAVE TO WORRY ABOUT LEAVING YOU HOME ALONE ANYMORE!
BUT IT'S BECOME OBVIOUS THAT I JUST CAN'T TRUST YOU OR YOUR BROTHER TO ACT LIKE RESPONSIBLE FULL-GROWN ADULTS!
...GRUMBLE...
...=SIGH=...
...DON'T WORRY, I'M NOT GOING TO KICK YOU OUT OF THE HOUSE...
GEE, THANKS.
BUT IT MIGHT BE A GOOD IDEA FOR YOU TO START LOOKING FOR A PLACE OF YOUR OWN, ANYWAY...
BECAUSE AFTER TODAY I'M MORE SERIOUS THAN EVER ABOUT MOVING TO FLORIDA AND SELLING THIS DUMP...
=GULP=

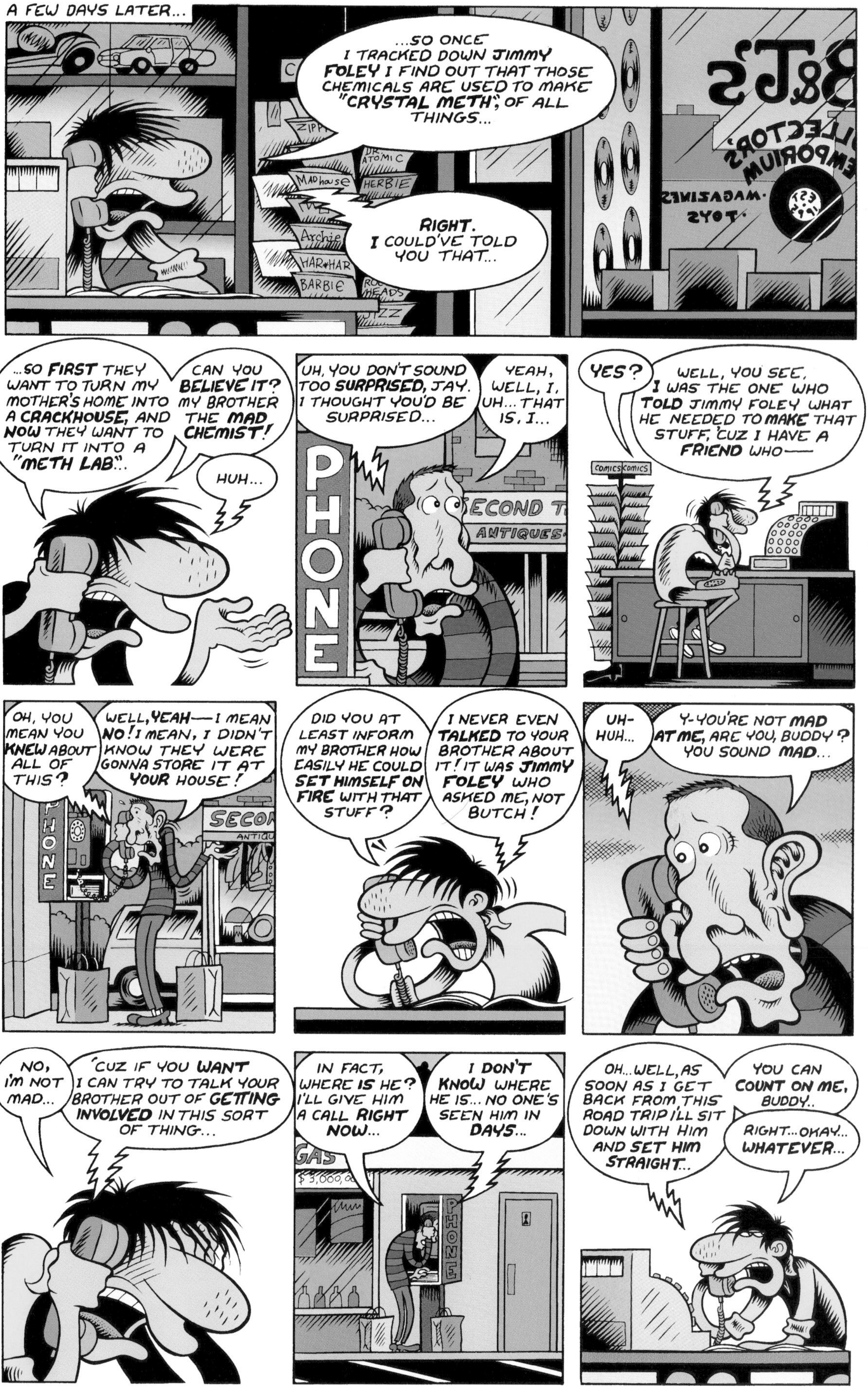
A FEW DAYS LATER...
...SO ONCE I TRACKED DOWN JIMMY FOLEY I FIND OUT THAT THOSE CHEMICALS ARE USED TO MAKE "CRYSTAL METH", OF ALL THINGS...
RIGHT. I COULD'VE TOLD YOU THAT...
MADhouse
DR. ATOMIC
HERBIE
Archie
HAR★HAR
BARBIE
ROCK HEADS
B&B'S
COLLECTORS' EMPORIUM
·MAGAZINES·
·TOYS·
...SO FIRST THEY WANT TO TURN MY MOTHER'S HOME INTO A CRACKHOUSE, AND NOW THEY WANT TO TURN IT INTO A "METH LAB"...
CAN YOU BELIEVE IT? MY BROTHER THE MAD CHEMIST!
HUH...
UH, YOU DON'T SOUND TOO SURPRISED, JAY. I THOUGHT YOU'D BE SURPRISED...
YEAH, WELL, I, UH... THAT IS, I...
PHONE
SECOND
ANTIQUES
YES?
WELL, YOU SEE, I WAS THE ONE WHO TOLD JIMMY FOLEY WHAT HE NEEDED TO MAKE THAT STUFF, 'CUZ I HAVE A FRIEND WHO——
COMICS COMICS
OH, YOU MEAN YOU KNEW ABOUT ALL OF THIS?
WELL, YEAH——I MEAN NO! I MEAN, I DIDN'T KNOW THEY WERE GONNA STORE IT AT YOUR HOUSE!
DID YOU AT LEAST INFORM MY BROTHER HOW EASILY HE COULD SET HIMSELF ON FIRE WITH THAT STUFF?
I NEVER EVEN TALKED TO YOUR BROTHER ABOUT IT! IT WAS JIMMY FOLEY WHO ASKED ME, NOT BUTCH!
UH-HUH...
Y-YOU'RE NOT MAD AT ME, ARE YOU, BUDDY? YOU SOUND MAD...
NO, I'M NOT MAD...
'CUZ IF YOU WANT I CAN TRY TO TALK YOUR BROTHER OUT OF GETTING INVOLVED IN THIS SORT OF THING...
IN FACT, WHERE IS HE? I'LL GIVE HIM A CALL RIGHT NOW...
I DON'T KNOW WHERE HE IS... NO ONE'S SEEN HIM IN DAYS...
GAS
PHONE
OH... WELL, AS SOON AS I GET BACK FROM THIS ROAD TRIP I'LL SIT DOWN WITH HIM AND SET HIM STRAIGHT...
YOU CAN COUNT ON ME, BUDDY..
RIGHT... OKAY... WHATEVER...

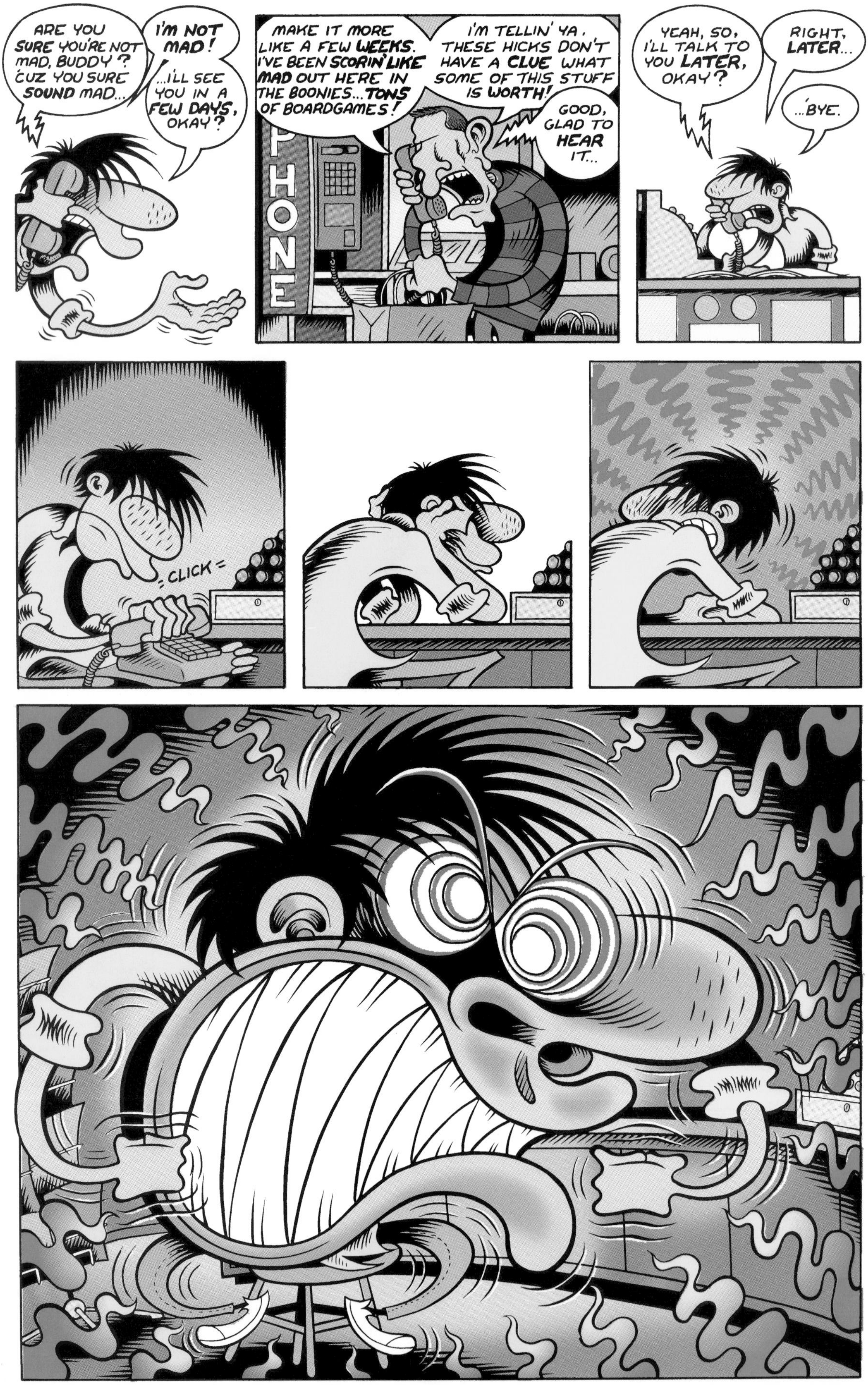
ARE YOU SURE YOU'RE NOT MAD, BUDDY? 'CUZ YOU SURE SOUND MAD...
I'M NOT MAD!
...I'LL SEE YOU IN A FEW DAYS, OKAY?
MAKE IT MORE LIKE A FEW WEEKS. I'VE BEEN SCORIN' LIKE MAD OUT HERE IN THE BOONIES...TONS OF BOARDGAMES!
I'M TELLIN' YA, THESE HICKS DON'T HAVE A CLUE WHAT SOME OF THIS STUFF IS WORTH!
PHONE
GOOD, GLAD TO HEAR IT...
YEAH, SO, I'LL TALK TO YOU LATER, OKAY?
RIGHT, LATER...
'...BYE.
=CLICK=

A WEEK OR SO LATER, AT POLICE H.Q...

HEY, TOM. I——

...HEY, BUDDY. THANKS FOR COMING DOWN...

——PENCILS?

≥SOB!≤

AWW, TAKE IT EASY, PAL....FOR ALL WE KNOW NOTHING BAD HAS HAPPENED...

JAKE IS DEAD! I JUST KNOW IT! ≥BWAAAH!≤

?!? JAKE?

BUT, I THOUGHT YOU SAID STINKY WAS MISSING...

HE IS, BUT SO IS JAKE, ACCORDING TO PENCILS, HERE...

≥WHIMPER≤

...APPARENTLY JAKE HAS FALLEN INTO ARREARS WITH HIS BOOKIE, AND INTIMATED TO PENCILS THAT HE FEARED FOR HIS SAFETY BECAUSE OF IT...

WHEN WAS THIS?

ABOUT A WEEK AGO —RIGHT, PENCILS?

I GUESS...

≥HONK!≤

...I TOLD HIM TO CALL THE POLICE, BUT HE LEFT TOWN INSTEAD.

NO ONE'S HEARD FROM HIM SINCE... ≥SNIFF≤

HUH...

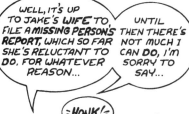

WELL, IT'S UP TO JAKE'S WIFE TO FILE A MISSING PERSON'S REPORT, WHICH SO FAR SHE'S RELUCTANT TO DO, FOR WHATEVER REASON...

UNTIL THEN THERE'S NOT MUCH I CAN DO, I'M SORRY TO SAY...

≥HONK!≤

33

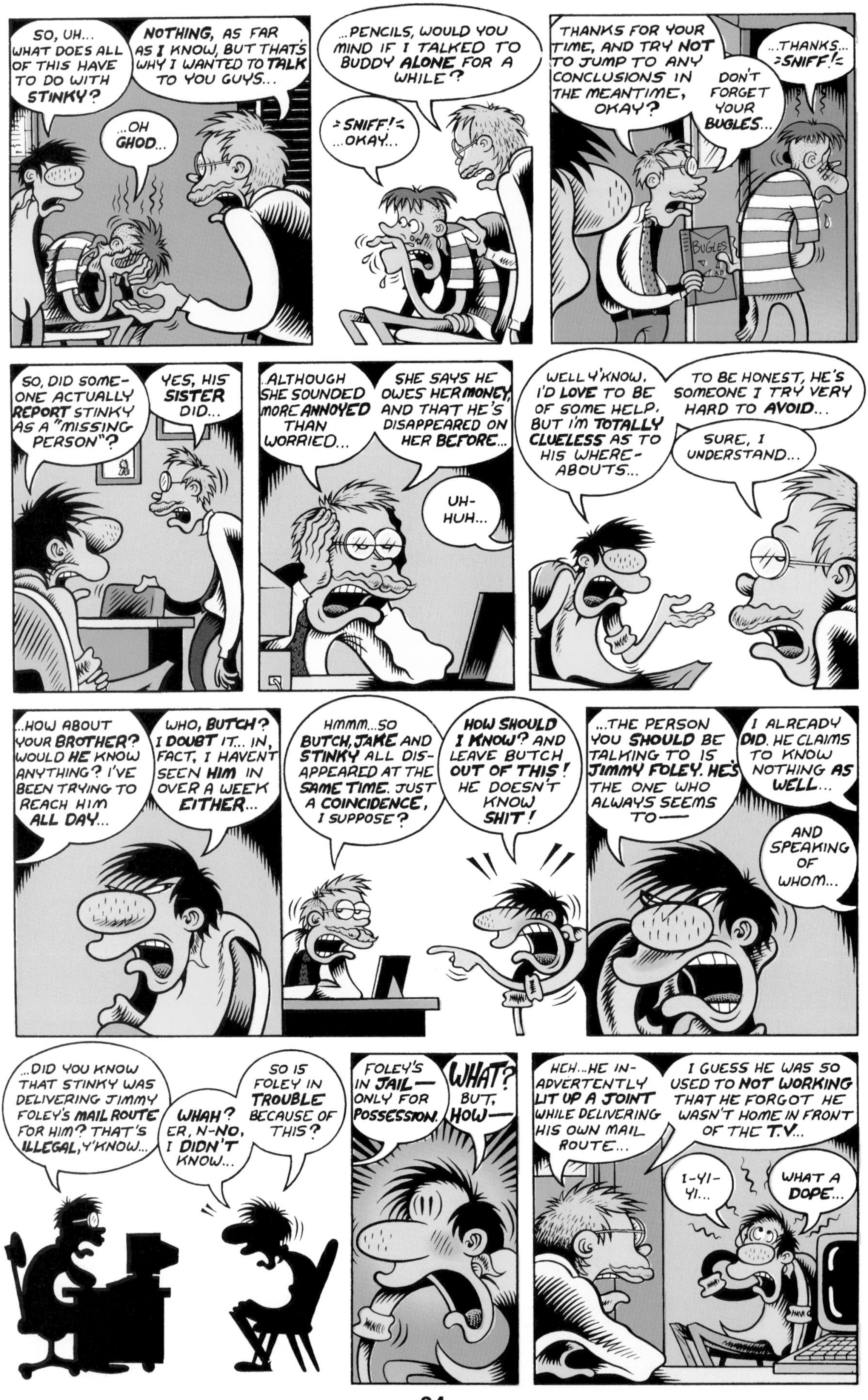
SO, UH... WHAT DOES ALL OF THIS HAVE TO DO WITH STINKY?
NOTHING, AS FAR AS I KNOW, BUT THAT'S WHY I WANTED TO TALK TO YOU GUYS...
...OH GHOD...
...PENCILS, WOULD YOU MIND IF I TALKED TO BUDDY ALONE FOR A WHILE?
SNIFF! ...OKAY...
THANKS FOR YOUR TIME, AND TRY NOT TO JUMP TO ANY CONCLUSIONS IN THE MEANTIME, OKAY?
DON'T FORGET YOUR BUGLES...
...THANKS... SNIFF!
BUGLES
SO, DID SOMEONE ACTUALLY REPORT STINKY AS A "MISSING PERSON"?
YES, HIS SISTER DID...
...ALTHOUGH SHE SOUNDED MORE ANNOYED THAN WORRIED...
SHE SAYS HE OWES HER MONEY, AND THAT HE'S DISAPPEARED ON HER BEFORE...
UH-HUH...
WELL Y'KNOW, I'D LOVE TO BE OF SOME HELP, BUT I'M TOTALLY CLUELESS AS TO HIS WHEREABOUTS...
TO BE HONEST, HE'S SOMEONE I TRY VERY HARD TO AVOID...
SURE, I UNDERSTAND...
...HOW ABOUT YOUR BROTHER? WOULD HE KNOW ANYTHING? I'VE BEEN TRYING TO REACH HIM ALL DAY...
WHO, BUTCH? I DOUBT IT... IN, FACT, I HAVEN'T SEEN HIM IN OVER A WEEK EITHER...
HMMM...SO BUTCH, JAKE AND STINKY ALL DISAPPEARED AT THE SAME TIME. JUST A COINCIDENCE, I SUPPOSE?
HOW SHOULD I KNOW? AND LEAVE BUTCH OUT OF THIS! HE DOESN'T KNOW SHIT!
...THE PERSON YOU SHOULD BE TALKING TO IS JIMMY FOLEY. HE'S THE ONE WHO ALWAYS SEEMS TO—
I ALREADY DID. HE CLAIMS TO KNOW NOTHING AS WELL...
AND SPEAKING OF WHOM...
...DID YOU KNOW THAT STINKY WAS DELIVERING JIMMY FOLEY'S MAIL ROUTE FOR HIM? THAT'S ILLEGAL, Y'KNOW...
WHAH? ER, N-NO, I DIDN'T KNOW...
SO IS FOLEY IN TROUBLE BECAUSE OF THIS?
FOLEY'S IN JAIL— ONLY FOR POSSESSION.
WHAT? BUT, HOW—
HEH...HE INADVERTENTLY LIT UP A JOINT WHILE DELIVERING HIS OWN MAIL ROUTE...
I GUESS HE WAS SO USED TO NOT WORKING THAT HE FORGOT HE WASN'T HOME IN FRONT OF THE T.V...
I-YI-YI...
WHAT A DOPE...

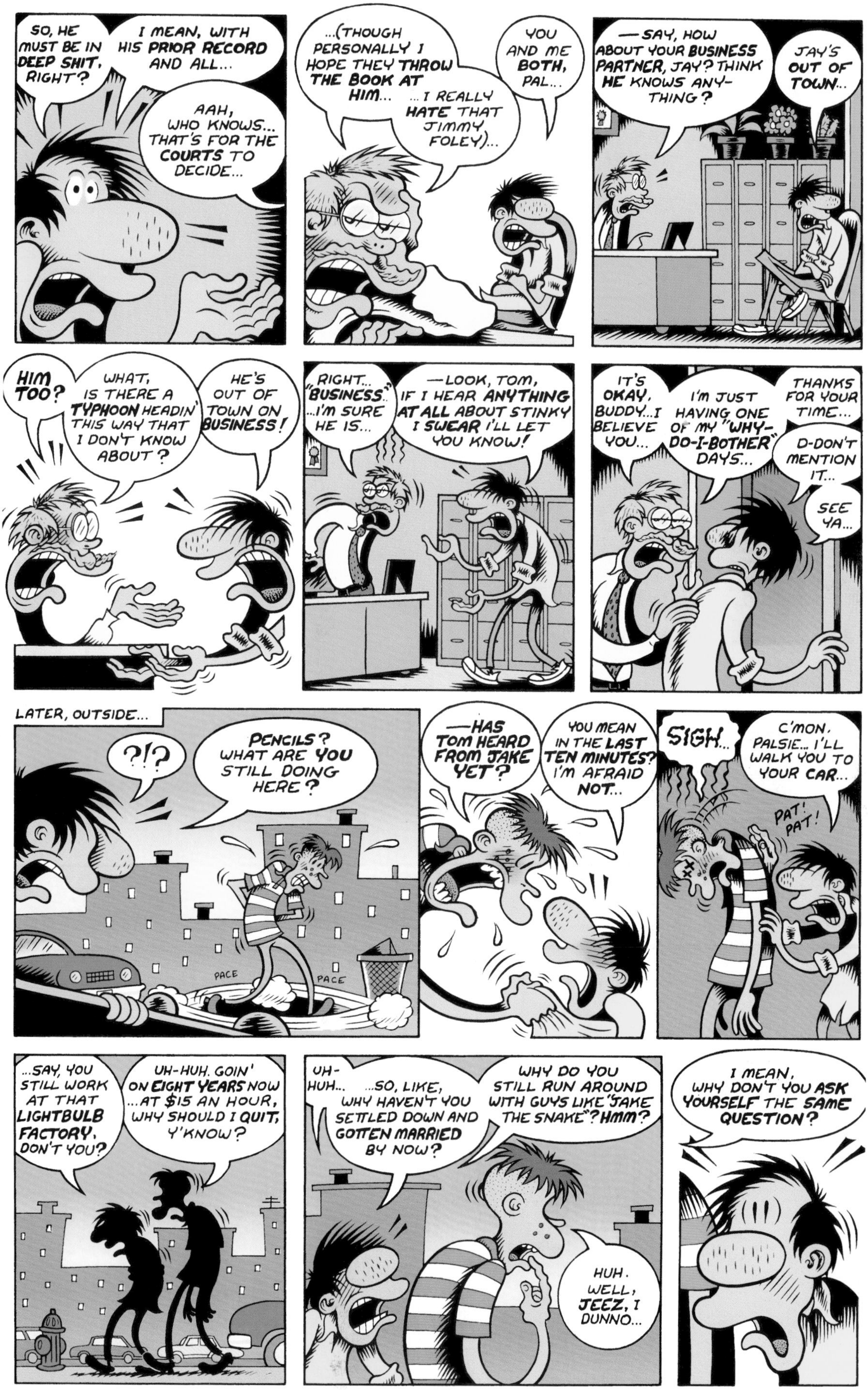
SO, HE MUST BE IN DEEP SHIT, RIGHT?
I MEAN, WITH HIS PRIOR RECORD AND ALL...
AAH, WHO KNOWS... THAT'S FOR THE COURTS TO DECIDE...
...(THOUGH PERSONALLY I HOPE THEY THROW THE BOOK AT HIM...
...I REALLY HATE THAT JIMMY FOLEY)...
YOU AND ME BOTH, PAL...
—SAY, HOW ABOUT YOUR BUSINESS PARTNER, JAY? THINK HE KNOWS ANYTHING?
JAY'S OUT OF TOWN...
HIM TOO?
WHAT, IS THERE A TYPHOON HEADIN' THIS WAY THAT I DON'T KNOW ABOUT?
HE'S OUT OF TOWN ON BUSINESS!
RIGHT... "BUSINESS"... I'M SURE HE IS...
—LOOK, TOM, IF I HEAR ANYTHING AT ALL ABOUT STINKY I SWEAR I'LL LET YOU KNOW!
IT'S OKAY, BUDDY...I BELIEVE YOU...
I'M JUST HAVING ONE OF MY "WHY-DO-I-BOTHER" DAYS...
THANKS FOR YOUR TIME...
D-DON'T MENTION IT...
SEE YA...
LATER, OUTSIDE...
?!?
PENCILS? WHAT ARE YOU STILL DOING HERE?
PACE
PACE
—HAS TOM HEARD FROM JAKE YET?
YOU MEAN IN THE LAST TEN MINUTES? I'M AFRAID NOT...
SIGH...
C'MON, PALSIE... I'LL WALK YOU TO YOUR CAR...
PAT! PAT!
...SAY, YOU STILL WORK AT THAT LIGHTBULB FACTORY, DON'T YOU?
UH-HUH. GOIN' ON EIGHT YEARS NOW ...AT $15 AN HOUR, WHY SHOULD I QUIT, Y'KNOW?
UH-HUH...
...SO, LIKE, WHY HAVEN'T YOU SETTLED DOWN AND GOTTEN MARRIED BY NOW?
WHY DO YOU STILL RUN AROUND WITH GUYS LIKE "JAKE THE SNAKE"? HMM?
HUH. WELL, JEEZ, I DUNNO...
I MEAN, WHY DON'T YOU ASK YOURSELF THE SAME QUESTION?

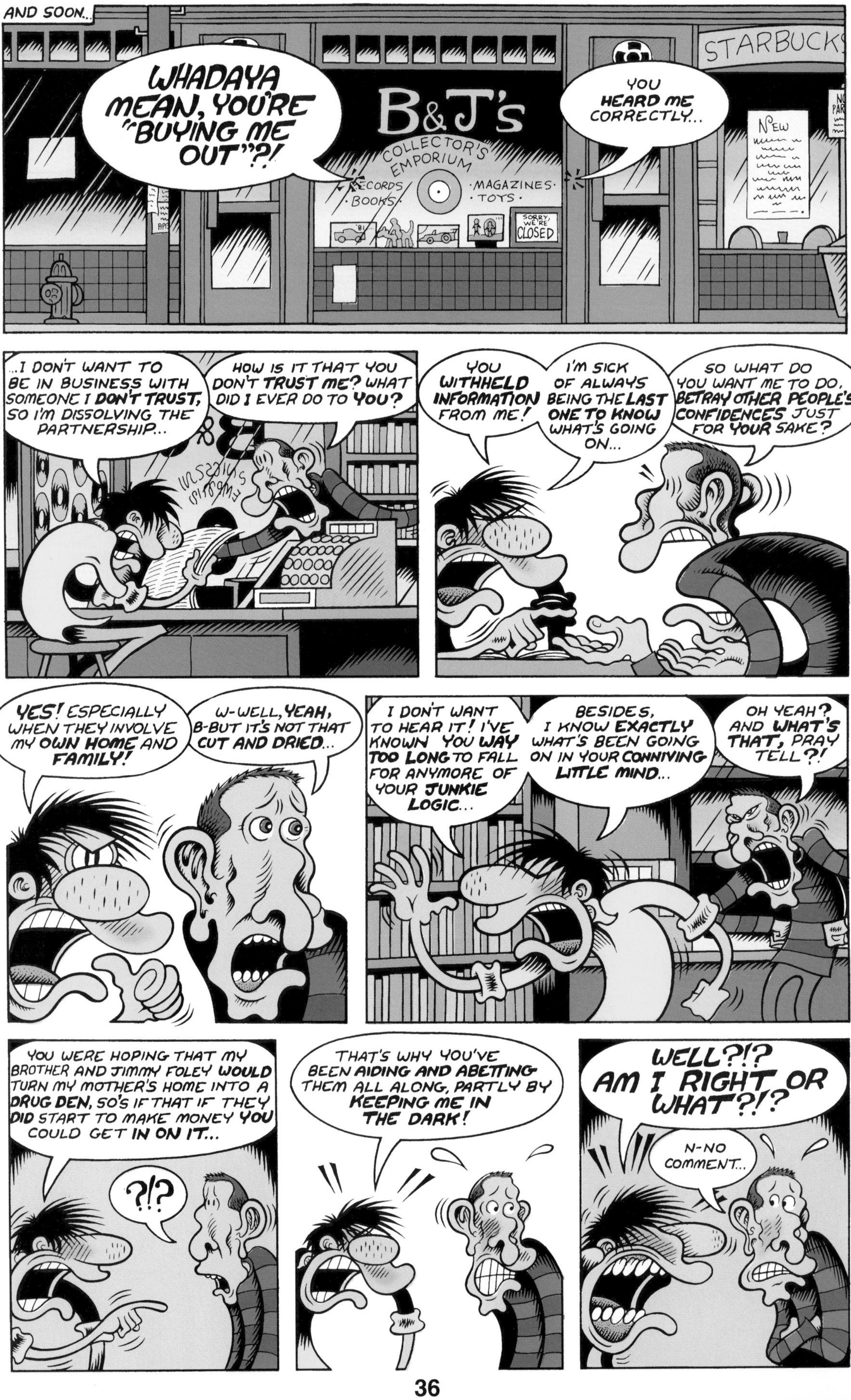
AND SOON...
WHADAYA MEAN, YOU'RE "BUYING ME OUT"?!
YOU HEARD ME CORRECTLY...
STARBUCKS
B&J's COLLECTOR'S EMPORIUM
RECORDS · BOOKS · MAGAZINES · TOYS
SORRY, WE'RE CLOSED
NEW
...I DON'T WANT TO BE IN BUSINESS WITH SOMEONE I DON'T TRUST, SO I'M DISSOLVING THE PARTNERSHIP...
HOW IS IT THAT YOU DON'T TRUST ME? WHAT DID I EVER DO TO YOU?
YOU WITHHELD INFORMATION FROM ME!
I'M SICK OF ALWAYS BEING THE LAST ONE TO KNOW WHAT'S GOING ON...
SO WHAT DO YOU WANT ME TO DO, BETRAY OTHER PEOPLE'S CONFIDENCES JUST FOR YOUR SAKE?
YES! ESPECIALLY WHEN THEY INVOLVE MY OWN HOME AND FAMILY!
W-WELL, YEAH, B-BUT IT'S NOT THAT CUT AND DRIED...
I DON'T WANT TO HEAR IT! I'VE KNOWN YOU WAY TOO LONG TO FALL FOR ANYMORE OF YOUR JUNKIE LOGIC...
BESIDES, I KNOW EXACTLY WHAT'S BEEN GOING ON IN YOUR CONNIVING LITTLE MIND...
OH YEAH? AND WHAT'S THAT, PRAY TELL?!
YOU WERE HOPING THAT MY BROTHER AND JIMMY FOLEY WOULD TURN MY MOTHER'S HOME INTO A DRUG DEN, SO'S IF THAT IF THEY DID START TO MAKE MONEY YOU COULD GET IN ON IT...
?!?
THAT'S WHY YOU'VE BEEN AIDING AND ABETTING THEM ALL ALONG, PARTLY BY KEEPING ME IN THE DARK!
WELL?!? AM I RIGHT OR WHAT?!?
N-NO COMMENT...

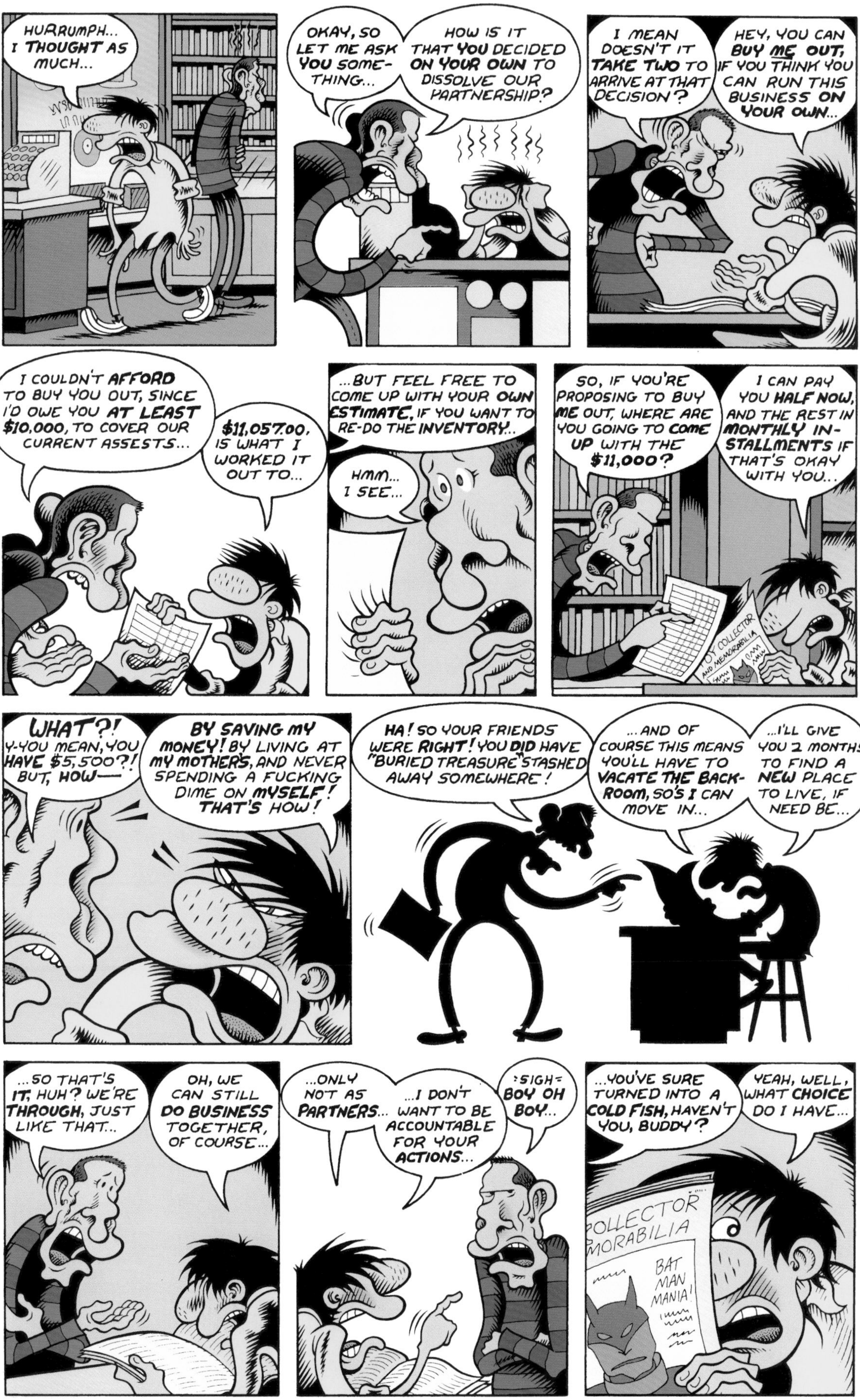
HURRUMPH... I THOUGHT AS MUCH...
OKAY, SO LET ME ASK YOU SOME-THING...
HOW IS IT THAT YOU DECIDED ON YOUR OWN TO DISSOLVE OUR PARTNERSHIP?
I MEAN DOESN'T IT TAKE TWO TO ARRIVE AT THAT DECISION?
HEY, YOU CAN BUY ME OUT, IF YOU THINK YOU CAN RUN THIS BUSINESS ON YOUR OWN...
I COULDN'T AFFORD TO BUY YOU OUT, SINCE I'D OWE YOU AT LEAST $10,000, TO COVER OUR CURRENT ASSESTS...
$11,057.00, IS WHAT I WORKED IT OUT TO...
...BUT FEEL FREE TO COME UP WITH YOUR OWN ESTIMATE, IF YOU WANT TO RE-DO THE INVENTORY...
HMM... I SEE...
SO, IF YOU'RE PROPOSING TO BUY ME OUT, WHERE ARE YOU GOING TO COME UP WITH THE $11,000?
I CAN PAY YOU HALF NOW, AND THE REST IN MONTHLY IN-STALLMENTS IF THAT'S OKAY WITH YOU...
TOY COLLECTOR AND MEMORABILIA
WHAT?! Y-YOU MEAN, YOU HAVE $5,500?! BUT, HOW—
BY SAVING MY MONEY! BY LIVING AT MY MOTHER'S, AND NEVER SPENDING A FUCKING DIME ON MYSELF! THAT'S HOW!
HA! SO YOUR FRIENDS WERE RIGHT! YOU DID HAVE "BURIED TREASURE" STASHED AWAY SOMEWHERE!
...AND OF COURSE THIS MEANS YOU'LL HAVE TO VACATE THE BACK-ROOM, SO'S I CAN MOVE IN...
...I'LL GIVE YOU 2 MONTHS TO FIND A NEW PLACE TO LIVE, IF NEED BE...
...SO THAT'S IT, HUH? WE'RE THROUGH, JUST LIKE THAT...
OH, WE CAN STILL DO BUSINESS TOGETHER, OF COURSE...
...ONLY NOT AS PARTNERS...
...I DON'T WANT TO BE ACCOUNTABLE FOR YOUR ACTIONS...
=SIGH= BOY OH BOY...
...YOU'VE SURE TURNED INTO A COLD FISH, HAVEN'T YOU, BUDDY?
YEAH, WELL, WHAT CHOICE DO I HAVE...
COLLECTOR MORABILIA
BAT MAN MANIA!

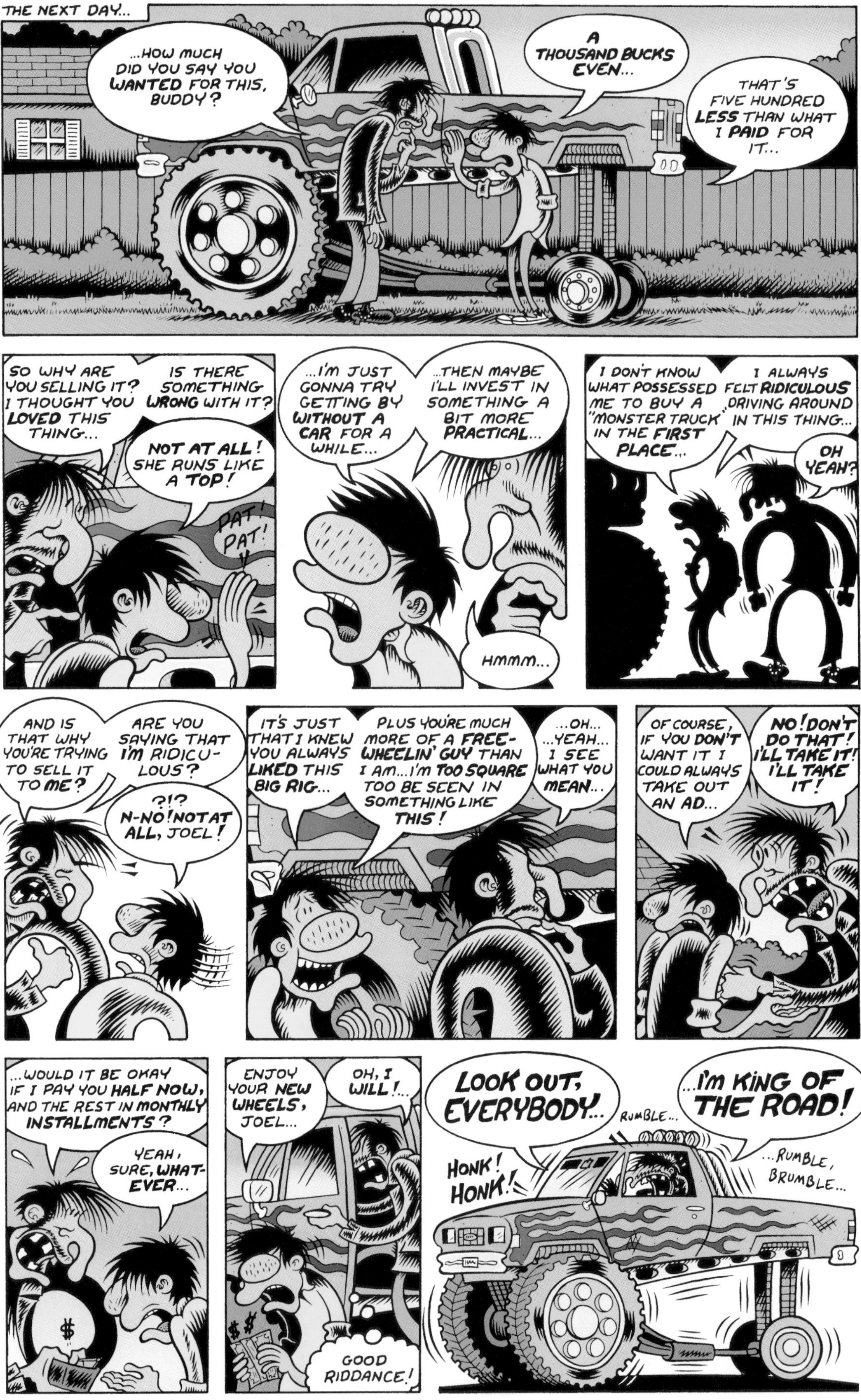
THE NEXT DAY...
...HOW MUCH DID YOU SAY YOU WANTED FOR THIS, BUDDY?
A THOUSAND BUCKS EVEN...
THAT'S FIVE HUNDRED LESS THAN WHAT I PAID FOR IT...
SO WHY ARE YOU SELLING IT? I THOUGHT YOU LOVED THIS THING...
IS THERE SOMETHING WRONG WITH IT?
NOT AT ALL! SHE RUNS LIKE A TOP!
PAT! PAT!
...I'M JUST GONNA TRY GETTING BY WITHOUT A CAR FOR A WHILE...
...THEN MAYBE I'LL INVEST IN SOMETHING A BIT MORE PRACTICAL...
HMMM...
I DON'T KNOW WHAT POSSESSED ME TO BUY A "MONSTER TRUCK" IN THE FIRST PLACE...
I ALWAYS FELT RIDICULOUS DRIVING AROUND IN THIS THING...
OH YEAH?
AND IS THAT WHY YOU'RE TRYING TO SELL IT TO ME?
ARE YOU SAYING THAT I'M RIDICULOUS?
?!? N-NO! NOT AT ALL, JOEL!
IT'S JUST THAT I KNEW YOU ALWAYS LIKED THIS BIG RIG...
PLUS YOU'RE MUCH MORE OF A FREE-WHEELIN' GUY THAN I AM... I'M TOO SQUARE TOO BE SEEN IN SOMETHING LIKE THIS!
...OH... ...YEAH... I SEE WHAT YOU MEAN...
OF COURSE, IF YOU DON'T WANT IT I COULD ALWAYS TAKE OUT AN AD...
NO! DON'T DO THAT! I'LL TAKE IT! I'LL TAKE IT!
...WOULD IT BE OKAY IF I PAY YOU HALF NOW, AND THE REST IN MONTHLY INSTALLMENTS?
YEAH, SURE, WHATEVER...
ENJOY YOUR NEW WHEELS, JOEL...
OH, I WILL!...
GOOD RIDDANCE!
LOOK OUT, EVERYBODY...
...I'M KING OF THE ROAD!
RUMBLE...
HONK! HONK!
...RUMBLE, BRUMBLE...

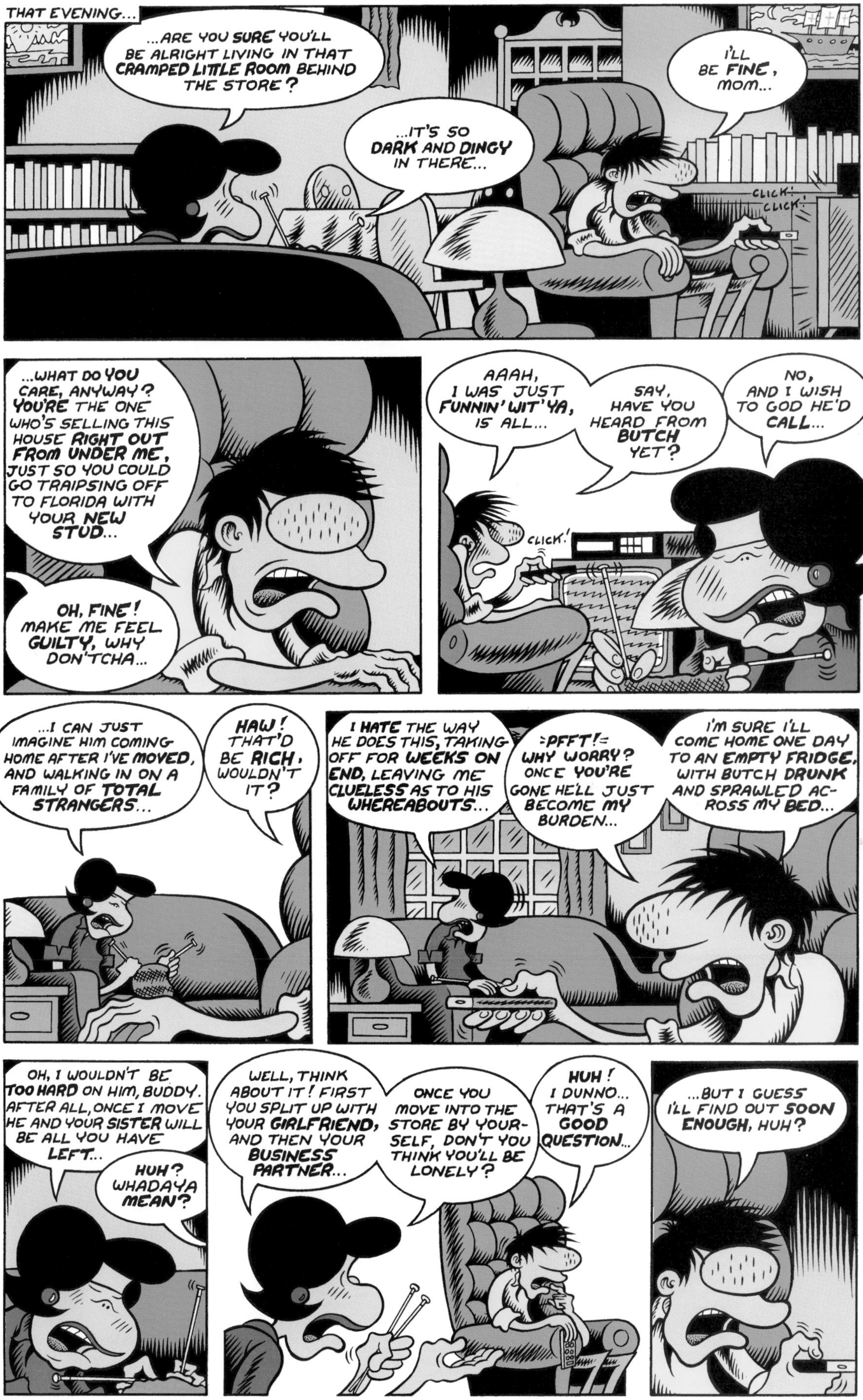
THAT EVENING...
...ARE YOU SURE YOU'LL BE ALRIGHT LIVING IN THAT CRAMPED LITTLE ROOM BEHIND THE STORE?
...IT'S SO DARK AND DINGY IN THERE...
I'LL BE FINE, MOM...
CLICK! CLICK!
...WHAT DO YOU CARE, ANYWAY? YOU'RE THE ONE WHO'S SELLING THIS HOUSE RIGHT OUT FROM UNDER ME, JUST SO YOU COULD GO TRAIPSING OFF TO FLORIDA WITH YOUR NEW STUD...
OH, FINE! MAKE ME FEEL GUILTY, WHY DON'TCHA...
AAAH, I WAS JUST FUNNIN' WIT'YA, IS ALL...
SAY, HAVE YOU HEARD FROM BUTCH YET?
NO, AND I WISH TO GOD HE'D CALL...
CLICK!
...I CAN JUST IMAGINE HIM COMING HOME AFTER I'VE MOVED, AND WALKING IN ON A FAMILY OF TOTAL STRANGERS...
HAW! THAT'D BE RICH, WOULDN'T IT?
I HATE THE WAY HE DOES THIS, TAKING OFF FOR WEEKS ON END, LEAVING ME CLUELESS AS TO HIS WHEREABOUTS...
=PFFT!= WHY WORRY? ONCE YOU'RE GONE HE'LL JUST BECOME MY BURDEN...
I'M SURE I'LL COME HOME ONE DAY TO AN EMPTY FRIDGE, WITH BUTCH DRUNK AND SPRAWLED ACROSS MY BED...
OH, I WOULDN'T BE TOO HARD ON HIM, BUDDY. AFTER ALL, ONCE I MOVE HE AND YOUR SISTER WILL BE ALL YOU HAVE LEFT...
HUH? WHADAYA MEAN?
WELL, THINK ABOUT IT! FIRST YOU SPLIT UP WITH YOUR GIRLFRIEND, AND THEN YOUR BUSINESS PARTNER...
ONCE YOU MOVE INTO THE STORE BY YOURSELF, DON'T YOU THINK YOU'LL BE LONELY?
HUH! I DUNNO... THAT'S A GOOD QUESTION...
...BUT I GUESS I'LL FIND OUT SOON ENOUGH, HUH?

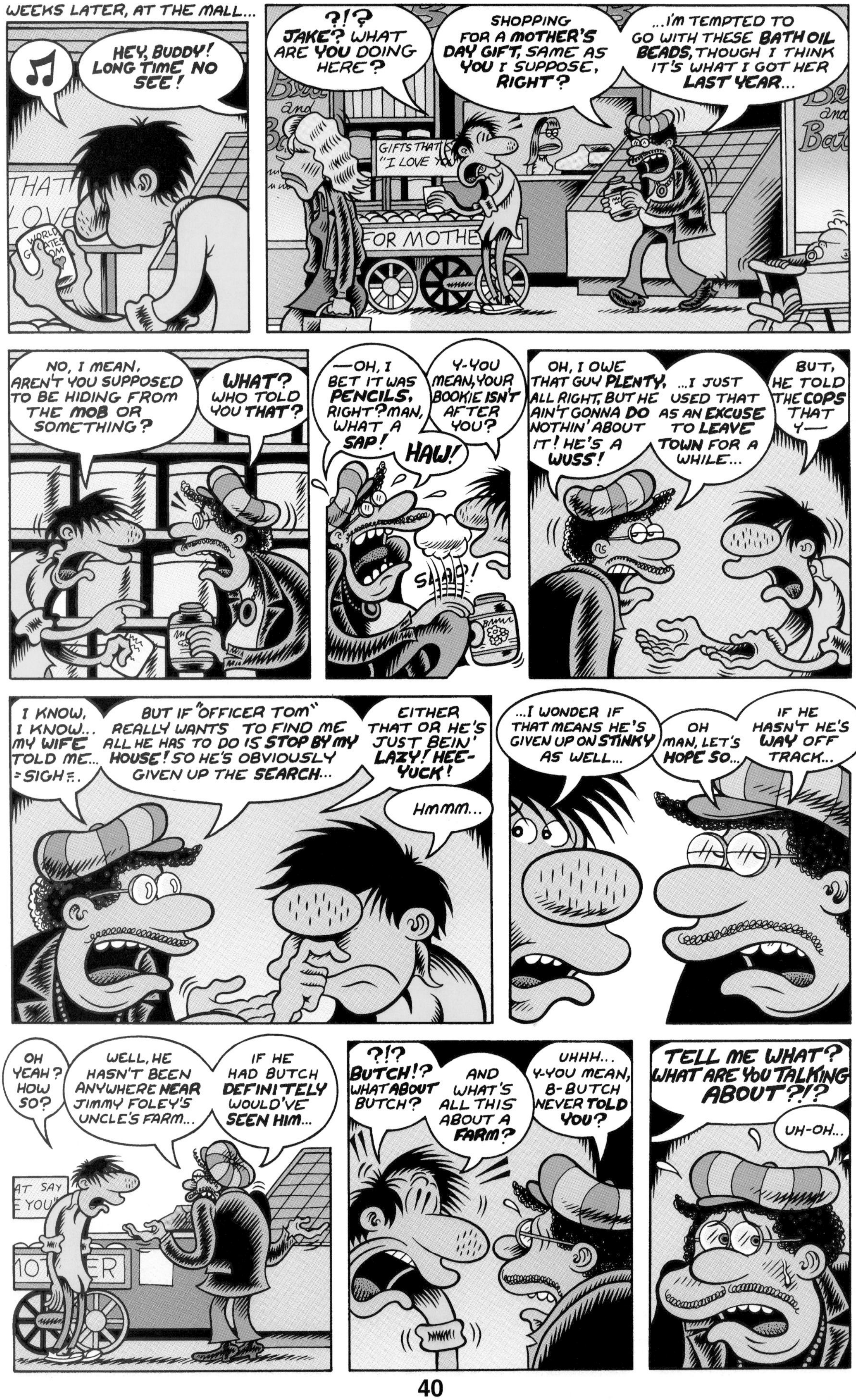
WEEKS LATER, AT THE MALL...
♫
HEY, BUDDY! LONG TIME NO SEE!
?!? JAKE? WHAT ARE YOU DOING HERE?
SHOPPING FOR A MOTHER'S DAY GIFT, SAME AS YOU I SUPPOSE, RIGHT?
...I'M TEMPTED TO GO WITH THESE BATH OIL BEADS, THOUGH I THINK IT'S WHAT I GOT HER LAST YEAR...
GIFTS THAT "I LOVE YOU"
FOR MOTHE
NO, I MEAN, AREN'T YOU SUPPOSED TO BE HIDING FROM THE MOB OR SOMETHING?
WHAT? WHO TOLD YOU THAT?
—OH, I BET IT WAS PENCILS, RIGHT? MAN, WHAT A SAP!
HAW!
Y-YOU MEAN, YOUR BOOKIE ISN'T AFTER YOU?
OH, I OWE THAT GUY PLENTY, ALL RIGHT, BUT HE AIN'T GONNA DO NOTHIN' ABOUT IT! HE'S A WUSS!
...I JUST USED THAT AS AN EXCUSE TO LEAVE TOWN FOR A WHILE...
BUT, HE TOLD THE COPS THAT Y—
I KNOW, I KNOW... MY WIFE TOLD ME... =SIGH=.
BUT IF "OFFICER TOM" REALLY WANTS TO FIND ME ALL HE HAS TO DO IS STOP BY MY HOUSE! SO HE'S OBVIOUSLY GIVEN UP THE SEARCH...
EITHER THAT OR HE'S JUST BEIN' LAZY! HEE-YUCK!
HMMM...
...I WONDER IF THAT MEANS HE'S GIVEN UP ON STINKY AS WELL...
OH MAN, LET'S HOPE SO...
IF HE HASN'T HE'S WAY OFF TRACK...
OH YEAH? HOW SO?
WELL, HE HASN'T BEEN ANYWHERE NEAR JIMMY FOLEY'S UNCLE'S FARM...
IF HE HAD BUTCH DEFINITELY WOULD'VE SEEN HIM...
?!? BUTCH!? WHAT ABOUT BUTCH?
AND WHAT'S ALL THIS ABOUT A FARM?
UHHH... Y-YOU MEAN, B-BUTCH NEVER TOLD YOU?
TELL ME WHAT? WHAT ARE YOU TALKING ABOUT?!?
UH-OH...

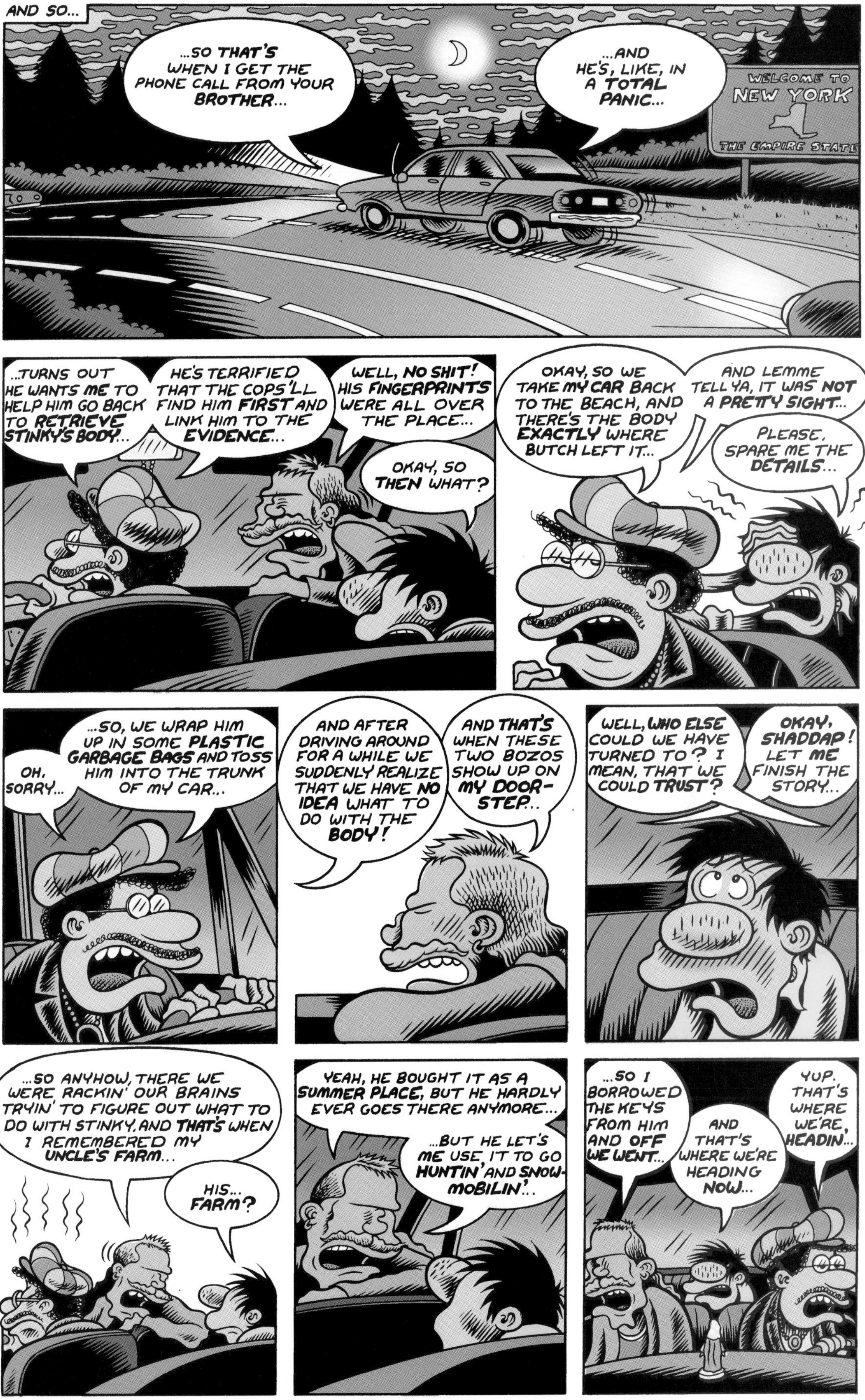
AND SO...
...SO THAT'S WHEN I GET THE PHONE CALL FROM YOUR BROTHER...
...AND HE'S, LIKE, IN A TOTAL PANIC...
WELCOME TO NEW YORK
THE EMPIRE STATE
...TURNS OUT HE WANTS ME TO HELP HIM GO BACK TO RETRIEVE STINKY'S BODY...
HE'S TERRIFIED THAT THE COPS'LL FIND HIM FIRST AND LINK HIM TO THE EVIDENCE...
WELL, NO SHIT! HIS FINGERPRINTS WERE ALL OVER THE PLACE...
OKAY, SO THEN WHAT?
OKAY, SO WE TAKE MY CAR BACK TO THE BEACH, AND THERE'S THE BODY EXACTLY WHERE BUTCH LEFT IT...
AND LEMME TELL YA, IT WAS NOT A PRETTY SIGHT...
PLEASE, SPARE ME THE DETAILS...
...SO, WE WRAP HIM UP IN SOME PLASTIC GARBAGE BAGS AND TOSS HIM INTO THE TRUNK OF MY CAR...
OH, SORRY...
AND AFTER DRIVING AROUND FOR A WHILE WE SUDDENLY REALIZE THAT WE HAVE NO IDEA WHAT TO DO WITH THE BODY!
AND THAT'S WHEN THESE TWO BOZOS SHOW UP ON MY DOOR-STEP...
WELL, WHO ELSE COULD WE HAVE TURNED TO? I MEAN, THAT WE COULD TRUST?
OKAY, SHADDAP! LET ME FINISH THE STORY...
...SO ANYHOW, THERE WE WERE RACKIN' OUR BRAINS TRYIN' TO FIGURE OUT WHAT TO DO WITH STINKY, AND THAT'S WHEN I REMEMBERED MY UNCLE'S FARM...
HIS... FARM?
YEAH, HE BOUGHT IT AS A SUMMER PLACE, BUT HE HARDLY EVER GOES THERE ANYMORE...
...BUT HE LET'S ME USE IT TO GO HUNTIN' AND SNOW-MOBILIN'...
...SO I BORROWED THE KEYS FROM HIM AND OFF WE WENT...
AND THAT'S WHERE WE'RE HEADING NOW...
YUP. THAT'S WHERE WE'RE HEADIN'...

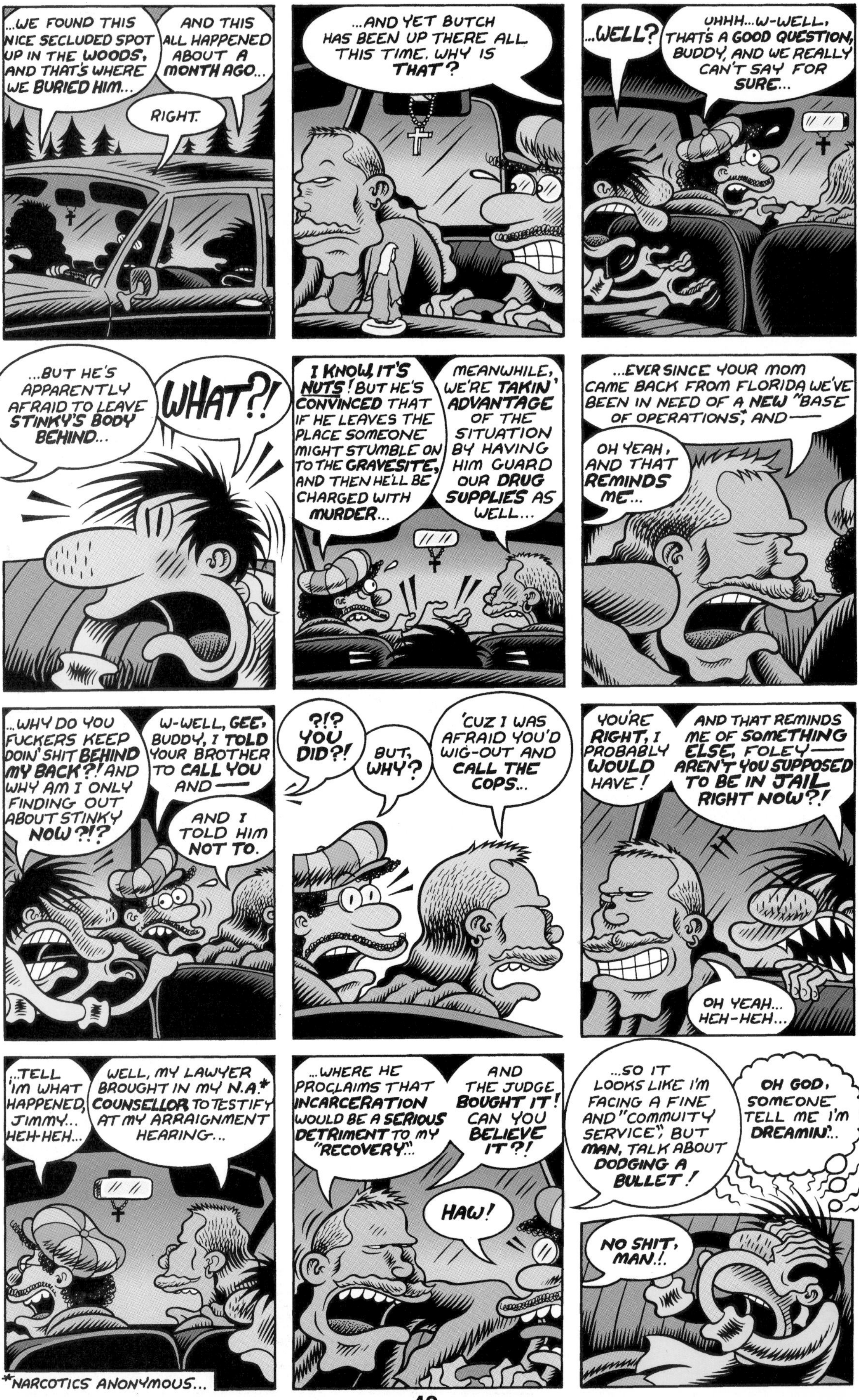
...WE FOUND THIS NICE SECLUDED SPOT UP IN THE WOODS, AND THAT'S WHERE WE BURIED HIM...
AND THIS ALL HAPPENED ABOUT A MONTH AGO...
RIGHT.
...AND YET BUTCH HAS BEEN UP THERE ALL THIS TIME. WHY IS THAT?
...WELL?
UHHH...W-WELL, THAT'S A GOOD QUESTION, BUDDY, AND WE REALLY CAN'T SAY FOR SURE...
...BUT HE'S APPARENTLY AFRAID TO LEAVE STINKY'S BODY BEHIND...
WHAT?!
I KNOW, IT'S NUTS! BUT HE'S CONVINCED THAT IF HE LEAVES THE PLACE SOMEONE MIGHT STUMBLE ON TO THE GRAVESITE, AND THEN HE'LL BE CHARGED WITH MURDER...
MEANWHILE, WE'RE TAKIN' ADVANTAGE OF THE SITUATION BY HAVING HIM GUARD OUR DRUG SUPPLIES AS WELL...
...EVER SINCE YOUR MOM CAME BACK FROM FLORIDA WE'VE BEEN IN NEED OF A NEW "BASE OF OPERATIONS", AND—
OH YEAH, AND THAT REMINDS ME...
...WHY DO YOU FUCKERS KEEP DOIN' SHIT BEHIND MY BACK?! AND WHY AM I ONLY FINDING OUT ABOUT STINKY NOW?!?
W-WELL, GEE, BUDDY, I TOLD YOUR BROTHER TO CALL YOU AND—
AND I TOLD HIM NOT TO.
?!? YOU DID?!
BUT, WHY?
'CUZ I WAS AFRAID YOU'D WIG-OUT AND CALL THE COPS...
YOU'RE RIGHT, I PROBABLY WOULD HAVE!
AND THAT REMINDS ME OF SOMETHING ELSE, FOLEY— AREN'T YOU SUPPOSED TO BE IN JAIL RIGHT NOW?!
OH YEAH... HEH-HEH...
...TELL 'IM WHAT HAPPENED, JIMMY... HEH-HEH...
WELL, MY LAWYER BROUGHT IN MY N.A.* COUNSELLOR TO TESTIFY AT MY ARRAIGNMENT HEARING...
...WHERE HE PROCLAIMS THAT INCARCERATION WOULD BE A SERIOUS DETRIMENT TO MY "RECOVERY"...
AND THE JUDGE BOUGHT IT! CAN YOU BELIEVE IT?!
HAW!
...SO IT LOOKS LIKE I'M FACING A FINE AND "COMMUITY SERVICE", BUT MAN, TALK ABOUT DODGING A BULLET!
OH GOD, SOMEONE TELL ME I'M DREAMIN'...
NO SHIT, MAN!.
*NARCOTICS ANONYMOUS...

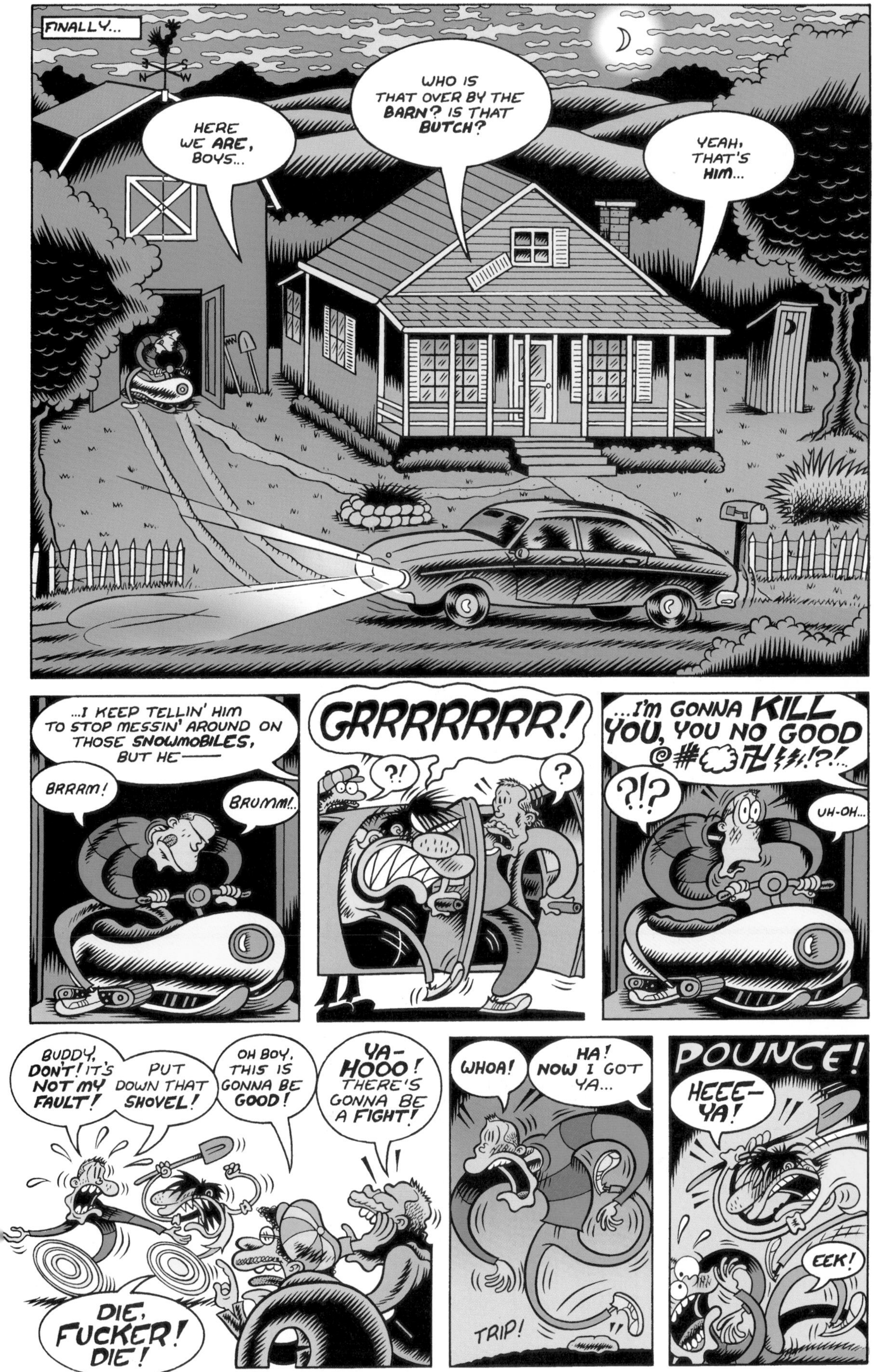
FINALLY...
HERE WE ARE, BOYS...
WHO IS THAT OVER BY THE BARN? IS THAT BUTCH?
YEAH, THAT'S HIM...
...I KEEP TELLIN' HIM TO STOP MESSIN' AROUND ON THOSE SNOWMOBILES, BUT HE——
BRRRM!
BRUMM!..
GRRRRRRR!
?!
?
...I'M GONNA KILL YOU, YOU NO GOOD @#☁卍⚡⚡!?!..
?!?
UH-OH...
BUDDY, DON'T! IT'S NOT MY FAULT!
PUT DOWN THAT SHOVEL!
OH BOY, THIS IS GONNA BE GOOD!
YA-HOOO! THERE'S GONNA BE A FIGHT!
DIE, FUCKER! DIE!
WHOA!
HA! NOW I GOT YA...
TRIP!
POUNCE!
HEEE-YA!
EEK!

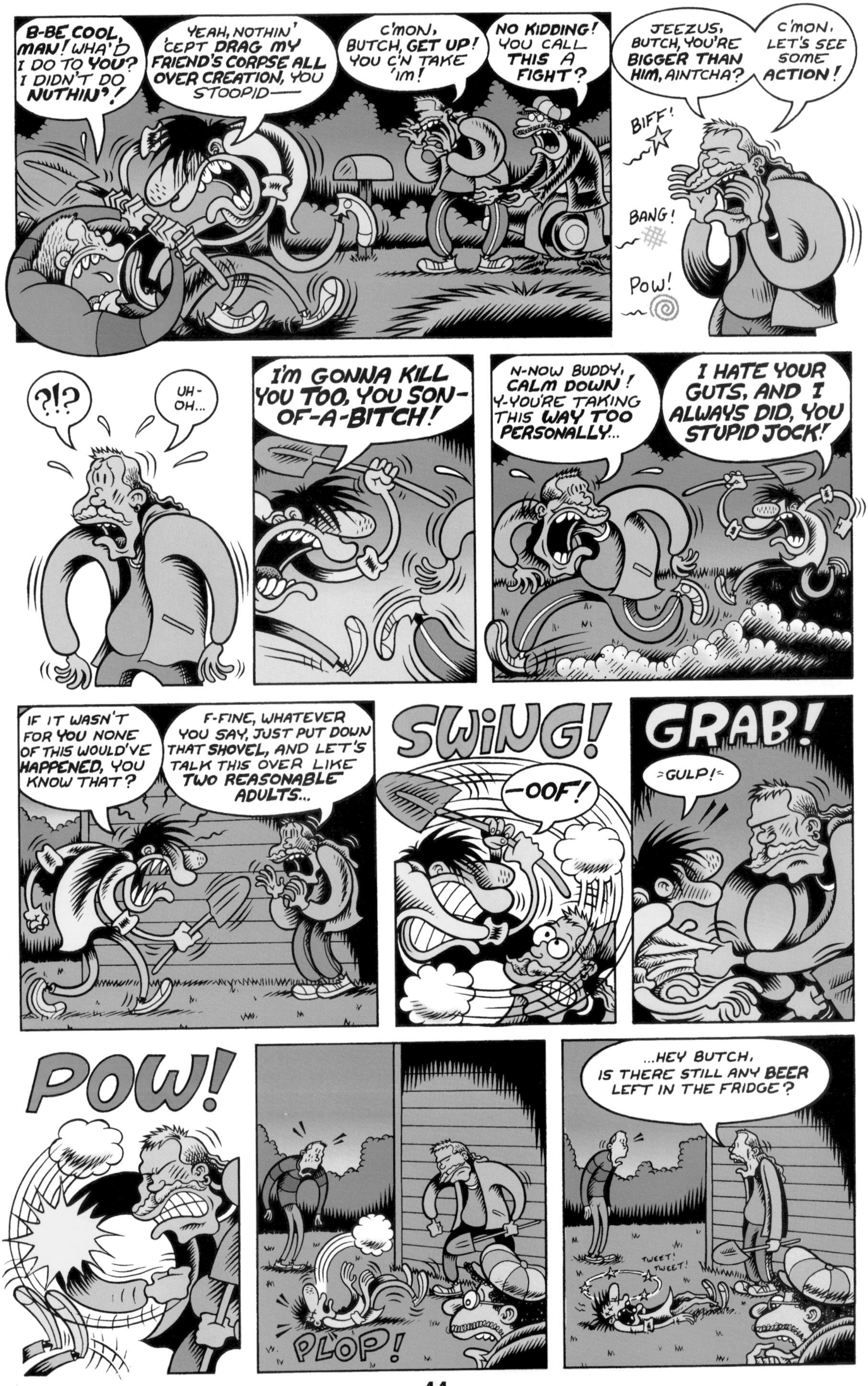
B-BE COOL, MAN! WHA'D I DO TO YOU? I DIDN'T DO NUTHIN'!
YEAH, NOTHIN' 'CEPT DRAG MY FRIEND'S CORPSE ALL OVER CREATION, YOU STOOPID—
C'MON, BUTCH, GET UP! YOU C'N TAKE 'IM!
NO KIDDING! YOU CALL THIS A FIGHT?
JEEZUS, BUTCH, YOU'RE BIGGER THAN HIM, AINTCHA?
C'MON, LET'S SEE SOME ACTION!
BIFF!
BANG!
POW!
?!?
UH-OH...
I'M GONNA KILL YOU TOO, YOU SON-OF-A-BITCH!
N-NOW BUDDY, CALM DOWN! Y-YOU'RE TAKING THIS WAY TOO PERSONALLY...
I HATE YOUR GUTS, AND I ALWAYS DID, YOU STUPID JOCK!
IF IT WASN'T FOR YOU NONE OF THIS WOULD'VE HAPPENED, YOU KNOW THAT?
F-FINE, WHATEVER YOU SAY, JUST PUT DOWN THAT SHOVEL, AND LET'S TALK THIS OVER LIKE TWO REASONABLE ADULTS...
SWING!
—OOF!
GRAB!
=GULP!=
POW!
PLOP!
TWEET! TWEET!
...HEY BUTCH, IS THERE STILL ANY BEER LEFT IN THE FRIDGE?

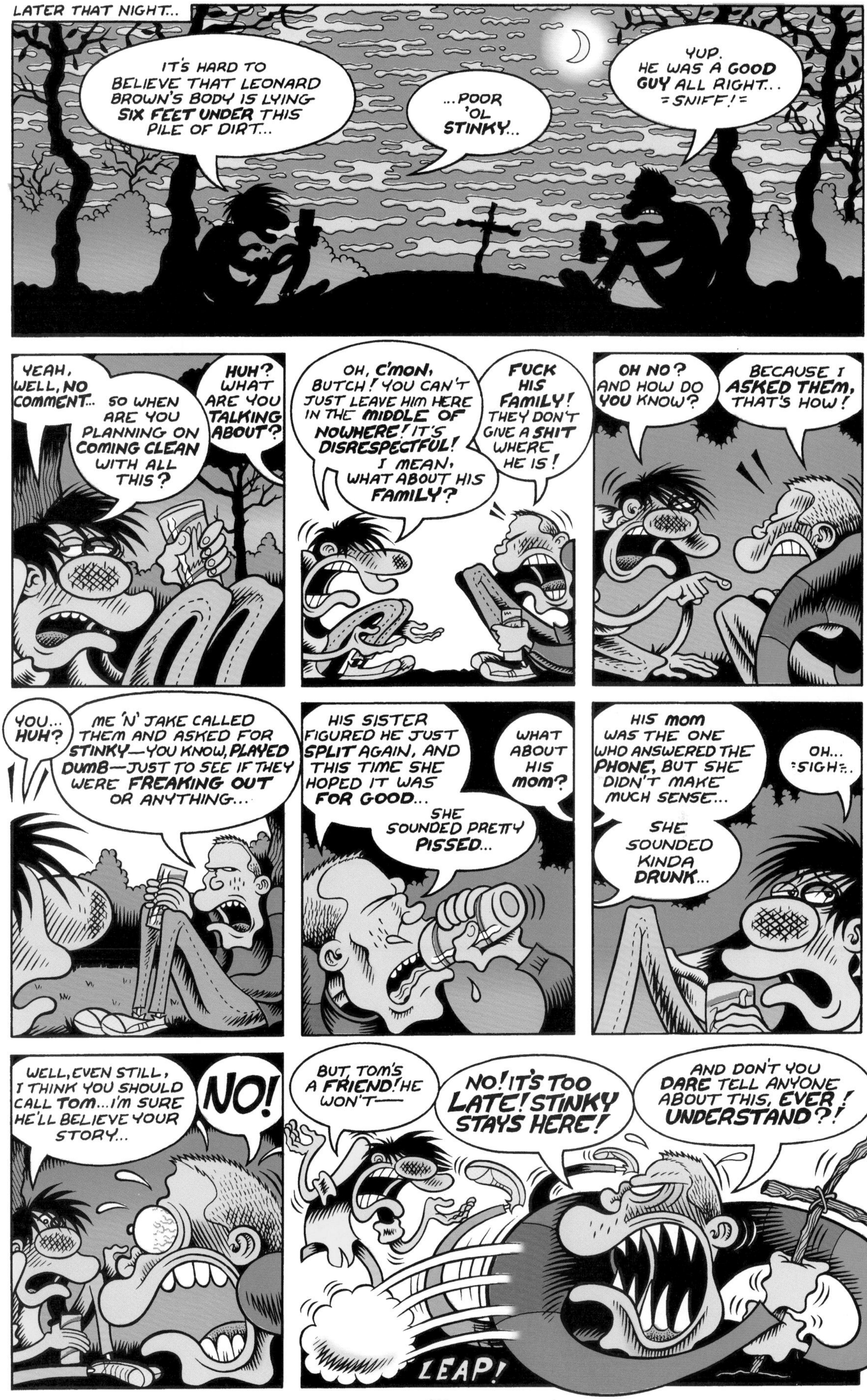
LATER THAT NIGHT...
IT'S HARD TO BELIEVE THAT LEONARD BROWN'S BODY IS LYING SIX FEET UNDER THIS PILE OF DIRT...
...POOR 'OL STINKY...
YUP. HE WAS A GOOD GUY ALL RIGHT... =SNIFF!=
YEAH, WELL, NO COMMENT... SO WHEN ARE YOU PLANNING ON COMING CLEAN WITH ALL THIS?
HUH? WHAT ARE YOU TALKING ABOUT?
OH, C'MON, BUTCH! YOU CAN'T JUST LEAVE HIM HERE IN THE MIDDLE OF NOWHERE! IT'S DISRESPECTFUL! I MEAN, WHAT ABOUT HIS FAMILY?
FUCK HIS FAMILY! THEY DON'T GIVE A SHIT WHERE HE IS!
OH NO? AND HOW DO YOU KNOW?
BECAUSE I ASKED THEM, THAT'S HOW!
YOU... HUH?
ME 'N' JAKE CALLED THEM AND ASKED FOR STINKY—YOU KNOW, PLAYED DUMB—JUST TO SEE IF THEY WERE FREAKING OUT OR ANYTHING...
HIS SISTER FIGURED HE JUST SPLIT AGAIN, AND THIS TIME SHE HOPED IT WAS FOR GOOD...
SHE SOUNDED PRETTY PISSED...
WHAT ABOUT HIS MOM?
HIS MOM WAS THE ONE WHO ANSWERED THE PHONE, BUT SHE DIDN'T MAKE MUCH SENSE...
SHE SOUNDED KINDA DRUNK...
OH... =SIGH=.
WELL, EVEN STILL, I THINK YOU SHOULD CALL TOM... I'M SURE HE'LL BELIEVE YOUR STORY...
NO!
BUT, TOM'S A FRIEND! HE WON'T—
NO! IT'S TOO LATE! STINKY STAYS HERE!
AND DON'T YOU DARE TELL ANYONE ABOUT THIS, EVER! UNDERSTAND?!
LEAP!

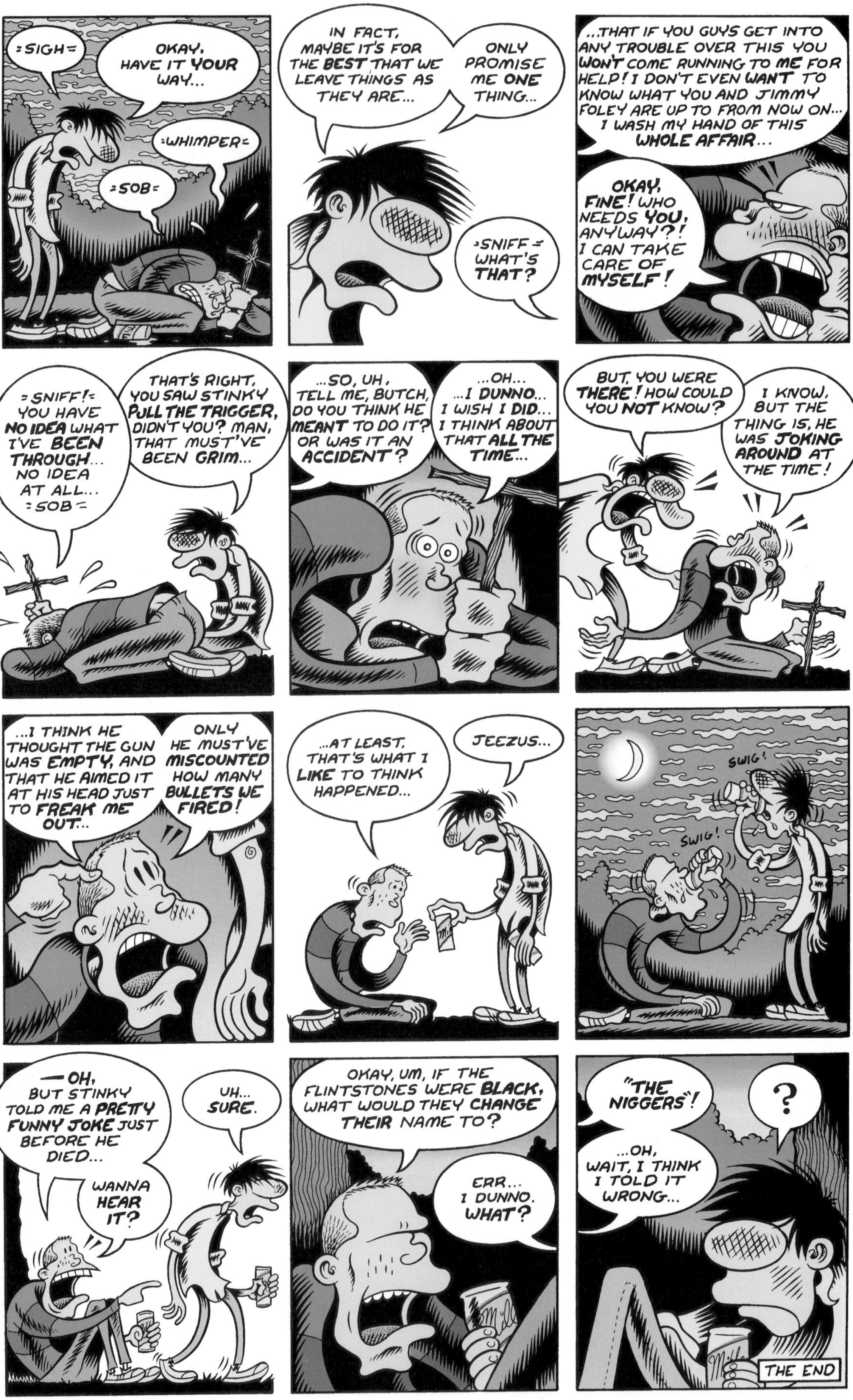
=SIGH=
OKAY, HAVE IT YOUR WAY...
=WHIMPER=
=SOB=
IN FACT, MAYBE IT'S FOR THE BEST THAT WE LEAVE THINGS AS THEY ARE...
ONLY PROMISE ME ONE THING...
=SNIFF= WHAT'S THAT?
...THAT IF YOU GUYS GET INTO ANY TROUBLE OVER THIS YOU WON'T COME RUNNING TO ME FOR HELP! I DON'T EVEN WANT TO KNOW WHAT YOU AND JIMMY FOLEY ARE UP TO FROM NOW ON... I WASH MY HAND OF THIS WHOLE AFFAIR...
OKAY, FINE! WHO NEEDS YOU, ANYWAY?! I CAN TAKE CARE OF MYSELF!
=SNIFF!= YOU HAVE NO IDEA WHAT I'VE BEEN THROUGH... NO IDEA AT ALL... =SOB=
THAT'S RIGHT, YOU SAW STINKY PULL THE TRIGGER, DIDN'T YOU? MAN, THAT MUST'VE BEEN GRIM...
...SO, UH, TELL ME, BUTCH, DO YOU THINK HE MEANT TO DO IT? OR WAS IT AN ACCIDENT?
...OH... ...I DUNNO... I WISH I DID... I THINK ABOUT THAT ALL THE TIME...
BUT, YOU WERE THERE! HOW COULD YOU NOT KNOW?
I KNOW, BUT THE THING IS, HE WAS JOKING AROUND AT THE TIME!
...I THINK HE THOUGHT THE GUN WAS EMPTY, AND THAT HE AIMED IT AT HIS HEAD JUST TO FREAK ME OUT...
ONLY HE MUST'VE MISCOUNTED HOW MANY BULLETS WE FIRED!
...AT LEAST, THAT'S WHAT I LIKE TO THINK HAPPENED...
JEEZUS...
SWIG!
SWIG!
—OH, BUT STINKY TOLD ME A PRETTY FUNNY JOKE JUST BEFORE HE DIED...
WANNA HEAR IT?
UH... SURE.
OKAY, UM, IF THE FLINTSTONES WERE BLACK, WHAT WOULD THEY CHANGE THEIR NAME TO?
ERR... I DUNNO. WHAT?
"THE NIGGERS"!
?
...OH, WAIT, I THINK I TOLD IT WRONG...
THE END

LISA LEAVENWORTH ON LIFE AND DEATH

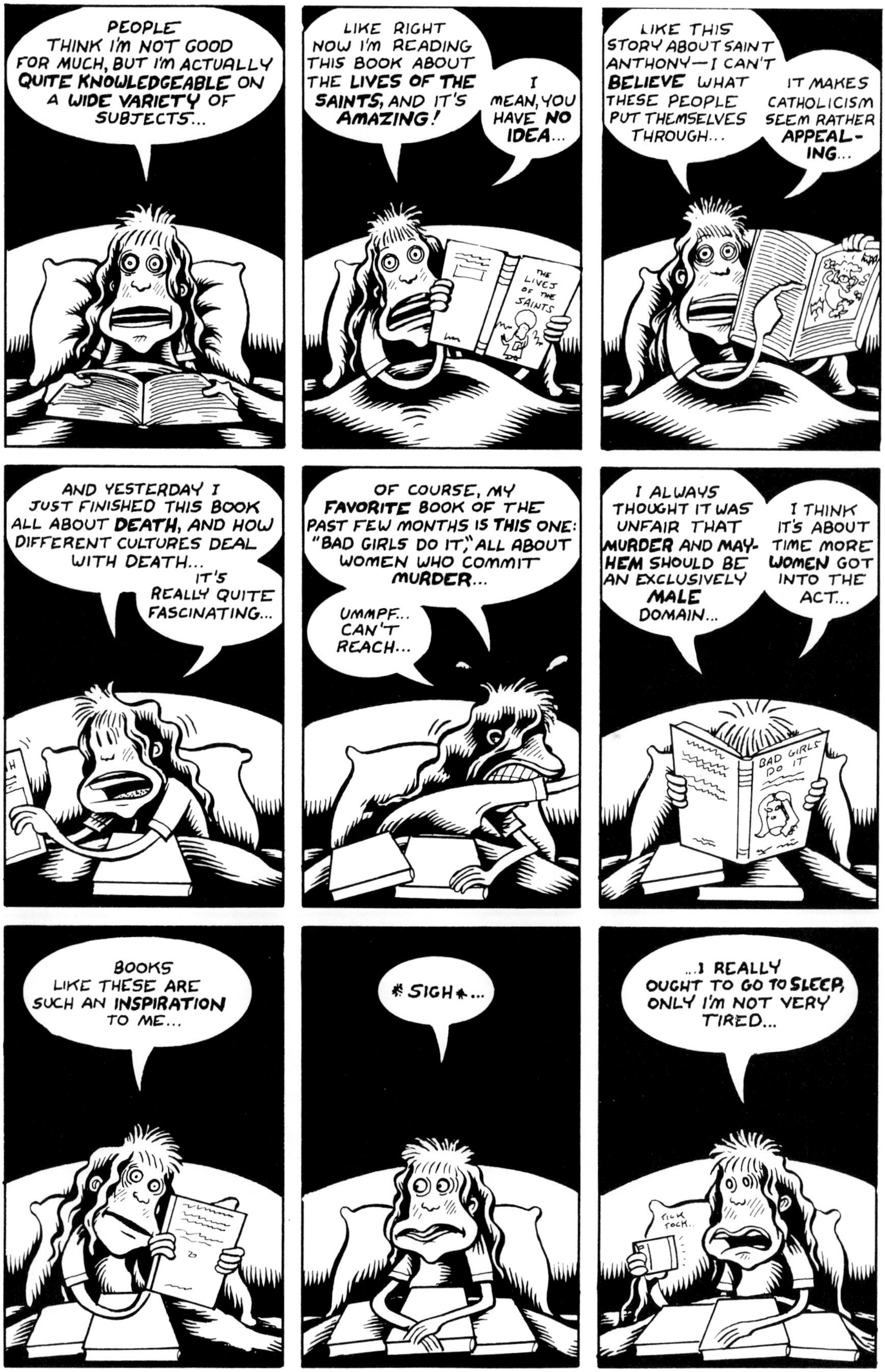
PEOPLE THINK I'M NOT GOOD FOR MUCH, BUT I'M ACTUALLY QUITE KNOWLEDGEABLE ON A WIDE VARIETY OF SUBJECTS...
LIKE RIGHT NOW I'M READING THIS BOOK ABOUT THE LIVES OF THE SAINTS, AND IT'S AMAZING!
I MEAN, YOU HAVE NO IDEA...
THE LIVES OF THE SAINTS
LIKE THIS STORY ABOUT SAINT ANTHONY—I CAN'T BELIEVE WHAT THESE PEOPLE PUT THEMSELVES THROUGH...
IT MAKES CATHOLICISM SEEM RATHER APPEALING...
AND YESTERDAY I JUST FINISHED THIS BOOK ALL ABOUT DEATH, AND HOW DIFFERENT CULTURES DEAL WITH DEATH...
IT'S REALLY QUITE FASCINATING...
OF COURSE, MY FAVORITE BOOK OF THE PAST FEW MONTHS IS THIS ONE: "BAD GIRLS DO IT," ALL ABOUT WOMEN WHO COMMIT MURDER...
UMMPF... CAN'T REACH...
I ALWAYS THOUGHT IT WAS UNFAIR THAT MURDER AND MAYHEM SHOULD BE AN EXCLUSIVELY MALE DOMAIN...
I THINK IT'S ABOUT TIME MORE WOMEN GOT INTO THE ACT...
BAD GIRLS DO IT
BOOKS LIKE THESE ARE SUCH AN INSPIRATION TO ME...
SIGH...
...I REALLY OUGHT TO GO TO SLEEP, ONLY I'M NOT VERY TIRED...
TICK TOCK..

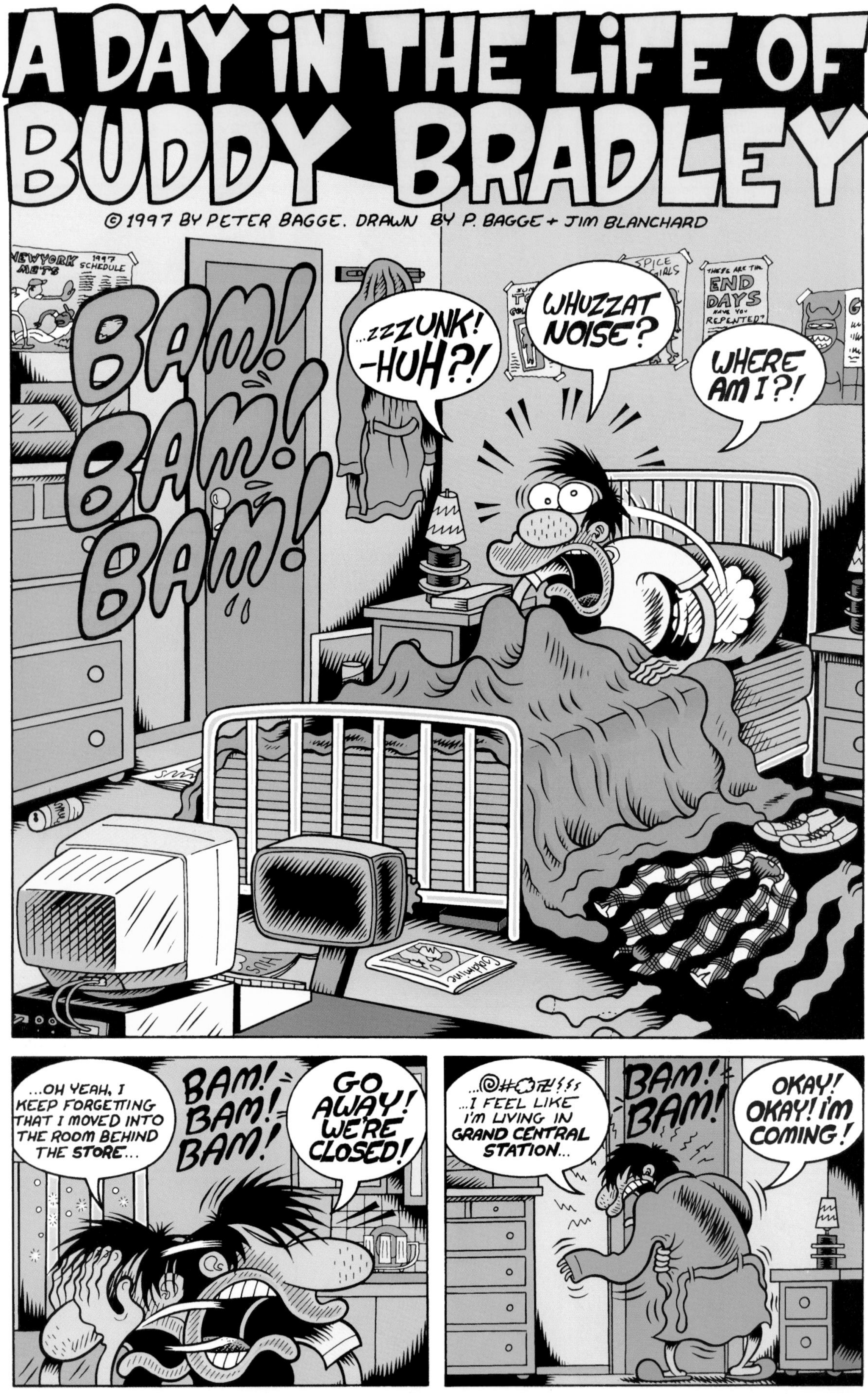

A DAY IN THE LIFE OF BUDDY BRADLEY
© 1997 BY PETER BAGGE. DRAWN BY P. BAGGE + JIM BLANCHARD
NEW YORK METS
1997 SCHEDULE
SPICE GIRLS
THESE ARE THE END DAYS HAVE YOU REPENTED?
BAM! BAM! BAM!
...ZZZUNK! -HUH?!
WHUZZAT NOISE?
WHERE AM I?!
...OH YEAH, I KEEP FORGETTING THAT I MOVED INTO THE ROOM BEHIND THE STORE...
BAM! BAM! BAM!
GO AWAY! WE'RE CLOSED!
...@#☼*!$$$ ...I FEEL LIKE I'M LIVING IN GRAND CENTRAL STATION...
BAM! BAM!
OKAY! OKAY! I'M COMING!

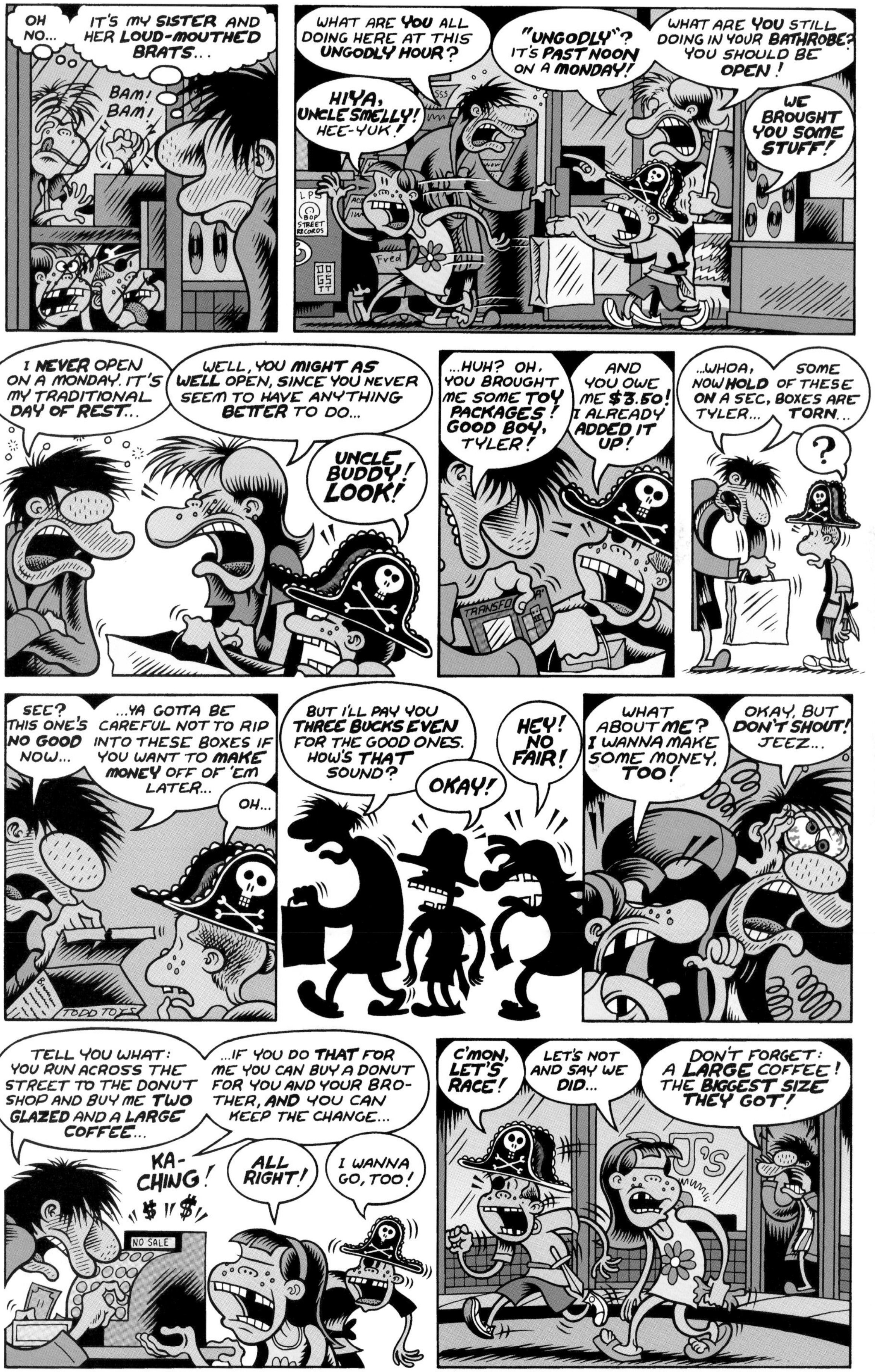
OH NO...
IT'S MY SISTER AND HER LOUD-MOUTHED BRATS...
BAM! BAM!
WHAT ARE YOU ALL DOING HERE AT THIS UNGODLY HOUR?
HIYA, UNCLE SMELLY! HEE-YUK!
"UNGODLY"? IT'S PAST NOON ON A MONDAY!
WHAT ARE YOU STILL DOING IN YOUR BATHROBE? YOU SHOULD BE OPEN!
WE BROUGHT YOU SOME STUFF!
BOP STREET RECORDS
Fred
I NEVER OPEN ON A MONDAY. IT'S MY TRADITIONAL DAY OF REST...
WELL, YOU MIGHT AS WELL OPEN, SINCE YOU NEVER SEEM TO HAVE ANYTHING BETTER TO DO...
UNCLE BUDDY! LOOK!
...HUH? OH, YOU BROUGHT ME SOME TOY PACKAGES! GOOD BOY, TYLER!
AND YOU OWE ME $3.50! I ALREADY ADDED IT UP!
...WHOA, NOW HOLD ON A SEC, TYLER...
SOME OF THESE BOXES ARE TORN...
?
SEE? THIS ONE'S NO GOOD NOW...
...YA GOTTA BE CAREFUL NOT TO RIP INTO THESE BOXES IF YOU WANT TO MAKE MONEY OFF OF 'EM LATER...
OH...
TODD TOYS
BUT I'LL PAY YOU THREE BUCKS EVEN FOR THE GOOD ONES. HOW'S THAT SOUND?
OKAY!
HEY! NO FAIR!
WHAT ABOUT ME? I WANNA MAKE SOME MONEY, TOO!
OKAY, BUT DON'T SHOUT! JEEZ...
TELL YOU WHAT: YOU RUN ACROSS THE STREET TO THE DONUT SHOP AND BUY ME TWO GLAZED AND A LARGE COFFEE...
...IF YOU DO THAT FOR ME YOU CAN BUY A DONUT FOR YOU AND YOUR BROTHER, AND YOU CAN KEEP THE CHANGE...
KA-CHING!
$ $
NO SALE
ALL RIGHT!
I WANNA GO, TOO!
C'MON, LET'S RACE!
LET'S NOT AND SAY WE DID...
DON'T FORGET: A LARGE COFFEE! THE BIGGEST SIZE THEY GOT!

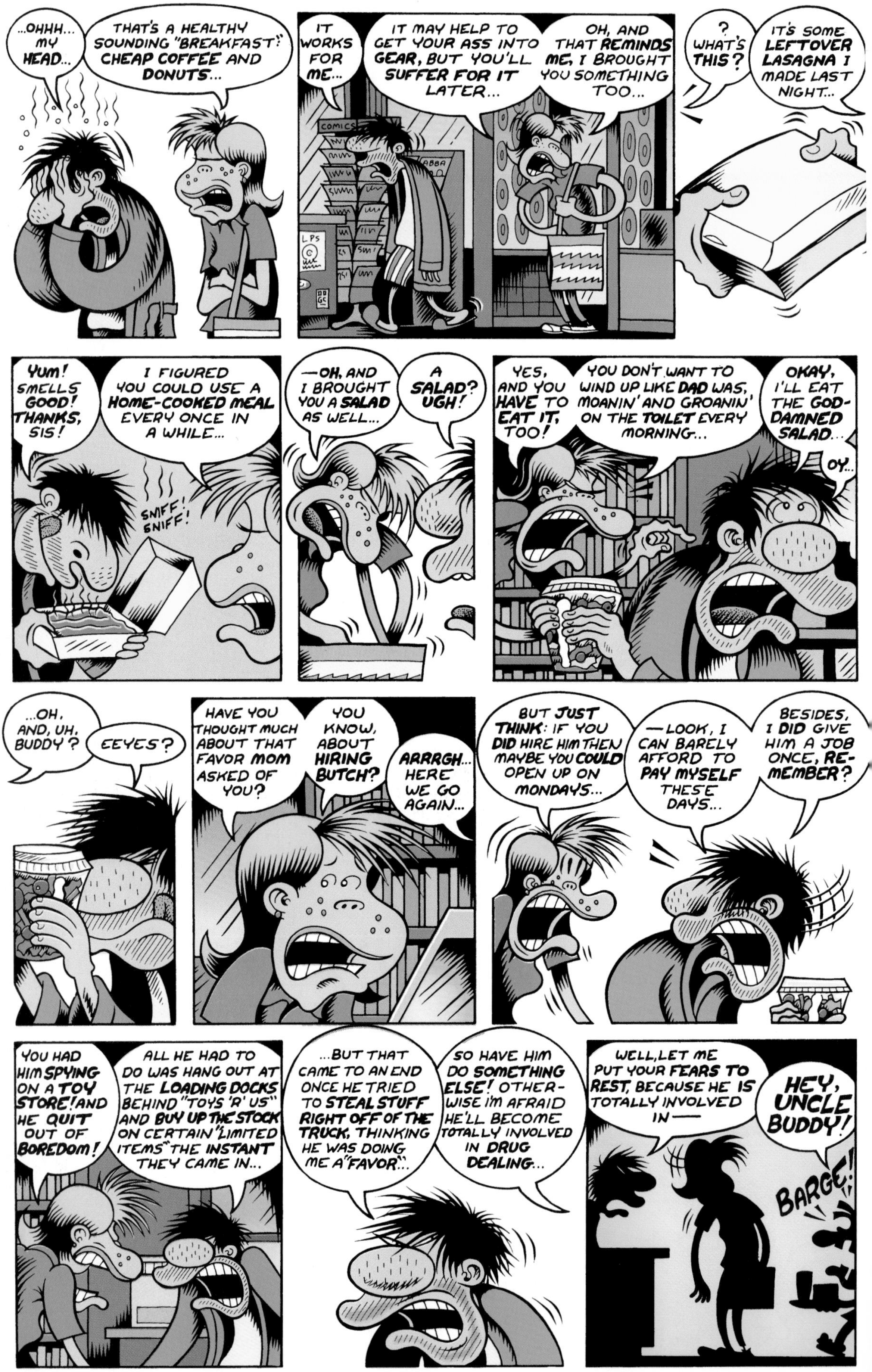
...OHHH... MY HEAD...
THAT'S A HEALTHY SOUNDING "BREAKFAST": CHEAP COFFEE AND DONUTS...
IT WORKS FOR ME...
IT MAY HELP TO GET YOUR ASS INTO GEAR, BUT YOU'LL SUFFER FOR IT LATER...
OH, AND THAT REMINDS ME, I BROUGHT YOU SOMETHING TOO...
COMICS
LPS
ABBA
? WHAT'S THIS?
IT'S SOME LEFTOVER LASAGNA I MADE LAST NIGHT...
YUM! SMELLS GOOD! THANKS, SIS!
I FIGURED YOU COULD USE A HOME-COOKED MEAL EVERY ONCE IN A WHILE...
SNIFF! SNIFF!
—OH, AND I BROUGHT YOU A SALAD AS WELL...
A SALAD? UGH!
YES, AND YOU HAVE TO EAT IT, TOO!
YOU DON'T WANT TO WIND UP LIKE DAD WAS, MOANIN' AND GROANIN' ON THE TOILET EVERY MORNING...
OKAY, I'LL EAT THE GOD-DAMNED SALAD...
OY...
...OH, AND, UH, BUDDY?
EEYES?
HAVE YOU THOUGHT MUCH ABOUT THAT FAVOR MOM ASKED OF YOU?
YOU KNOW, ABOUT HIRING BUTCH?
ARRRGH... HERE WE GO AGAIN...
BUT JUST THINK: IF YOU DID HIRE HIM THEN MAYBE YOU COULD OPEN UP ON MONDAYS...
—LOOK, I CAN BARELY AFFORD TO PAY MYSELF THESE DAYS...
BESIDES, I DID GIVE HIM A JOB ONCE, REMEMBER?
YOU HAD HIM SPYING ON A TOY STORE! AND HE QUIT OUT OF BOREDOM!
ALL HE HAD TO DO WAS HANG OUT AT THE LOADING DOCKS BEHIND "TOYS 'R' US" AND BUY UP THE STOCK ON CERTAIN "LIMITED ITEMS" THE INSTANT THEY CAME IN...
...BUT THAT CAME TO AN END ONCE HE TRIED TO STEAL STUFF RIGHT OFF OF THE TRUCK, THINKING HE WAS DOING ME A "FAVOR"...
SO HAVE HIM DO SOMETHING ELSE! OTHERWISE I'M AFRAID HE'LL BECOME TOTALLY INVOLVED IN DRUG DEALING...
WELL, LET ME PUT YOUR FEARS TO REST, BECAUSE HE IS TOTALLY INVOLVED IN—
HEY, UNCLE BUDDY!
BARGE!

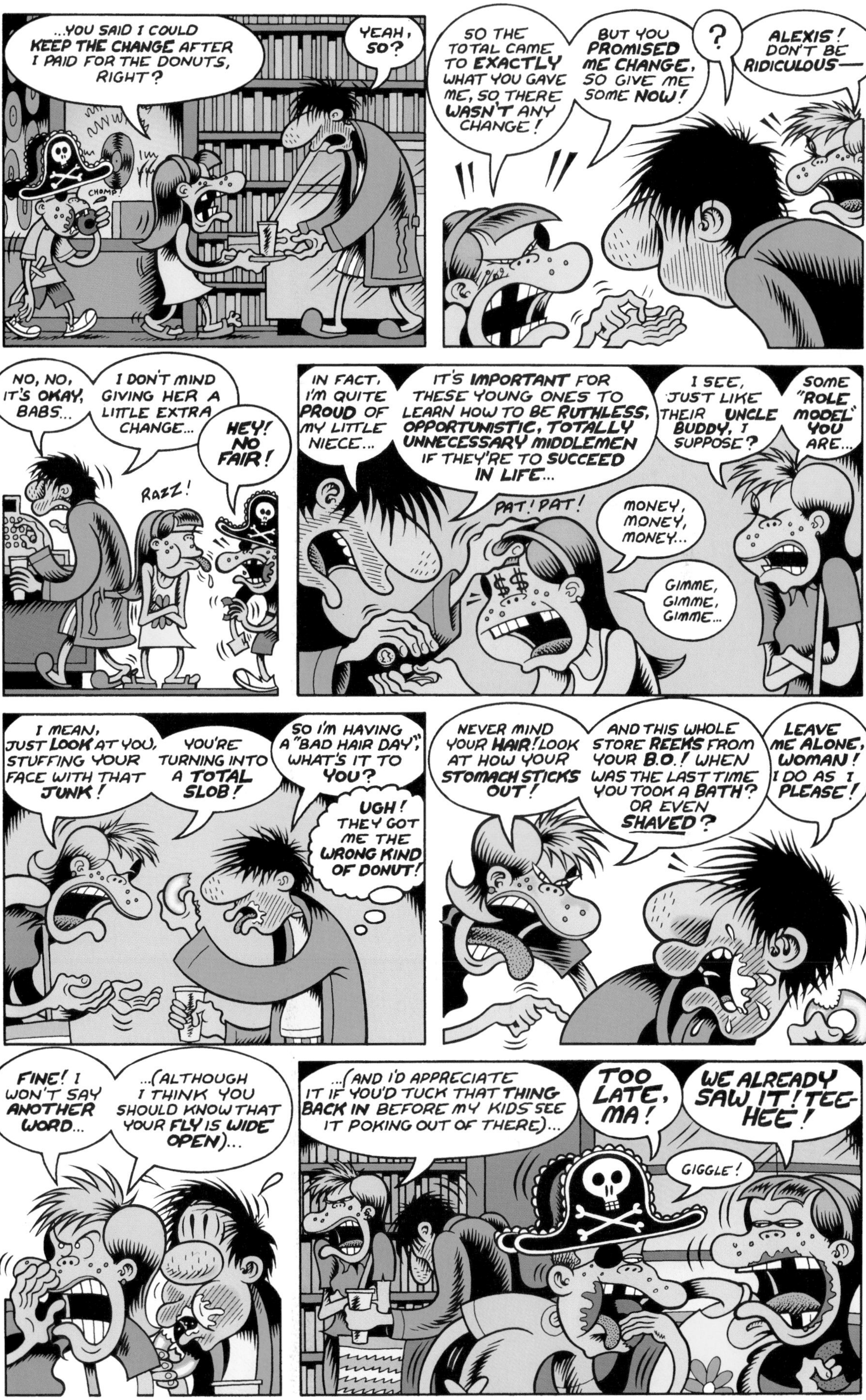
...YOU SAID I COULD KEEP THE CHANGE AFTER I PAID FOR THE DONUTS, RIGHT?
YEAH, SO?
CHOMP!
SO THE TOTAL CAME TO EXACTLY WHAT YOU GAVE ME, SO THERE WASN'T ANY CHANGE!
BUT YOU PROMISED ME CHANGE, SO GIVE ME SOME NOW!
?
ALEXIS! DON'T BE RIDICULOUS—
NO, NO, IT'S OKAY, BABS...
I DON'T MIND GIVING HER A LITTLE EXTRA CHANGE...
HEY! NO FAIR!
RAZZ!
IN FACT, I'M QUITE PROUD OF MY LITTLE NIECE...
IT'S IMPORTANT FOR THESE YOUNG ONES TO LEARN HOW TO BE RUTHLESS, OPPORTUNISTIC, TOTALLY UNNECESSARY MIDDLEMEN IF THEY'RE TO SUCCEED IN LIFE...
I SEE, JUST LIKE THEIR UNCLE BUDDY, I SUPPOSE?
SOME "ROLE MODEL" YOU ARE...
PAT! PAT!
MONEY, MONEY, MONEY...
GIMME, GIMME, GIMME...
I MEAN, JUST LOOK AT YOU, STUFFING YOUR FACE WITH THAT JUNK!
YOU'RE TURNING INTO A TOTAL SLOB!
SO I'M HAVING A "BAD HAIR DAY", WHAT'S IT TO YOU?
UGH! THEY GOT ME THE WRONG KIND OF DONUT!
NEVER MIND YOUR HAIR! LOOK AT HOW YOUR STOMACH STICKS OUT!
AND THIS WHOLE STORE REEKS FROM YOUR B.O.! WHEN WAS THE LAST TIME YOU TOOK A BATH? OR EVEN SHAVED?
LEAVE ME ALONE, WOMAN! I DO AS I PLEASE!
FINE! I WON'T SAY ANOTHER WORD...
...(ALTHOUGH I THINK YOU SHOULD KNOW THAT YOUR FLY IS WIDE OPEN)...
...(AND I'D APPRECIATE IT IF YOU'D TUCK THAT THING BACK IN BEFORE MY KIDS SEE IT POKING OUT OF THERE)...
TOO LATE, MA!
WE ALREADY SAW IT! TEE-HEE!
GIGGLE!

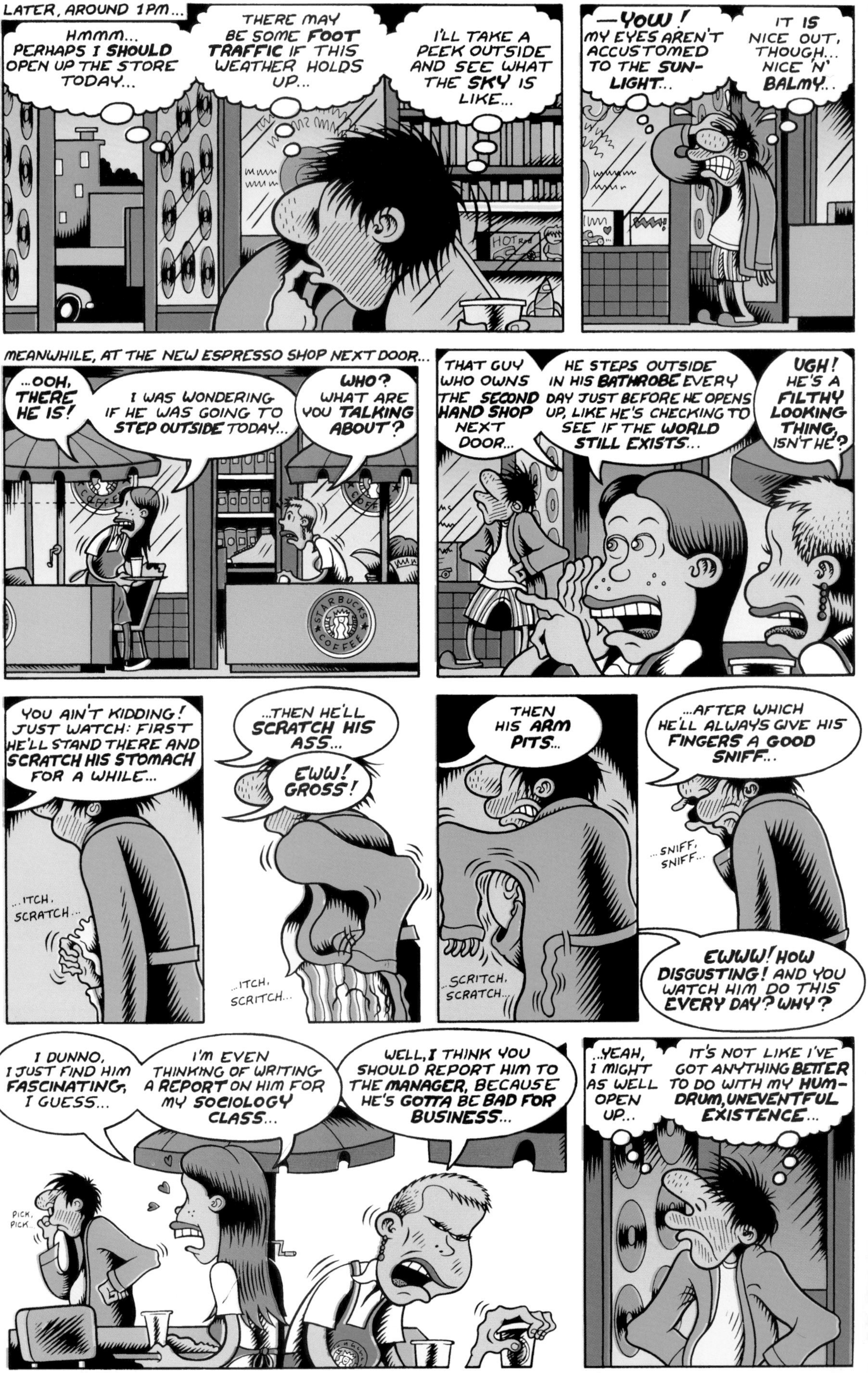
LATER, AROUND 1PM...
HMMM... PERHAPS I SHOULD OPEN UP THE STORE TODAY...
THERE MAY BE SOME FOOT TRAFFIC IF THIS WEATHER HOLDS UP...
I'LL TAKE A PEEK OUTSIDE AND SEE WHAT THE SKY IS LIKE...
—YOW! MY EYES AREN'T ACCUSTOMED TO THE SUN-LIGHT...
IT IS NICE OUT, THOUGH... NICE 'N' BALMY...
MEANWHILE, AT THE NEW ESPRESSO SHOP NEXT DOOR...
...OOH, THERE HE IS!
I WAS WONDERING IF HE WAS GOING TO STEP OUTSIDE TODAY...
WHO? WHAT ARE YOU TALKING ABOUT?
STARBUCKS COFFEE
THAT GUY WHO OWNS THE SECOND HAND SHOP NEXT DOOR...
HE STEPS OUTSIDE IN HIS BATHROBE EVERY DAY JUST BEFORE HE OPENS UP, LIKE HE'S CHECKING TO SEE IF THE WORLD STILL EXISTS...
UGH! HE'S A FILTHY LOOKING THING, ISN'T HE?
YOU AIN'T KIDDING! JUST WATCH: FIRST HE'LL STAND THERE AND SCRATCH HIS STOMACH FOR A WHILE...
...ITCH, SCRATCH...
...THEN HE'LL SCRATCH HIS ASS...
EWW! GROSS!
...ITCH, SCRITCH...
THEN HIS ARM PITS...
...SCRITCH, SCRATCH...
...AFTER WHICH HE'LL ALWAYS GIVE HIS FINGERS A GOOD SNIFF...
...SNIFF, SNIFF...
EWWW! HOW DISGUSTING! AND YOU WATCH HIM DO THIS EVERY DAY? WHY?
I DUNNO, I JUST FIND HIM FASCINATING, I GUESS...
I'M EVEN THINKING OF WRITING A REPORT ON HIM FOR MY SOCIOLOGY CLASS...
WELL, I THINK YOU SHOULD REPORT HIM TO THE MANAGER, BECAUSE HE'S GOTTA BE BAD FOR BUSINESS...
PICK, PICK...
...YEAH, I MIGHT AS WELL OPEN UP...
IT'S NOT LIKE I'VE GOT ANYTHING BETTER TO DO WITH MY HUM-DRUM, UNEVENTFUL EXISTENCE...

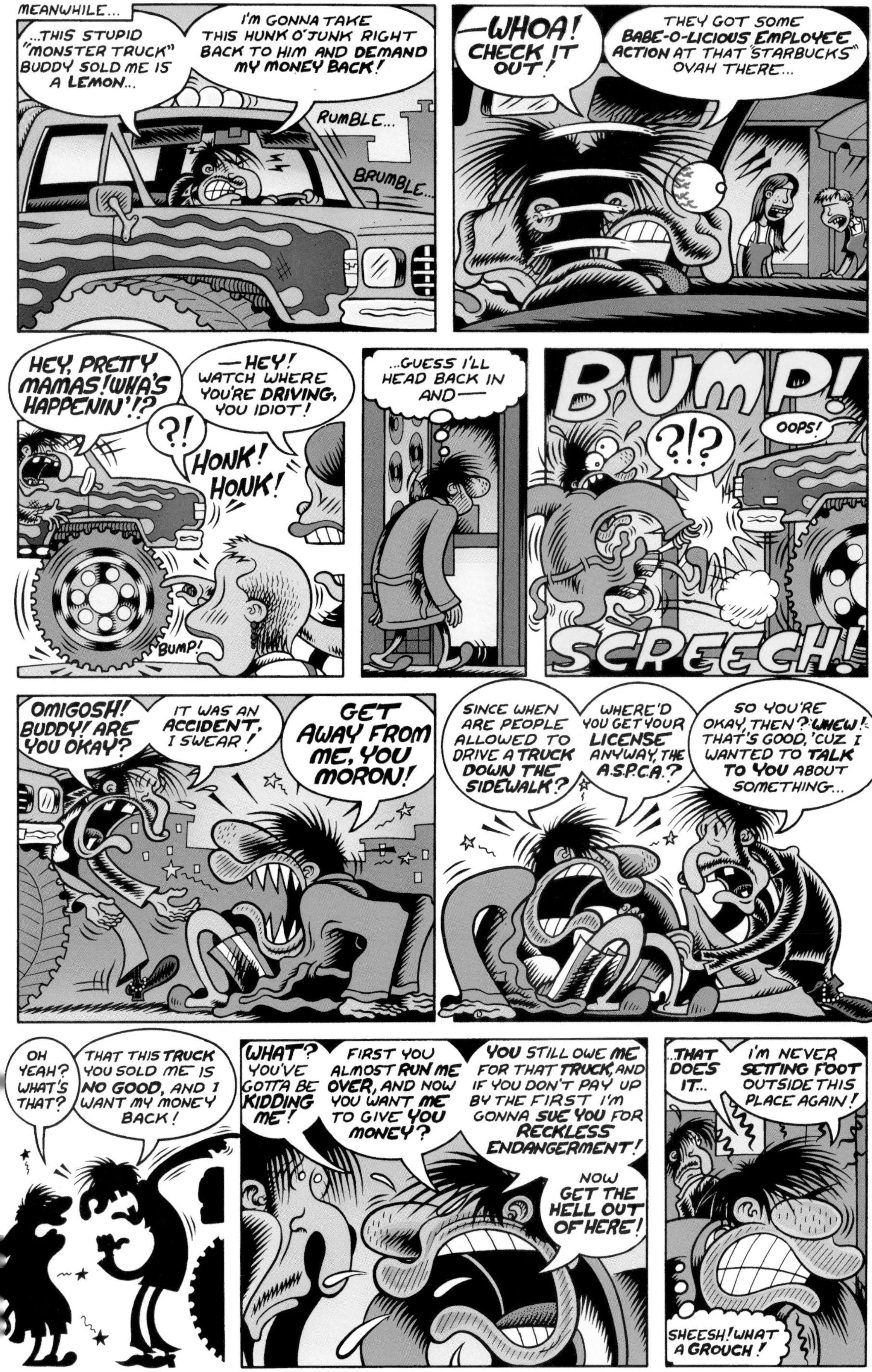

MEANWHILE...
...THIS STUPID "MONSTER TRUCK" BUDDY SOLD ME IS A LEMON...
I'M GONNA TAKE THIS HUNK O'JUNK RIGHT BACK TO HIM AND DEMAND MY MONEY BACK!
RUMBLE...
BRUMBLE...
—WHOA! CHECK IT OUT!
THEY GOT SOME BABE-O-LICIOUS EMPLOYEE ACTION AT THAT "STARBUCKS" OVAH THERE...
HEY, PRETTY MAMAS! WHA'S HAPPENIN'!?
—HEY! WATCH WHERE YOU'RE DRIVING, YOU IDIOT!
?!
HONK! HONK!
BUMP!
...GUESS I'LL HEAD BACK IN AND—
BUMP!
?!?
OOPS!
SCREECH!
OMIGOSH! BUDDY! ARE YOU OKAY?
IT WAS AN ACCIDENT, I SWEAR!
GET AWAY FROM ME, YOU MORON!
SINCE WHEN ARE PEOPLE ALLOWED TO DRIVE A TRUCK DOWN THE SIDEWALK?
WHERE'D YOU GET YOUR LICENSE ANYWAY, THE A.S.P.C.A.?
SO YOU'RE OKAY, THEN? WHEW! THAT'S GOOD, 'CUZ I WANTED TO TALK TO YOU ABOUT SOMETHING...
OH YEAH? WHAT'S THAT?
THAT THIS TRUCK YOU SOLD ME IS NO GOOD, AND I WANT MY MONEY BACK!
WHAT? YOU'VE GOTTA BE KIDDING ME!
FIRST YOU ALMOST RUN ME OVER, AND NOW YOU WANT ME TO GIVE YOU MONEY?
YOU STILL OWE ME FOR THAT TRUCK, AND IF YOU DON'T PAY UP BY THE FIRST I'M GONNA SUE YOU FOR RECKLESS ENDANGERMENT!
NOW GET THE HELL OUT OF HERE!
...THAT DOES IT...
I'M NEVER SETTING FOOT OUTSIDE THIS PLACE AGAIN!
SHEESH! WHAT A GROUCH!

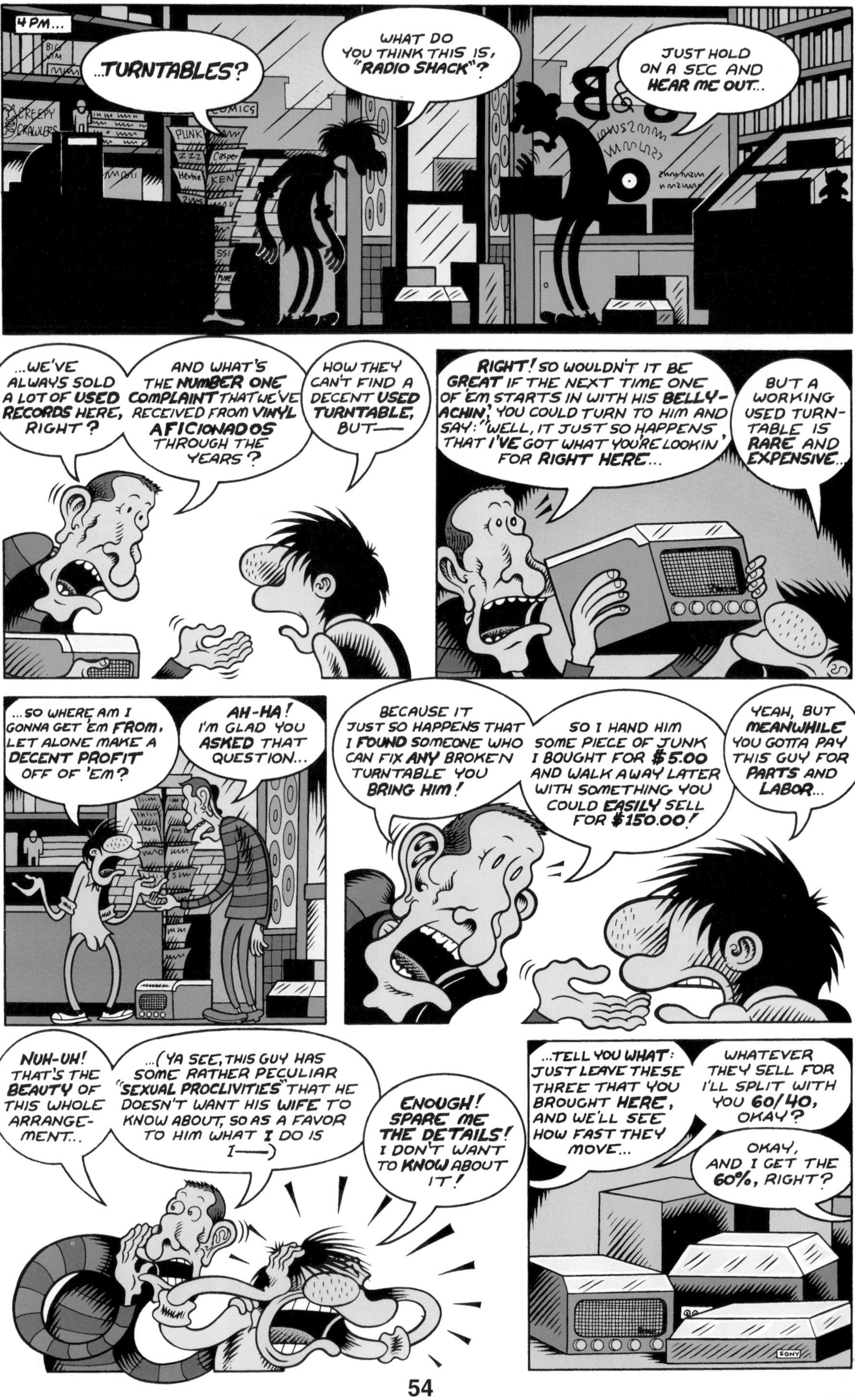
4 PM...
...TURNTABLES?
WHAT DO YOU THINK THIS IS, "RADIO SHACK"?
JUST HOLD ON A SEC AND HEAR ME OUT...
...WE'VE ALWAYS SOLD A LOT OF USED RECORDS HERE, RIGHT?
AND WHAT'S THE NUMBER ONE COMPLAINT THAT WE'VE RECEIVED FROM VINYL AFICIONADOS THROUGH THE YEARS?
HOW THEY CAN'T FIND A DECENT USED TURNTABLE, BUT—
RIGHT! SO WOULDN'T IT BE GREAT IF THE NEXT TIME ONE OF 'EM STARTS IN WITH HIS BELLY-ACHIN', YOU COULD TURN TO HIM AND SAY: "WELL, IT JUST SO HAPPENS THAT I'VE GOT WHAT YOU'RE LOOKIN' FOR RIGHT HERE...
BUT A WORKING USED TURN-TABLE IS RARE AND EXPENSIVE...
...SO WHERE AM I GONNA GET 'EM FROM, LET ALONE MAKE A DECENT PROFIT OFF OF 'EM?
AH-HA! I'M GLAD YOU ASKED THAT QUESTION...
BECAUSE IT JUST SO HAPPENS THAT I FOUND SOMEONE WHO CAN FIX ANY BROKEN TURNTABLE YOU BRING HIM!
SO I HAND HIM SOME PIECE OF JUNK I BOUGHT FOR $5.00 AND WALK AWAY LATER WITH SOMETHING YOU COULD EASILY SELL FOR $150.00!
YEAH, BUT MEANWHILE YOU GOTTA PAY THIS GUY FOR PARTS AND LABOR...
NUH-UH! THAT'S THE BEAUTY OF THIS WHOLE ARRANGE-MENT...
...(YA SEE, THIS GUY HAS SOME RATHER PECULIAR "SEXUAL PROCLIVITIES" THAT HE DOESN'T WANT HIS WIFE TO KNOW ABOUT, SO AS A FAVOR TO HIM WHAT I DO IS I—)
ENOUGH! SPARE ME THE DETAILS! I DON'T WANT TO KNOW ABOUT IT!
...TELL YOU WHAT: JUST LEAVE THESE THREE THAT YOU BROUGHT HERE, AND WE'LL SEE HOW FAST THEY MOVE...
WHATEVER THEY SELL FOR I'LL SPLIT WITH YOU 60/40, OKAY?
OKAY, AND I GET THE 60%, RIGHT?

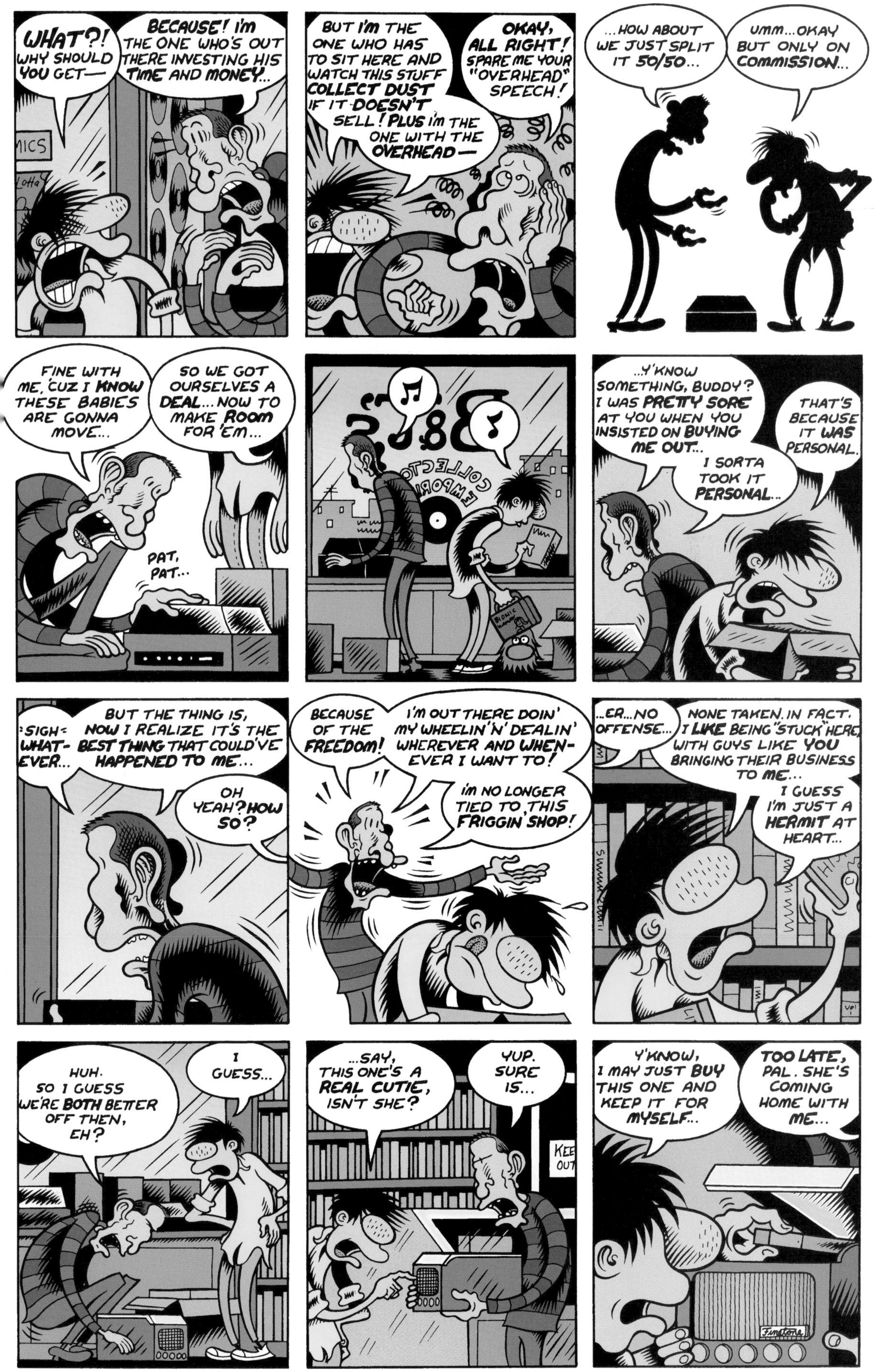
WHAT?! WHY SHOULD YOU GET—
BECAUSE! I'M THE ONE WHO'S OUT THERE INVESTING HIS TIME AND MONEY...
BUT I'M THE ONE WHO HAS TO SIT HERE AND WATCH THIS STUFF COLLECT DUST IF IT DOESN'T SELL! PLUS I'M THE ONE WITH THE OVERHEAD—
OKAY, ALL RIGHT! SPARE ME YOUR "OVERHEAD" SPEECH!
...HOW ABOUT WE JUST SPLIT IT 50/50...
UMM...OKAY BUT ONLY ON COMMISSION...
FINE WITH ME, 'CUZ I KNOW THESE BABIES ARE GONNA MOVE...
SO WE GOT OURSELVES A DEAL... NOW TO MAKE ROOM FOR 'EM...
PAT, PAT...
...Y'KNOW SOMETHING, BUDDY? I WAS PRETTY SORE AT YOU WHEN YOU INSISTED ON BUYING ME OUT...
I SORTA TOOK IT PERSONAL...
THAT'S BECAUSE IT WAS PERSONAL.
:SIGH: WHAT-EVER...
BUT THE THING IS, NOW I REALIZE IT'S THE BEST THING THAT COULD'VE HAPPENED TO ME...
OH YEAH? HOW SO?
BECAUSE OF THE FREEDOM!
I'M OUT THERE DOIN' MY WHEELIN' 'N' DEALIN' WHEREVER AND WHEN-EVER I WANT TO!
I'M NO LONGER TIED TO THIS FRIGGIN' SHOP!
...ER...NO OFFENSE...
NONE TAKEN. IN FACT, I LIKE BEING "STUCK" HERE, WITH GUYS LIKE YOU BRINGING THEIR BUSINESS TO ME...
I GUESS I'M JUST A HERMIT AT HEART...
HUH. SO I GUESS WE'RE BOTH BETTER OFF THEN, EH?
I GUESS...
...SAY, THIS ONE'S A REAL CUTIE, ISN'T SHE?
YUP. SURE IS...
KEEP OUT
Y'KNOW, I MAY JUST BUY THIS ONE AND KEEP IT FOR MYSELF...
TOO LATE, PAL. SHE'S COMING HOME WITH ME...
Finetone

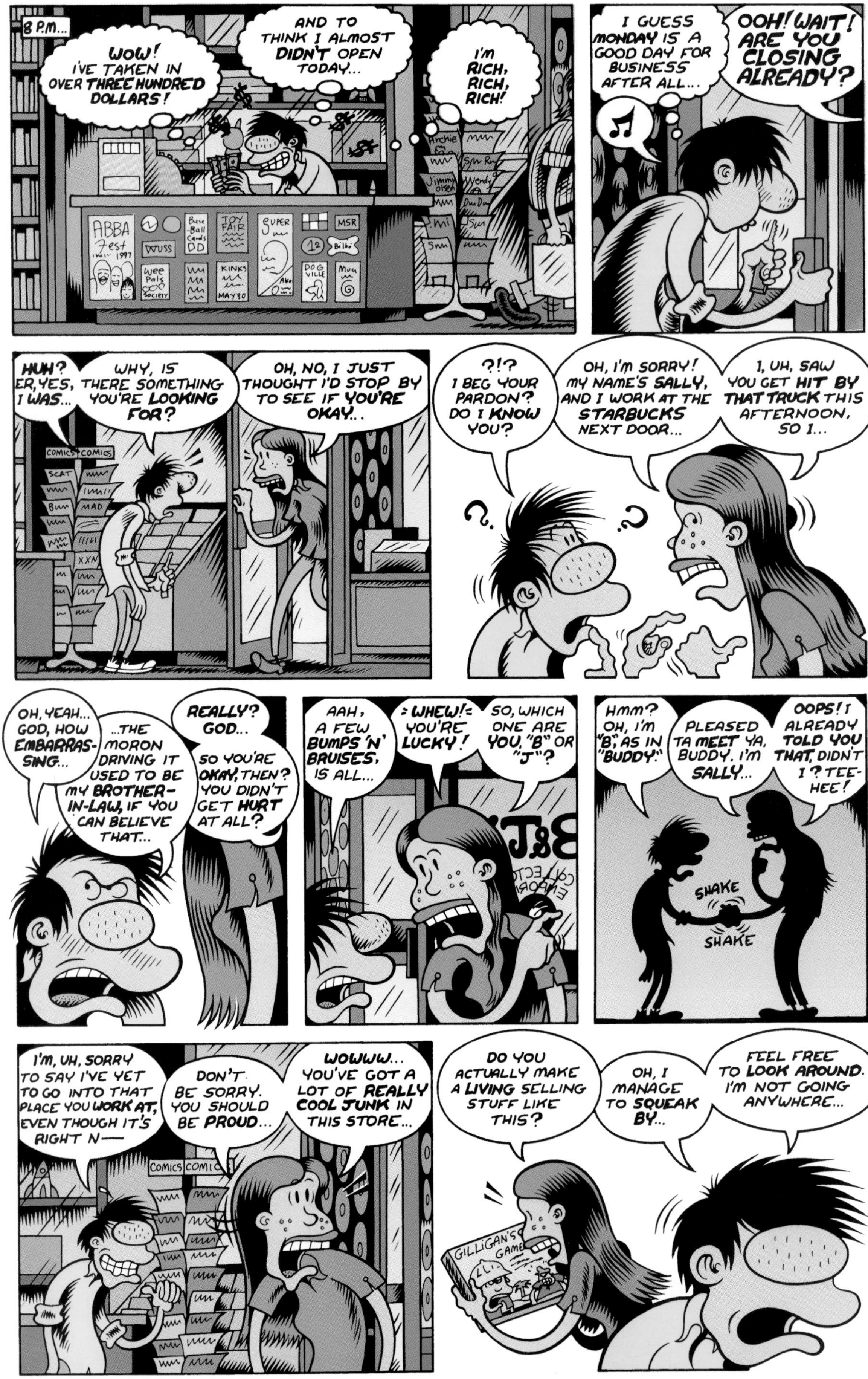
8 P.M...
WOW! I'VE TAKEN IN OVER THREE HUNDRED DOLLARS!
AND TO THINK I ALMOST DIDN'T OPEN TODAY...
I'M RICH, RICH, RICH!
I GUESS MONDAY IS A GOOD DAY FOR BUSINESS AFTER ALL...
OOH! WAIT! ARE YOU CLOSING ALREADY?
HUH? ER, YES, I WAS...
WHY, IS THERE SOMETHING YOU'RE LOOKING FOR?
OH, NO, I JUST THOUGHT I'D STOP BY TO SEE IF YOU'RE OKAY...
?!? I BEG YOUR PARDON? DO I KNOW YOU?
OH, I'M SORRY! MY NAME'S SALLY, AND I WORK AT THE STARBUCKS NEXT DOOR...
I, UH, SAW YOU GET HIT BY THAT TRUCK THIS AFTERNOON, SO I...
OH, YEAH... GOD, HOW EMBARRASSING...
...THE MORON DRIVING IT USED TO BE MY BROTHER-IN-LAW, IF YOU CAN BELIEVE THAT...
REALLY? GOD...
SO YOU'RE OKAY, THEN? YOU DIDN'T GET HURT AT ALL?
AAH, A FEW BUMPS 'N' BRUISES, IS ALL...
WHEW! YOU'RE LUCKY!
SO, WHICH ONE ARE YOU, "B" OR "J"?
HMM? OH, I'M "B," AS IN "BUDDY."
PLEASED TA MEET YA, BUDDY. I'M SALLY...
OOPS! I ALREADY TOLD YOU THAT, DIDN'T I? TEE-HEE!
SHAKE
SHAKE
I'M, UH, SORRY TO SAY I'VE YET TO GO INTO THAT PLACE YOU WORK AT, EVEN THOUGH IT'S RIGHT N—
DON'T. BE SORRY. YOU SHOULD BE PROUD...
WOWWW... YOU'VE GOT A LOT OF REALLY COOL JUNK IN THIS STORE...
DO YOU ACTUALLY MAKE A LIVING SELLING STUFF LIKE THIS?
OH, I MANAGE TO SQUEAK BY...
FEEL FREE TO LOOK AROUND. I'M NOT GOING ANYWHERE...

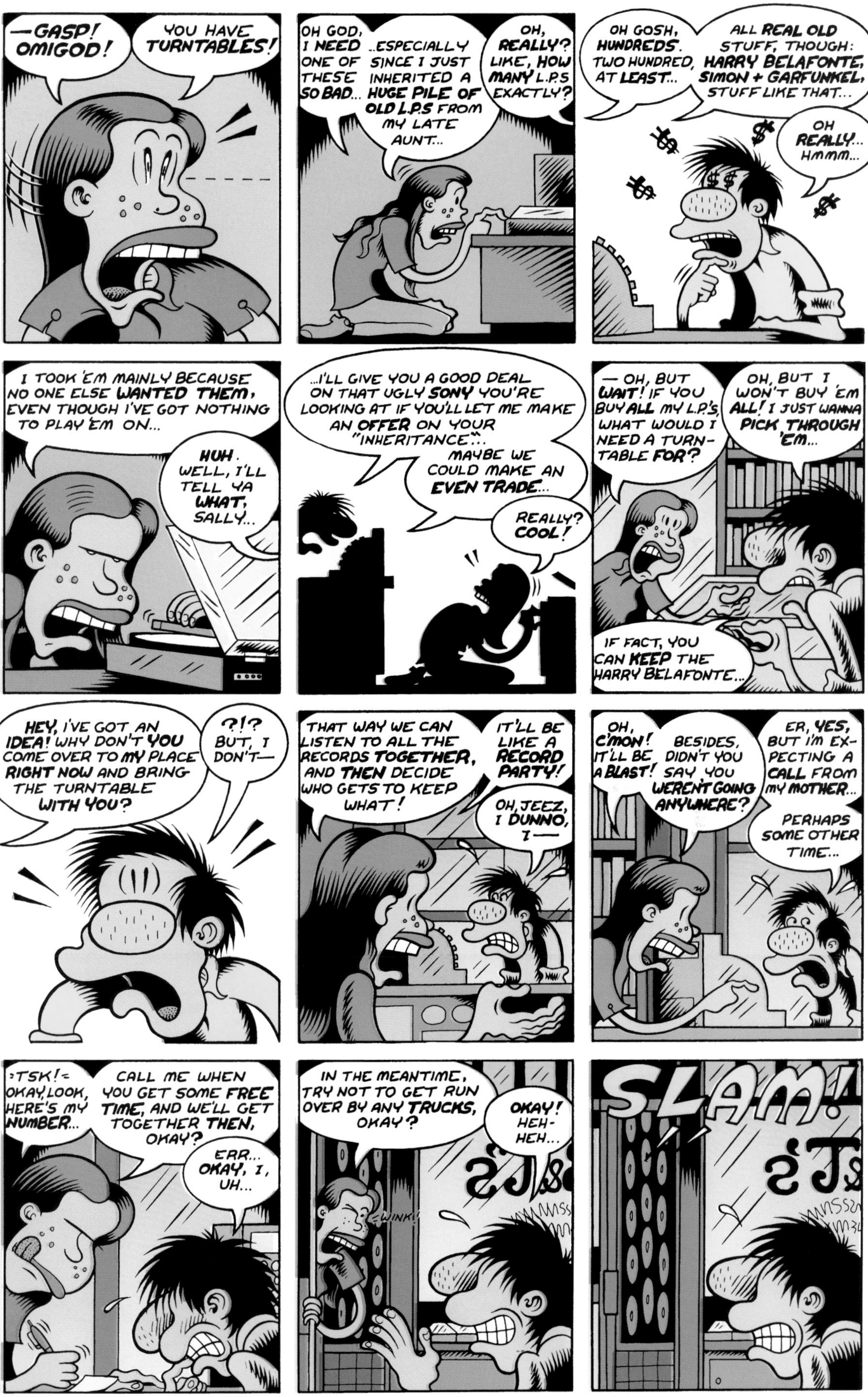
—GASP! OMIGOD!
YOU HAVE TURNTABLES!
OH GOD, I NEED ONE OF THESE SO BAD...
..ESPECIALLY SINCE I JUST INHERITED A HUGE PILE OF OLD L.P.S FROM MY LATE AUNT...
OH, REALLY? LIKE, HOW MANY L.P.S EXACTLY?
OH GOSH, HUNDREDS. TWO HUNDRED, AT LEAST...
ALL REAL OLD STUFF, THOUGH: HARRY BELAFONTE, SIMON + GARFUNKEL, STUFF LIKE THAT...
OH REALLY... HMMM...
I TOOK 'EM MAINLY BECAUSE NO ONE ELSE WANTED THEM, EVEN THOUGH I'VE GOT NOTHING TO PLAY 'EM ON...
HUH. WELL, I'LL TELL YA WHAT, SALLY...
...I'LL GIVE YOU A GOOD DEAL ON THAT UGLY SONY YOU'RE LOOKING AT IF YOU'LL LET ME MAKE AN OFFER ON YOUR "INHERITANCE"...
MAYBE WE COULD MAKE AN EVEN TRADE...
REALLY? COOL!
— OH, BUT WAIT! IF YOU BUY ALL MY L.P.'S, WHAT WOULD I NEED A TURNTABLE FOR?
OH, BUT I WON'T BUY 'EM ALL! I JUST WANNA PICK THROUGH 'EM...
IF FACT, YOU CAN KEEP THE HARRY BELAFONTE...
HEY, I'VE GOT AN IDEA! WHY DON'T YOU COME OVER TO MY PLACE RIGHT NOW AND BRING THE TURNTABLE WITH YOU?
?!? BUT, I DON'T—
THAT WAY WE CAN LISTEN TO ALL THE RECORDS TOGETHER, AND THEN DECIDE WHO GETS TO KEEP WHAT!
IT'LL BE LIKE A RECORD PARTY!
OH, JEEZ, I DUNNO, I—
OH, C'MON! IT'LL BE A BLAST!
BESIDES, DIDN'T YOU SAY YOU WEREN'T GOING ANYWHERE?
ER, YES, BUT I'M EXPECTING A CALL FROM MY MOTHER...
PERHAPS SOME OTHER TIME...
=TSK!= OKAY, LOOK, HERE'S MY NUMBER...
CALL ME WHEN YOU GET SOME FREE TIME, AND WE'LL GET TOGETHER THEN, OKAY?
ERR... OKAY, I, UH...
IN THE MEANTIME, TRY NOT TO GET RUN OVER BY ANY TRUCKS, OKAY?
WINK!
OKAY! HEH-HEH...
SLAM!

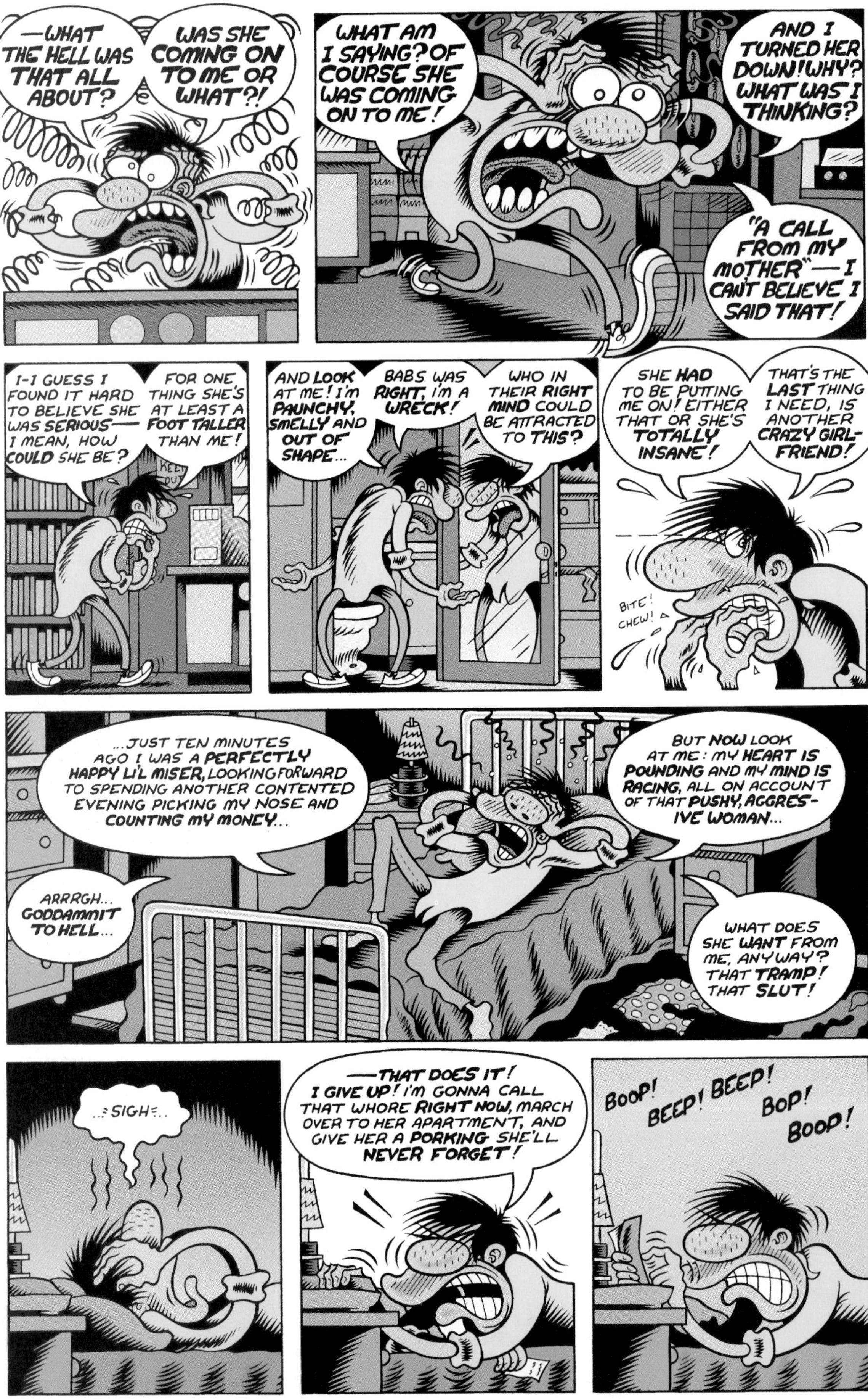
—WHAT THE HELL WAS THAT ALL ABOUT?
WAS SHE COMING ON TO ME OR WHAT?!
WHAT AM I SAYING? OF COURSE SHE WAS COMING ON TO ME!
AND I TURNED HER DOWN! WHY? WHAT WAS I THINKING?
"A CALL FROM MY MOTHER"—I CAN'T BELIEVE I SAID THAT!
I-I GUESS I FOUND IT HARD TO BELIEVE SHE WAS SERIOUS— I MEAN, HOW COULD SHE BE?
FOR ONE THING SHE'S AT LEAST A FOOT TALLER THAN ME!
AND LOOK AT ME! I'M PAUNCHY, SMELLY AND OUT OF SHAPE...
BABS WAS RIGHT, I'M A WRECK!
WHO IN THEIR RIGHT MIND COULD BE ATTRACTED TO THIS?
SHE HAD TO BE PUTTING ME ON! EITHER THAT OR SHE'S TOTALLY INSANE!
THAT'S THE LAST THING I NEED, IS ANOTHER CRAZY GIRL-FRIEND!
BITE! CHEW!
...JUST TEN MINUTES AGO I WAS A PERFECTLY HAPPY LI'L MISER, LOOKING FORWARD TO SPENDING ANOTHER CONTENTED EVENING PICKING MY NOSE AND COUNTING MY MONEY...
BUT NOW LOOK AT ME: MY HEART IS POUNDING AND MY MIND IS RACING, ALL ON ACCOUNT OF THAT PUSHY, AGGRES-IVE WOMAN...
ARRRGH... GODDAMNIT TO HELL...
WHAT DOES SHE WANT FROM ME, ANYWAY? THAT TRAMP! THAT SLUT!
...SIGH...
—THAT DOES IT! I GIVE UP! I'M GONNA CALL THAT WHORE RIGHT NOW, MARCH OVER TO HER APARTMENT, AND GIVE HER A PORKING SHE'LL NEVER FORGET!
BOOP! BEEP! BEEP! BOP! BOOP!

...ON SECOND THOUGHT, MAYBE I WON'T...

CLICK

BESIDES, WHO AM I KIDDING? I AIN'T NO STUD...

"A PORKING SHE'LL NEVER FORGET." YEAH, RIGHT!

...IN FACT, IT'S BEEN SO LONG SINCE I'VE "DONE IT" THAT I'M AFRAID I'VE FORGOTTEN HOW!

WHAT IF I CAN'T GET IT UP?

AND EVEN IF I DID I'D PROBABLY COME IN TWO SECONDS...

...PLUS WHAT IF I GET CRABS FROM HER? OR WORSE?

WHAT IF SHE GOT PREGNANT AND DECIDED TO KEEP IT?!

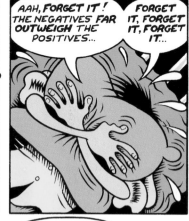

AAH, FORGET IT! THE NEGATIVES FAR OUTWEIGH THE POSITIVES...

FORGET IT, FORGET IT, FORGET IT...

MY BIGGEST PROBLEM NOW IS THAT I'VE TOTALLY GOT SEX-ON-THE-BRAIN, AND I CAN'T THINK OF ANYTHING ELSE!

MY INSIDES ARE ON FIRE!

I'VE GOT TO GET MY ROCKS OFF OTHER THAN THE USUAL WAY, BUT HOW?

ESPECIALLY SINCE I DON'T WANT TO LEAVE THIS ROOM...

...I'D DIAL ONE OF THOSE 1-900 NUMBERS, BUT I'M AFRAID THAT MIGHT BECOME A HABIT...

AN EXPENSIVE ONE, AT THAT...

HEY, MAYBE I COULD ENGAGE THIS SALLY CHICK IN SOME GOOD OL' FASHIONED PHONE SEX!

AFTER ALL, SHE SEEMS LIKE THE "UP-FOR ANYTHING" TYPE!

—NO, BAD IDEA. SHE'LL JUST SAY: "WHY DON'T YOU COME OVER INSTEAD?"

BESIDES, I DON'T EVEN KNOW THIS WOMAN! HOW COULD I BE SO PRESUMPTUOUS?

...OY...

...THINK... THINK...

TAP TAP

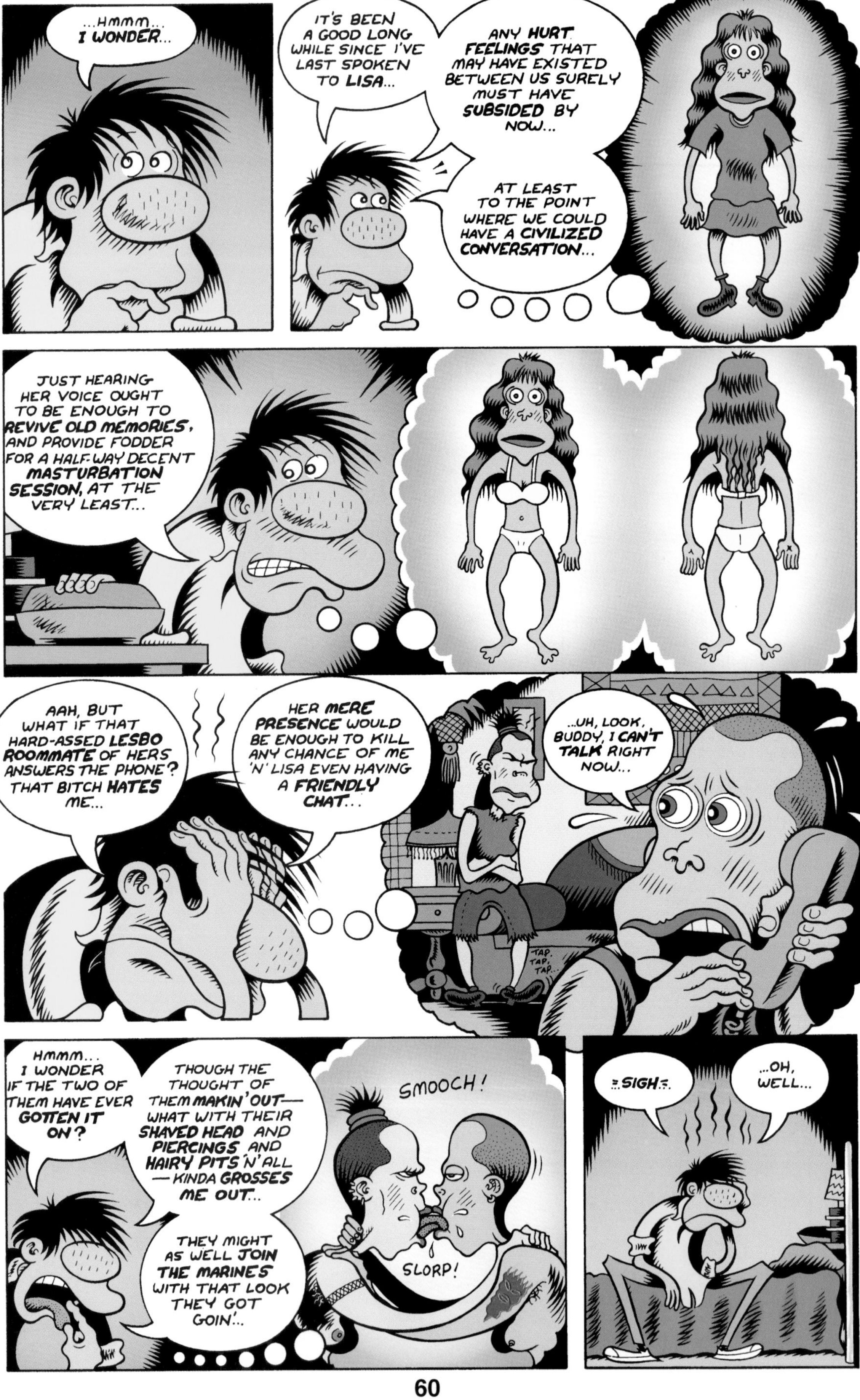
...HMMM...
I WONDER...
IT'S BEEN A GOOD LONG WHILE SINCE I'VE LAST SPOKEN TO LISA...
ANY HURT FEELINGS THAT MAY HAVE EXISTED BETWEEN US SURELY MUST HAVE SUBSIDED BY NOW...
AT LEAST TO THE POINT WHERE WE COULD HAVE A CIVILIZED CONVERSATION...
JUST HEARING HER VOICE OUGHT TO BE ENOUGH TO REVIVE OLD MEMORIES, AND PROVIDE FODDER FOR A HALF-WAY DECENT MASTURBATION SESSION, AT THE VERY LEAST...
AAH, BUT WHAT IF THAT HARD-ASSED LESBO ROOMMATE OF HERS ANSWERS THE PHONE? THAT BITCH HATES ME...
HER MERE PRESENCE WOULD BE ENOUGH TO KILL ANY CHANCE OF ME 'N' LISA EVEN HAVING A FRIENDLY CHAT...
...UH, LOOK, BUDDY, I CAN'T TALK RIGHT NOW...
TAP, TAP, TAP...
HMMM... I WONDER IF THE TWO OF THEM HAVE EVER GOTTEN IT ON?
THOUGH THE THOUGHT OF THEM MAKIN' OUT— WHAT WITH THEIR SHAVED HEAD AND PIERCINGS AND HAIRY PITS 'N' ALL —KINDA GROSSES ME OUT...
SMOOCH!
SLORP!
THEY MIGHT AS WELL JOIN THE MARINES WITH THAT LOOK THEY GOT GOIN'...
SIGH
...OH, WELL...

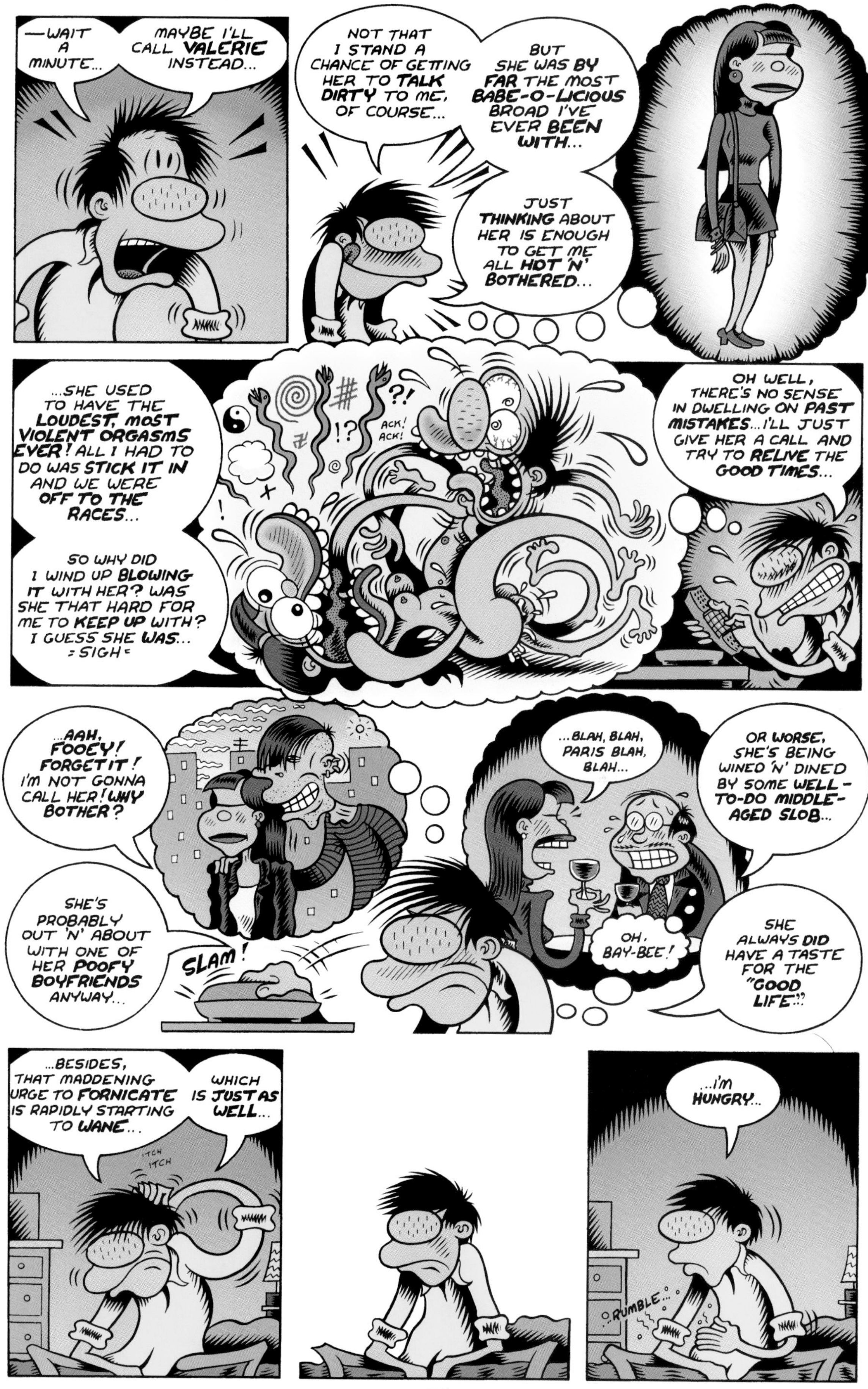
—WAIT A MINUTE...
MAYBE I'LL CALL VALERIE INSTEAD...
NOT THAT I STAND A CHANCE OF GETTING HER TO TALK DIRTY TO ME, OF COURSE...
BUT SHE WAS BY FAR THE MOST BABE-O-LICIOUS BROAD I'VE EVER BEEN WITH...
JUST THINKING ABOUT HER IS ENOUGH TO GET ME ALL HOT 'N' BOTHERED...
...SHE USED TO HAVE THE LOUDEST, MOST VIOLENT ORGASMS EVER! ALL I HAD TO DO WAS STICK IT IN AND WE WERE OFF TO THE RACES...
?!
!?
ACK! ACK!
!
SO WHY DID I WIND UP BLOWING IT WITH HER? WAS SHE THAT HARD FOR ME TO KEEP UP WITH? I GUESS SHE WAS... =SIGH=
OH WELL, THERE'S NO SENSE IN DWELLING ON PAST MISTAKES... I'LL JUST GIVE HER A CALL AND TRY TO RELIVE THE GOOD TIMES...
...AAH, FOOEY! FORGET IT! I'M NOT GONNA CALL HER! WHY BOTHER?
SHE'S PROBABLY OUT 'N' ABOUT WITH ONE OF HER POOFY BOYFRIENDS ANYWAY...
SLAM!
...BLAH, BLAH, PARIS BLAH, BLAH...
OH, BAY-BEE!
OR WORSE, SHE'S BEING WINED 'N' DINED BY SOME WELL-TO-DO MIDDLE-AGED SLOB...
SHE ALWAYS DID HAVE A TASTE FOR THE "GOOD LIFE"!?
...BESIDES, THAT MADDENING URGE TO FORNICATE IS RAPIDLY STARTING TO WANE...
WHICH IS JUST AS WELL...
ITCH ITCH
...I'M HUNGRY...
...RUMBLE...

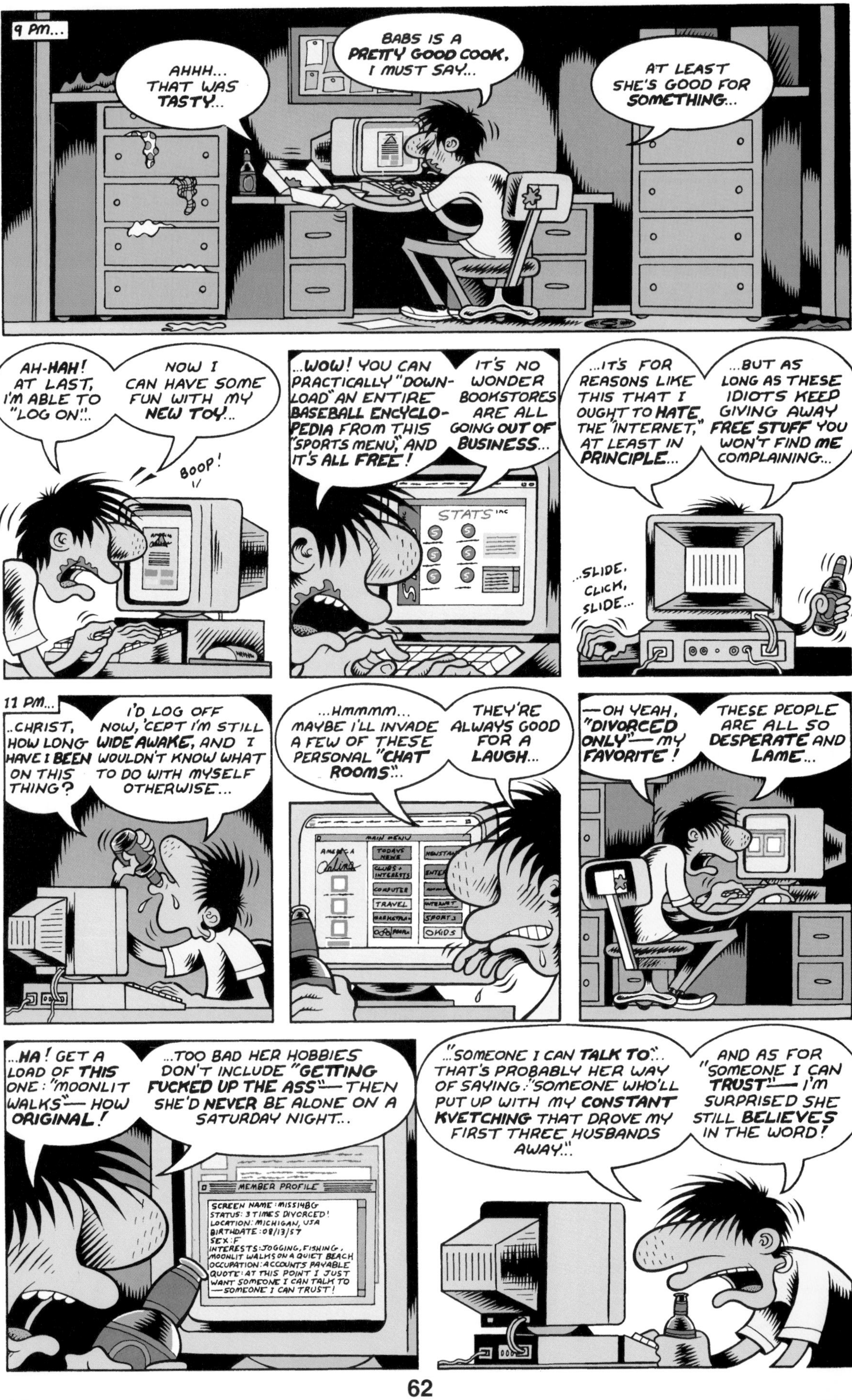
9 PM...
AHHH... THAT WAS TASTY...
BABS IS A PRETTY GOOD COOK, I MUST SAY...
AT LEAST SHE'S GOOD FOR SOMETHING...
AH-HAH! AT LAST, I'M ABLE TO "LOG ON"...
NOW I CAN HAVE SOME FUN WITH MY NEW TOY...
BOOP!
...WOW! YOU CAN PRACTICALLY "DOWNLOAD" AN ENTIRE BASEBALL ENCYCLOPEDIA FROM THIS "SPORTS MENU," AND IT'S ALL FREE!
IT'S NO WONDER BOOKSTORES ARE ALL GOING OUT OF BUSINESS...
STATS INC
...IT'S FOR REASONS LIKE THIS THAT I OUGHT TO HATE THE "INTERNET," AT LEAST IN PRINCIPLE...
...BUT AS LONG AS THESE IDIOTS KEEP GIVING AWAY FREE STUFF YOU WON'T FIND ME COMPLAINING...
...SLIDE, CLICK, SLIDE...
11 PM...
..CHRIST, HOW LONG HAVE I BEEN ON THIS THING?
I'D LOG OFF NOW, 'CEPT I'M STILL WIDE AWAKE, AND I WOULDN'T KNOW WHAT TO DO WITH MYSELF OTHERWISE...
...HMMMM... MAYBE I'LL INVADE A FEW OF THESE PERSONAL "CHAT ROOMS"...
THEY'RE ALWAYS GOOD FOR A LAUGH...
MAIN MENU
TRAVEL
SPORTS
KIDS
—OH YEAH, "DIVORCED ONLY"— MY FAVORITE!
THESE PEOPLE ARE ALL SO DESPERATE AND LAME...
...HA! GET A LOAD OF THIS ONE: "MOONLIT WALKS"— HOW ORIGINAL!
...TOO BAD HER HOBBIES DON'T INCLUDE "GETTING FUCKED UP THE ASS"— THEN SHE'D NEVER BE ALONE ON A SATURDAY NIGHT...
MEMBER PROFILE
SCREEN NAME: MISS14BG
STATUS: 3 TIMES DIVORCED!
LOCATION: MICHIGAN, USA
BIRTHDATE: 08/13/57
SEX: F
INTERESTS: JOGGING, FISHING, MOONLIT WALKS ON A QUIET BEACH
OCCUPATION: ACCOUNTS PAYABLE
QUOTE: AT THIS POINT I JUST WANT SOMEONE I CAN TALK TO —SOMEONE I CAN TRUST!
..."SOMEONE I CAN TALK TO"... THAT'S PROBABLY HER WAY OF SAYING: "SOMEONE WHO'LL PUT UP WITH MY CONSTANT KVETCHING THAT DROVE MY FIRST THREE HUSBANDS AWAY"...
AND AS FOR "SOMEONE I CAN TRUST"— I'M SURPRISED SHE STILL BELIEVES IN THE WORD!

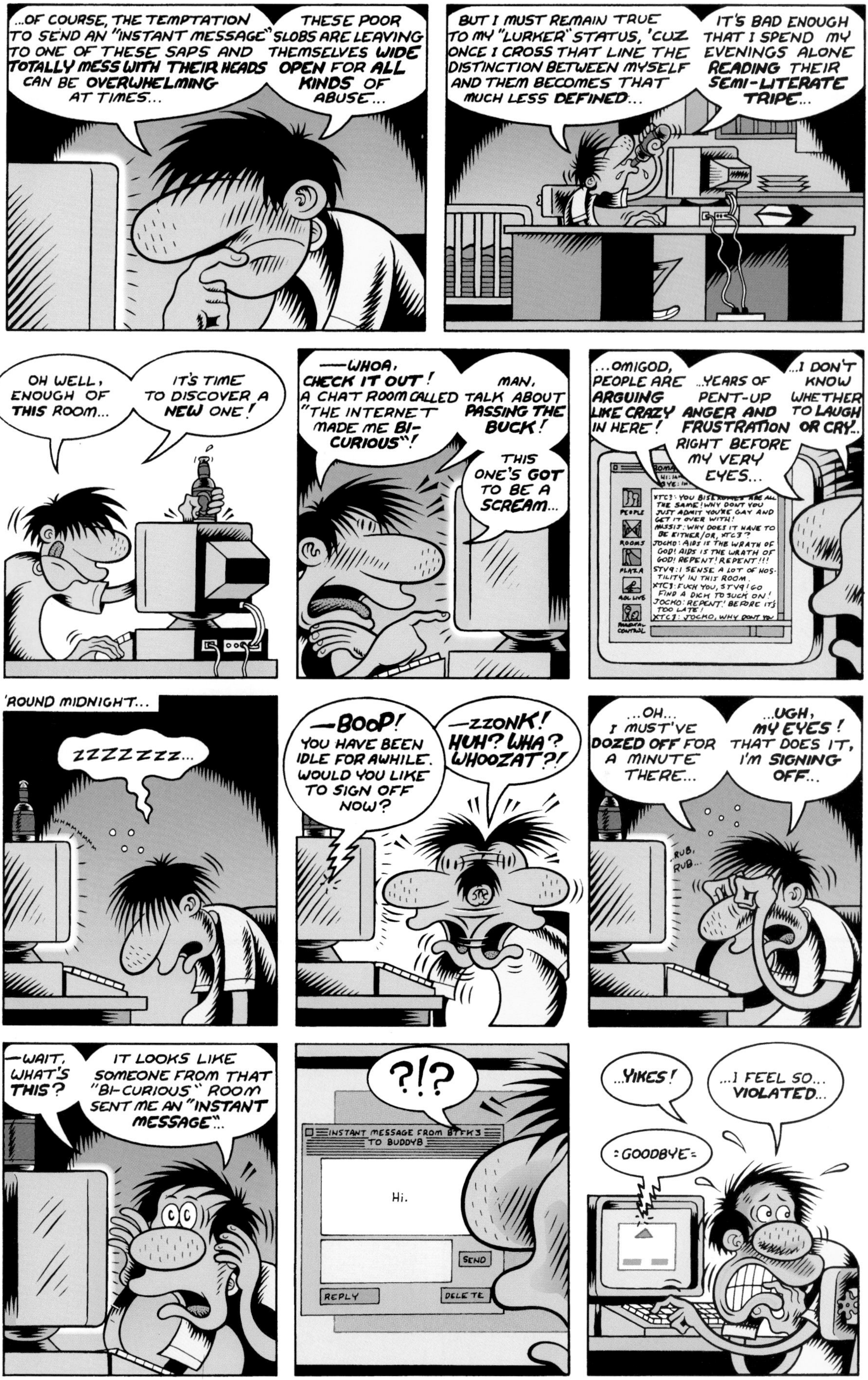
...OF COURSE, THE TEMPTATION TO SEND AN "INSTANT MESSAGE" TO ONE OF THESE SAPS AND TOTALLY MESS WITH THEIR HEADS CAN BE OVERWHELMING AT TIMES...
THESE POOR SLOBS ARE LEAVING THEMSELVES WIDE OPEN FOR ALL KINDS OF ABUSE...
BUT I MUST REMAIN TRUE TO MY "LURKER" STATUS, 'CUZ ONCE I CROSS THAT LINE THE DISTINCTION BETWEEN MYSELF AND THEM BECOMES THAT MUCH LESS DEFINED...
IT'S BAD ENOUGH THAT I SPEND MY EVENINGS ALONE READING THEIR SEMI-LITERATE TRIPE...
OH WELL, ENOUGH OF THIS ROOM...
IT'S TIME TO DISCOVER A NEW ONE!
—WHOA, CHECK IT OUT! A CHAT ROOM CALLED "THE INTERNET MADE ME BI-CURIOUS"!
MAN, TALK ABOUT PASSING THE BUCK!
THIS ONE'S GOT TO BE A SCREAM...
...OMIGOD, PEOPLE ARE ARGUING LIKE CRAZY IN HERE!
...YEARS OF PENT-UP ANGER AND FRUSTRATION RIGHT BEFORE MY VERY EYES...
...I DON'T KNOW WHETHER TO LAUGH OR CRY...
PEOPLE
ROOMS
PLAZA
AOL LIVE
PARENTAL CONTROL
XTC3: YOU BISE... ARE ALL THE SAME! WHY DONT YOU JUST ADMIT YOU'RE GAY AND GET IT OVER WITH!
MISSIJ: WHY DOES IT HAVE TO BE EITHER/OR, XTC3?
JOCKO: AIDS IS THE WRATH OF GOD! AIDS IS THE WRATH OF GOD! REPENT! REPENT!!!
STV9: I SENSE A LOT OF HOSTILITY IN THIS ROOM.
XTC3: FUCK YOU, STV9! GO FIND A DICK TO SUCK ON!
JOCKO: REPENT! BEFORE IT'S TOO LATE!
XTC3: JOCKO, WHY DONT YOU
'ROUND MIDNIGHT...
ZZZZZZZ...
—BOOP! YOU HAVE BEEN IDLE FOR AWHILE. WOULD YOU LIKE TO SIGN OFF NOW?
—ZZONK! HUH? WHA? WHOOZAT?!
...OH... I MUST'VE DOZED OFF FOR A MINUTE THERE...
...UGH, MY EYES! THAT DOES IT, I'M SIGNING OFF...
RUB, RUB...
—WAIT, WHAT'S THIS?
IT LOOKS LIKE SOMEONE FROM THAT "BI-CURIOUS" ROOM SENT ME AN "INSTANT MESSAGE"...
?!?
INSTANT MESSAGE FROM BTFK3 TO BUDDYB
Hi.
SEND
REPLY
DELETE
...YIKES!
...I FEEL SO... VIOLATED...
=GOODBYE=

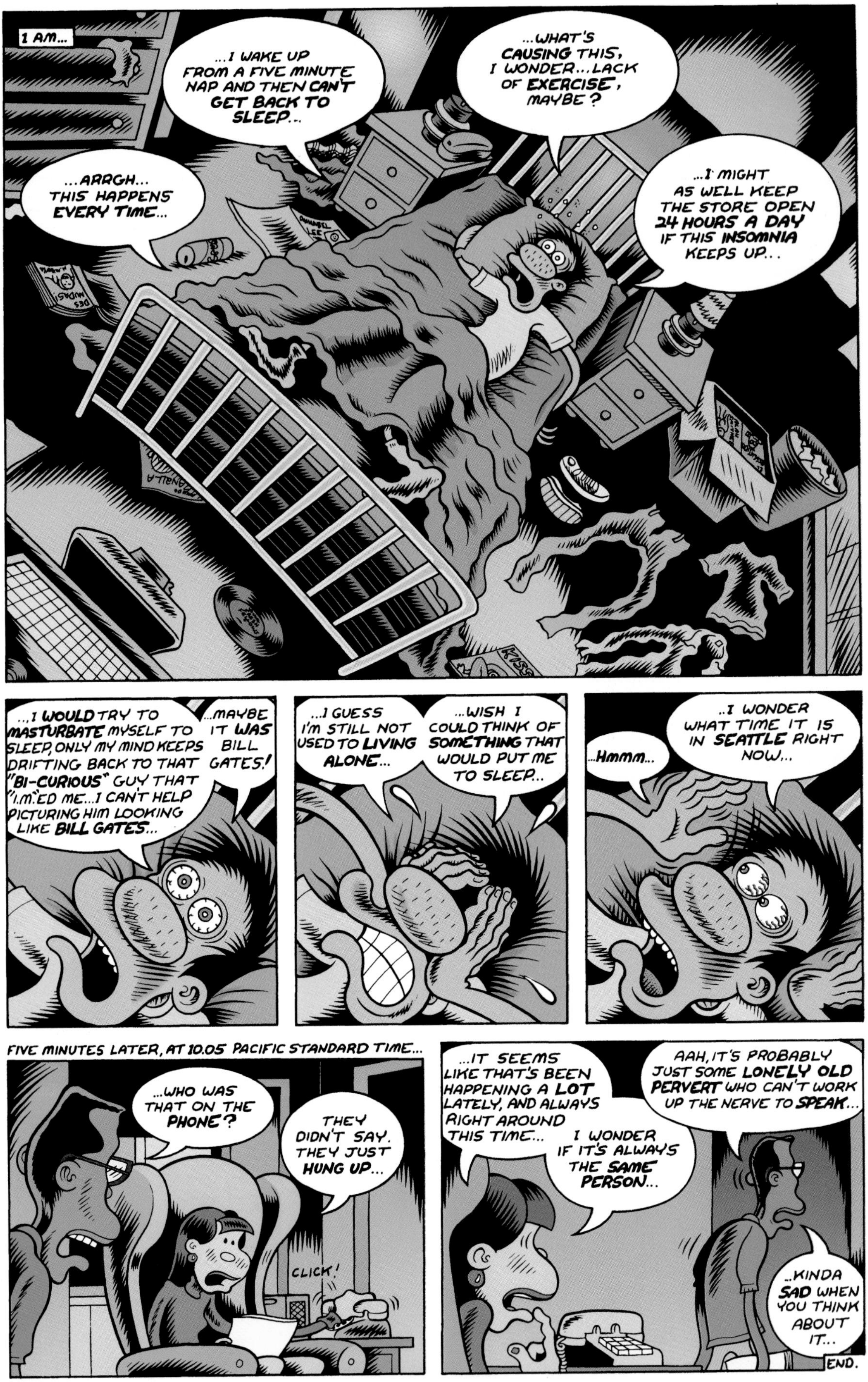
1 AM...
...ARRGH... THIS HAPPENS EVERY TIME...
...I WAKE UP FROM A FIVE MINUTE NAP AND THEN CAN'T GET BACK TO SLEEP...
...WHAT'S CAUSING THIS, I WONDER... LACK OF EXERCISE, MAYBE?
...I MIGHT AS WELL KEEP THE STORE OPEN 24 HOURS A DAY IF THIS INSOMNIA KEEPS UP...
...I WOULD TRY TO MASTURBATE MYSELF TO SLEEP, ONLY MY MIND KEEPS DRIFTING BACK TO THAT "BI-CURIOUS" GUY THAT "I.M."ED ME... I CAN'T HELP PICTURING HIM LOOKING LIKE BILL GATES...
...MAYBE IT WAS BILL GATES!
...I GUESS I'M STILL NOT USED TO LIVING ALONE...
...WISH I COULD THINK OF SOMETHING THAT WOULD PUT ME TO SLEEP...
...Hmmm...
..I WONDER WHAT TIME IT IS IN SEATTLE RIGHT NOW...
FIVE MINUTES LATER, AT 10.05 PACIFIC STANDARD TIME...
...WHO WAS THAT ON THE PHONE?
THEY DIDN'T SAY. THEY JUST HUNG UP...
CLICK!
...IT SEEMS LIKE THAT'S BEEN HAPPENING A LOT LATELY, AND ALWAYS RIGHT AROUND THIS TIME...
I WONDER IF IT'S ALWAYS THE SAME PERSON...
AAH, IT'S PROBABLY JUST SOME LONELY OLD PERVERT WHO CAN'T WORK UP THE NERVE TO SPEAK...
..KINDA SAD WHEN YOU THINK ABOUT IT...
END.

A DAY IN THE LIFE OF BUTCH BRADLEY

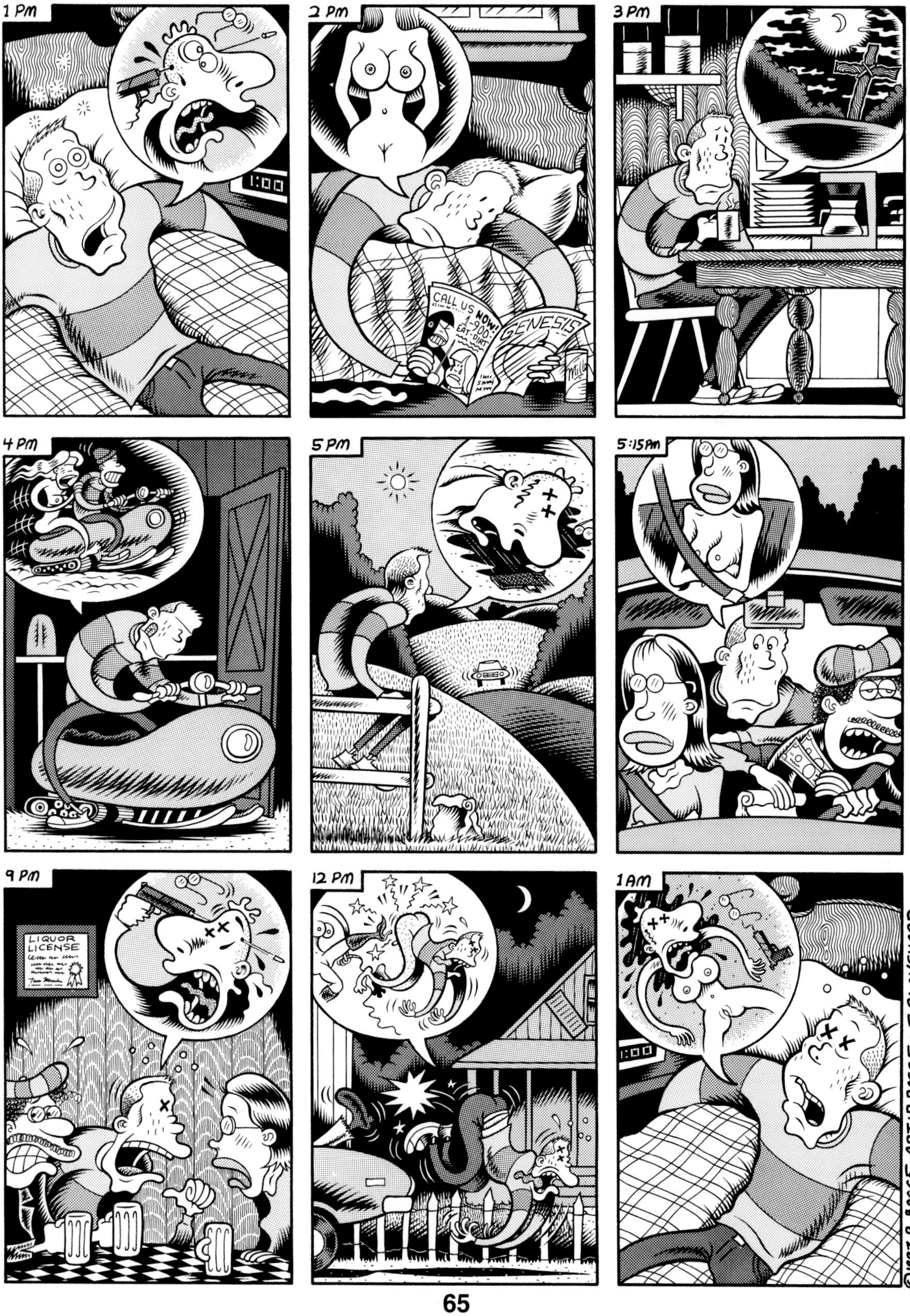
1 PM
1:00
2 PM
CALL US NOW!
1-900-EAT-DIRT
GENESIS
3 PM
4 PM
5 PM
5:15PM
9 PM
LIQUOR LICENSE
12 PM
1AM
1:00

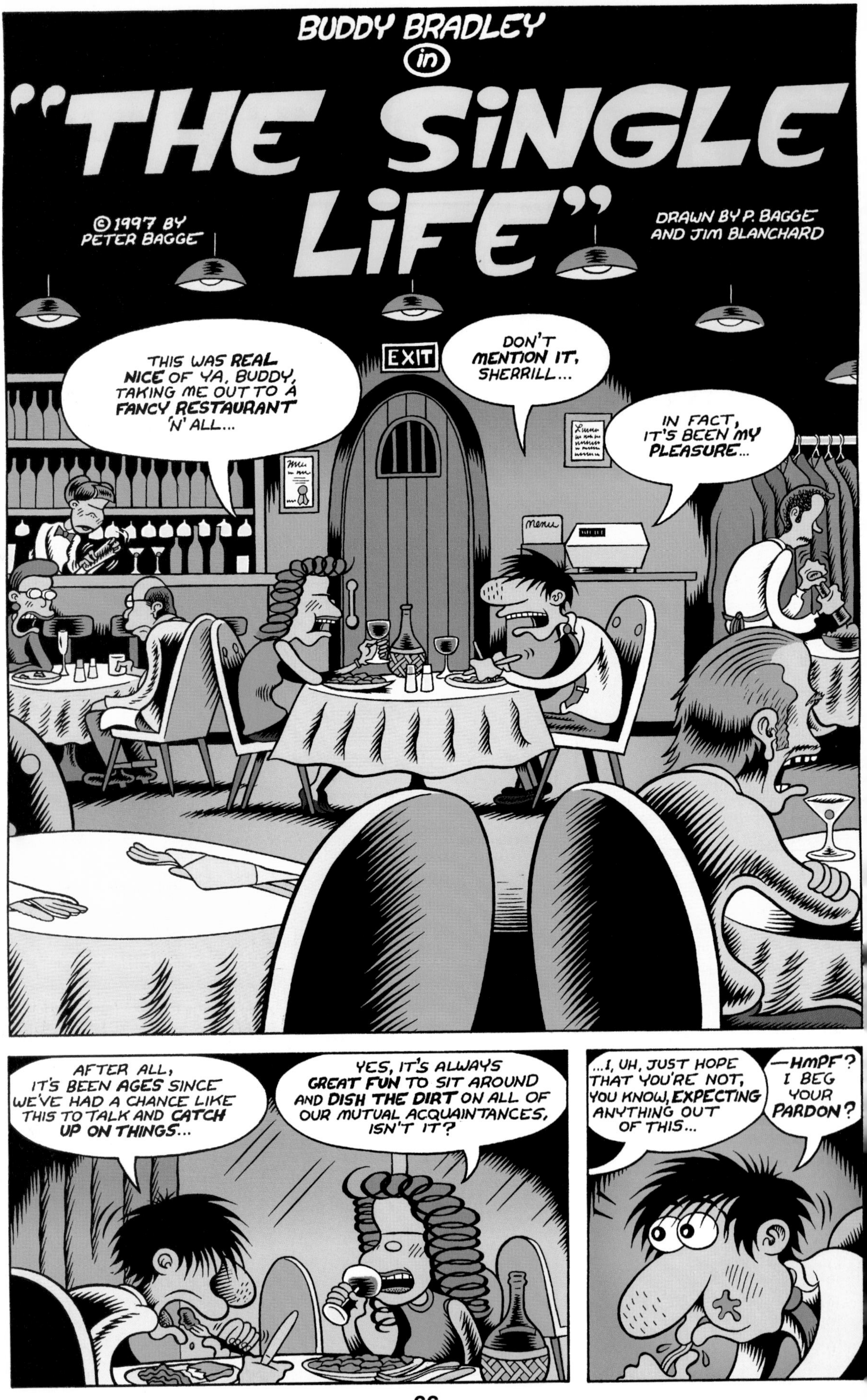
BUDDY BRADLEY
in
"THE SINGLE LIFE"
©1997 BY PETER BAGGE
DRAWN BY P. BAGGE AND JIM BLANCHARD
EXIT
THIS WAS REAL NICE OF YA, BUDDY, TAKING ME OUT TO A FANCY RESTAURANT 'N' ALL...
DON'T MENTION IT, SHERRILL...
IN FACT, IT'S BEEN MY PLEASURE...
AFTER ALL, IT'S BEEN AGES SINCE WE'VE HAD A CHANCE LIKE THIS TO TALK AND CATCH UP ON THINGS...
YES, IT'S ALWAYS GREAT FUN TO SIT AROUND AND DISH THE DIRT ON ALL OF OUR MUTUAL ACQUAINTANCES, ISN'T IT?
...I, UH, JUST HOPE THAT YOU'RE NOT, YOU KNOW, EXPECTING ANYTHING OUT OF THIS...
—HMPF? I BEG YOUR PARDON?

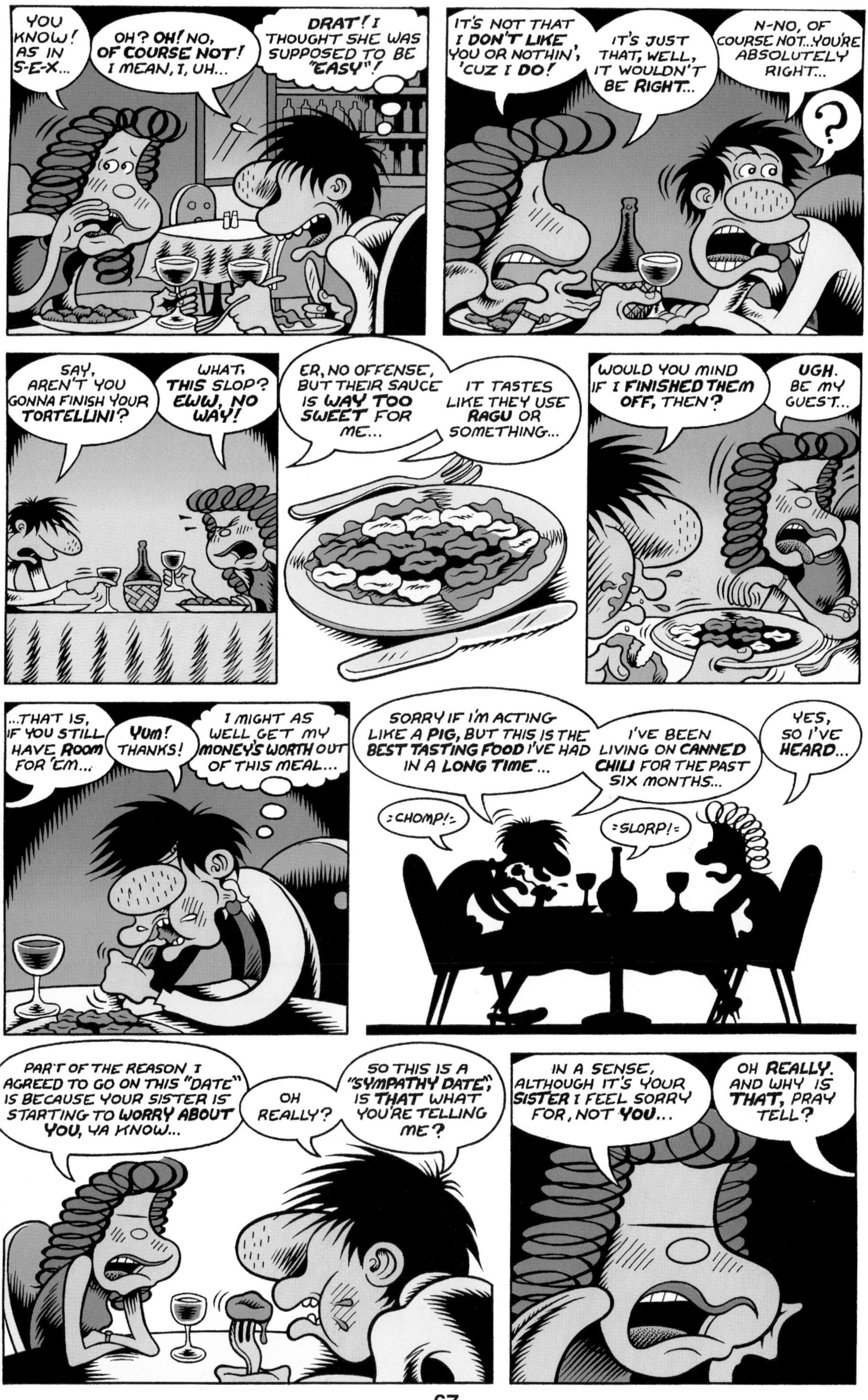
YOU KNOW! AS IN S-E-X...
OH? OH! NO, OF COURSE NOT! I MEAN, I, UH...
DRAT! I THOUGHT SHE WAS SUPPOSED TO BE "EASY"!
IT'S NOT THAT I DON'T LIKE YOU OR NOTHIN', 'CUZ I DO!
IT'S JUST THAT, WELL, IT WOULDN'T BE RIGHT...
N-NO, OF COURSE NOT...YOU'RE ABSOLUTELY RIGHT...
?
SAY, AREN'T YOU GONNA FINISH YOUR TORTELLINI?
WHAT, THIS SLOP? EWW, NO WAY!
ER, NO OFFENSE, BUT THEIR SAUCE IS WAY TOO SWEET FOR ME...
IT TASTES LIKE THEY USE RAGU OR SOMETHING...
WOULD YOU MIND IF I FINISHED THEM OFF, THEN?
UGH. BE MY GUEST...
...THAT IS, IF YOU STILL HAVE ROOM FOR 'EM...
YUM! THANKS!
I MIGHT AS WELL GET MY MONEY'S WORTH OUT OF THIS MEAL...
SORRY IF I'M ACTING LIKE A PIG, BUT THIS IS THE BEST TASTING FOOD I'VE HAD IN A LONG TIME...
I'VE BEEN LIVING ON CANNED CHILI FOR THE PAST SIX MONTHS...
YES, SO I'VE HEARD...
CHOMP!
SLORP!
PART OF THE REASON I AGREED TO GO ON THIS "DATE" IS BECAUSE YOUR SISTER IS STARTING TO WORRY ABOUT YOU, YA KNOW...
OH REALLY?
SO THIS IS A "SYMPATHY DATE", IS THAT WHAT YOU'RE TELLING ME?
IN A SENSE, ALTHOUGH IT'S YOUR SISTER I FEEL SORRY FOR, NOT YOU...
OH REALLY. AND WHY IS THAT, PRAY TELL?

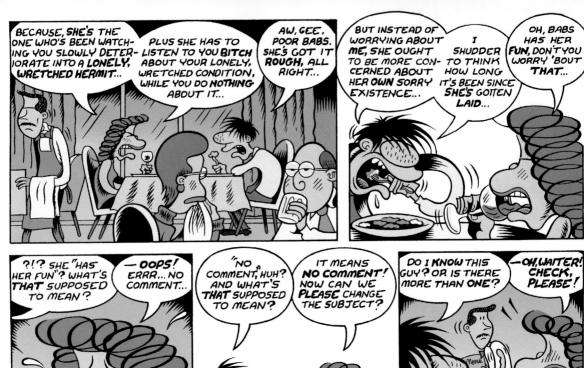

Panel 1: BECAUSE, SHE'S THE ONE WHO'S BEEN WATCHING YOU SLOWLY DETERIORATE INTO A *LONELY, WRETCHED HERMIT*...

PLUS SHE HAS TO LISTEN TO YOU *BITCH* ABOUT YOUR LONELY, WRETCHED CONDITION, WHILE YOU DO *NOTHING* ABOUT IT...

AW, GEE, POOR BABS. SHE'S GOT IT *ROUGH*, ALL RIGHT...

Panel 2: BUT INSTEAD OF WORRYING ABOUT *ME*, SHE OUGHT TO BE MORE CONCERNED ABOUT HER *OWN* SORRY EXISTENCE...

I *SHUDDER* TO THINK HOW LONG IT'S BEEN SINCE SHE'S GOTTEN *LAID*...

OH, *BABS* HAS HER *FUN*, DON'T YOU WORRY 'BOUT *THAT*...

?!? SHE "HAS HER FUN"? WHAT'S *THAT* SUPPOSED TO MEAN?

— *OOPS!* ERRR... NO COMMENT...

"NO COMMENT, HUH? AND WHAT'S *THAT* SUPPOSED TO MEAN?

IT MEANS *NO COMMENT!* NOW CAN WE *PLEASE* CHANGE THE SUBJECT?

DO I *KNOW* THIS GUY? OR IS THERE MORE THAN ONE?

— OH, *WAITER!* CHECK, PLEASE!

HERE YOU GO, MA'AM...

GIVE IT TO *HIM*. HE'S PAYIN'!

— *I AM?* AREN'T WE AT LEAST GOIN' "HALFSIES"?

HEY, *YOU'RE* THE ONE WHO ASKED *ME* OUT, REMEMBER? THAT MEANS *YOU* PAY! RULES ARE RULES!

RIGHT, RIGHT... I FORGOT ABOUT THE "RULES"...

WELCOME TO THE WORLD OF "DATING"...

YOU DIDN'T FINISH THE *TORTELLINI*, EITHER. AREN'T YOU GOING TO "DOGGIE-BAG" IT?

NAH. YOU WERE RIGHT, IT *IS* GROSS.

SUIT YOURSELF. AFTER ALL, *YOU* PAID FOR IT! NYUK! NYUK!

HEH-HEH...

— OOH, HE'S HELPING ME WITH MY *COAT!* HOW GENTLEMAN-LIKE...

ARRGH! I'M GONNA GIVE *BABS* HELL FOR FIXING ME UP WITH THIS *NO-SEX, CHEAPSKATE* FRIEND OF HERS!

PLUS I GOTTA FIND OUT WHO THIS "*NO COMMENT*" IS!

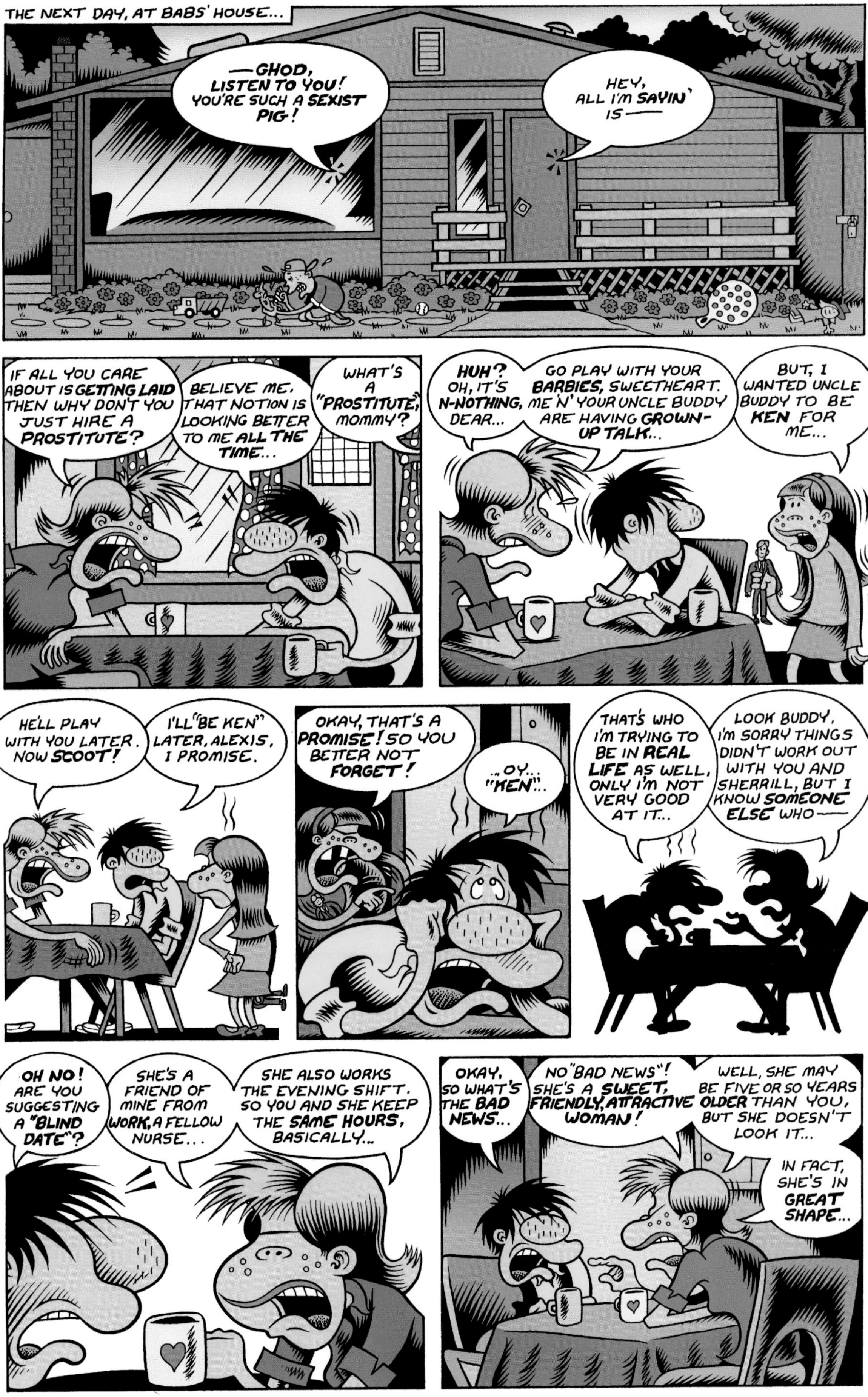
THE NEXT DAY, AT BABS' HOUSE...
—GHOD, LISTEN TO YOU! YOU'RE SUCH A SEXIST PIG!
HEY, ALL I'M SAYIN' IS—
IF ALL YOU CARE ABOUT IS GETTING LAID THEN WHY DON'T YOU JUST HIRE A PROSTITUTE?
BELIEVE ME, THAT NOTION IS LOOKING BETTER TO ME ALL THE TIME...
WHAT'S A "PROSTITUTE," MOMMY?
HUH? OH, IT'S N-NOTHING, DEAR...
GO PLAY WITH YOUR BARBIES, SWEETHEART. ME 'N' YOUR UNCLE BUDDY ARE HAVING GROWN-UP TALK...
BUT, I WANTED UNCLE BUDDY TO BE KEN FOR ME...
HE'LL PLAY WITH YOU LATER. NOW SCOOT!
I'LL "BE KEN" LATER, ALEXIS, I PROMISE.
OKAY, THAT'S A PROMISE! SO YOU BETTER NOT FORGET!
...OY... "KEN"...
THAT'S WHO I'M TRYING TO BE IN REAL LIFE AS WELL, ONLY I'M NOT VERY GOOD AT IT...
LOOK BUDDY, I'M SORRY THINGS DIDN'T WORK OUT WITH YOU AND SHERRILL, BUT I KNOW SOMEONE ELSE WHO—
OH NO! ARE YOU SUGGESTING A "BLIND DATE"?
SHE'S A FRIEND OF MINE FROM WORK, A FELLOW NURSE...
SHE ALSO WORKS THE EVENING SHIFT, SO YOU AND SHE KEEP THE SAME HOURS, BASICALLY...
OKAY, SO WHAT'S THE BAD NEWS...
NO "BAD NEWS"! SHE'S A SWEET, FRIENDLY, ATTRACTIVE WOMAN!
WELL, SHE MAY BE FIVE OR SO YEARS OLDER THAN YOU, BUT SHE DOESN'T LOOK IT...
IN FACT, SHE'S IN GREAT SHAPE...

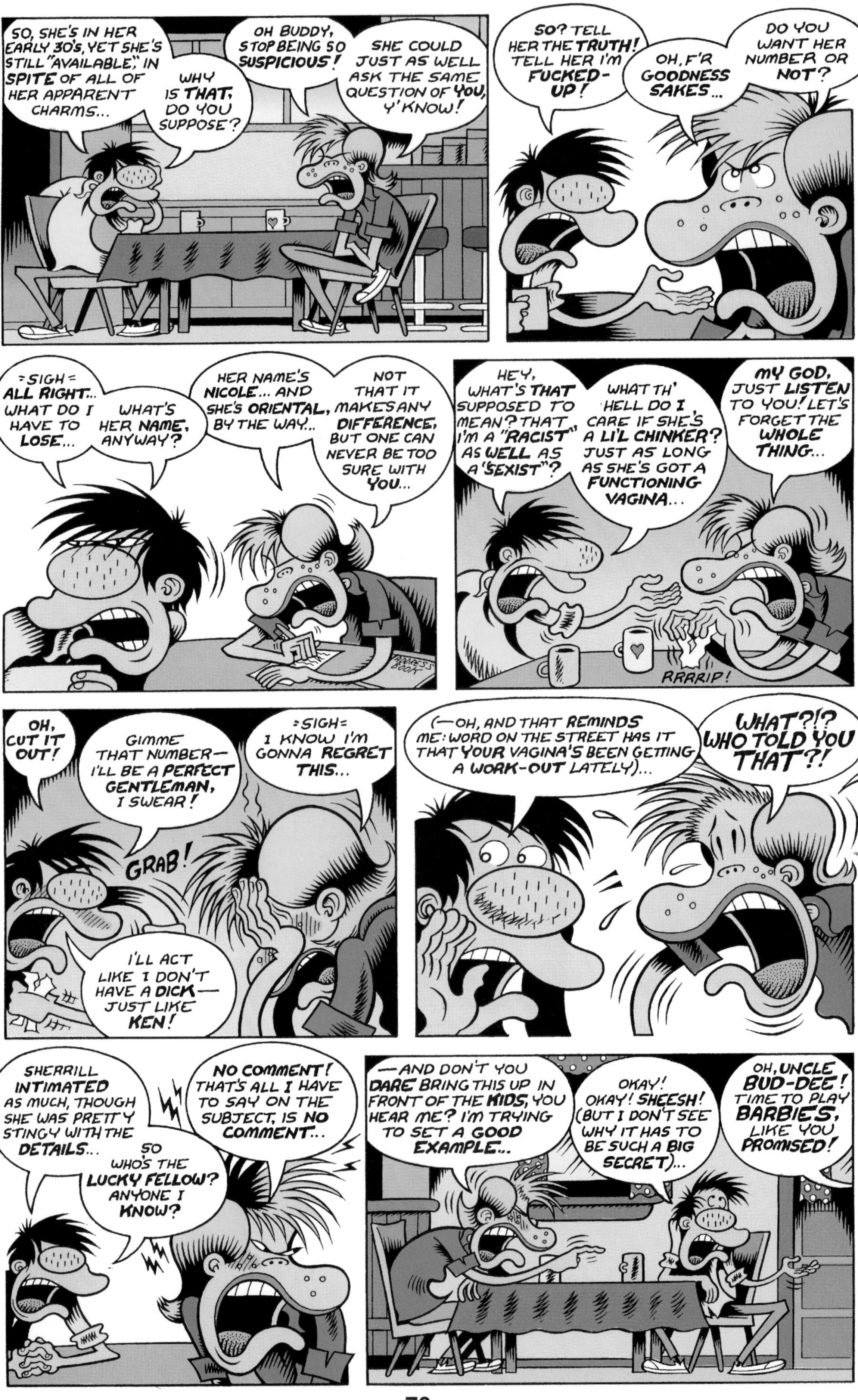

SO, SHE'S IN HER EARLY 30'S, YET SHE'S STILL "AVAILABLE," IN SPITE OF ALL OF HER APPARENT CHARMS...
WHY IS THAT, DO YOU SUPPOSE?
OH BUDDY, STOP BEING SO SUSPICIOUS!
SHE COULD JUST AS WELL ASK THE SAME QUESTION OF YOU, Y' KNOW!
SO? TELL HER THE TRUTH! TELL HER I'M FUCKED-UP!
OH, F'R GOODNESS SAKES...
DO YOU WANT HER NUMBER OR NOT?
=SIGH= ALL RIGHT... WHAT DO I HAVE TO LOSE...
WHAT'S HER NAME, ANYWAY?
HER NAME'S NICOLE... AND SHE'S ORIENTAL, BY THE WAY...
NOT THAT IT MAKES ANY DIFFERENCE, BUT ONE CAN NEVER BE TOO SURE WITH YOU...
ADDRESS BOOK
HEY, WHAT'S THAT SUPPOSED TO MEAN? THAT I'M A "RACIST" AS WELL AS A "SEXIST"?
WHAT TH' HELL DO I CARE IF SHE'S A LI'L CHINKER? JUST AS LONG AS SHE'S GOT A FUNCTIONING VAGINA...
MY GOD, JUST LISTEN TO YOU! LET'S FORGET THE WHOLE THING...
RRRRIP!
OH, CUT IT OUT!
GIMME THAT NUMBER— I'LL BE A PERFECT GENTLEMAN, I SWEAR!
=SIGH= I KNOW I'M GONNA REGRET THIS...
GRAB!
I'LL ACT LIKE I DON'T HAVE A DICK— JUST LIKE KEN!
(—OH, AND THAT REMINDS ME: WORD ON THE STREET HAS IT THAT YOUR VAGINA'S BEEN GETTING A WORK-OUT LATELY)...
WHAT?!? WHO TOLD YOU THAT?!
SHERRILL INTIMATED AS MUCH, THOUGH SHE WAS PRETTY STINGY WITH THE DETAILS...
SO WHO'S THE LUCKY FELLOW? ANYONE I KNOW?
NO COMMENT! THAT'S ALL I HAVE TO SAY ON THE SUBJECT, IS NO COMMENT...
—AND DON'T YOU DARE BRING THIS UP IN FRONT OF THE KIDS, YOU HEAR ME? I'M TRYING TO SET A GOOD EXAMPLE...
OKAY! OKAY! SHEESH! (BUT I DON'T SEE WHY IT HAS TO BE SUCH A BIG SECRET)...
OH, UNCLE BUD-DEE! TIME TO PLAY BARBIES, LIKE YOU PROMISED!

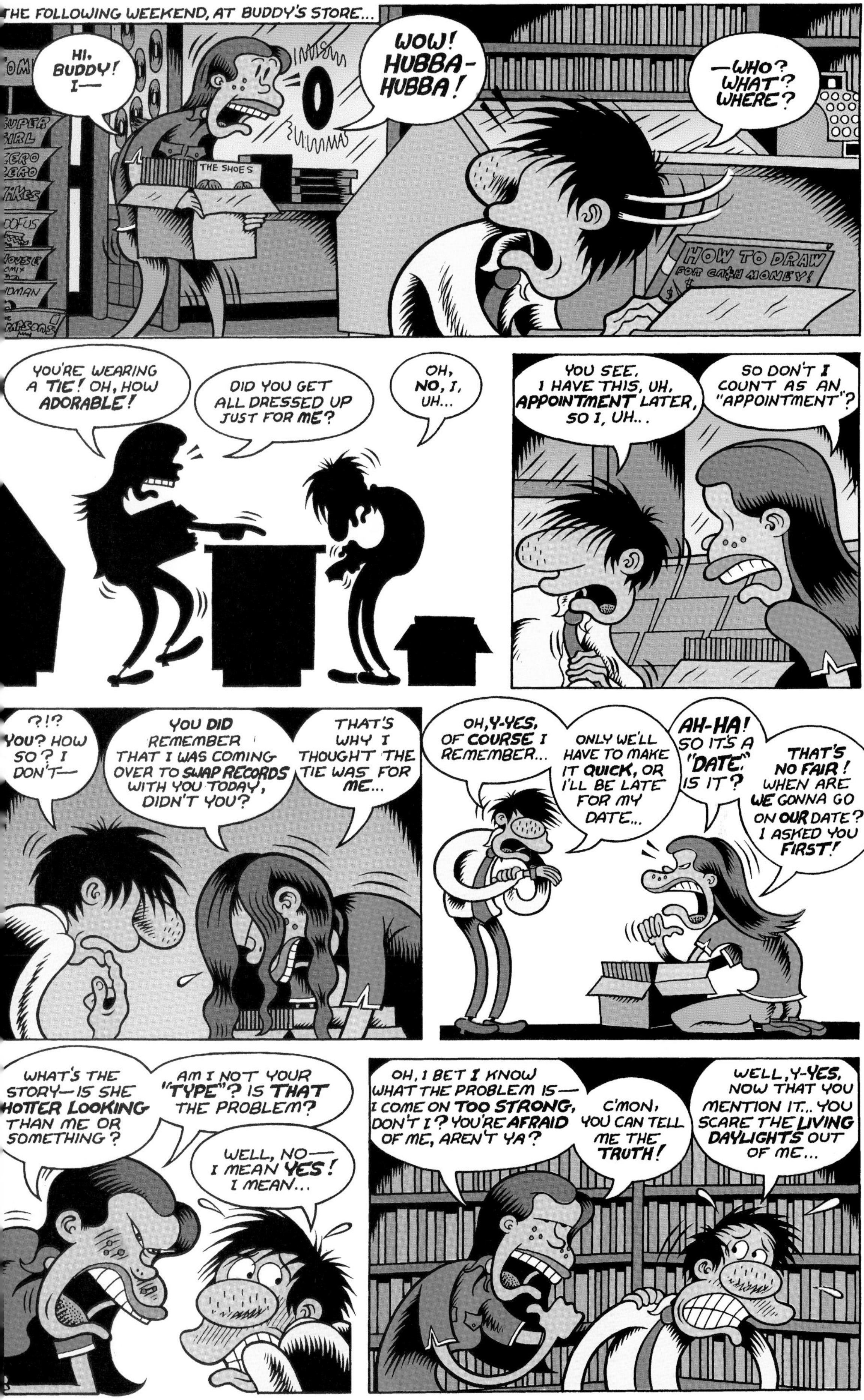
THE FOLLOWING WEEKEND, AT BUDDY'S STORE...
HI, BUDDY! I—
WOW! HUBBA-HUBBA!
—WHO? WHAT? WHERE?
THE SHOES
HOW TO DRAW FOR CA$H MONEY!
YOU'RE WEARING A TIE! OH, HOW ADORABLE!
DID YOU GET ALL DRESSED UP JUST FOR ME?
OH, NO, I, UH...
YOU SEE, I HAVE THIS, UH, APPOINTMENT LATER, SO I, UH...
SO DON'T I COUNT AS AN "APPOINTMENT"?
?!? YOU? HOW SO? I DON'T—
YOU DID REMEMBER THAT I WAS COMING OVER TO SWAP RECORDS WITH YOU TODAY, DIDN'T YOU?
THAT'S WHY I THOUGHT THE TIE WAS FOR ME...
OH, Y-YES, OF COURSE I REMEMBER...
ONLY WE'LL HAVE TO MAKE IT QUICK, OR I'LL BE LATE FOR MY DATE...
AH-HA! SO IT'S A "DATE," IS IT?
THAT'S NO FAIR! WHEN ARE WE GONNA GO ON OUR DATE? I ASKED YOU FIRST!
WHAT'S THE STORY—IS SHE HOTTER LOOKING THAN ME OR SOMETHING?
AM I NOT YOUR "TYPE"? IS THAT THE PROBLEM?
WELL, NO— I MEAN YES! I MEAN...
OH, I BET I KNOW WHAT THE PROBLEM IS— I COME ON TOO STRONG, DON'T I? YOU'RE AFRAID OF ME, AREN'T YA?
C'MON, YOU CAN TELL ME THE TRUTH!
WELL, Y-YES, NOW THAT YOU MENTION IT... YOU SCARE THE LIVING DAYLIGHTS OUT OF ME...

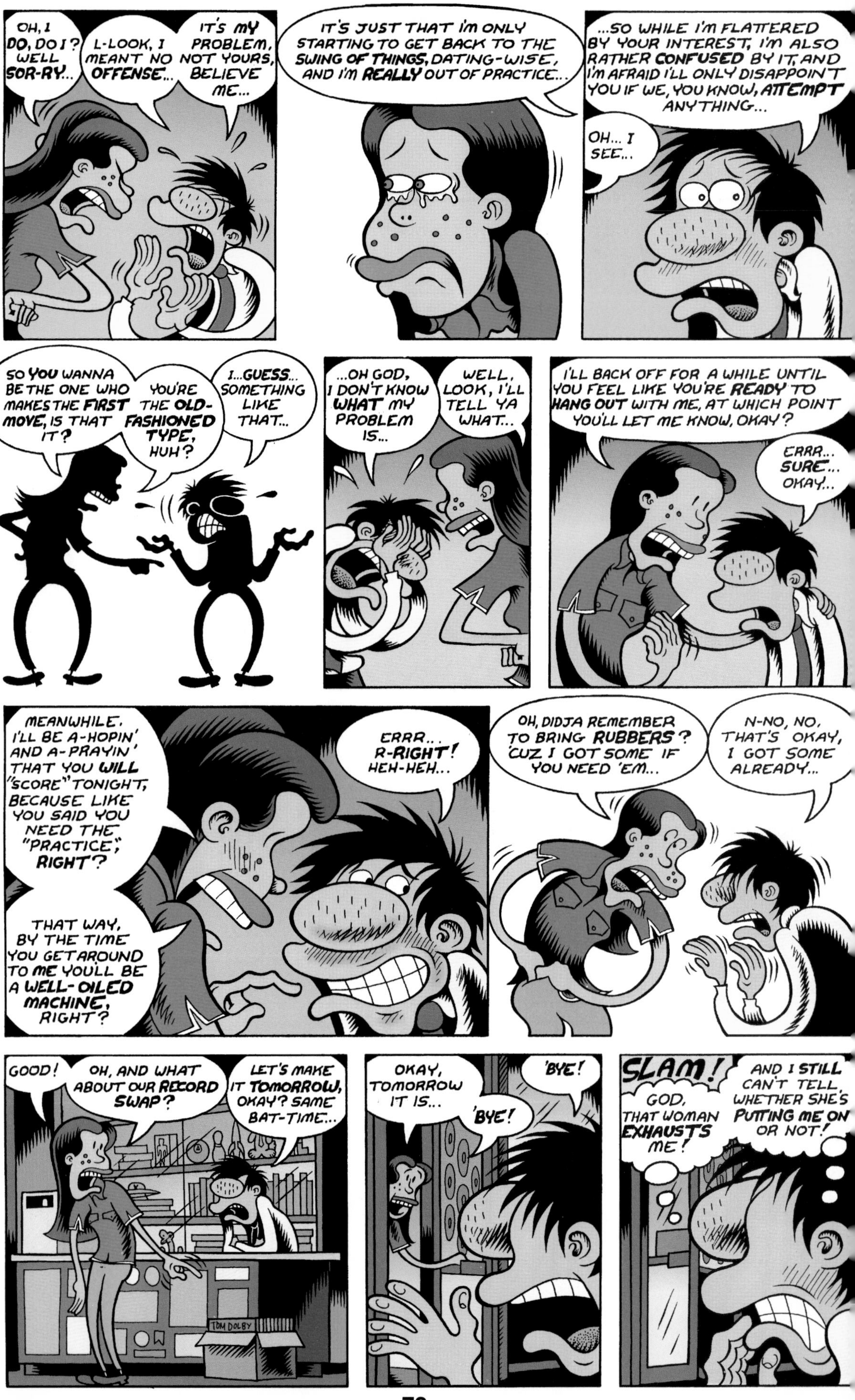
OH, I DO, DO I? WELL SOR-RY...
L-LOOK, I MEANT NO OFFENSE...
IT'S MY PROBLEM, NOT YOURS, BELIEVE ME...
IT'S JUST THAT I'M ONLY STARTING TO GET BACK TO THE SWING OF THINGS, DATING-WISE, AND I'M REALLY OUT OF PRACTICE...
...SO WHILE I'M FLATTERED BY YOUR INTEREST, I'M ALSO RATHER CONFUSED BY IT, AND I'M AFRAID I'LL ONLY DISAPPOINT YOU IF WE, YOU KNOW, ATTEMPT ANYTHING...
OH... I SEE...
SO YOU WANNA BE THE ONE WHO MAKES THE FIRST MOVE, IS THAT IT?
YOU'RE THE OLD-FASHIONED TYPE, HUH?
I...GUESS... SOMETHING LIKE THAT...
...OH GOD, I DON'T KNOW WHAT MY PROBLEM IS...
WELL, LOOK, I'LL TELL YA WHAT...
I'LL BACK OFF FOR A WHILE UNTIL YOU FEEL LIKE YOU'RE READY TO HANG OUT WITH ME, AT WHICH POINT YOU'LL LET ME KNOW, OKAY?
ERRR... SURE... OKAY...
MEANWHILE, I'LL BE A-HOPIN' AND A-PRAYIN' THAT YOU WILL "SCORE" TONIGHT, BECAUSE LIKE YOU SAID YOU NEED THE "PRACTICE," RIGHT?
ERRR... R-RIGHT! HEH-HEH...
THAT WAY, BY THE TIME YOU GET AROUND TO ME YOU'LL BE A WELL-OILED MACHINE, RIGHT?
OH, DIDJA REMEMBER TO BRING RUBBERS? 'CUZ I GOT SOME IF YOU NEED 'EM...
N-NO, NO, THAT'S OKAY, I GOT SOME ALREADY...
GOOD!
OH, AND WHAT ABOUT OUR RECORD SWAP?
LET'S MAKE IT TOMORROW, OKAY? SAME BAT-TIME...
TOM DOLBY
OKAY, TOMORROW IT IS...
'BYE!
'BYE!
SLAM!
GOD, THAT WOMAN EXHAUSTS ME!
AND I STILL CAN'T TELL WHETHER SHE'S PUTTING ME ON OR NOT!

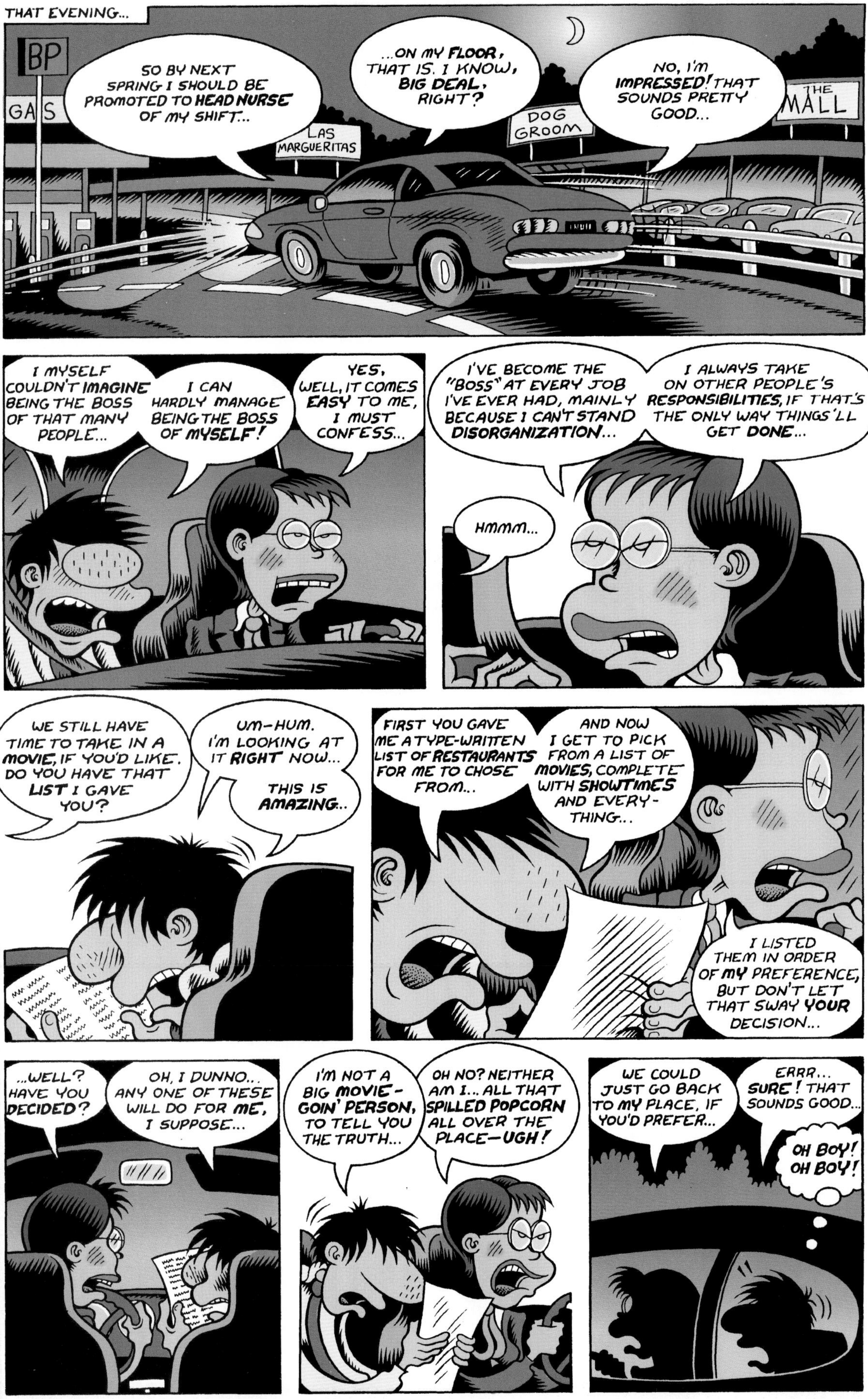
THAT EVENING...
BP
GAS
LAS MARGUERITAS
DOG GROOM
THE MALL
SO BY NEXT SPRING I SHOULD BE PROMOTED TO HEAD NURSE OF MY SHIFT...
...ON MY FLOOR, THAT IS. I KNOW, BIG DEAL, RIGHT?
NO, I'M IMPRESSED! THAT SOUNDS PRETTY GOOD...
I MYSELF COULDN'T IMAGINE BEING THE BOSS OF THAT MANY PEOPLE...
I CAN HARDLY MANAGE BEING THE BOSS OF MYSELF!
YES, WELL, IT COMES EASY TO ME, I MUST CONFESS...
I'VE BECOME THE "BOSS" AT EVERY JOB I'VE EVER HAD, MAINLY BECAUSE I CAN'T STAND DISORGANIZATION...
I ALWAYS TAKE ON OTHER PEOPLE'S RESPONSIBILITIES, IF THAT'S THE ONLY WAY THINGS'LL GET DONE...
HMMM...
WE STILL HAVE TIME TO TAKE IN A MOVIE, IF YOU'D LIKE. DO YOU HAVE THAT LIST I GAVE YOU?
UM-HUM. I'M LOOKING AT IT RIGHT NOW...
THIS IS AMAZING...
FIRST YOU GAVE ME A TYPE-WRITTEN LIST OF RESTAURANTS FOR ME TO CHOSE FROM...
AND NOW I GET TO PICK FROM A LIST OF MOVIES, COMPLETE WITH SHOWTIMES AND EVERY-THING...
I LISTED THEM IN ORDER OF MY PREFERENCE, BUT DON'T LET THAT SWAY YOUR DECISION...
...WELL? HAVE YOU DECIDED?
OH, I DUNNO... ANY ONE OF THESE WILL DO FOR ME, I SUPPOSE...
I'M NOT A BIG MOVIE-GOIN' PERSON, TO TELL YOU THE TRUTH...
OH NO? NEITHER AM I... ALL THAT SPILLED POPCORN ALL OVER THE PLACE—UGH!
WE COULD JUST GO BACK TO MY PLACE, IF YOU'D PREFER...
ERRR... SURE! THAT SOUNDS GOOD...
OH BOY! OH BOY!

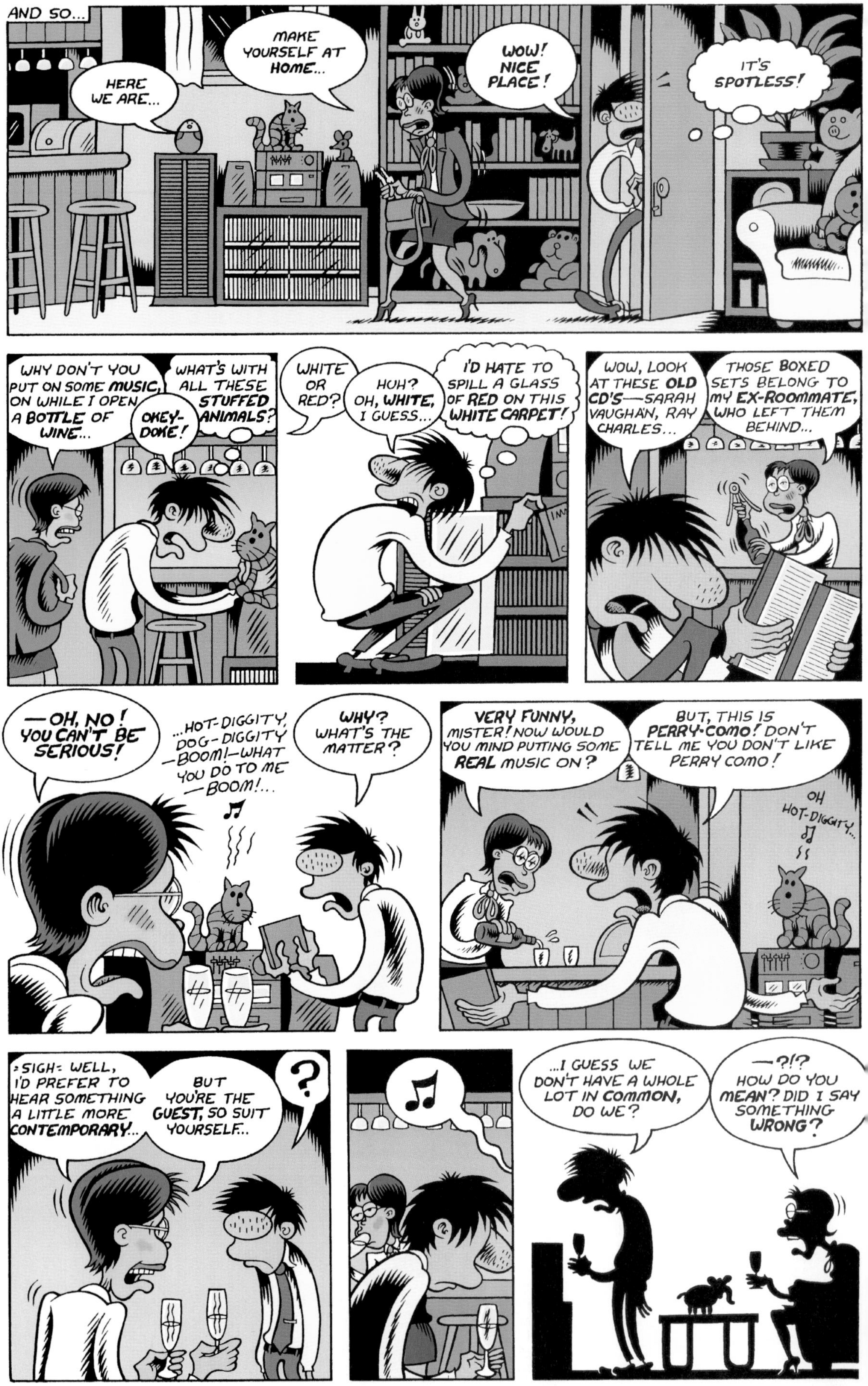
AND SO...
HERE WE ARE...
MAKE YOURSELF AT HOME...
WOW! NICE PLACE!
IT'S SPOTLESS!
WHY DON'T YOU PUT ON SOME MUSIC, ON WHILE I OPEN A BOTTLE OF WINE...
WHAT'S WITH ALL THESE STUFFED ANIMALS?
OKEY-DOKE!
WHITE OR RED?
HUH? OH, WHITE, I GUESS...
I'D HATE TO SPILL A GLASS OF RED ON THIS WHITE CARPET!
WOW, LOOK AT THESE OLD CD'S—SARAH VAUGHAN, RAY CHARLES...
THOSE BOXED SETS BELONG TO MY EX-ROOMMATE, WHO LEFT THEM BEHIND...
—OH, NO! YOU CAN'T BE SERIOUS!
...HOT-DIGGITY, DOG-DIGGITY —BOOM!—WHAT YOU DO TO ME —BOOM!...
WHY? WHAT'S THE MATTER?
VERY FUNNY, MISTER! NOW WOULD YOU MIND PUTTING SOME REAL MUSIC ON?
BUT, THIS IS PERRY-COMO! DON'T TELL ME YOU DON'T LIKE PERRY COMO!
OH HOT-DIGGITY...
=SIGH= WELL, I'D PREFER TO HEAR SOMETHING A LITTLE MORE CONTEMPORARY...
BUT YOU'RE THE GUEST, SO SUIT YOURSELF..
?
...I GUESS WE DON'T HAVE A WHOLE LOT IN COMMON, DO WE?
—?!? HOW DO YOU MEAN? DID I SAY SOMETHING WRONG?

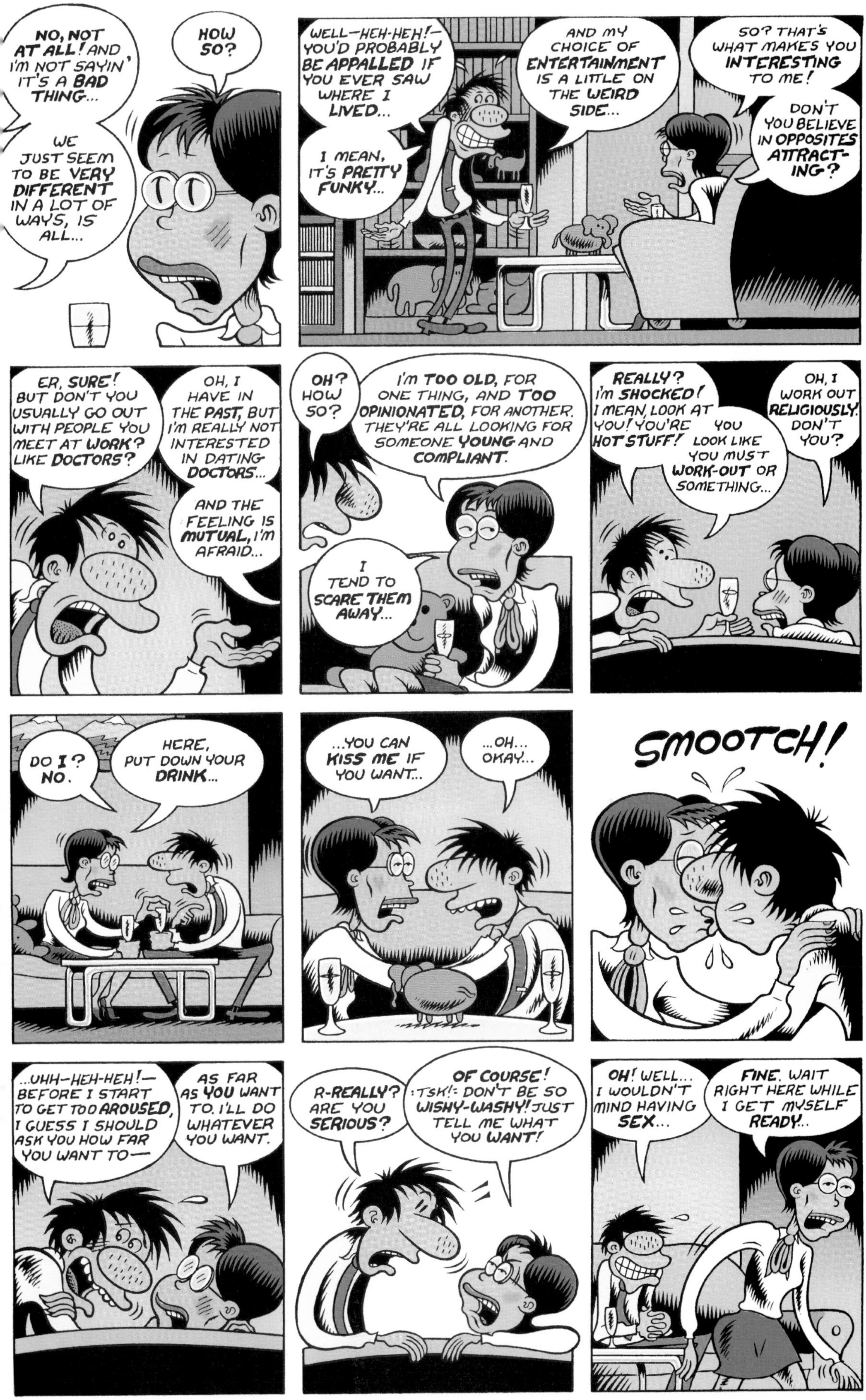
NO, NOT AT ALL! AND I'M NOT SAYIN' IT'S A BAD THING...
WE JUST SEEM TO BE VERY DIFFERENT IN A LOT OF WAYS, IS ALL...
HOW SO?
WELL—HEH-HEH!— YOU'D PROBABLY BE APPALLED IF YOU EVER SAW WHERE I LIVED...
I MEAN, IT'S PRETTY FUNKY...
AND MY CHOICE OF ENTERTAINMENT IS A LITTLE ON THE WEIRD SIDE...
SO? THAT'S WHAT MAKES YOU INTERESTING TO ME!
DON'T YOU BELIEVE IN OPPOSITES ATTRACT-ING?
ER, SURE! BUT DON'T YOU USUALLY GO OUT WITH PEOPLE YOU MEET AT WORK? LIKE DOCTORS?
OH, I HAVE IN THE PAST, BUT I'M REALLY NOT INTERESTED IN DATING DOCTORS...
AND THE FEELING IS MUTUAL, I'M AFRAID...
OH? HOW SO?
I'M TOO OLD, FOR ONE THING, AND TOO OPINIONATED, FOR ANOTHER. THEY'RE ALL LOOKING FOR SOMEONE YOUNG AND COMPLIANT.
I TEND TO SCARE THEM AWAY...
REALLY? I'M SHOCKED! I MEAN, LOOK AT YOU! YOU'RE HOT STUFF!
YOU LOOK LIKE YOU MUST WORK-OUT OR SOMETHING...
OH, I WORK OUT RELIGIOUSLY. DON'T YOU?
DO I? NO.
HERE, PUT DOWN YOUR DRINK...
...YOU CAN KISS ME IF YOU WANT...
...OH... OKAY...
SMOOTCH!
...UHH—HEH-HEH!— BEFORE I START TO GET TOO AROUSED, I GUESS I SHOULD ASK YOU HOW FAR YOU WANT TO—
AS FAR AS YOU WANT TO. I'LL DO WHATEVER YOU WANT.
R-REALLY? ARE YOU SERIOUS?
OF COURSE! :TSK!: DON'T BE SO WISHY-WASHY! JUST TELL ME WHAT YOU WANT!
OH! WELL... I WOULDN'T MIND HAVING SEX...
FINE. WAIT RIGHT HERE WHILE I GET MYSELF READY...

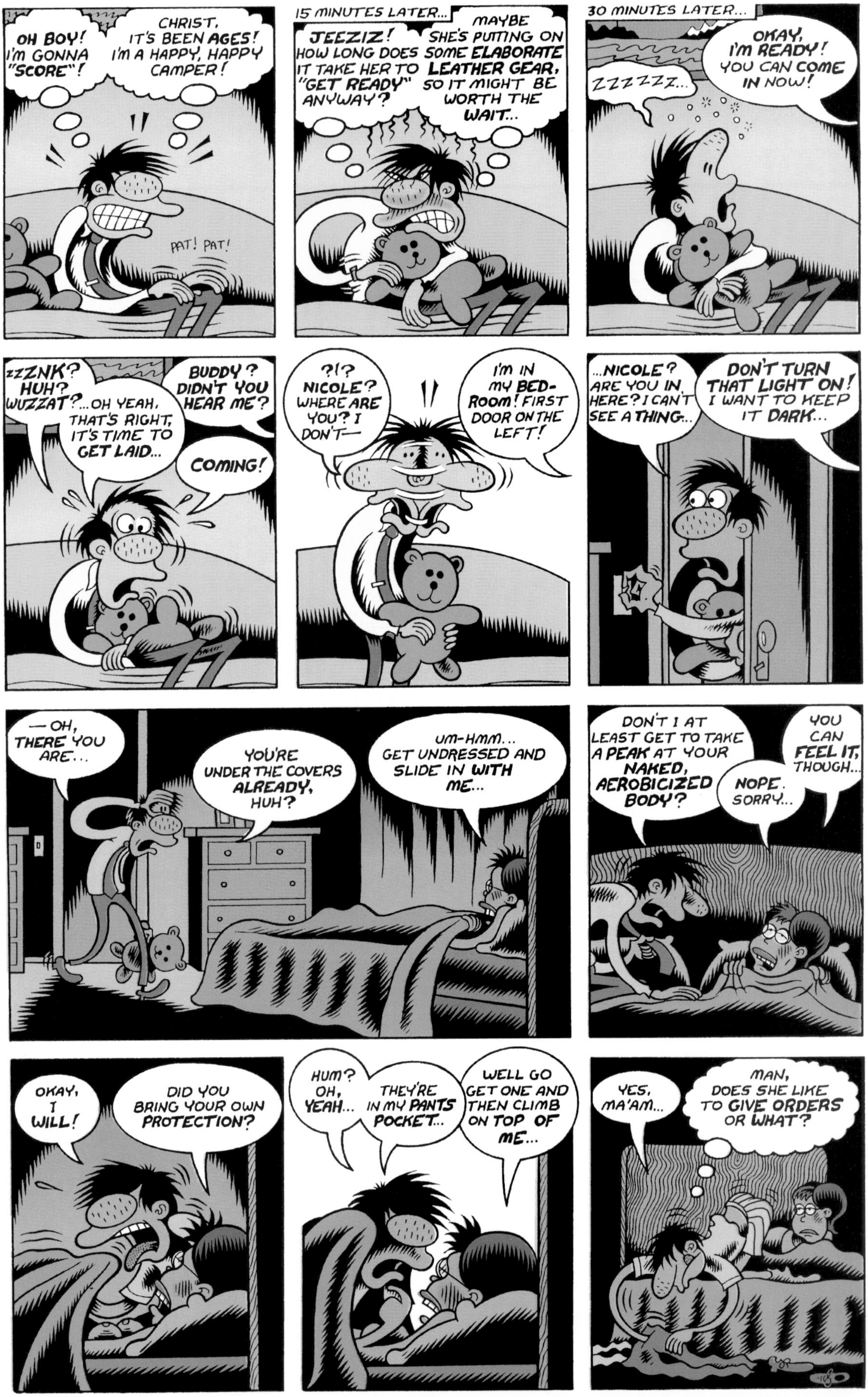
OH BOY! I'M GONNA "SCORE"!
CHRIST, IT'S BEEN AGES! I'M A HAPPY, HAPPY CAMPER!
PAT! PAT!
15 MINUTES LATER...
JEEZIZ! HOW LONG DOES IT TAKE HER TO "GET READY" ANYWAY?
MAYBE SHE'S PUTTING ON SOME ELABORATE LEATHER GEAR, SO IT MIGHT BE WORTH THE WAIT...
30 MINUTES LATER...
ZZZZZZ...
OKAY, I'M READY! YOU CAN COME IN NOW!
ZZZNK? HUH? WUZZAT?...OH YEAH, THAT'S RIGHT, IT'S TIME TO GET LAID...
BUDDY? DIDN'T YOU HEAR ME?
COMING!
?!? NICOLE? WHERE ARE YOU? I DON'T—
I'M IN MY BED-ROOM! FIRST DOOR ON THE LEFT!
...NICOLE? ARE YOU IN HERE? I CAN'T SEE A THING...
DON'T TURN THAT LIGHT ON! I WANT TO KEEP IT DARK...
—OH, THERE YOU ARE...
YOU'RE UNDER THE COVERS ALREADY, HUH?
UM-HMM... GET UNDRESSED AND SLIDE IN WITH ME...
DON'T I AT LEAST GET TO TAKE A PEAK AT YOUR NAKED, AEROBICIZED BODY?
NOPE. SORRY...
YOU CAN FEEL IT, THOUGH...
OKAY, I WILL!
DID YOU BRING YOUR OWN PROTECTION?
HUM? OH, YEAH...
THEY'RE IN MY PANTS POCKET...
WELL GO GET ONE AND THEN CLIMB ON TOP OF ME...
YES, MA'AM...
MAN, DOES SHE LIKE TO GIVE ORDERS OR WHAT?

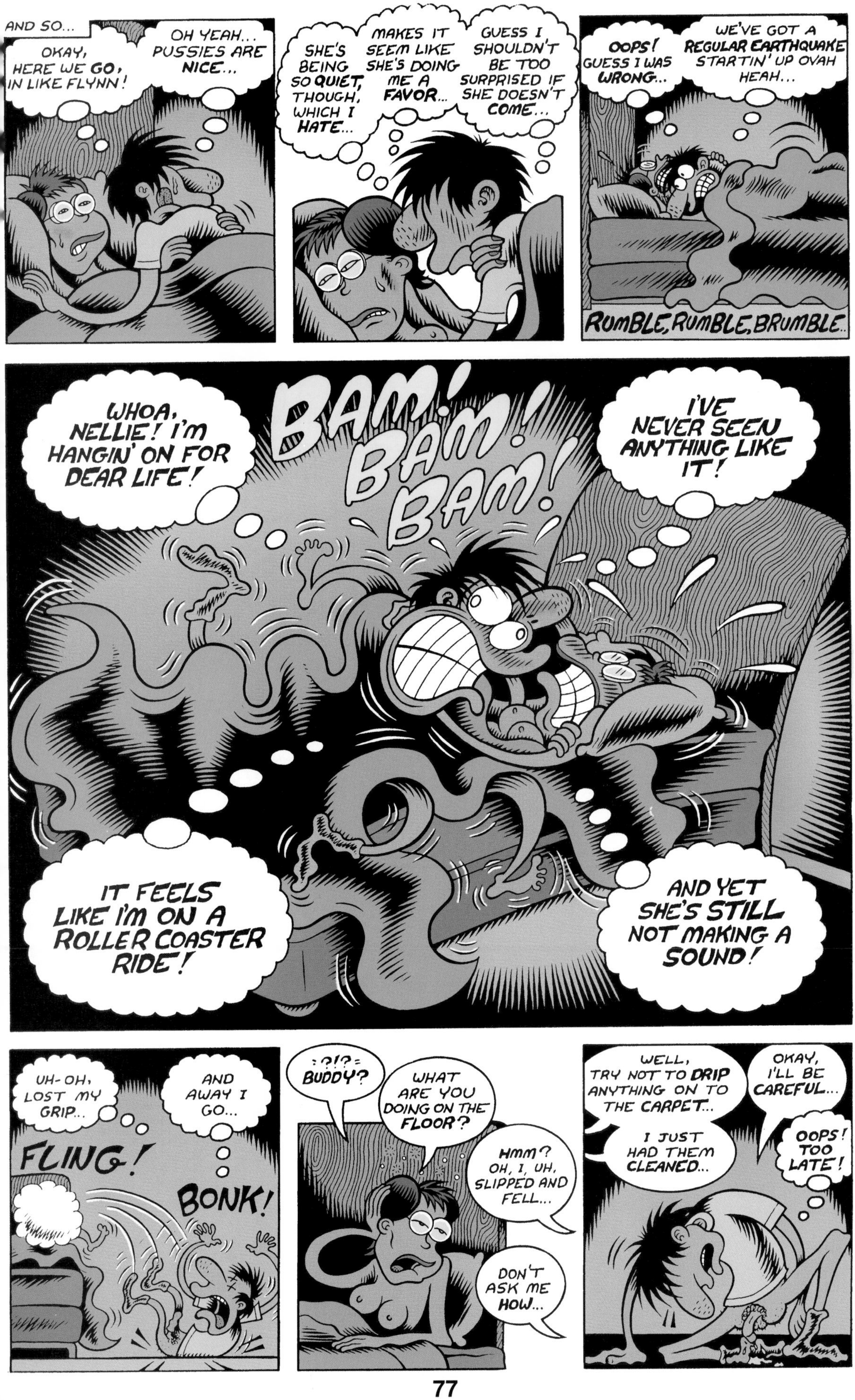
AND SO...
OKAY, HERE WE GO, IN LIKE FLYNN!
OH YEAH... PUSSIES ARE NICE...
SHE'S BEING SO QUIET, THOUGH, WHICH I HATE...
MAKES IT SEEM LIKE SHE'S DOING ME A FAVOR...
GUESS I SHOULDN'T BE TOO SURPRISED IF SHE DOESN'T COME...
OOPS! GUESS I WAS WRONG...
WE'VE GOT A REGULAR EARTHQUAKE STARTIN' UP OVAH HEAH...
RUMBLE, RUMBLE, BRUMBLE...
WHOA, NELLIE! I'M HANGIN' ON FOR DEAR LIFE!
BAM! BAM! BAM!
I'VE NEVER SEEN ANYTHING LIKE IT!
IT FEELS LIKE I'M ON A ROLLER COASTER RIDE!
AND YET SHE'S STILL NOT MAKING A SOUND!
UH-OH, LOST MY GRIP...
AND AWAY I GO...
FLING!
BONK!
?!?= BUDDY?
WHAT ARE YOU DOING ON THE FLOOR?
HMM? OH, I, UH, SLIPPED AND FELL...
DON'T ASK ME HOW...
WELL, TRY NOT TO DRIP ANYTHING ON TO THE CARPET...
I JUST HAD THEM CLEANED...
OKAY, I'LL BE CAREFUL...
OOPS! TOO LATE!

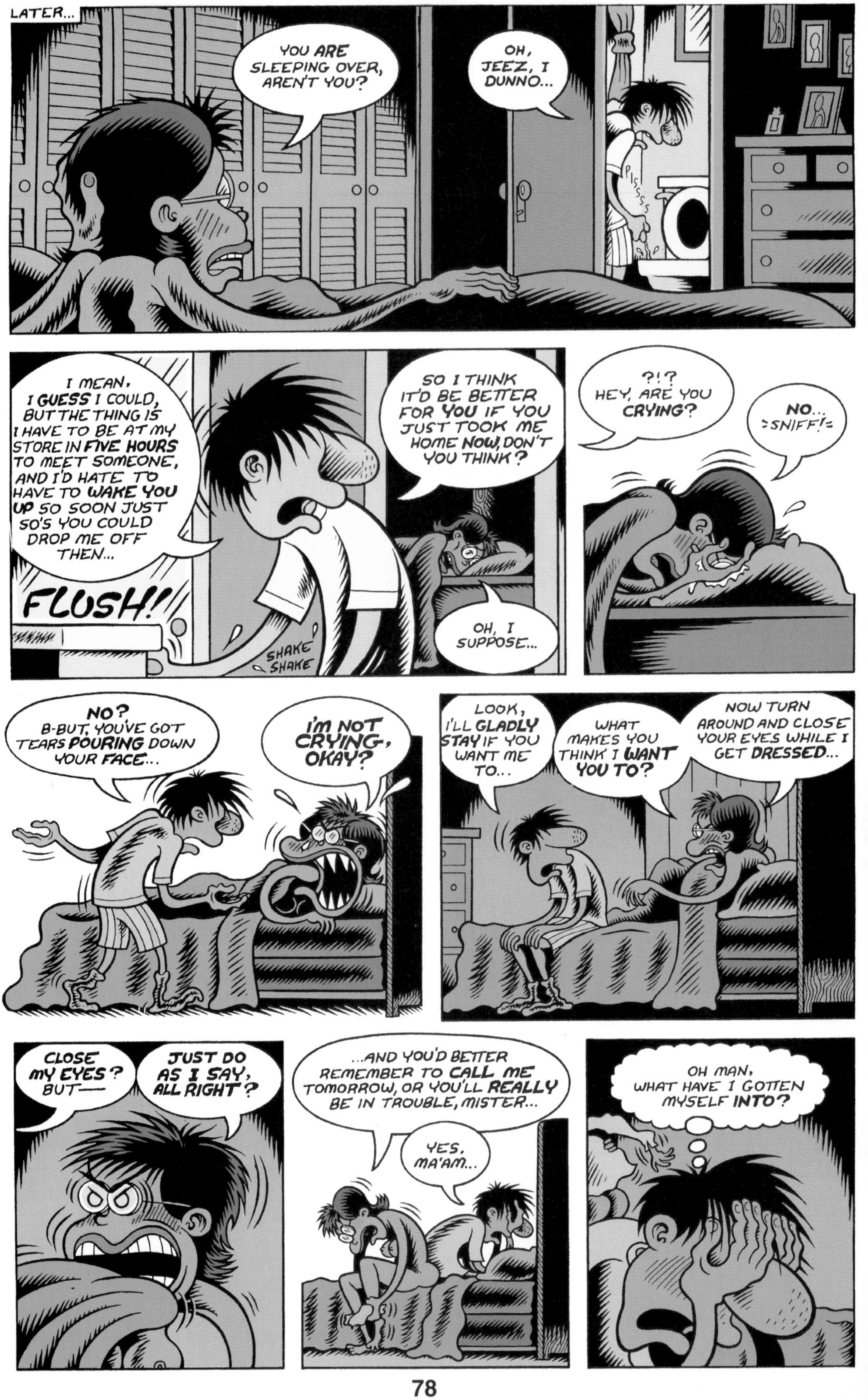
LATER...
YOU ARE SLEEPING OVER, AREN'T YOU?
OH, JEEZ, I DUNNO...
PISSSS
I MEAN, I GUESS I COULD, BUT THE THING IS I HAVE TO BE AT MY STORE IN FIVE HOURS TO MEET SOMEONE, AND I'D HATE TO HAVE TO WAKE YOU UP SO SOON JUST SO'S YOU COULD DROP ME OFF THEN...
FLUSH!
SHAKE SHAKE
SO I THINK IT'D BE BETTER FOR YOU IF YOU JUST TOOK ME HOME NOW, DON'T YOU THINK?
OH, I SUPPOSE...
?!? HEY, ARE YOU CRYING?
NO... =SNIFF!=
NO? B-BUT, YOU'VE GOT TEARS POURING DOWN YOUR FACE...
I'M NOT CRYING, OKAY?
LOOK, I'LL GLADLY STAY IF YOU WANT ME TO...
WHAT MAKES YOU THINK I WANT YOU TO?
NOW TURN AROUND AND CLOSE YOUR EYES WHILE I GET DRESSED...
CLOSE MY EYES? BUT—
JUST DO AS I SAY, ALL RIGHT?
...AND YOU'D BETTER REMEMBER TO CALL ME TOMORROW, OR YOU'LL REALLY BE IN TROUBLE, MISTER...
YES, MA'AM...
OH MAN, WHAT HAVE I GOTTEN MYSELF INTO?

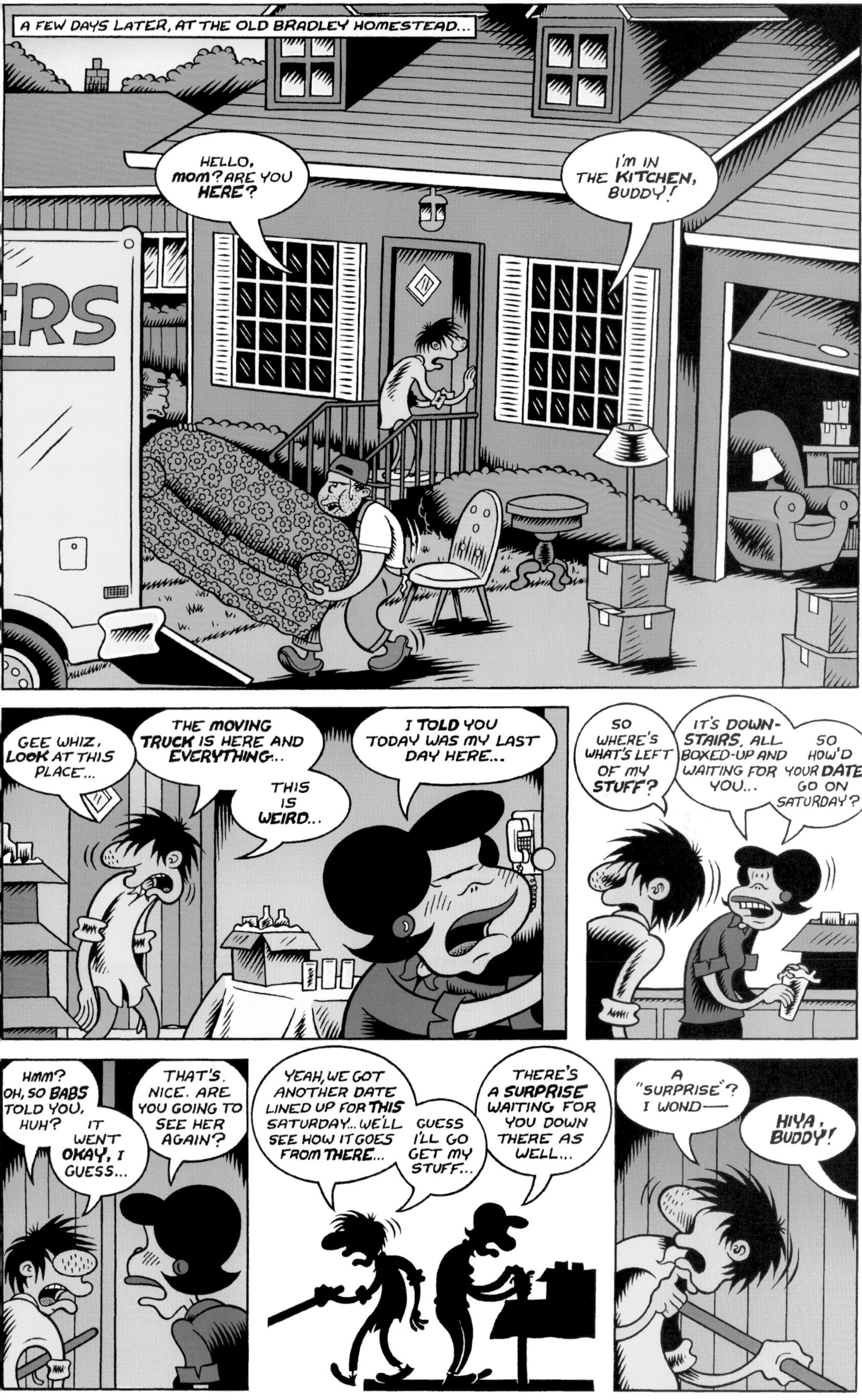
A FEW DAYS LATER, AT THE OLD BRADLEY HOMESTEAD...
HELLO, MOM? ARE YOU HERE?
I'M IN THE KITCHEN, BUDDY!
ERS
GEE WHIZ, LOOK AT THIS PLACE...
THE MOVING TRUCK IS HERE AND EVERYTHING...
THIS IS WEIRD...
I TOLD YOU TODAY WAS MY LAST DAY HERE...
SO WHERE'S WHAT'S LEFT OF MY STUFF?
IT'S DOWN-STAIRS, ALL BOXED-UP AND WAITING FOR YOU...
SO HOW'D YOUR DATE GO ON SATURDAY?
HMM? OH, SO BABS TOLD YOU, HUH?
IT WENT OKAY, I GUESS...
THAT'S NICE. ARE YOU GOING TO SEE HER AGAIN?
YEAH, WE GOT ANOTHER DATE LINED UP FOR THIS SATURDAY... WE'LL SEE HOW IT GOES FROM THERE...
GUESS I'LL GO GET MY STUFF...
THERE'S A SURPRISE WAITING FOR YOU DOWN THERE AS WELL...
A "SURPRISE"? I WOND—
HIYA, BUDDY!

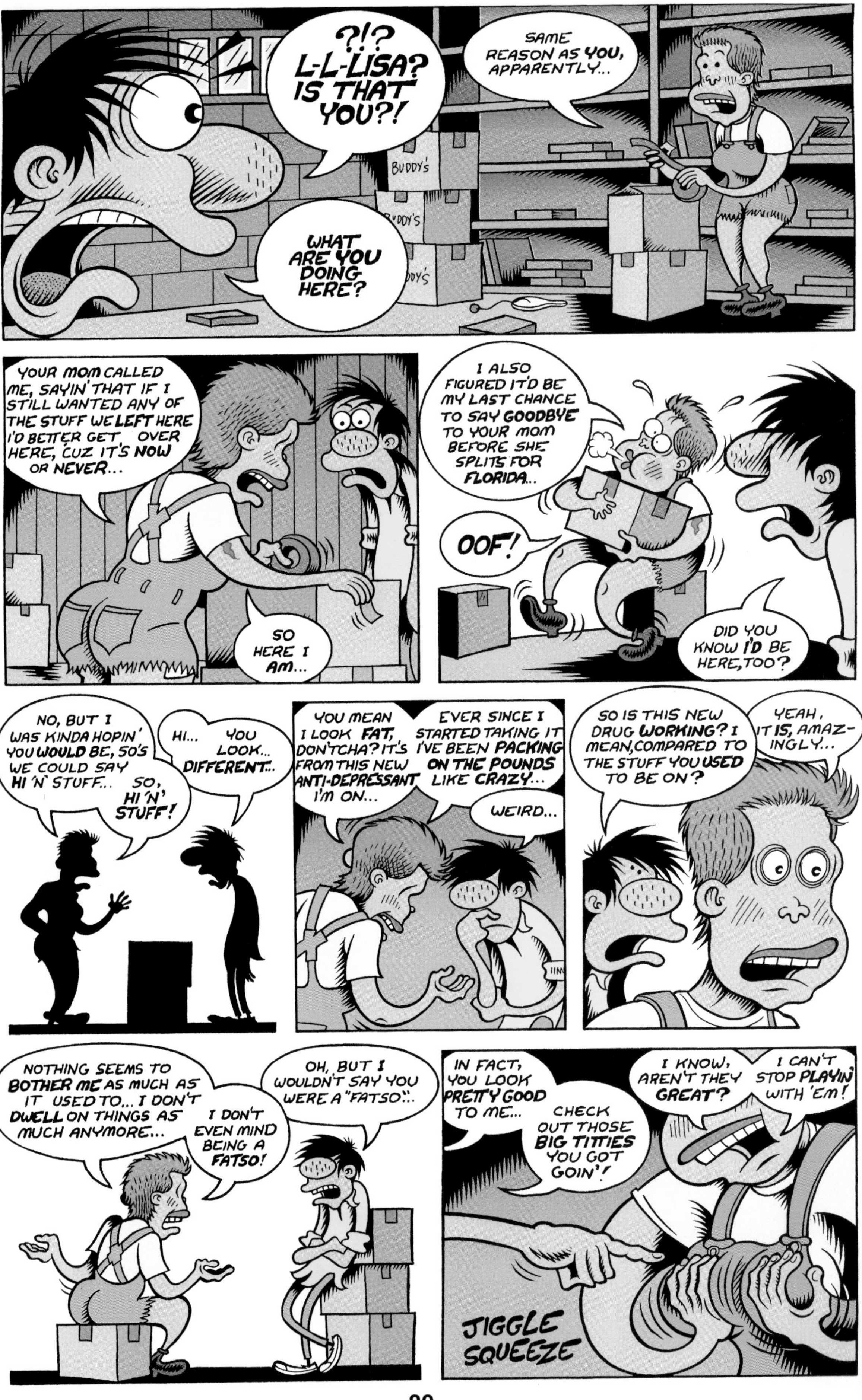
?!? L-L-LISA? IS THAT YOU?!
WHAT ARE YOU DOING HERE?
SAME REASON AS YOU, APPARENTLY...
BUDDY'S
YOUR MOM CALLED ME, SAYIN' THAT IF I STILL WANTED ANY OF THE STUFF WE LEFT HERE I'D BETTER GET OVER HERE, 'CUZ IT'S NOW OR NEVER...
SO HERE I AM...
I ALSO FIGURED IT'D BE MY LAST CHANCE TO SAY GOODBYE TO YOUR MOM BEFORE SHE SPLITS FOR FLORIDA...
OOF!
DID YOU KNOW I'D BE HERE, TOO?
NO, BUT I WAS KINDA HOPIN' YOU WOULD BE, SO'S WE COULD SAY HI 'N' STUFF...
SO, HI 'N' STUFF!
HI... YOU LOOK... DIFFERENT...
YOU MEAN I LOOK FAT, DON'TCHA? IT'S FROM THIS NEW ANTI-DEPRESSANT I'M ON...
EVER SINCE I STARTED TAKING IT I'VE BEEN PACKING ON THE POUNDS LIKE CRAZY...
WEIRD...
SO IS THIS NEW DRUG WORKING? I MEAN, COMPARED TO THE STUFF YOU USED TO BE ON?
YEAH, IT IS, AMAZINGLY...
NOTHING SEEMS TO BOTHER ME AS MUCH AS IT USED TO... I DON'T DWELL ON THINGS AS MUCH ANYMORE...
I DON'T EVEN MIND BEING A FATSO!
OH, BUT I WOULDN'T SAY YOU WERE A "FATSO"...
IN FACT, YOU LOOK PRETTY GOOD TO ME...
CHECK OUT THOSE BIG TITTIES YOU GOT GOIN'!
I KNOW, AREN'T THEY GREAT?
I CAN'T STOP PLAYIN' WITH 'EM!
JIGGLE
SQUEEZE

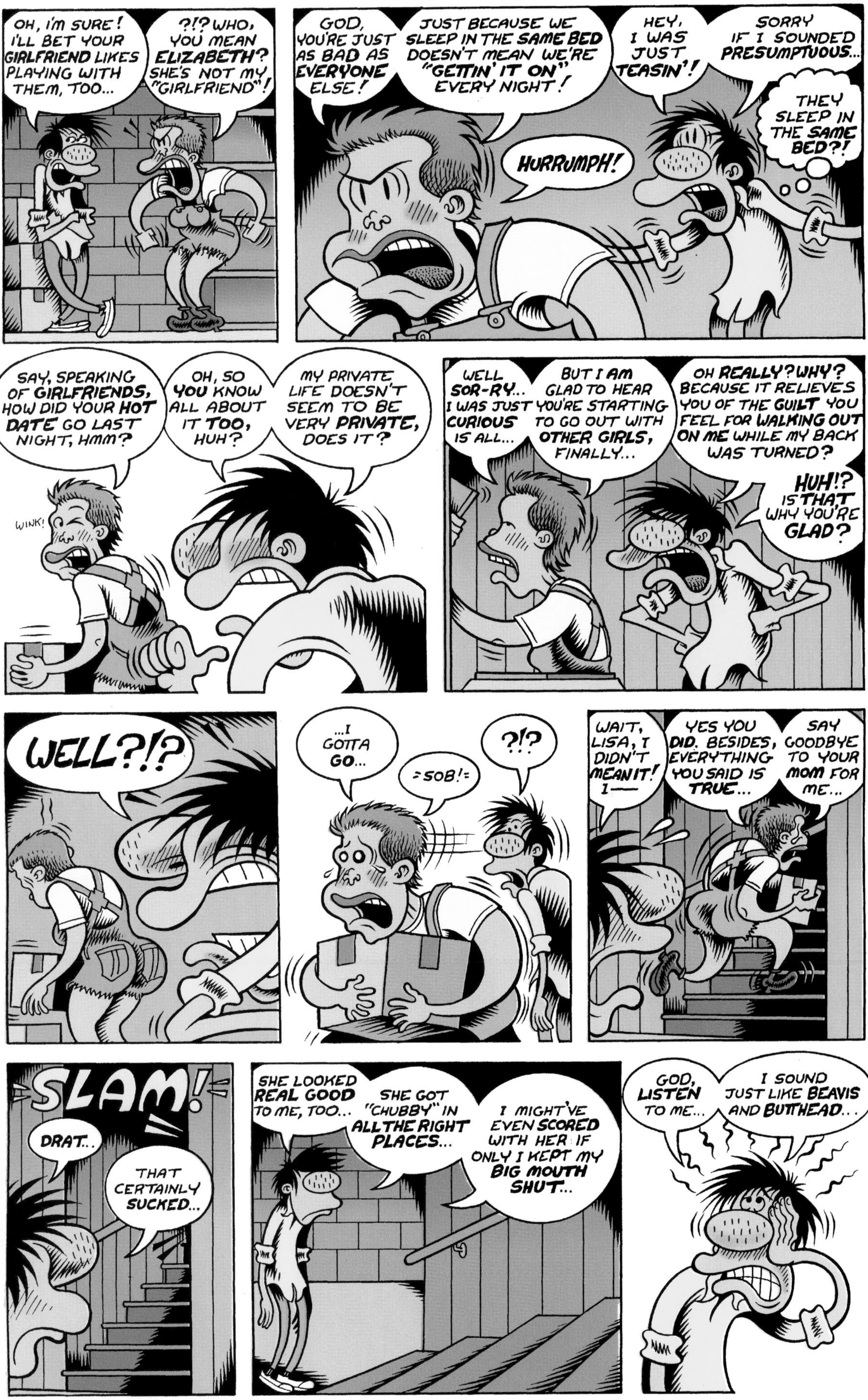

OH, I'M SURE! I'LL BET YOUR GIRLFRIEND LIKES PLAYING WITH THEM, TOO...
?!? WHO, YOU MEAN ELIZABETH? SHE'S NOT MY "GIRLFRIEND"!
GOD, YOU'RE JUST AS BAD AS EVERYONE ELSE!
JUST BECAUSE WE SLEEP IN THE SAME BED DOESN'T MEAN WE'RE "GETTIN' IT ON" EVERY NIGHT!
HURRUMPH!
HEY, I WAS JUST TEASIN'!
SORRY IF I SOUNDED PRESUMPTUOUS...
THEY SLEEP IN THE SAME BED?!
SAY, SPEAKING OF GIRLFRIENDS, HOW DID YOUR HOT DATE GO LAST NIGHT, HMM?
WINK!
OH, SO YOU KNOW ALL ABOUT IT TOO, HUH?
MY PRIVATE LIFE DOESN'T SEEM TO BE VERY PRIVATE, DOES IT?
WELL SOR-RY... I WAS JUST CURIOUS IS ALL...
BUT I AM GLAD TO HEAR YOU'RE STARTING TO GO OUT WITH OTHER GIRLS, FINALLY...
OH REALLY? WHY? BECAUSE IT RELIEVES YOU OF THE GUILT YOU FEEL FOR WALKING OUT ON ME WHILE MY BACK WAS TURNED?
HUH!? IS THAT WHY YOU'RE GLAD?
WELL?!?
...I GOTTA GO...
=SOB!=
?!?
WAIT, LISA, I DIDN'T MEAN IT! I—
YES YOU DID. BESIDES, EVERYTHING YOU SAID IS TRUE...
SAY GOODBYE TO YOUR MOM FOR ME...
SLAM!
DRAT...
THAT CERTAINLY SUCKED...
SHE LOOKED REAL GOOD TO ME, TOO...
SHE GOT "CHUBBY" IN ALL THE RIGHT PLACES...
I MIGHT'VE EVEN SCORED WITH HER IF ONLY I KEPT MY BIG MOUTH SHUT...
GOD, LISTEN TO ME...
I SOUND JUST LIKE BEAVIS AND BUTTHEAD...

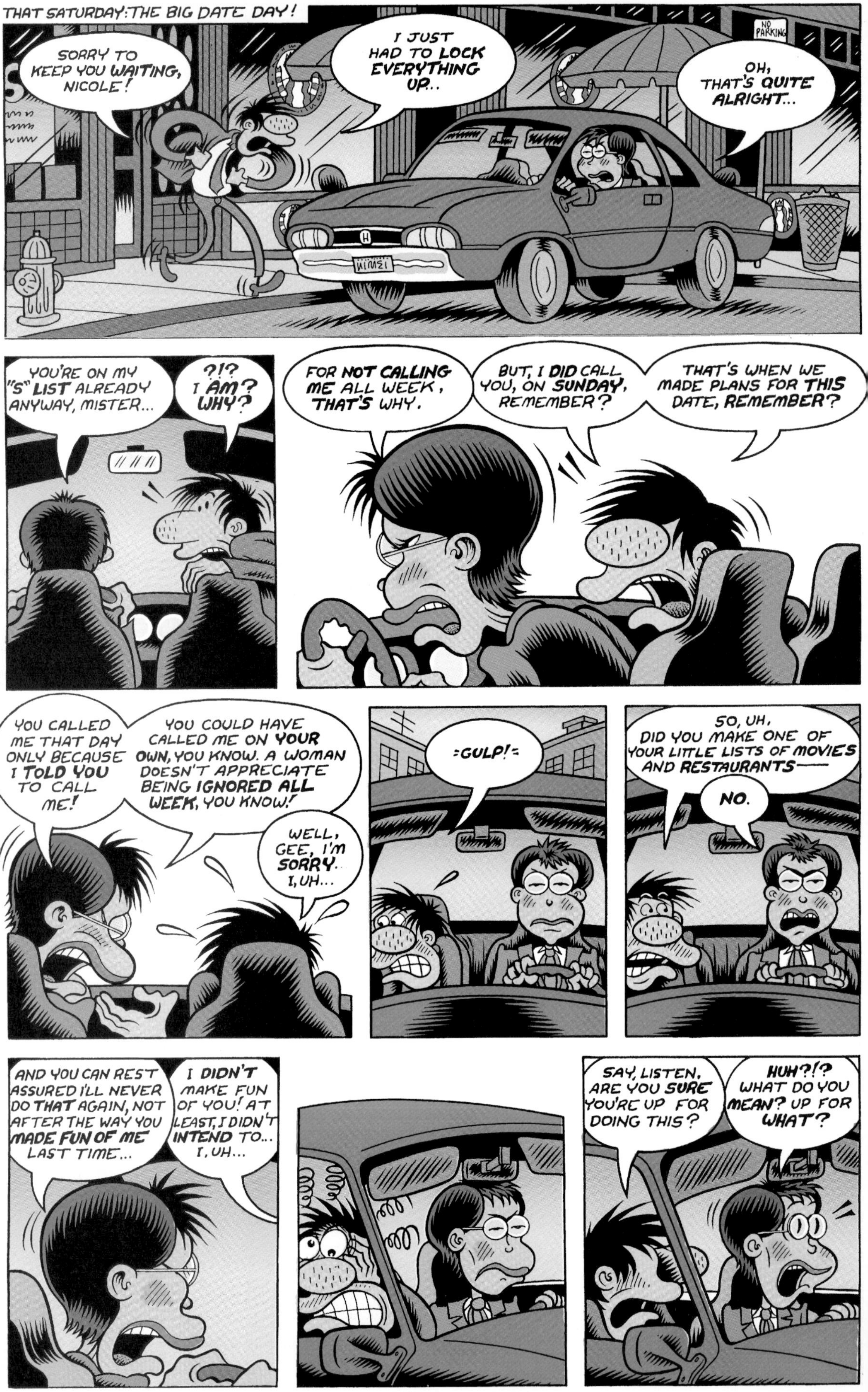

THAT SATURDAY: THE BIG DATE DAY!
SORRY TO KEEP YOU WAITING, NICOLE!
I JUST HAD TO LOCK EVERYTHING UP...
NO PARKING
OH, THAT'S QUITE ALRIGHT...
YOU'RE ON MY "S" LIST ALREADY ANYWAY, MISTER...
?!? I AM? WHY?
FOR NOT CALLING ME ALL WEEK, THAT'S WHY.
BUT, I DID CALL YOU, ON SUNDAY, REMEMBER?
THAT'S WHEN WE MADE PLANS FOR THIS DATE, REMEMBER?
YOU CALLED ME THAT DAY ONLY BECAUSE I TOLD YOU TO CALL ME!
YOU COULD HAVE CALLED ME ON YOUR OWN, YOU KNOW. A WOMAN DOESN'T APPRECIATE BEING IGNORED ALL WEEK, YOU KNOW!
WELL, GEE, I'M SORRY. I, UH...
=GULP!=
SO, UH, DID YOU MAKE ONE OF YOUR LITTLE LISTS OF MOVIES AND RESTAURANTS——
NO.
AND YOU CAN REST ASSURED I'LL NEVER DO THAT AGAIN, NOT AFTER THE WAY YOU MADE FUN OF ME LAST TIME...
I DIDN'T MAKE FUN OF YOU! AT LEAST, I DIDN'T INTEND TO... I, UH...
SAY, LISTEN, ARE YOU SURE YOU'RE UP FOR DOING THIS?
HUH?!? WHAT DO YOU MEAN? UP FOR WHAT?

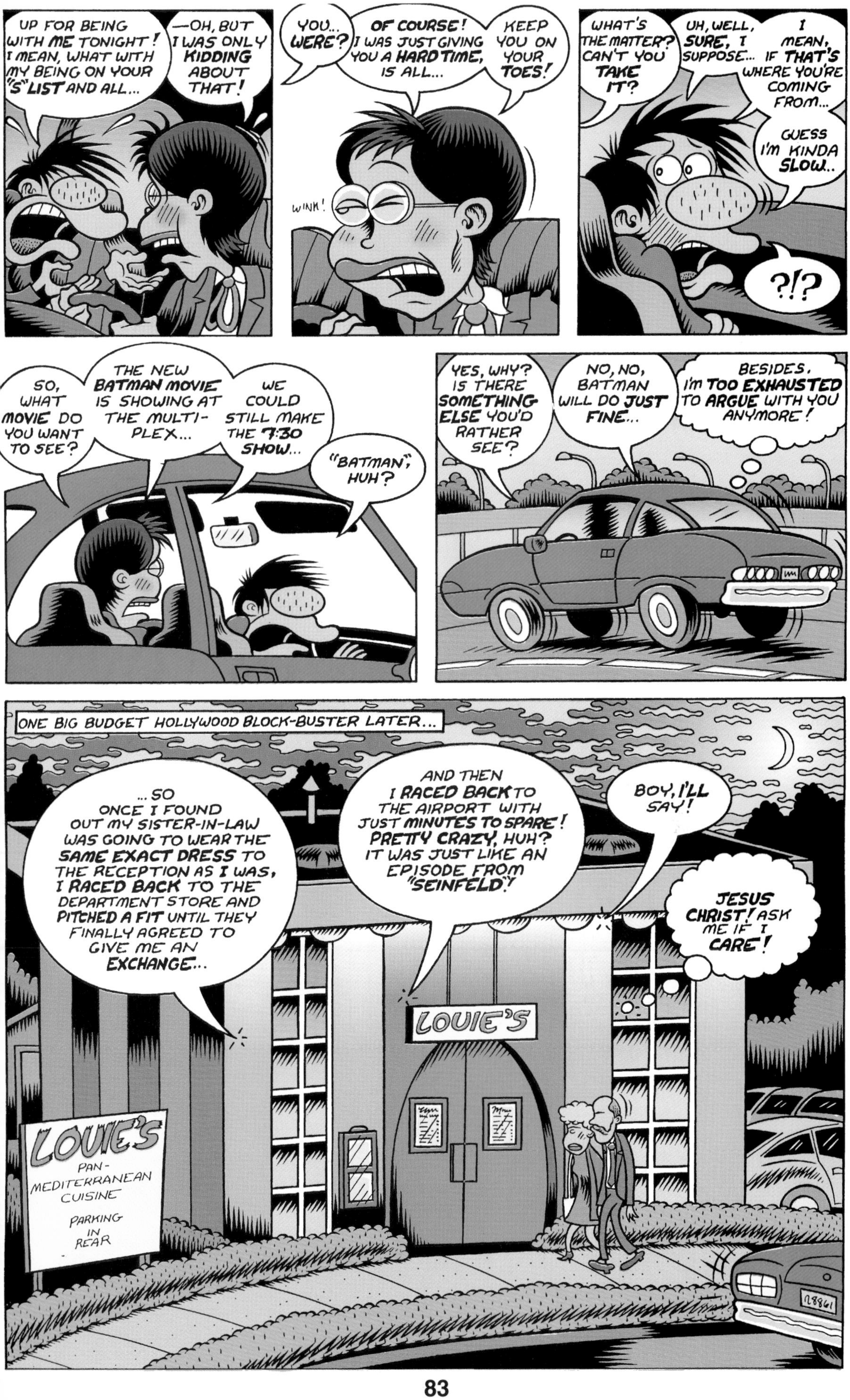
UP FOR BEING WITH ME TONIGHT! I MEAN, WHAT WITH MY BEING ON YOUR "S" LIST AND ALL...
—OH, BUT I WAS ONLY KIDDING ABOUT THAT!
YOU... WERE?
OF COURSE! I WAS JUST GIVING YOU A HARD TIME, IS ALL...
KEEP YOU ON YOUR TOES!
WINK!
WHAT'S THE MATTER? CAN'T YOU TAKE IT?
UH, WELL, SURE, I SUPPOSE...
I MEAN, IF THAT'S WHERE YOU'RE COMING FROM...
GUESS I'M KINDA SLOW..
?!?
SO, WHAT MOVIE DO YOU WANT TO SEE?
THE NEW BATMAN MOVIE IS SHOWING AT THE MULTI-PLEX...
WE COULD STILL MAKE THE 7:30 SHOW...
"BATMAN", HUH?
YES, WHY? IS THERE SOMETHING ELSE YOU'D RATHER SEE?
NO, NO, BATMAN WILL DO JUST FINE...
BESIDES, I'M TOO EXHAUSTED TO ARGUE WITH YOU ANYMORE!
ONE BIG BUDGET HOLLYWOOD BLOCK-BUSTER LATER...
... SO ONCE I FOUND OUT MY SISTER-IN-LAW WAS GOING TO WEAR THE SAME EXACT DRESS TO THE RECEPTION AS I WAS, I RACED BACK TO THE DEPARTMENT STORE AND PITCHED A FIT UNTIL THEY FINALLY AGREED TO GIVE ME AN EXCHANGE...
AND THEN I RACED BACK TO THE AIRPORT WITH JUST MINUTES TO SPARE! PRETTY CRAZY, HUH? IT WAS JUST LIKE AN EPISODE FROM "SEINFELD"!
BOY, I'LL SAY!
JESUS CHRIST! ASK ME IF I CARE!
LOUIE'S
LOUIE'S PAN-MEDITERRANEAN CUISINE
PARKING IN REAR

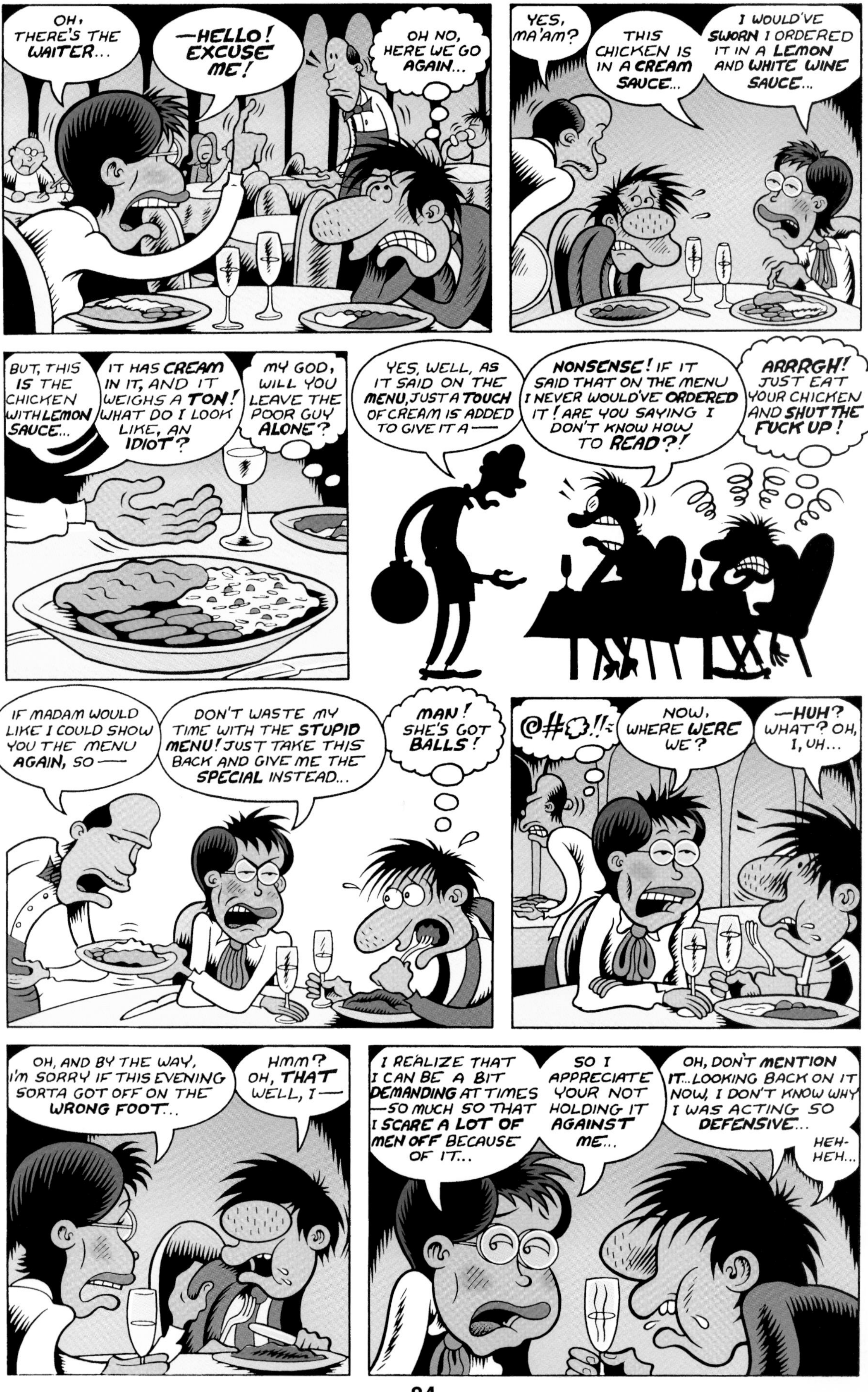
OH, THERE'S THE WAITER...
—HELLO! EXCUSE ME!
OH NO, HERE WE GO AGAIN...
YES, MA'AM?
THIS CHICKEN IS IN A CREAM SAUCE...
I WOULD'VE SWORN I ORDERED IT IN A LEMON AND WHITE WINE SAUCE...
BUT, THIS IS THE CHICKEN WITH LEMON SAUCE...
IT HAS CREAM IN IT, AND IT WEIGHS A TON! WHAT DO I LOOK LIKE, AN IDIOT?
MY GOD, WILL YOU LEAVE THE POOR GUY ALONE?
YES, WELL, AS IT SAID ON THE MENU, JUST A TOUCH OF CREAM IS ADDED TO GIVE IT A—
NONSENSE! IF IT SAID THAT ON THE MENU I NEVER WOULD'VE ORDERED IT! ARE YOU SAYING I DON'T KNOW HOW TO READ?!
ARRRGH! JUST EAT YOUR CHICKEN AND SHUT THE FUCK UP!
IF MADAM WOULD LIKE I COULD SHOW YOU THE MENU AGAIN, SO—
DON'T WASTE MY TIME WITH THE STUPID MENU! JUST TAKE THIS BACK AND GIVE ME THE SPECIAL INSTEAD...
MAN! SHE'S GOT BALLS!
@#✿!!
NOW, WHERE WERE WE?
—HUH? WHAT? OH, I, UH...
OH, AND BY THE WAY, I'M SORRY IF THIS EVENING SORTA GOT OFF ON THE WRONG FOOT...
HMM? OH, THAT WELL, I—
I REALIZE THAT I CAN BE A BIT DEMANDING AT TIMES —SO MUCH SO THAT I SCARE A LOT OF MEN OFF BECAUSE OF IT...
SO I APPRECIATE YOUR NOT HOLDING IT AGAINST ME...
OH, DON'T MENTION IT... LOOKING BACK ON IT NOW, I DON'T KNOW WHY I WAS ACTING SO DEFENSIVE...
HEH-HEH...

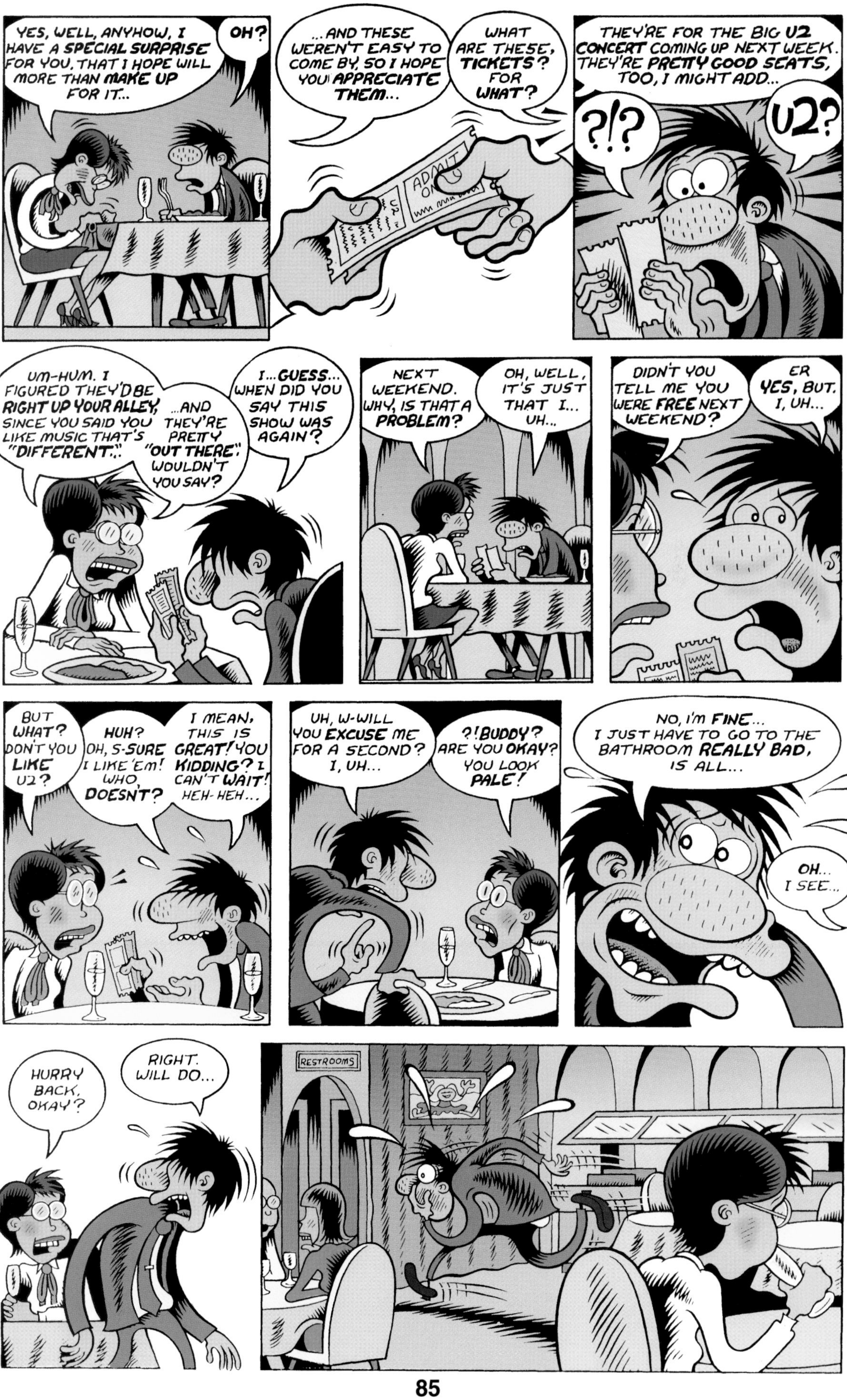
YES, WELL, ANYHOW, I HAVE A SPECIAL SURPRISE FOR YOU, THAT I HOPE WILL MORE THAN MAKE UP FOR IT...
OH?
...AND THESE WEREN'T EASY TO COME BY, SO I HOPE YOU APPRECIATE THEM...
WHAT ARE THESE, TICKETS? FOR WHAT?
ADMIT ONE
U2
THEY'RE FOR THE BIG U2 CONCERT COMING UP NEXT WEEK. THEY'RE PRETTY GOOD SEATS, TOO, I MIGHT ADD...
?!?
U2?
UM-HUM. I FIGURED THEY'D BE RIGHT UP YOUR ALLEY, SINCE YOU SAID YOU LIKE MUSIC THAT'S "DIFFERENT."
...AND THEY'RE PRETTY "OUT THERE," WOULDN'T YOU SAY?
I...GUESS... WHEN DID YOU SAY THIS SHOW WAS AGAIN?
NEXT WEEKEND. WHY, IS THAT A PROBLEM?
OH, WELL, IT'S JUST THAT I... UH...
DIDN'T YOU TELL ME YOU WERE FREE NEXT WEEKEND?
ER YES, BUT. I, UH...
BUT WHAT? DON'T YOU LIKE U2?
HUH? OH, S-SURE I LIKE 'EM! WHO DOESN'T?
I MEAN, THIS IS GREAT! YOU KIDDING? I CAN'T WAIT! HEH-HEH...
UH, W-WILL YOU EXCUSE ME FOR A SECOND? I, UH...
?!BUDDY? ARE YOU OKAY? YOU LOOK PALE!
NO, I'M FINE... I JUST HAVE TO GO TO THE BATHROOM REALLY BAD, IS ALL...
OH... I SEE...
HURRY BACK, OKAY?
RIGHT. WILL DO...
RESTROOMS

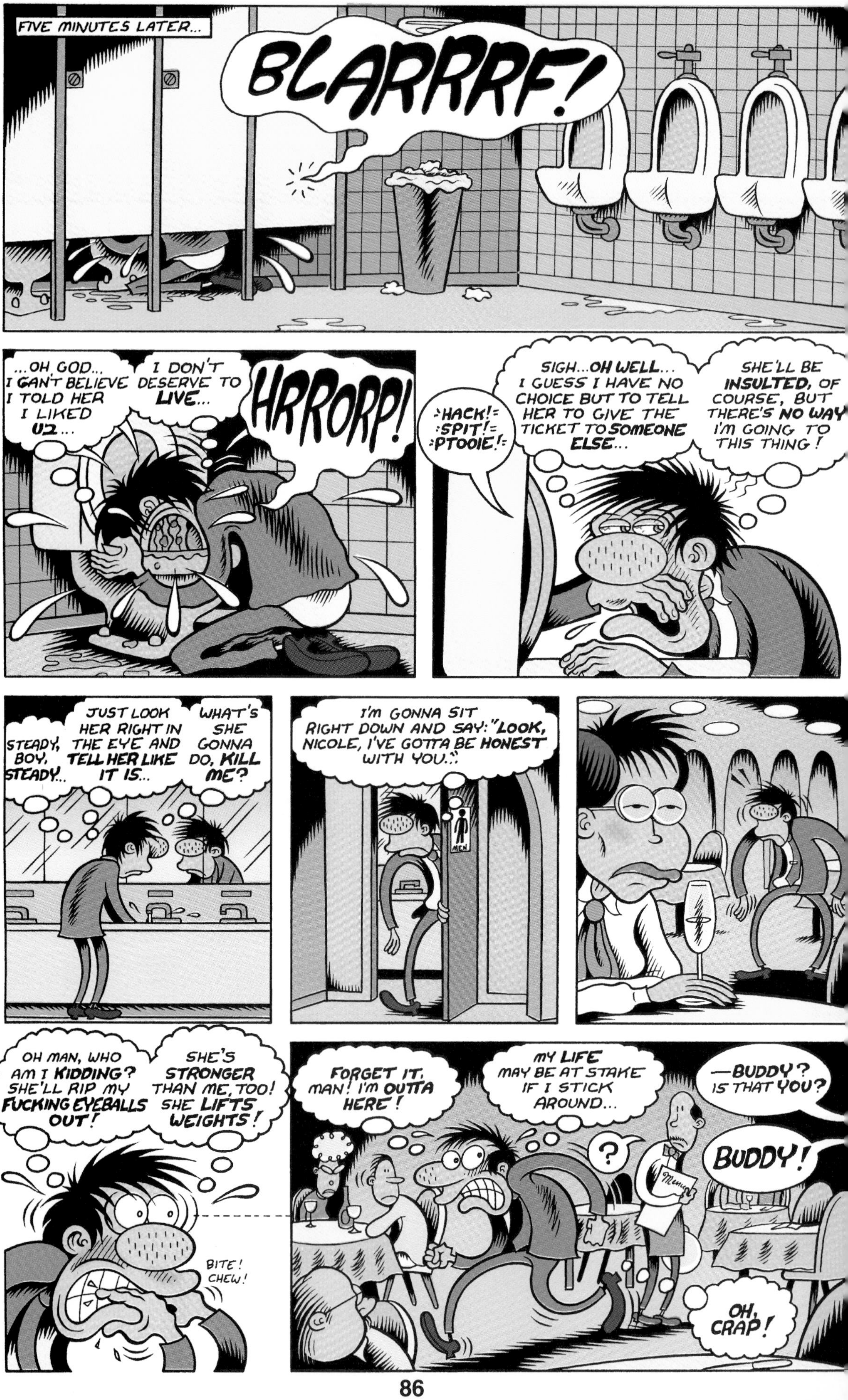
FIVE MINUTES LATER...
BLARRRF!
...OH GOD... I CAN'T BELIEVE I TOLD HER I LIKED U2...
I DON'T DESERVE TO LIVE...
HRRORP!
HACK! SPIT! PTOOIE!
SIGH...OH WELL... I GUESS I HAVE NO CHOICE BUT TO TELL HER TO GIVE THE TICKET TO SOMEONE ELSE...
SHE'LL BE INSULTED, OF COURSE, BUT THERE'S NO WAY I'M GOING TO THIS THING!
STEADY, BOY, STEADY...
JUST LOOK HER RIGHT IN THE EYE AND TELL HER LIKE IT IS...
WHAT'S SHE GONNA DO, KILL ME?
I'M GONNA SIT RIGHT DOWN AND SAY: "LOOK, NICOLE, I'VE GOTTA BE HONEST WITH YOU..."
MEN
OH MAN, WHO AM I KIDDING? SHE'LL RIP MY FUCKING EYEBALLS OUT!
SHE'S STRONGER THAN ME, TOO! SHE LIFTS WEIGHTS!
BITE! CHEW!
FORGET IT, MAN! I'M OUTTA HERE!
MY LIFE MAY BE AT STAKE IF I STICK AROUND...
?
Menu
—BUDDY? IS THAT YOU?
BUDDY!
OH, CRAP!

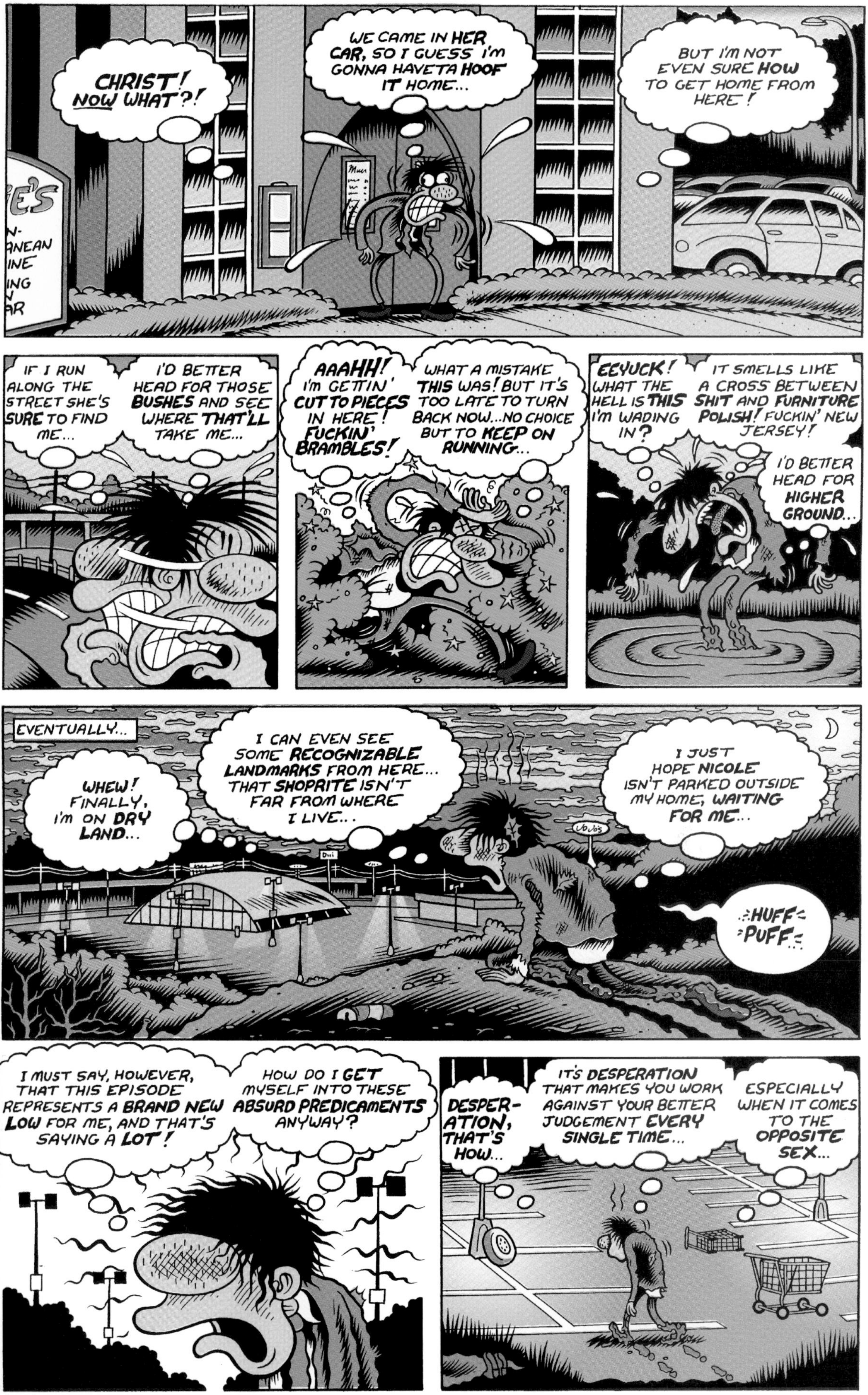
CHRIST! NOW WHAT?!
WE CAME IN HER CAR, SO I GUESS I'M GONNA HAVETA HOOF IT HOME...
BUT I'M NOT EVEN SURE HOW TO GET HOME FROM HERE!
IF I RUN ALONG THE STREET SHE'S SURE TO FIND ME...
I'D BETTER HEAD FOR THOSE BUSHES AND SEE WHERE THAT'LL TAKE ME...
AAAHH! I'M GETTIN' CUT TO PIECES IN HERE! FUCKIN' BRAMBLES!
WHAT A MISTAKE THIS WAS! BUT IT'S TOO LATE TO TURN BACK NOW...NO CHOICE BUT TO KEEP ON RUNNING...
EEYUCK! WHAT THE HELL IS THIS I'M WADING IN?
IT SMELLS LIKE A CROSS BETWEEN SHIT AND FURNITURE POLISH! FUCKIN' NEW JERSEY!
I'D BETTER HEAD FOR HIGHER GROUND...
EVENTUALLY...
WHEW! FINALLY, I'M ON DRY LAND...
I CAN EVEN SEE SOME RECOGNIZABLE LANDMARKS FROM HERE... THAT SHOPRITE ISN'T FAR FROM WHERE I LIVE...
I JUST HOPE NICOLE ISN'T PARKED OUTSIDE MY HOME, WAITING FOR ME...
HUFF PUFF
I MUST SAY, HOWEVER, THAT THIS EPISODE REPRESENTS A BRAND NEW LOW FOR ME, AND THAT'S SAYING A LOT!
HOW DO I GET MYSELF INTO THESE ABSURD PREDICAMENTS ANYWAY?
DESPER-ATION, THAT'S HOW...
IT'S DESPERATION THAT MAKES YOU WORK AGAINST YOUR BETTER JUDGEMENT EVERY SINGLE TIME...
ESPECIALLY WHEN IT COMES TO THE OPPOSITE SEX...

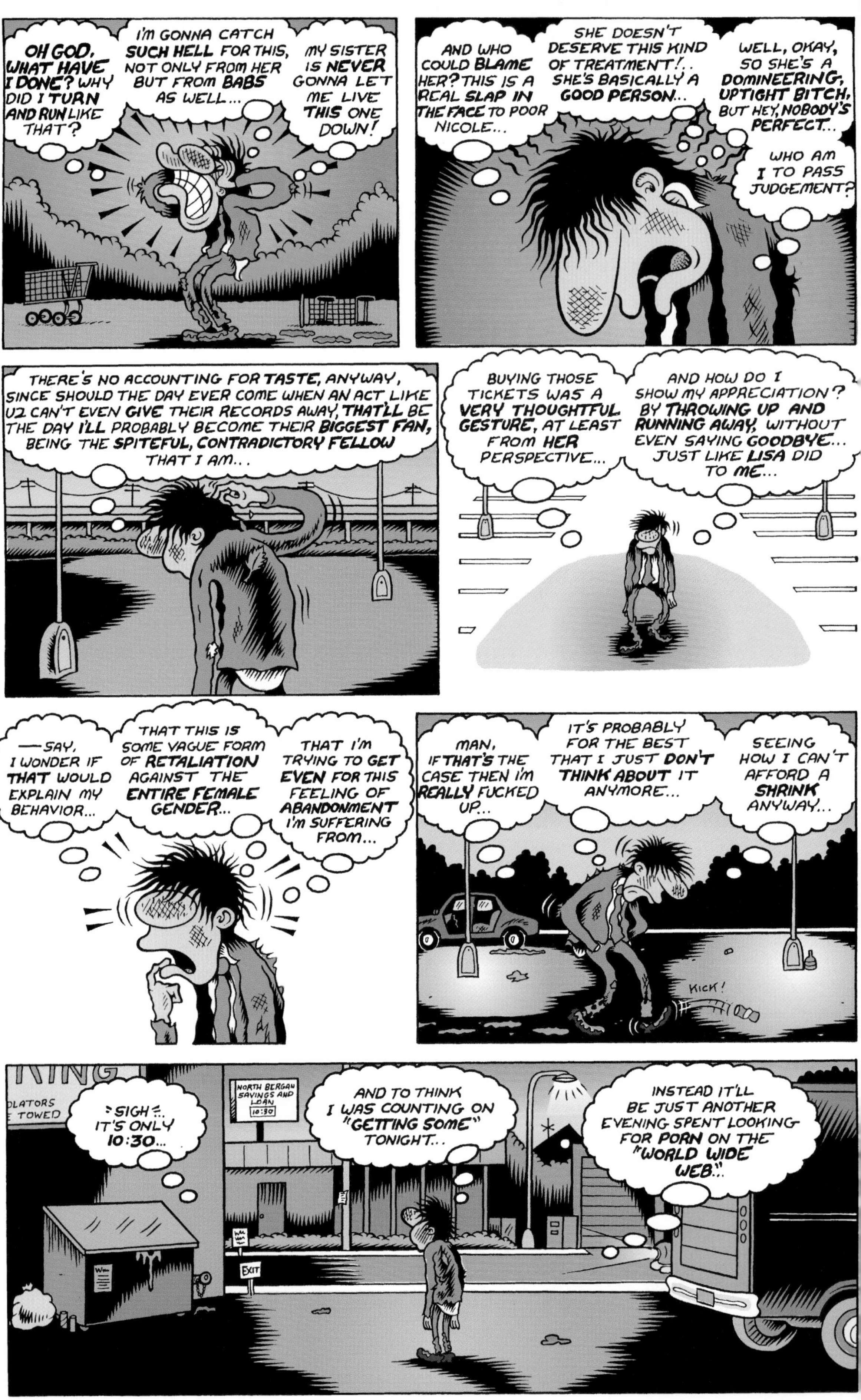

OH GOD, WHAT HAVE I DONE? WHY DID I TURN AND RUN LIKE THAT?
I'M GONNA CATCH SUCH HELL FOR THIS, NOT ONLY FROM HER BUT FROM BABS AS WELL...
MY SISTER IS NEVER GONNA LET ME LIVE THIS ONE DOWN!
AND WHO COULD BLAME HER? THIS IS A REAL SLAP IN THE FACE TO POOR NICOLE...
SHE DOESN'T DESERVE THIS KIND OF TREATMENT!.. SHE'S BASICALLY A GOOD PERSON...
WELL, OKAY, SO SHE'S A DOMINEERING, UPTIGHT BITCH, BUT HEY, NOBODY'S PERFECT...
WHO AM I TO PASS JUDGEMENT?
THERE'S NO ACCOUNTING FOR TASTE, ANYWAY, SINCE SHOULD THE DAY EVER COME WHEN AN ACT LIKE U2 CAN'T EVEN GIVE THEIR RECORDS AWAY, THAT'LL BE THE DAY I'LL PROBABLY BECOME THEIR BIGGEST FAN, BEING THE SPITEFUL, CONTRADICTORY FELLOW THAT I AM...
BUYING THOSE TICKETS WAS A VERY THOUGHTFUL GESTURE, AT LEAST FROM HER PERSPECTIVE...
AND HOW DO I SHOW MY APPRECIATION? BY THROWING UP AND RUNNING AWAY, WITHOUT EVEN SAYING GOODBYE... JUST LIKE LISA DID TO ME...
—SAY, I WONDER IF THAT WOULD EXPLAIN MY BEHAVIOR...
THAT THIS IS SOME VAGUE FORM OF RETALIATION AGAINST THE ENTIRE FEMALE GENDER...
THAT I'M TRYING TO GET EVEN FOR THIS FEELING OF ABANDONMENT I'M SUFFERING FROM...
MAN, IF THAT'S THE CASE THEN I'M REALLY FUCKED UP...
IT'S PROBABLY FOR THE BEST THAT I JUST DON'T THINK ABOUT IT ANYMORE...
SEEING HOW I CAN'T AFFORD A SHRINK ANYWAY...
KICK!
OLATORS
E TOWED
NORTH BERGAN SAVINGS AND LOAN 10:30
EXIT
=SIGH=.. IT'S ONLY 10:30...
AND TO THINK I WAS COUNTING ON "GETTING SOME" TONIGHT...
INSTEAD IT'LL BE JUST ANOTHER EVENING SPENT LOOKING FOR PORN ON THE "WORLD WIDE WEB."..

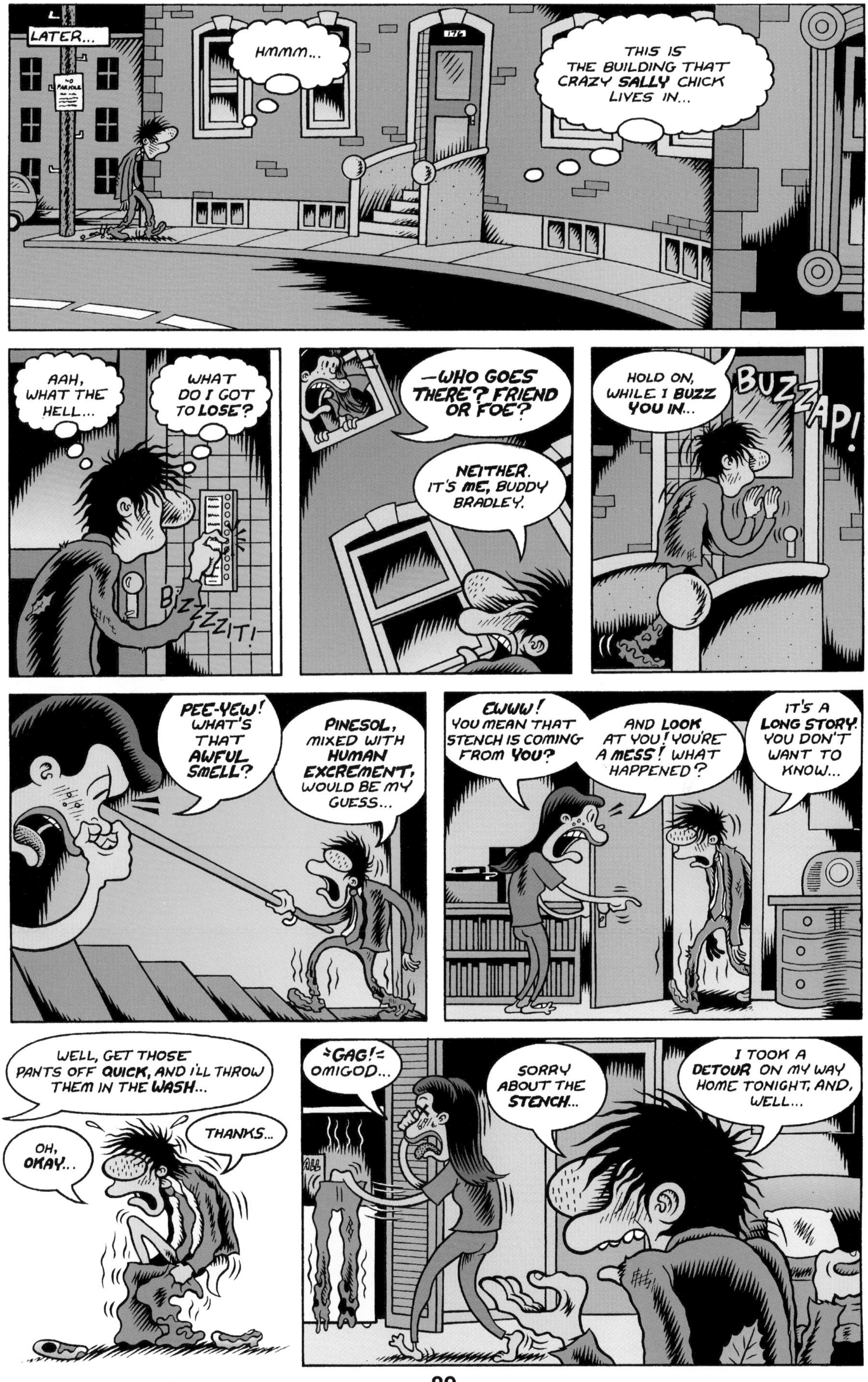
LATER...
HMMM...
THIS IS THE BUILDING THAT CRAZY SALLY CHICK LIVES IN...
AAH, WHAT THE HELL...
WHAT DO I GOT TO LOSE?
BZZZZIT!
—WHO GOES THERE? FRIEND OR FOE?
NEITHER. IT'S ME, BUDDY BRADLEY.
HOLD ON, WHILE I BUZZ YOU IN...
BUZZAP!
PEE-YEW! WHAT'S THAT AWFUL SMELL?
PINESOL, MIXED WITH HUMAN EXCREMENT, WOULD BE MY GUESS...
EWWW! YOU MEAN THAT STENCH IS COMING FROM YOU?
AND LOOK AT YOU! YOU'RE A MESS! WHAT HAPPENED?
IT'S A LONG STORY. YOU DON'T WANT TO KNOW...
WELL, GET THOSE PANTS OFF QUICK, AND I'LL THROW THEM IN THE WASH...
OH, OKAY...
THANKS...
GAG! OMIGOD...
SORRY ABOUT THE STENCH...
I TOOK A DETOUR ON MY WAY HOME TONIGHT, AND, WELL...

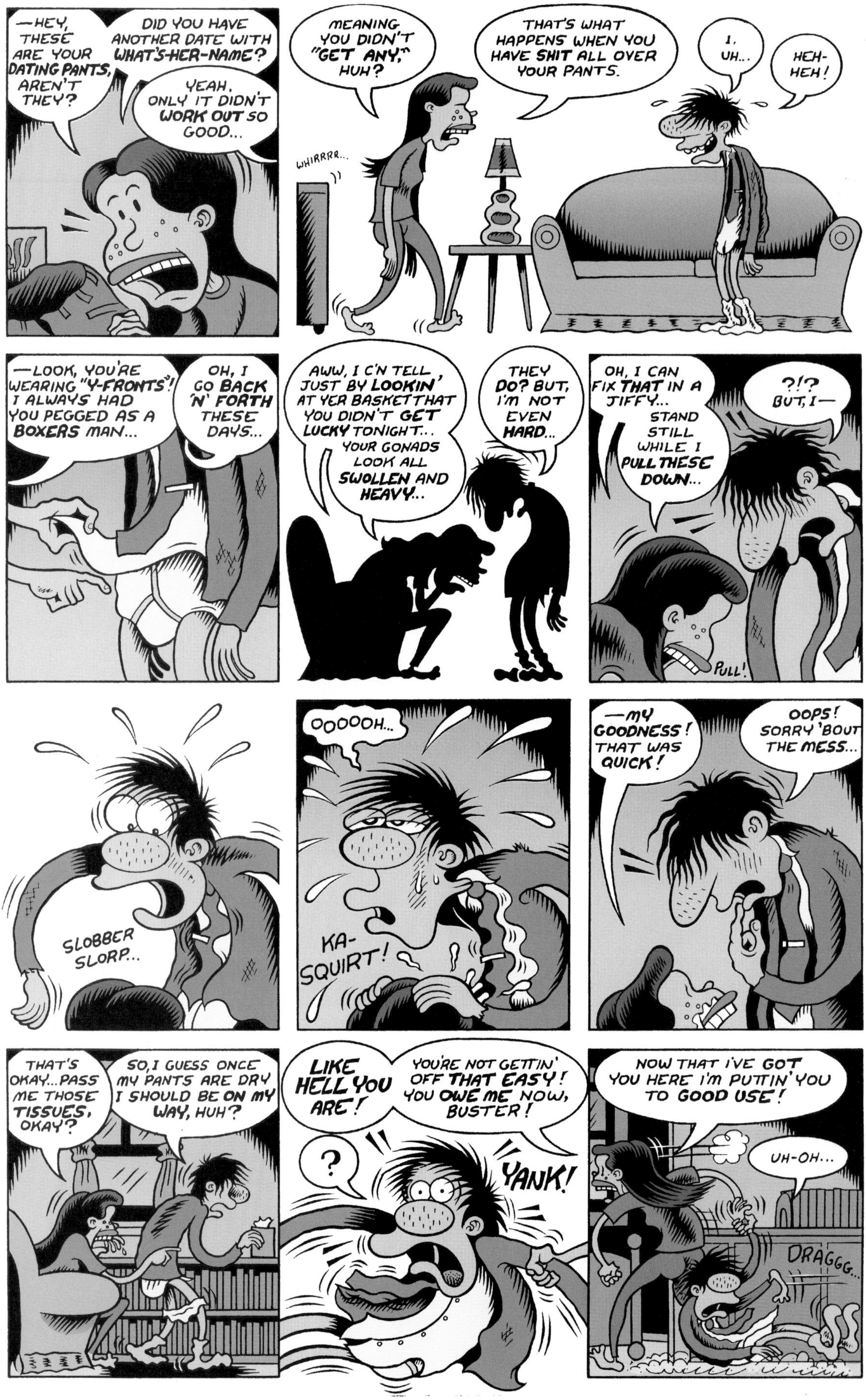
—HEY, THESE ARE YOUR DATING PANTS, AREN'T THEY?
DID YOU HAVE ANOTHER DATE WITH WHAT'S-HER-NAME?
YEAH, ONLY IT DIDN'T WORK OUT SO GOOD...
MEANING YOU DIDN'T "GET ANY," HUH?
WHIRRRR...
THAT'S WHAT HAPPENS WHEN YOU HAVE SHIT ALL OVER YOUR PANTS.
I, UH...
HEH-HEH!
—LOOK, YOU'RE WEARING "Y-FRONTS"! I ALWAYS HAD YOU PEGGED AS A BOXERS MAN...
OH, I GO BACK 'N' FORTH THESE DAYS...
AWW, I C'N TELL, JUST BY LOOKIN' AT YER BASKET THAT YOU DIDN'T GET LUCKY TONIGHT...
YOUR GONADS LOOK ALL SWOLLEN AND HEAVY...
THEY DO? BUT, I'M NOT EVEN HARD...
OH, I CAN FIX THAT IN A JIFFY...
STAND STILL WHILE I PULL THESE DOWN...
?!? BUT, I—
PULL!
SLOBBER SLORP...
OOOOOH...
KA-SQUIRT!
—MY GOODNESS! THAT WAS QUICK!
OOPS! SORRY 'BOUT THE MESS...
THAT'S OKAY...PASS ME THOSE TISSUES, OKAY?
SO, I GUESS ONCE MY PANTS ARE DRY I SHOULD BE ON MY WAY, HUH?
LIKE HELL YOU ARE!
YOU'RE NOT GETTIN' OFF THAT EASY! YOU OWE ME NOW, BUSTER!
?
YANK!
NOW THAT I'VE GOT YOU HERE I'M PUTTIN' YOU TO GOOD USE!
UH-OH...
DRAGGG...

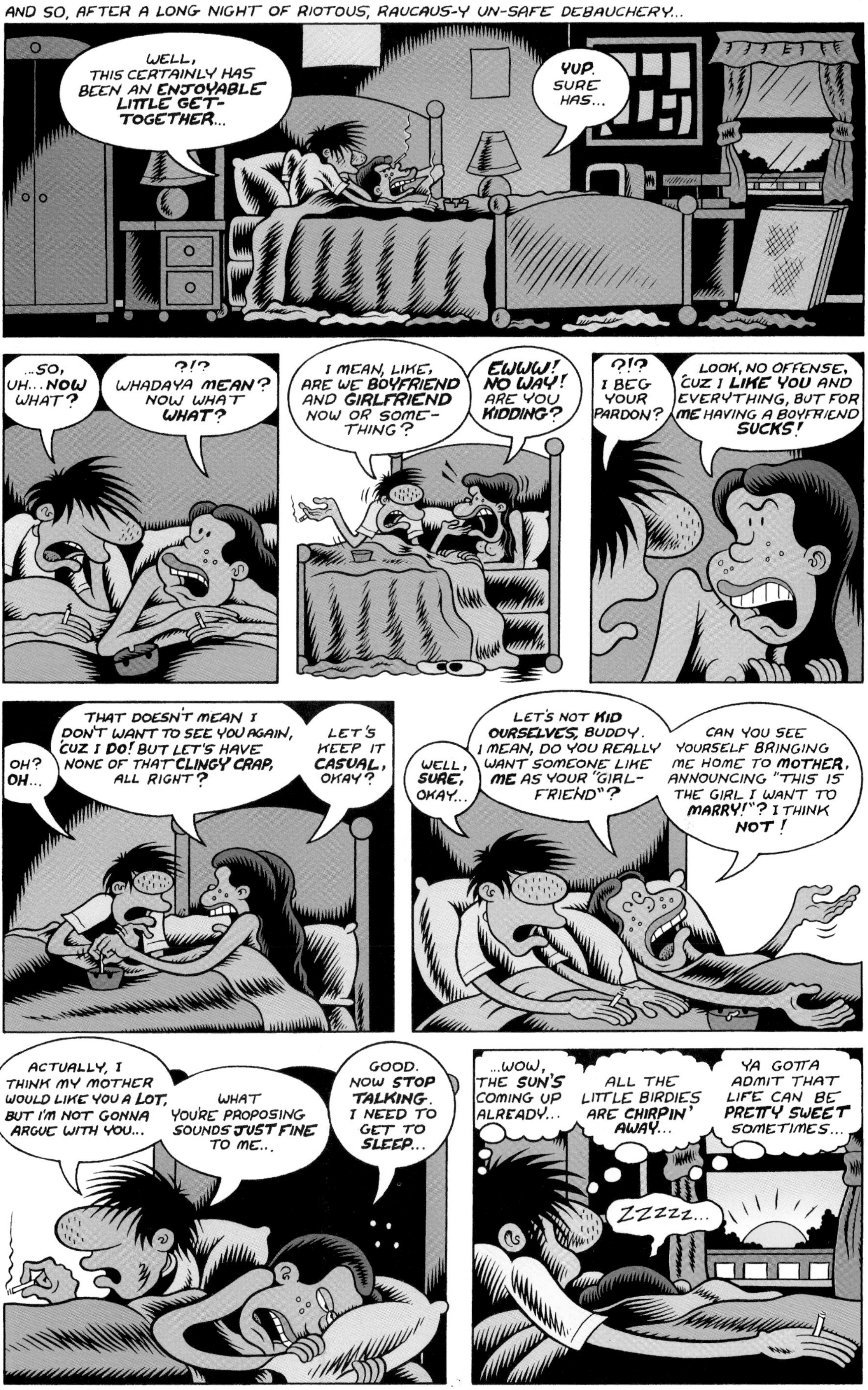

AND SO, AFTER A LONG NIGHT OF RIOTOUS, RAUCAUS-Y UN-SAFE DEBAUCHERY...
WELL, THIS CERTAINLY HAS BEEN AN ENJOYABLE LITTLE GET-TOGETHER...
YUP. SURE HAS...
...SO, UH... NOW WHAT?
?!? WHADAYA MEAN? NOW WHAT WHAT?
I MEAN, LIKE, ARE WE BOYFRIEND AND GIRLFRIEND NOW OR SOME-THING?
EWWW! NO WAY! ARE YOU KIDDING?
?!? I BEG YOUR PARDON?
LOOK, NO OFFENSE, 'CUZ I LIKE YOU AND EVERYTHING, BUT FOR ME HAVING A BOYFRIEND SUCKS!
OH? OH...
THAT DOESN'T MEAN I DON'T WANT TO SEE YOU AGAIN, 'CUZ I DO! BUT LET'S HAVE NONE OF THAT CLINGY CRAP, ALL RIGHT?
LET'S KEEP IT CASUAL, OKAY?
WELL, SURE, OKAY...
LET'S NOT KID OURSELVES, BUDDY. I MEAN, DO YOU REALLY WANT SOMEONE LIKE ME AS YOUR "GIRL-FRIEND"?
CAN YOU SEE YOURSELF BRINGING ME HOME TO MOTHER, ANNOUNCING "THIS IS THE GIRL I WANT TO MARRY!"? I THINK NOT!
ACTUALLY, I THINK MY MOTHER WOULD LIKE YOU A LOT, BUT I'M NOT GONNA ARGUE WITH YOU...
WHAT YOU'RE PROPOSING SOUNDS JUST FINE TO ME...
GOOD. NOW STOP TALKING. I NEED TO GET TO SLEEP...
...WOW, THE SUN'S COMING UP ALREADY...
ALL THE LITTLE BIRDIES ARE CHIRPIN' AWAY...
YA GOTTA ADMIT THAT LIFE CAN BE PRETTY SWEET SOMETIMES...
ZZZZZ...

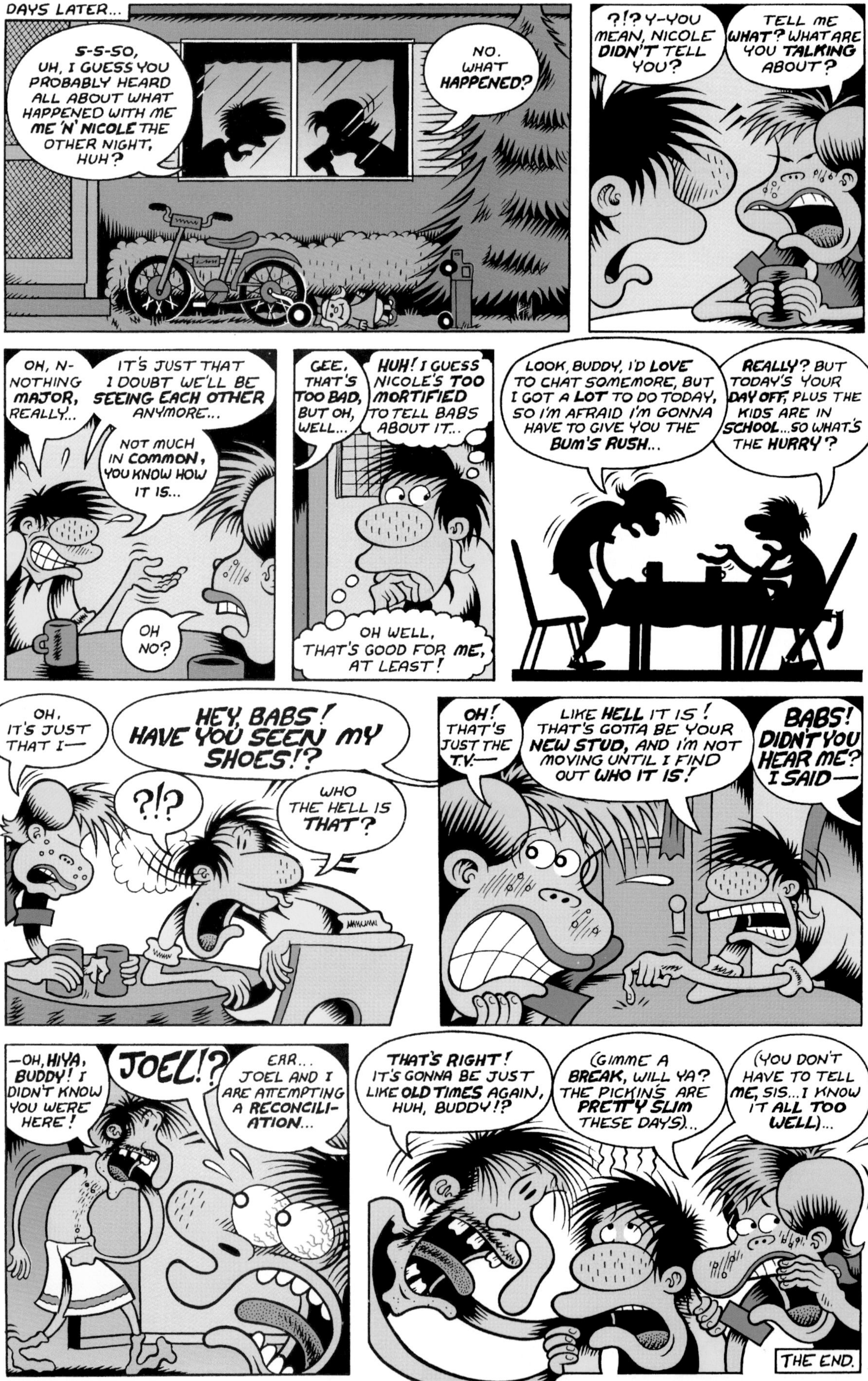
DAYS LATER...
S-S-SO, UH, I GUESS YOU PROBABLY HEARD ALL ABOUT WHAT HAPPENED WITH ME ME 'N' NICOLE THE OTHER NIGHT, HUH?
NO. WHAT HAPPENED?
?!? Y-YOU MEAN, NICOLE DIDN'T TELL YOU?
TELL ME WHAT? WHAT ARE YOU TALKING ABOUT?
OH, N-NOTHING MAJOR, REALLY...
IT'S JUST THAT I DOUBT WE'LL BE SEEING EACH OTHER ANYMORE...
NOT MUCH IN COMMON, YOU KNOW HOW IT IS...
OH NO?
GEE, THAT'S TOO BAD, BUT OH, WELL...
HUH! I GUESS NICOLE'S TOO MORTIFIED TO TELL BABS ABOUT IT...
OH WELL, THAT'S GOOD FOR ME, AT LEAST!
LOOK, BUDDY, I'D LOVE TO CHAT SOMEMORE, BUT I GOT A LOT TO DO TODAY, SO I'M AFRAID I'M GONNA HAVE TO GIVE YOU THE BUM'S RUSH...
REALLY? BUT TODAY'S YOUR DAY OFF, PLUS THE KIDS ARE IN SCHOOL...SO WHAT'S THE HURRY?
OH, IT'S JUST THAT I—
HEY, BABS! HAVE YOU SEEN MY SHOES!?
?!?
WHO THE HELL IS THAT?
OH! THAT'S JUST THE T.V.—
LIKE HELL IT IS! THAT'S GOTTA BE YOUR NEW STUD, AND I'M NOT MOVING UNTIL I FIND OUT WHO IT IS!
BABS! DIDN'T YOU HEAR ME? I SAID—
—OH, HIYA, BUDDY! I DIDN'T KNOW YOU WERE HERE!
JOEL!?
ERR... JOEL AND I ARE ATTEMPTING A RECONCILI-ATION...
THAT'S RIGHT! IT'S GONNA BE JUST LIKE OLD TIMES AGAIN, HUH, BUDDY!?
(GIMME A BREAK, WILL YA? THE PICKIN'S ARE PRETTY SLIM THESE DAYS)...
(YOU DON'T HAVE TO TELL ME, SIS...I KNOW IT ALL TOO WELL)...
THE END.

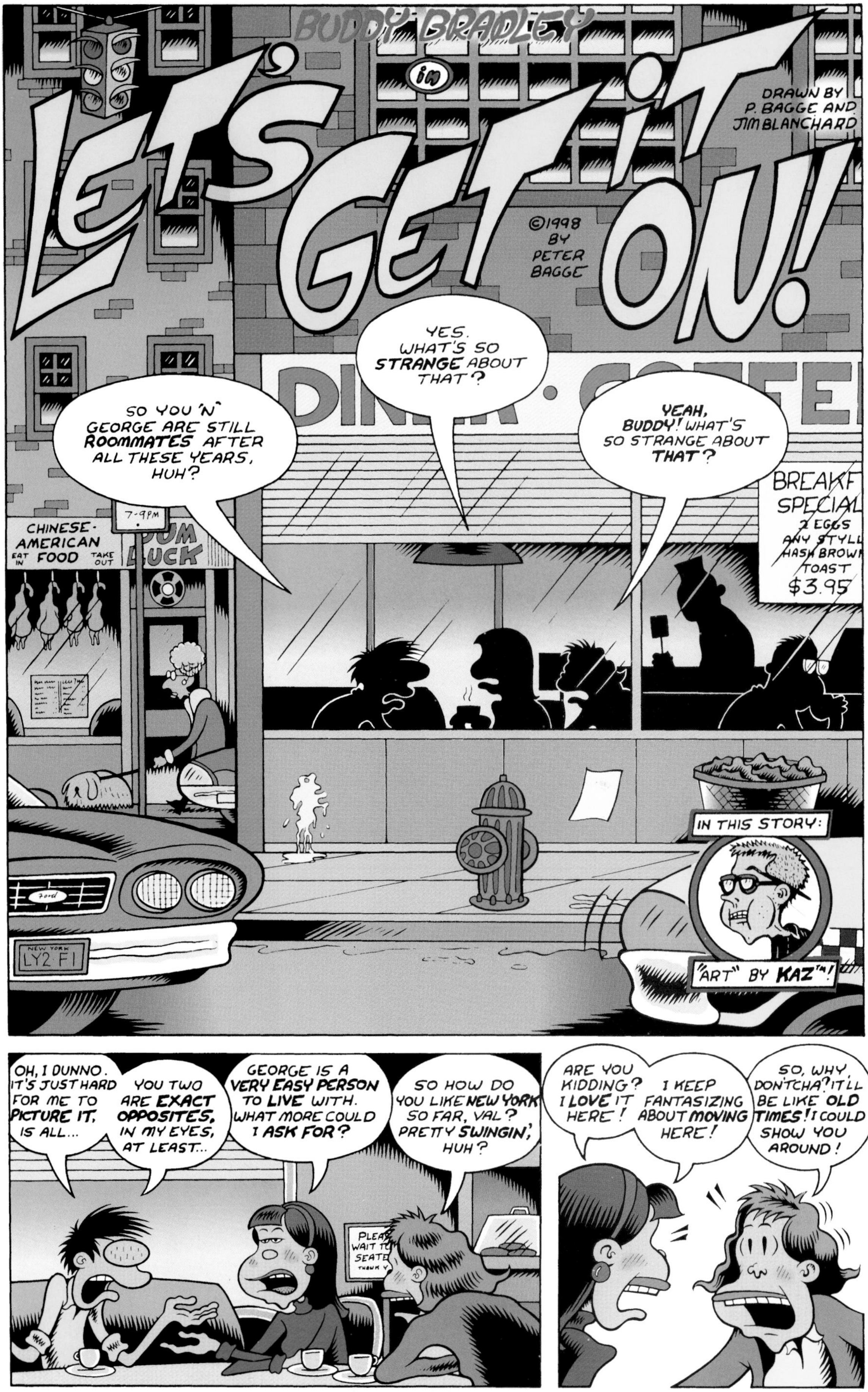

BUDDY BRADLEY
in
LET'S GET IT ON!
DRAWN BY P. BAGGE AND JIM BLANCHARD
©1998 BY PETER BAGGE
SO YOU 'N' GEORGE ARE STILL ROOMMATES AFTER ALL THESE YEARS, HUH?
YES. WHAT'S SO STRANGE ABOUT THAT?
YEAH, BUDDY! WHAT'S SO STRANGE ABOUT THAT?
DINER · COFFEE
BREAKF SPECIAL 2 EGGS ANY STYLE HASH BROWN TOAST $3.95
CHINESE-AMERICAN FOOD EAT IN TAKE OUT
7-9PM
NEW YORK LY2·F1
IN THIS STORY:
"ART" BY KAZ™!
OH, I DUNNO. IT'S JUST HARD FOR ME TO PICTURE IT, IS ALL...
YOU TWO ARE EXACT OPPOSITES, IN MY EYES, AT LEAST...
GEORGE IS A VERY EASY PERSON TO LIVE WITH. WHAT MORE COULD I ASK FOR?
SO HOW DO YOU LIKE NEW YORK SO FAR, VAL? PRETTY SWINGIN', HUH?
ARE YOU KIDDING? I LOVE IT HERE!
I KEEP FANTASIZING ABOUT MOVING HERE!
SO, WHY DON'TCHA? IT'LL BE LIKE OLD TIMES! I COULD SHOW YOU AROUND!

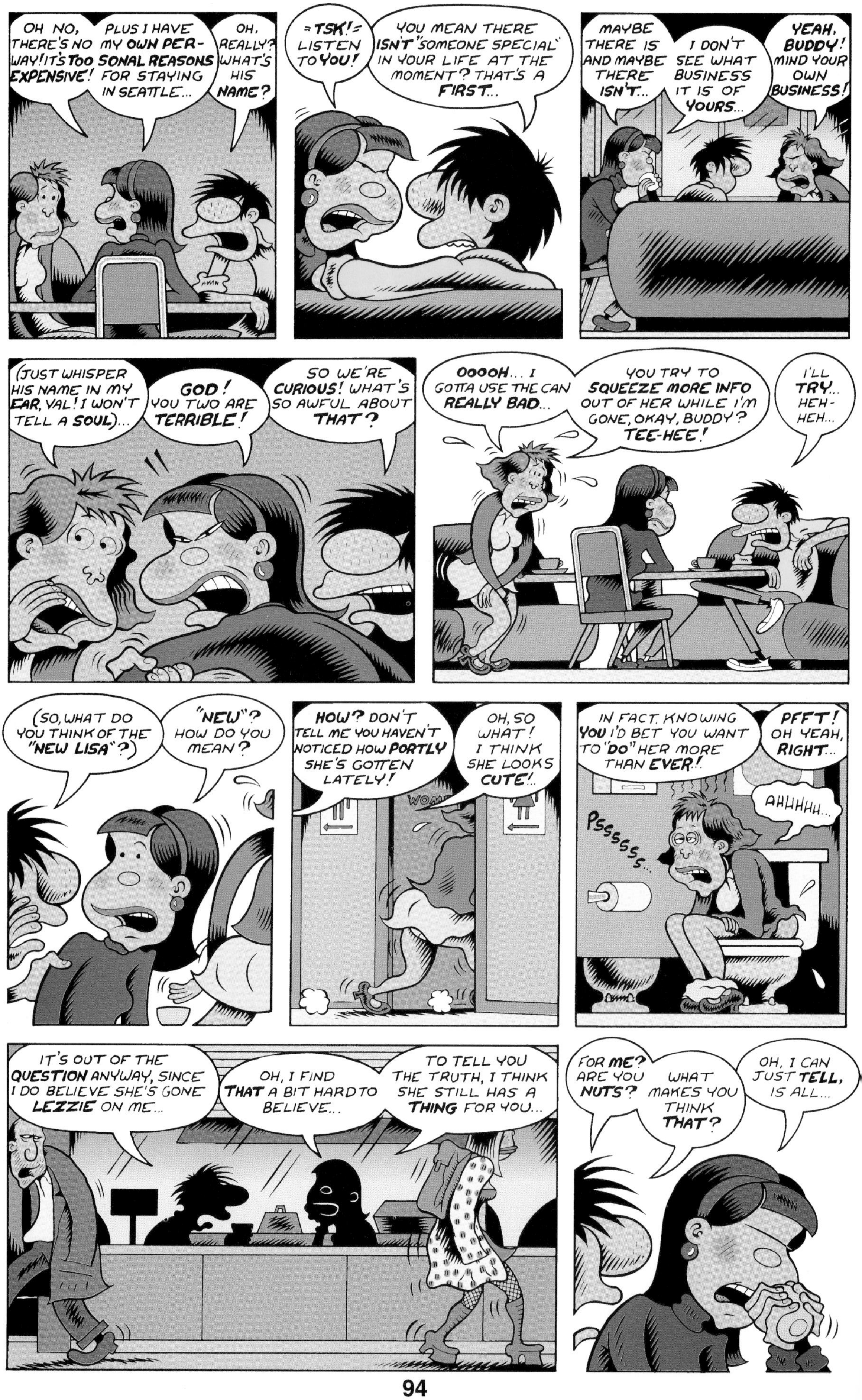

OH NO, THERE'S NO WAY! IT'S TOO EXPENSIVE!
PLUS I HAVE MY OWN PERSONAL REASONS FOR STAYING IN SEATTLE...
OH, REALLY? WHAT'S HIS NAME?
=TSK!= LISTEN TO YOU!
YOU MEAN THERE ISN'T "SOMEONE SPECIAL" IN YOUR LIFE AT THE MOMENT? THAT'S A FIRST...
MAYBE THERE IS AND MAYBE THERE ISN'T...
I DON'T SEE WHAT BUSINESS IT IS OF YOURS...
YEAH, BUDDY! MIND YOUR OWN BUSINESS!
(JUST WHISPER HIS NAME IN MY EAR, VAL! I WON'T TELL A SOUL)...
GOD! YOU TWO ARE TERRIBLE!
SO WE'RE CURIOUS! WHAT'S SO AWFUL ABOUT THAT?
OOOOH... I GOTTA USE THE CAN REALLY BAD...
YOU TRY TO SQUEEZE MORE INFO OUT OF HER WHILE I'M GONE, OKAY, BUDDY? TEE-HEE!
I'LL TRY... HEH-HEH...
(SO, WHAT DO YOU THINK OF THE "NEW LISA"?)
"NEW"? HOW DO YOU MEAN?
HOW? DON'T TELL ME YOU HAVEN'T NOTICED HOW PORTLY SHE'S GOTTEN LATELY!
OH, SO WHAT! I THINK SHE LOOKS CUTE!..
IN FACT, KNOWING YOU I'D BET YOU WANT TO "DO" HER MORE THAN EVER!.
PFFT! OH YEAH, RIGHT...
AHHHHH...
PSSSSSS...
IT'S OUT OF THE QUESTION ANYWAY, SINCE I DO BELIEVE SHE'S GONE LEZZIE ON ME...
OH, I FIND THAT A BIT HARD TO BELIEVE...
TO TELL YOU THE TRUTH, I THINK SHE STILL HAS A THING FOR YOU...
FOR ME? ARE YOU NUTS?
WHAT MAKES YOU THINK THAT?
OH, I CAN JUST TELL, IS ALL...

...HOW ABOUT *YOU*? DO YOU STILL HAVE A *"THING"* FOR ME, TOO? HEH-HEH...

OH YEAH, RIGHT! DREAM ON, PAL.

Y'KNOW, YOU 'N' ME SHOULD HAVE A *PRIVATE* GET-TOGETHER BEFORE YOU GO BACK TO SEATTLE...

OH WE *SHOULD*, SHOULD WE?

RUB, RUB...

SURE! WHY NOT? AFTER ALL, WE'RE BOTH *"FREE AGENTS"* AT THE MOMENT...

WHO SAYS I'M A *"FREE AGENT"*...

—AND WILL YOU *PLEASE* KEEP YOUR *HANDS* OFF OF MY *KNEE*!?

OW!

SLAP!

JEEZ! SOR-RY!

I CAN'T *HELP* IT, THOUGH! IT'S A *PAVLOVIAN* RESPONSE!

"PAVLOVIAN" MY ASS! WHAT ARE YOU, A *DOG*?

IT'S *TRUE*, THOUGH! I—

OH *FORGET IT!* SORRY I ASKED...

LOOK, I'M SORRY IF I DASHED ANY *HOPES* YOU MAY HAVE BEEN HARBORING, BUDDY...

BUT I DON'T WANT TO GET INTO SOME *MESSY SITUATION* WHERE WE—

(—OOPS! HERE COMES LISA)...

(OOPS!)

I'M *BACK!*

DID YOU *FIND OUT* ANYTHING, BUDDY?

MEN

ONLY THAT SHE'S DATING THE *POPE!*

OOOH! JUICY!

HA-HA.

SPEAKING OF WHICH, I HAVE AN *"AUDIENCE"* WITH THE POPE IN 15 MINUTES...

I REALLY SHOULD BE GOING SOON...

AWW! AL-READY?

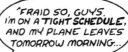

'FRAID SO, GUYS. I'M ON A *TIGHT SCHEDULE*, AND MY PLANE LEAVES TOMORROW MORNING...

WELL, GEE WHIZ! THAT SURE *SUCKS!*

NEXT TIME GIVE US MORE OF AN *ADVANCE WARNING* SO WE CAN MAKE PLANS TO *PAINT THE TOWN RED!*

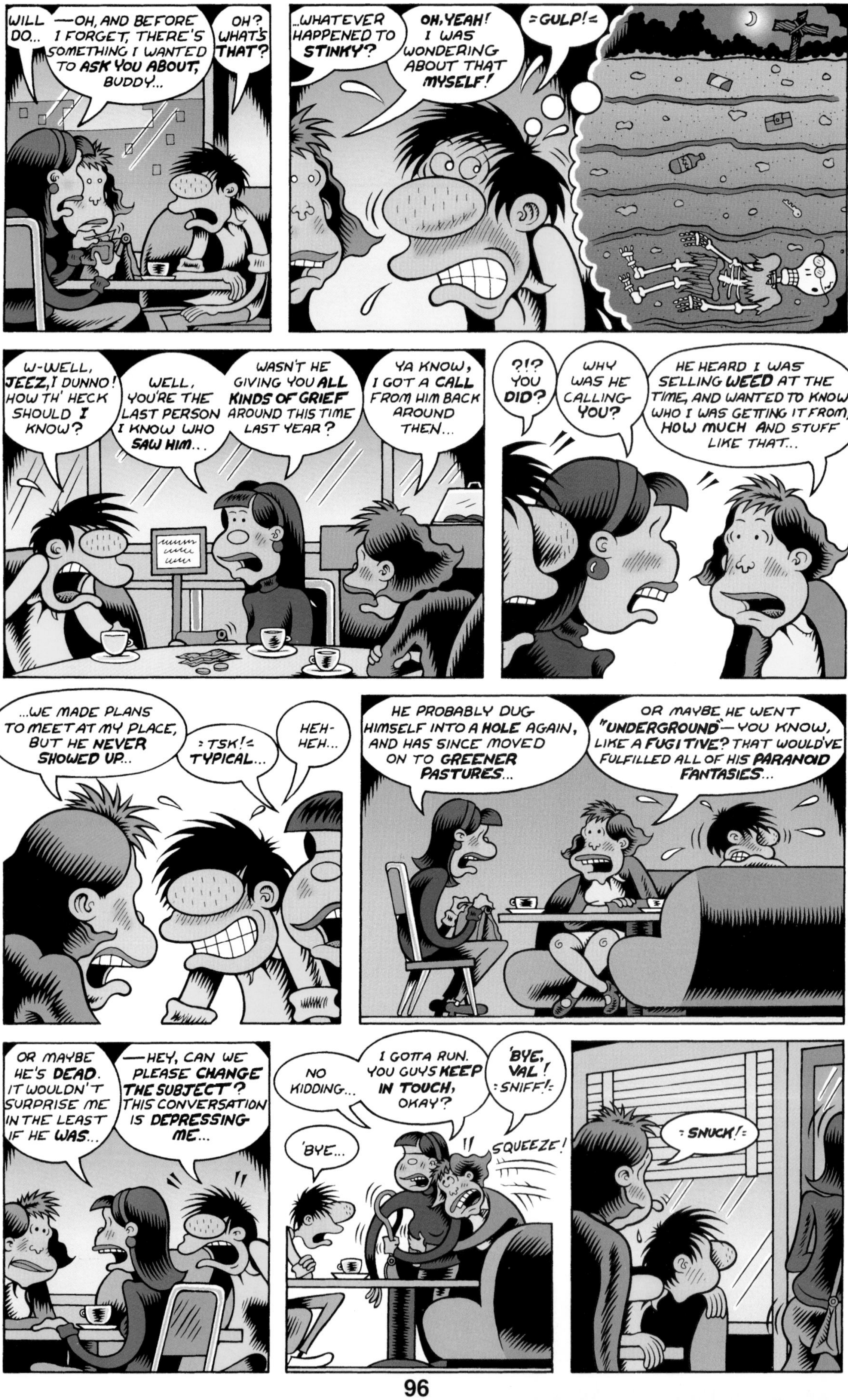
WILL DO...
—OH, AND BEFORE I FORGET, THERE'S SOMETHING I WANTED TO ASK YOU ABOUT, BUDDY...
OH? WHAT'S THAT?
...WHATEVER HAPPENED TO STINKY?
OH, YEAH! I WAS WONDERING ABOUT THAT MYSELF!
=GULP!=
W-WELL, JEEZ, I DUNNO! HOW TH' HECK SHOULD I KNOW?
WELL, YOU'RE THE LAST PERSON I KNOW WHO SAW HIM...
WASN'T HE GIVING YOU ALL KINDS OF GRIEF AROUND THIS TIME LAST YEAR?
YA KNOW, I GOT A CALL FROM HIM BACK AROUND THEN...
?!? YOU DID?
WHY WAS HE CALLING YOU?
HE HEARD I WAS SELLING WEED AT THE TIME, AND WANTED TO KNOW WHO I WAS GETTING IT FROM, HOW MUCH AND STUFF LIKE THAT...
...WE MADE PLANS TO MEET AT MY PLACE, BUT HE NEVER SHOWED UP...
=TSK!= TYPICAL...
HEH-HEH...
HE PROBABLY DUG HIMSELF INTO A HOLE AGAIN, AND HAS SINCE MOVED ON TO GREENER PASTURES...
OR MAYBE HE WENT "UNDERGROUND"—YOU KNOW, LIKE A FUGITIVE? THAT WOULD'VE FULFILLED ALL OF HIS PARANOID FANTASIES...
OR MAYBE HE'S DEAD. IT WOULDN'T SURPRISE ME IN THE LEAST IF HE WAS...
—HEY, CAN WE PLEASE CHANGE THE SUBJECT? THIS CONVERSATION IS DEPRESSING ME...
NO KIDDING...
I GOTTA RUN. YOU GUYS KEEP IN TOUCH, OKAY?
'BYE, VAL! =SNIFF!=
'BYE...
SQUEEZE!
=SNUCK!=

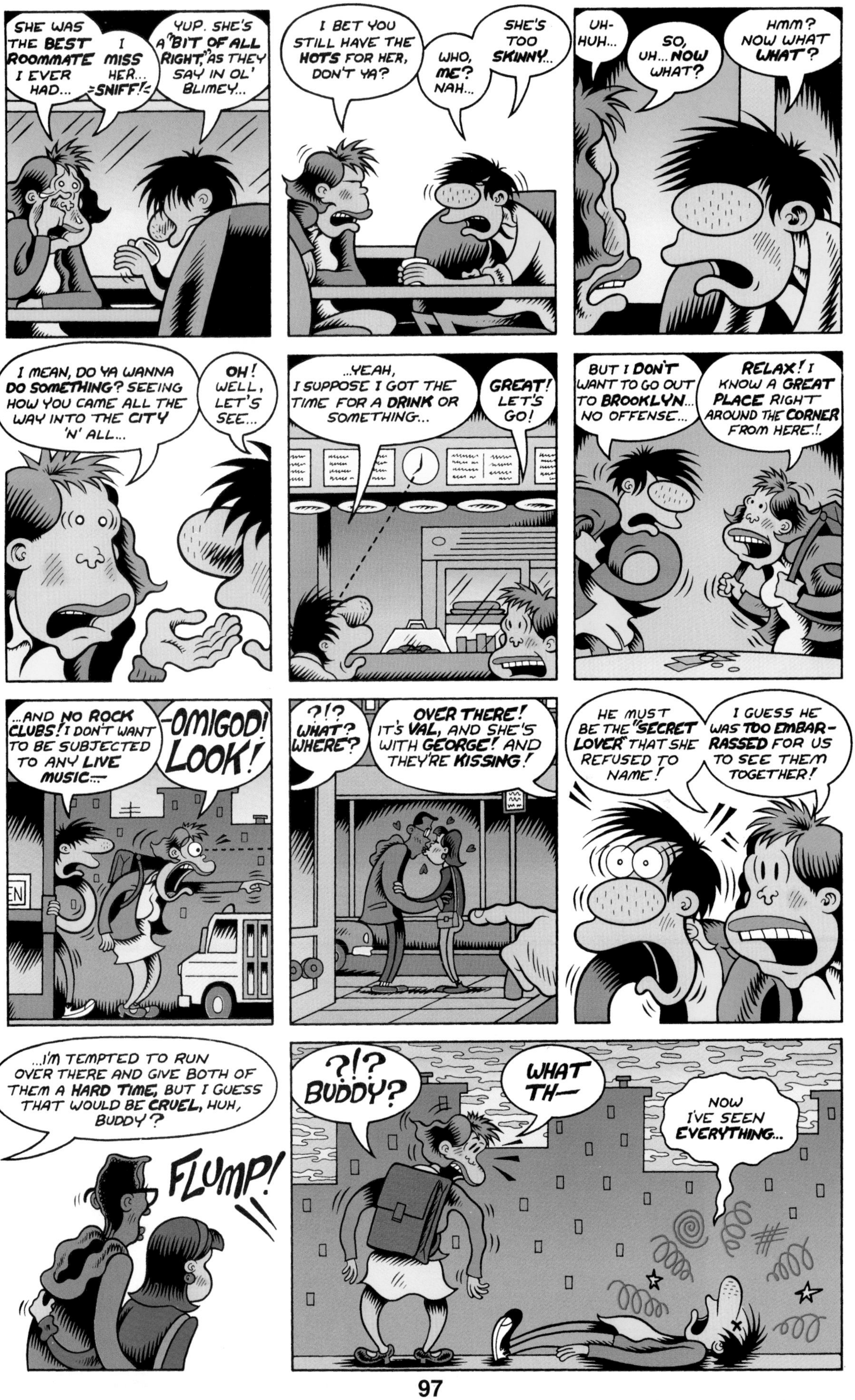

SHE WAS THE BEST ROOMMATE I EVER HAD...
I MISS HER... =SNIFF!=
YUP. SHE'S A "BIT OF ALL RIGHT," AS THEY SAY IN OL' BLIMEY...
I BET YOU STILL HAVE THE HOTS FOR HER, DON'T YA?
WHO, ME? NAH...
SHE'S TOO SKINNY...
UH-HUH...
SO, UH... NOW WHAT?
HMM? NOW WHAT WHAT?
I MEAN, DO YA WANNA DO SOMETHING? SEEING HOW YOU CAME ALL THE WAY INTO THE CITY 'N' ALL...
OH! WELL, LET'S SEE...
...YEAH, I SUPPOSE I GOT THE TIME FOR A DRINK OR SOMETHING...
GREAT! LET'S GO!
BUT I DON'T WANT TO GO OUT TO BROOKLYN... NO OFFENSE...
RELAX! I KNOW A GREAT PLACE RIGHT AROUND THE CORNER FROM HERE!.
...AND NO ROCK CLUBS! I DON'T WANT TO BE SUBJECTED TO ANY LIVE MUSIC...—
-OMIGOD! LOOK!
?!? WHAT? WHERE?
OVER THERE! IT'S VAL, AND SHE'S WITH GEORGE! AND THEY'RE KISSING!
HE MUST BE THE "SECRET LOVER" THAT SHE REFUSED TO NAME!
I GUESS HE WAS TOO EMBARRASSED FOR US TO SEE THEM TOGETHER!
...I'M TEMPTED TO RUN OVER THERE AND GIVE BOTH OF THEM A HARD TIME, BUT I GUESS THAT WOULD BE CRUEL, HUH, BUDDY?
FLUMP!
?!? BUDDY?
WHAT TH—
NOW I'VE SEEN EVERYTHING...

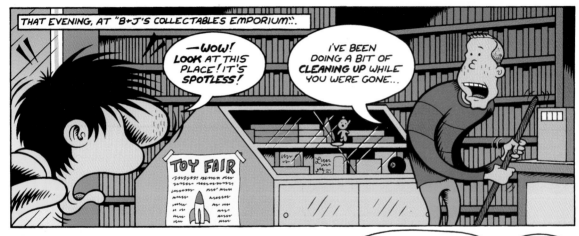

—WOW! **LOOK** AT THIS PLACE! IT'S **SPOTLESS!**

I'VE BEEN DOING A BIT OF **CLEANING UP** WHILE YOU WERE GONE...

TOY FAIR

BOY, I'LL SAY!

THIS PLACE HAS **NEVER** LOOKED THIS GOOD...

I ALSO ALPHABETIZED **EVERYTHING:** THE BOOKS, THE RECORDS...

...IT MAKES THINGS A LOT EASIER FOR **ME**, SINCE I DON'T HAVE THE STOCK **MEMORIZED** LIKE YOU DO...

HMMM... SO I SEE...

...YOU ALPHABETIZED THESE L.P.'S BY **TITLE**, THOUGH. YOU'RE SUPPOSED TO FILE THEM BY THE RECORDING ARTIST'S **NAME**...

REALLY?

SOME GIRLS
THE ROLLING STONES
TODD RUN...
THE BEATLES SOMETHING NEW
SOMETIME IN NEW YORK CITY
WALT DISNEY'S SONGS OF THE SOUTH!
SOUL FINGE...
SMILEY
SWING!
SWOO...

BUT, YOU TOLD ME TO RACK ALL THE **COMICS** AND **MAGAZINES** BY THEIR TITLES...

I KNOW, BUT BOOKS AND RECORDS ARE **DIFFERENT.**

WHY?

WHY? UH...GEE, I **DUNNO** WHY!

BUT DON'T SWEAT IT. AT LEAST THEY'RE IN **SOME** KIND OF ORDER NOW...

I'LL FIX 'EM **RIGHT NOW**, IF YOU WANT...

NO! LEAVE 'EM! THEY'RE **FINE! REALLY!**

AND WILL YOU **PLEASE** STOP **WORKING** SO HARD? YOU'RE MAKING ME NERVOUS!

WELL, JEEZ! I'M JUST TRYING TO DO A **GOOD** JOB, IS ALL!

I DON'T WANT ANYONE TO THINK YOU HIRED ME JUST BECAUSE **MOM MADE** YOU...

YOU'RE WORKING OUT **FINE**, BELIEVE **ME!** SO YOU CAN STOP TRYING TO **IMPRESS ME** NOW...

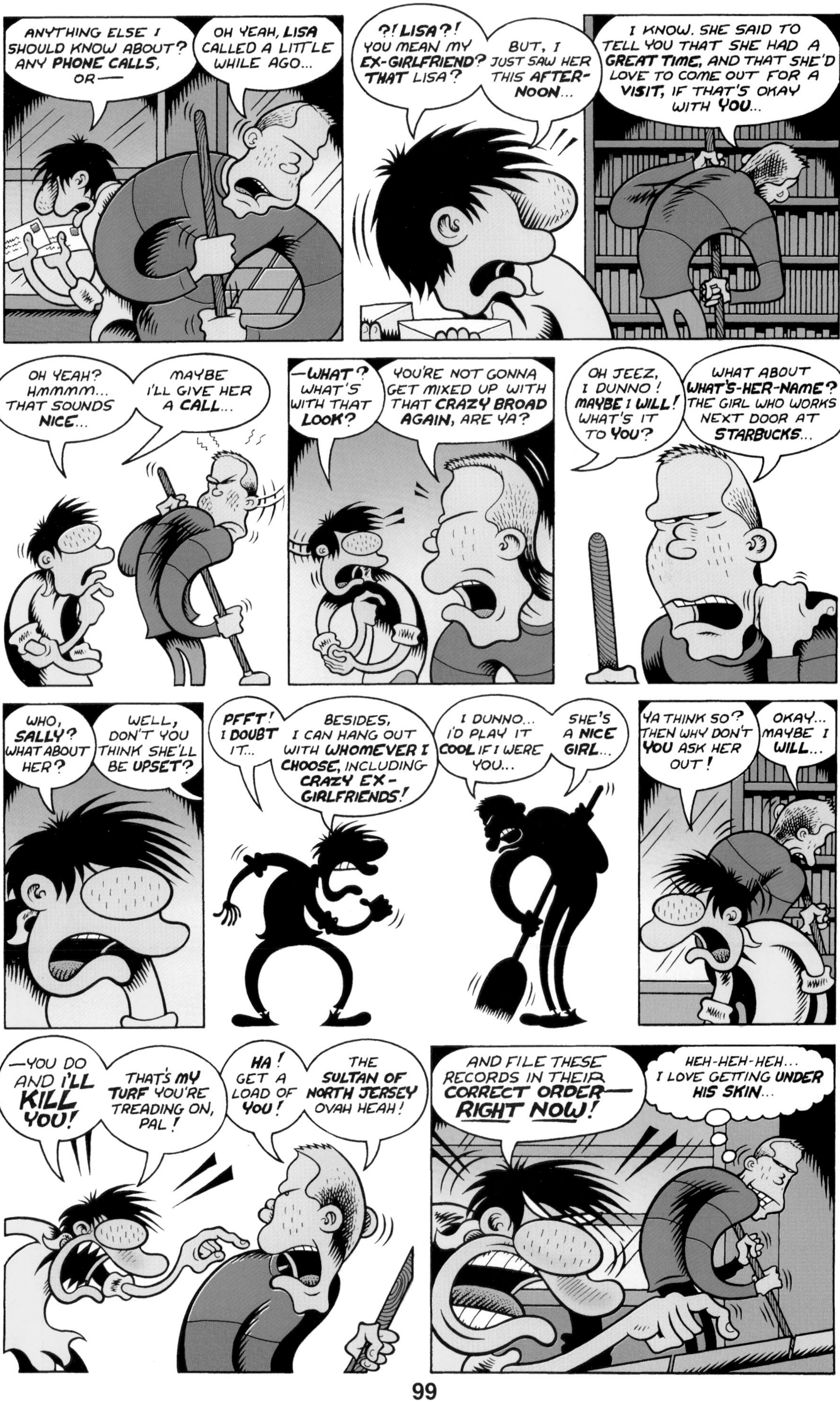
ANYTHING ELSE I SHOULD KNOW ABOUT? ANY PHONE CALLS, OR—
OH YEAH, LISA CALLED A LITTLE WHILE AGO...
?! LISA?! YOU MEAN MY EX-GIRLFRIEND? THAT LISA?
BUT, I JUST SAW HER THIS AFTERNOON...
I KNOW. SHE SAID TO TELL YOU THAT SHE HAD A GREAT TIME, AND THAT SHE'D LOVE TO COME OUT FOR A VISIT, IF THAT'S OKAY WITH YOU...
OH YEAH? HMMMM... THAT SOUNDS NICE...
MAYBE I'LL GIVE HER A CALL...
—WHAT? WHAT'S WITH THAT LOOK?
YOU'RE NOT GONNA GET MIXED UP WITH THAT CRAZY BROAD AGAIN, ARE YA?
OH JEEZ, I DUNNO! MAYBE I WILL! WHAT'S IT TO YOU?
WHAT ABOUT WHAT'S-HER-NAME? THE GIRL WHO WORKS NEXT DOOR AT STARBUCKS...
WHO, SALLY? WHAT ABOUT HER?
WELL, DON'T YOU THINK SHE'LL BE UPSET?
PFFT! I DOUBT IT...
BESIDES, I CAN HANG OUT WITH WHOMEVER I CHOOSE, INCLUDING CRAZY EX-GIRLFRIENDS!
I DUNNO... I'D PLAY IT COOL IF I WERE YOU...
SHE'S A NICE GIRL...
YA THINK SO? THEN WHY DON'T YOU ASK HER OUT!
OKAY... MAYBE I WILL...
—YOU DO AND I'LL KILL YOU!
THAT'S MY TURF YOU'RE TREADING ON, PAL!
HA! GET A LOAD OF YOU!
THE SULTAN OF NORTH JERSEY OVAH HEAH!
AND FILE THESE RECORDS IN THEIR CORRECT ORDER— RIGHT NOW!
HEH-HEH-HEH... I LOVE GETTING UNDER HIS SKIN...

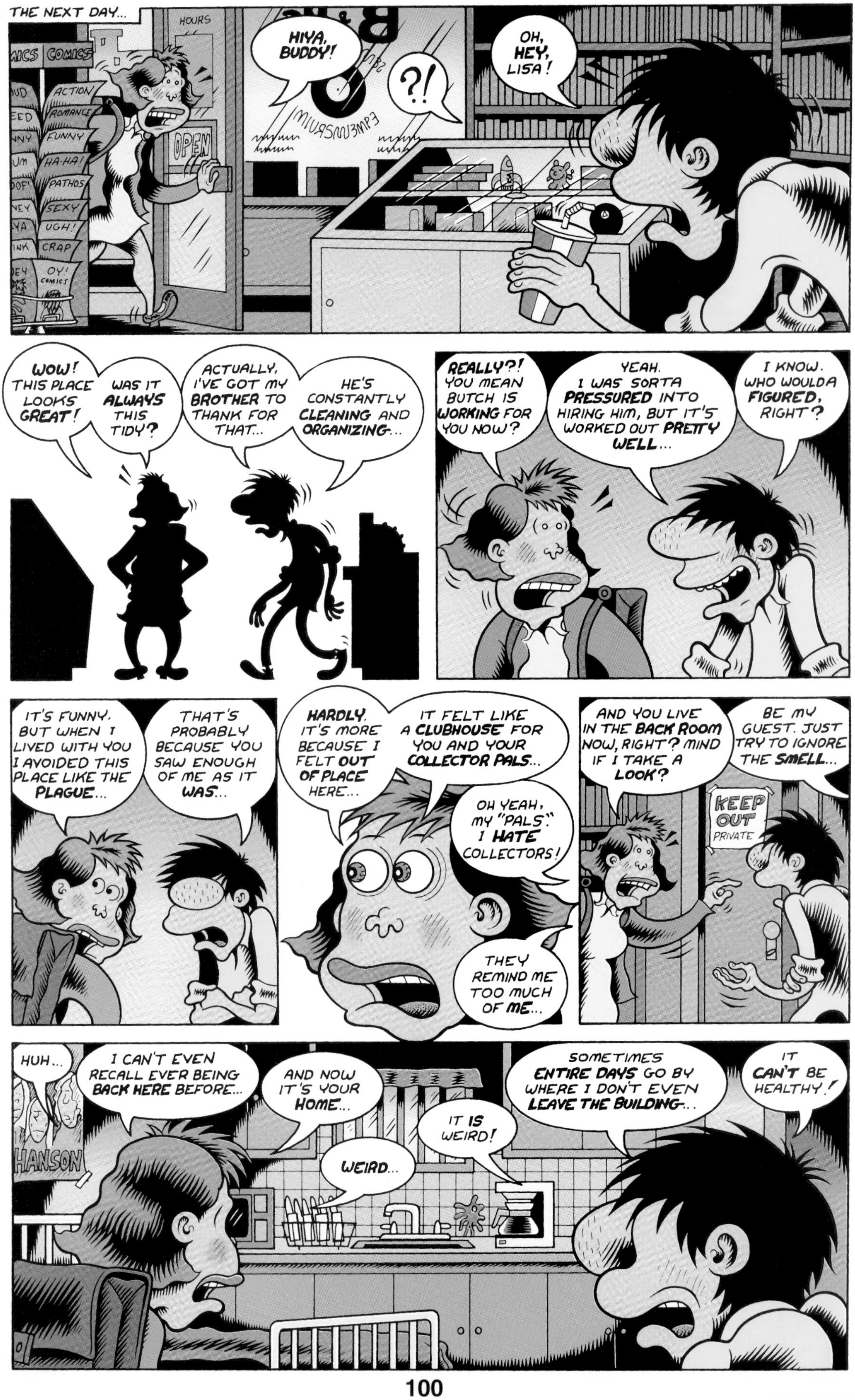
THE NEXT DAY...
HIYA, BUDDY!
?!
OH, HEY, LISA!
WOW! THIS PLACE LOOKS GREAT!
WAS IT ALWAYS THIS TIDY?
ACTUALLY, I'VE GOT MY BROTHER TO THANK FOR THAT...
HE'S CONSTANTLY CLEANING AND ORGANIZING...
REALLY?! YOU MEAN BUTCH IS WORKING FOR YOU NOW?
YEAH. I WAS SORTA PRESSURED INTO HIRING HIM, BUT IT'S WORKED OUT PRETTY WELL...
I KNOW. WHO WOULDA FIGURED, RIGHT?
IT'S FUNNY, BUT WHEN I LIVED WITH YOU I AVOIDED THIS PLACE LIKE THE PLAGUE...
THAT'S PROBABLY BECAUSE YOU SAW ENOUGH OF ME AS IT WAS...
HARDLY. IT'S MORE BECAUSE I FELT OUT OF PLACE HERE...
IT FELT LIKE A CLUBHOUSE FOR YOU AND YOUR COLLECTOR PALS...
OH YEAH, MY "PALS." I HATE COLLECTORS!
THEY REMIND ME TOO MUCH OF ME...
AND YOU LIVE IN THE BACK ROOM NOW, RIGHT? MIND IF I TAKE A LOOK?
BE MY GUEST. JUST TRY TO IGNORE THE SMELL...
KEEP OUT PRIVATE
HUH...
I CAN'T EVEN RECALL EVER BEING BACK HERE BEFORE...
AND NOW IT'S YOUR HOME...
WEIRD...
IT IS WEIRD!
SOMETIMES ENTIRE DAYS GO BY WHERE I DON'T EVEN LEAVE THE BUILDING...
IT CAN'T BE HEALTHY!
HANSON

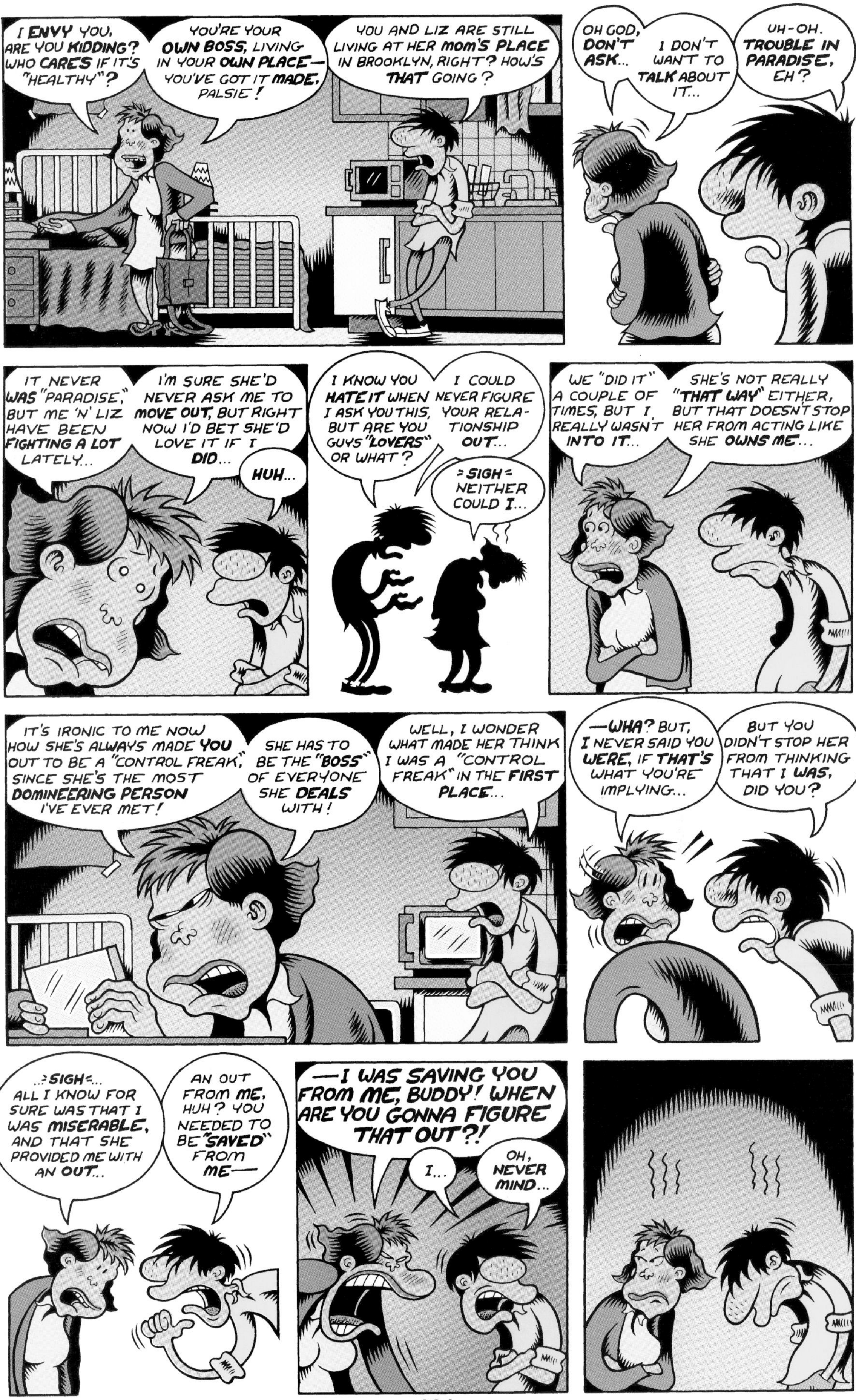
I ENVY YOU, ARE YOU KIDDING? WHO CARES IF IT'S "HEALTHY"?
YOU'RE YOUR OWN BOSS, LIVING IN YOUR OWN PLACE— YOU'VE GOT IT MADE, PALSIE!
YOU AND LIZ ARE STILL LIVING AT HER MOM'S PLACE IN BROOKLYN, RIGHT? HOW'S THAT GOING?
OH GOD, DON'T ASK...
I DON'T WANT TO TALK ABOUT IT...
UH-OH. TROUBLE IN PARADISE, EH?
IT NEVER WAS "PARADISE," BUT ME 'N' LIZ HAVE BEEN FIGHTING A LOT LATELY...
I'M SURE SHE'D NEVER ASK ME TO MOVE OUT, BUT RIGHT NOW I'D BET SHE'D LOVE IT IF I DID...
HUH...
I KNOW YOU HATE IT WHEN I ASK YOU THIS, BUT ARE YOU GUYS "LOVERS" OR WHAT?
I COULD NEVER FIGURE YOUR RELATIONSHIP OUT...
=SIGH= NEITHER COULD I...
WE "DID IT" A COUPLE OF TIMES, BUT I REALLY WASN'T INTO IT...
SHE'S NOT REALLY "THAT WAY" EITHER, BUT THAT DOESN'T STOP HER FROM ACTING LIKE SHE OWNS ME...
IT'S IRONIC TO ME NOW HOW SHE'S ALWAYS MADE YOU OUT TO BE A "CONTROL FREAK," SINCE SHE'S THE MOST DOMINEERING PERSON I'VE EVER MET!
SHE HAS TO BE THE "BOSS" OF EVERYONE SHE DEALS WITH!
WELL, I WONDER WHAT MADE HER THINK I WAS A "CONTROL FREAK" IN THE FIRST PLACE...
—WHA? BUT, I NEVER SAID YOU WERE, IF THAT'S WHAT YOU'RE IMPLYING...
BUT YOU DIDN'T STOP HER FROM THINKING THAT I WAS, DID YOU?
..=SIGH=... ALL I KNOW FOR SURE WAS THAT I WAS MISERABLE, AND THAT SHE PROVIDED ME WITH AN OUT...
AN OUT FROM ME, HUH? YOU NEEDED TO BE "SAVED" FROM ME—
—I WAS SAVING YOU FROM ME, BUDDY! WHEN ARE YOU GONNA FIGURE THAT OUT?!
I...
OH, NEVER MIND...

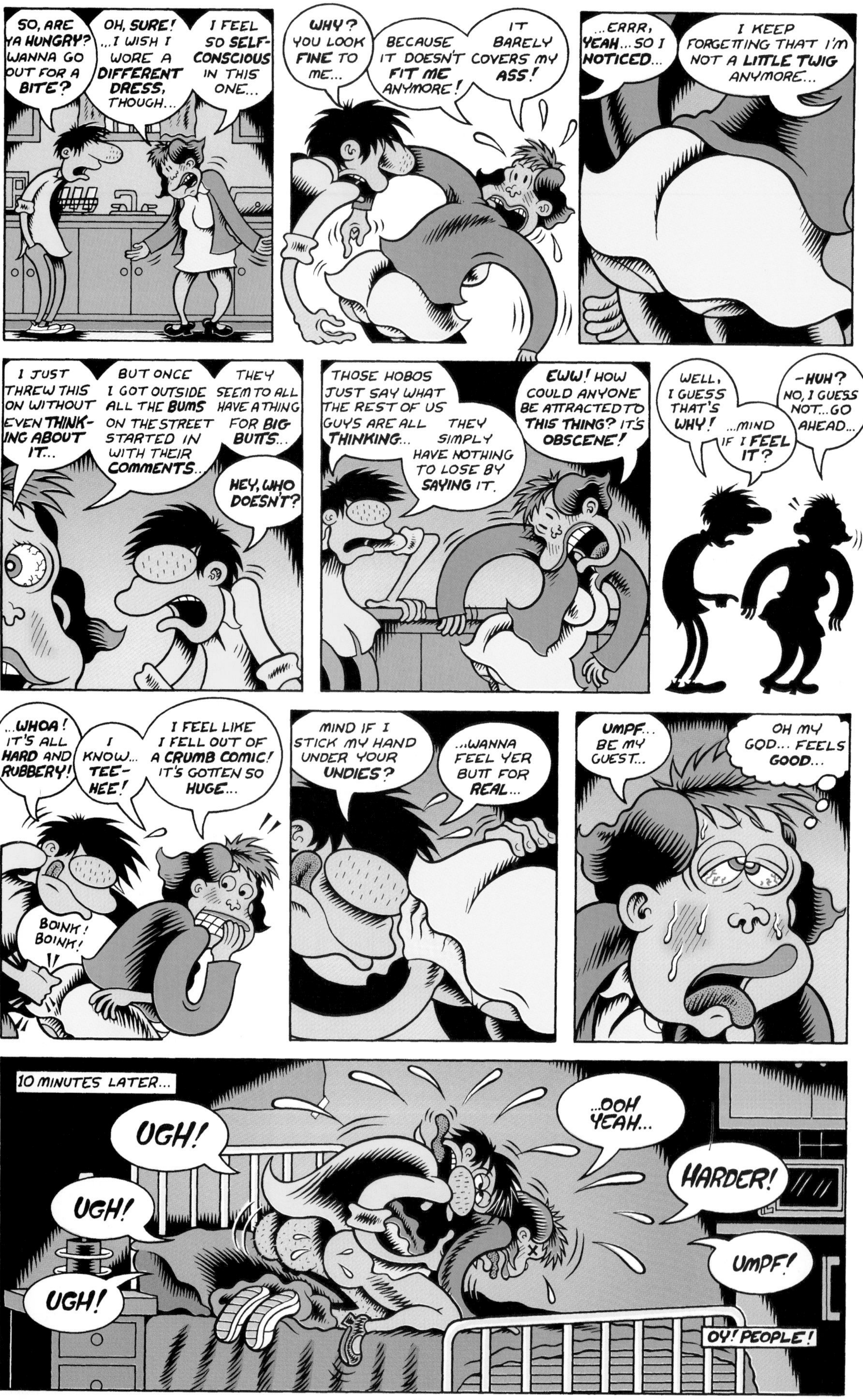
SO, ARE YA HUNGRY? WANNA GO OUT FOR A BITE?
OH, SURE! ...I WISH I WORE A DIFFERENT DRESS, THOUGH...
I FEEL SO SELF-CONSCIOUS IN THIS ONE...
WHY? YOU LOOK FINE TO ME...
BECAUSE IT DOESN'T FIT ME ANYMORE!
IT BARELY COVERS MY ASS!
...ERRR, YEAH... SO I NOTICED...
I KEEP FORGETTING THAT I'M NOT A LITTLE TWIG ANYMORE...
I JUST THREW THIS ON WITHOUT EVEN THINKING ABOUT IT...
BUT ONCE I GOT OUTSIDE ALL THE BUMS ON THE STREET STARTED IN WITH THEIR COMMENTS...
THEY SEEM TO ALL HAVE A THING FOR BIG BUTTS...
HEY, WHO DOESN'T?
THOSE HOBOS JUST SAY WHAT THE REST OF US GUYS ARE ALL THINKING...
THEY SIMPLY HAVE NOTHING TO LOSE BY SAYING IT.
EWW! HOW COULD ANYONE BE ATTRACTED TO THIS THING? IT'S OBSCENE!
WELL, I GUESS THAT'S WHY!
...MIND IF I FEEL IT?
-HUH? NO, I GUESS NOT... GO AHEAD...
...WHOA! IT'S ALL HARD AND RUBBERY!
I KNOW... TEE-HEE!
I FEEL LIKE I FELL OUT OF A CRUMB COMIC! IT'S GOTTEN SO HUGE...
BOINK! BOINK!
MIND IF I STICK MY HAND UNDER YOUR UNDIES?
...WANNA FEEL YER BUTT FOR REAL...
UMPF... BE MY GUEST...
OH MY GOD... FEELS GOOD...
10 MINUTES LATER...
UGH!
UGH!
UGH!
...OOH YEAH...
HARDER!
UMPF!
OY! PEOPLE!

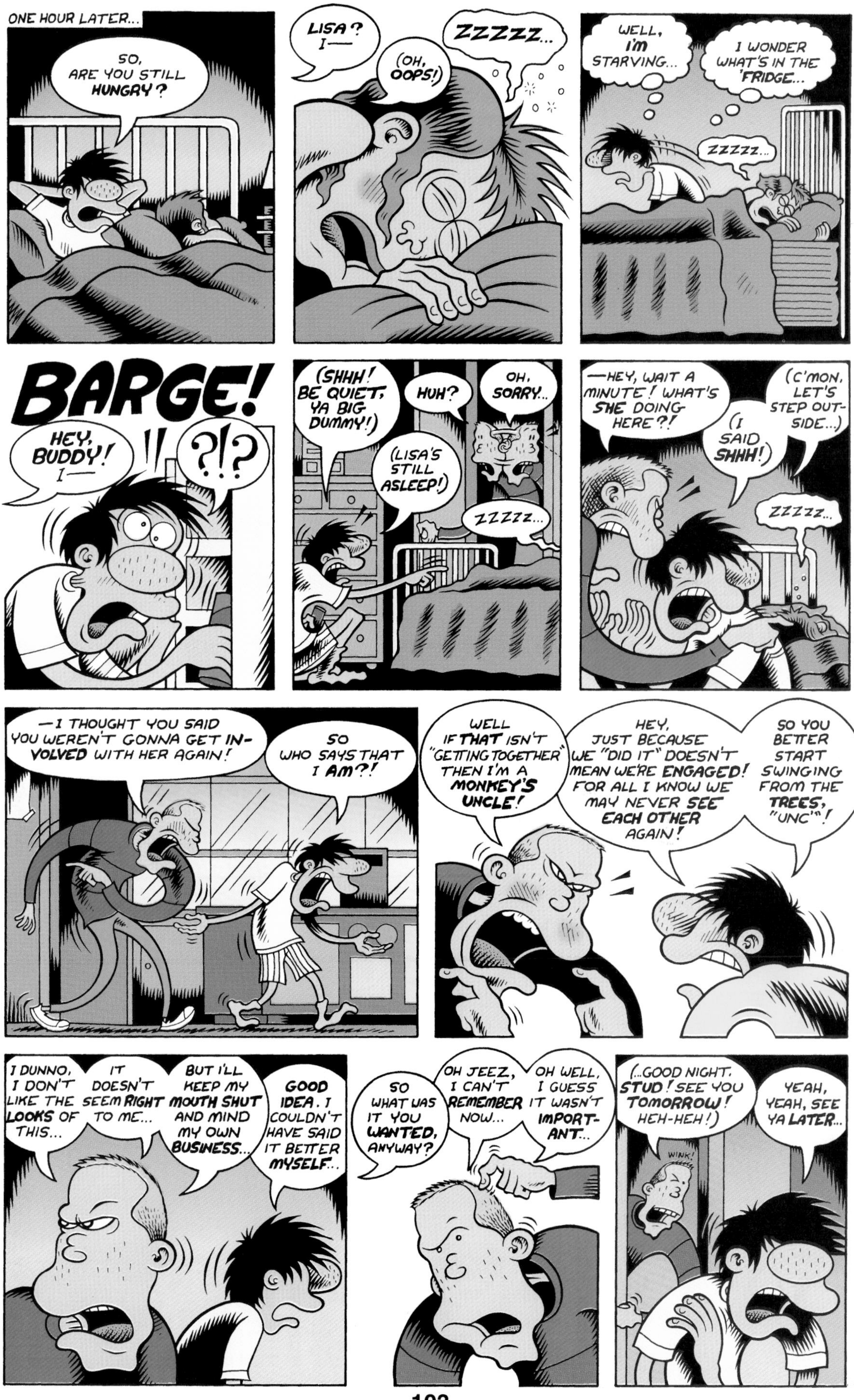
ONE HOUR LATER...
SO, ARE YOU STILL HUNGRY?
LISA? I—
(OH, OOPS!)
ZZZZZ...
WELL, I'M STARVING...
I WONDER WHAT'S IN THE 'FRIDGE...
ZZZZZ...
BARGE!
HEY, BUDDY! I—
?!?
(SHHH! BE QUIET, YA BIG DUMMY!)
HUH?
OH, SORRY...
(LISA'S STILL ASLEEP!)
ZZZZZ...
—HEY, WAIT A MINUTE! WHAT'S SHE DOING HERE?!
(C'MON, LET'S STEP OUT-SIDE...)
(I SAID SHHH!)
ZZZZZ...
—I THOUGHT YOU SAID YOU WEREN'T GONNA GET IN-VOLVED WITH HER AGAIN!
SO WHO SAYS THAT I AM?!
WELL IF THAT ISN'T "GETTING TOGETHER" THEN I'M A MONKEY'S UNCLE!
HEY, JUST BECAUSE WE "DID IT" DOESN'T MEAN WE'RE ENGAGED! FOR ALL I KNOW WE MAY NEVER SEE EACH OTHER AGAIN!
SO YOU BETTER START SWINGING FROM THE TREES, "UNC"!
I DUNNO, I DON'T LIKE THE LOOKS OF THIS...
IT DOESN'T SEEM RIGHT TO ME...
BUT I'LL KEEP MY MOUTH SHUT AND MIND MY OWN BUSINESS...
GOOD IDEA. I COULDN'T HAVE SAID IT BETTER MYSELF...
SO WHAT WAS IT YOU WANTED, ANYWAY?
OH JEEZ, I CAN'T REMEMBER NOW...
OH WELL, I GUESS IT WASN'T IMPORT-ANT...
(...GOOD NIGHT, STUD! SEE YOU TOMORROW! HEH-HEH!)
WINK!
YEAH, YEAH, SEE YA LATER...

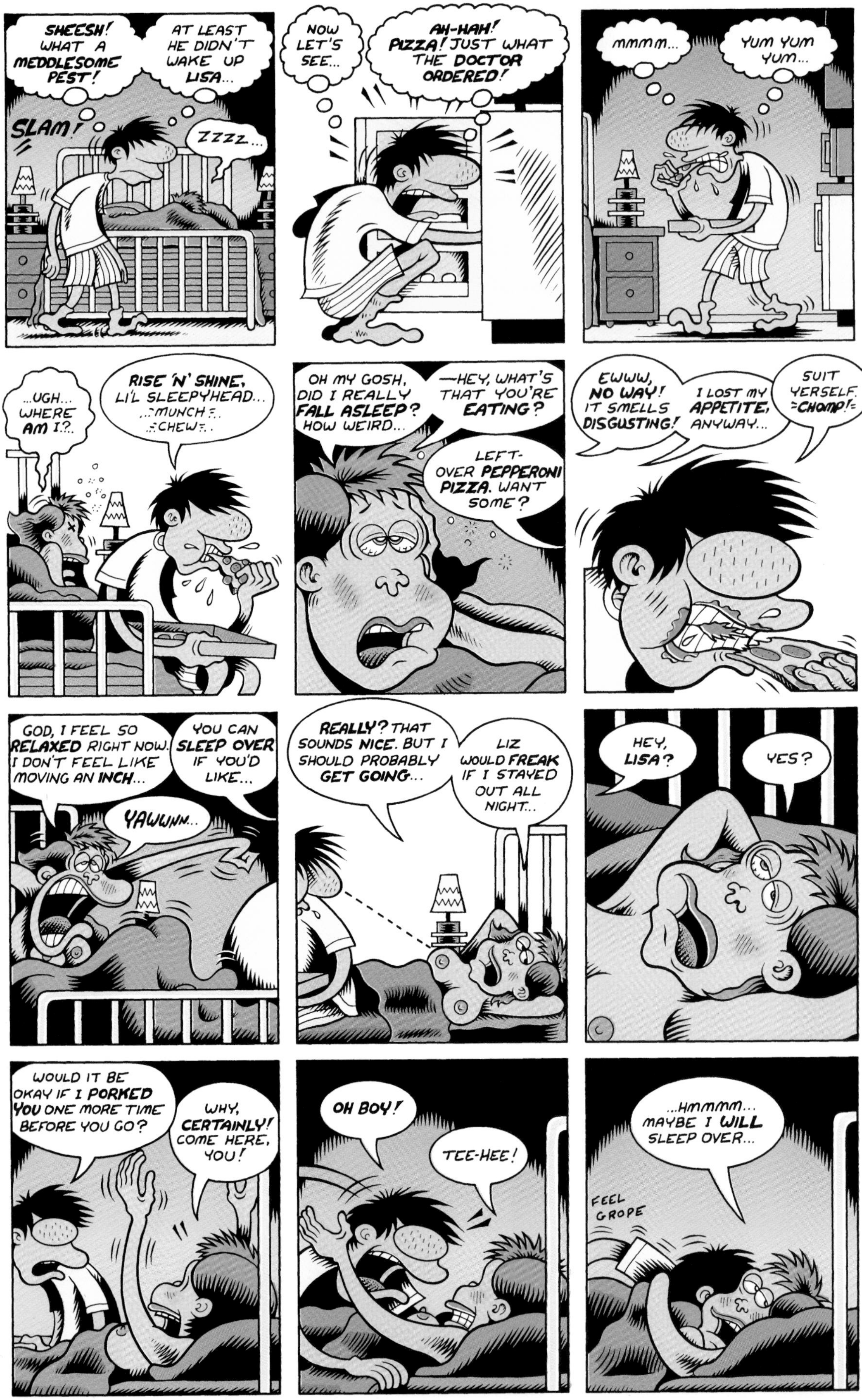
SHEESH! WHAT A MEDDLESOME PEST!
AT LEAST HE DIDN'T WAKE UP LISA...
SLAM!
ZZZZ...
NOW LET'S SEE...
AH-HAH! PIZZA! JUST WHAT THE DOCTOR ORDERED!
MMMM...
YUM YUM YUM...
...UGH... WHERE AM I?..
RISE 'N' SHINE, LI'L SLEEPYHEAD... MUNCH CHEW
OH MY GOSH, DID I REALLY FALL ASLEEP? HOW WEIRD...
—HEY, WHAT'S THAT YOU'RE EATING?
LEFT-OVER PEPPERONI PIZZA. WANT SOME?
EWWW, NO WAY! IT SMELLS DISGUSTING!
I LOST MY APPETITE, ANYWAY...
SUIT YERSELF. CHOMP!
GOD, I FEEL SO RELAXED RIGHT NOW. I DON'T FEEL LIKE MOVING AN INCH...
YOU CAN SLEEP OVER IF YOU'D LIKE...
YAWWNN...
REALLY? THAT SOUNDS NICE. BUT I SHOULD PROBABLY GET GOING...
LIZ WOULD FREAK IF I STAYED OUT ALL NIGHT...
HEY, LISA?
YES?
WOULD IT BE OKAY IF I PORKED YOU ONE MORE TIME BEFORE YOU GO?
WHY, CERTAINLY! COME HERE, YOU!
OH BOY!
TEE-HEE!
...HMMMM... MAYBE I WILL SLEEP OVER...
FEEL GROPE

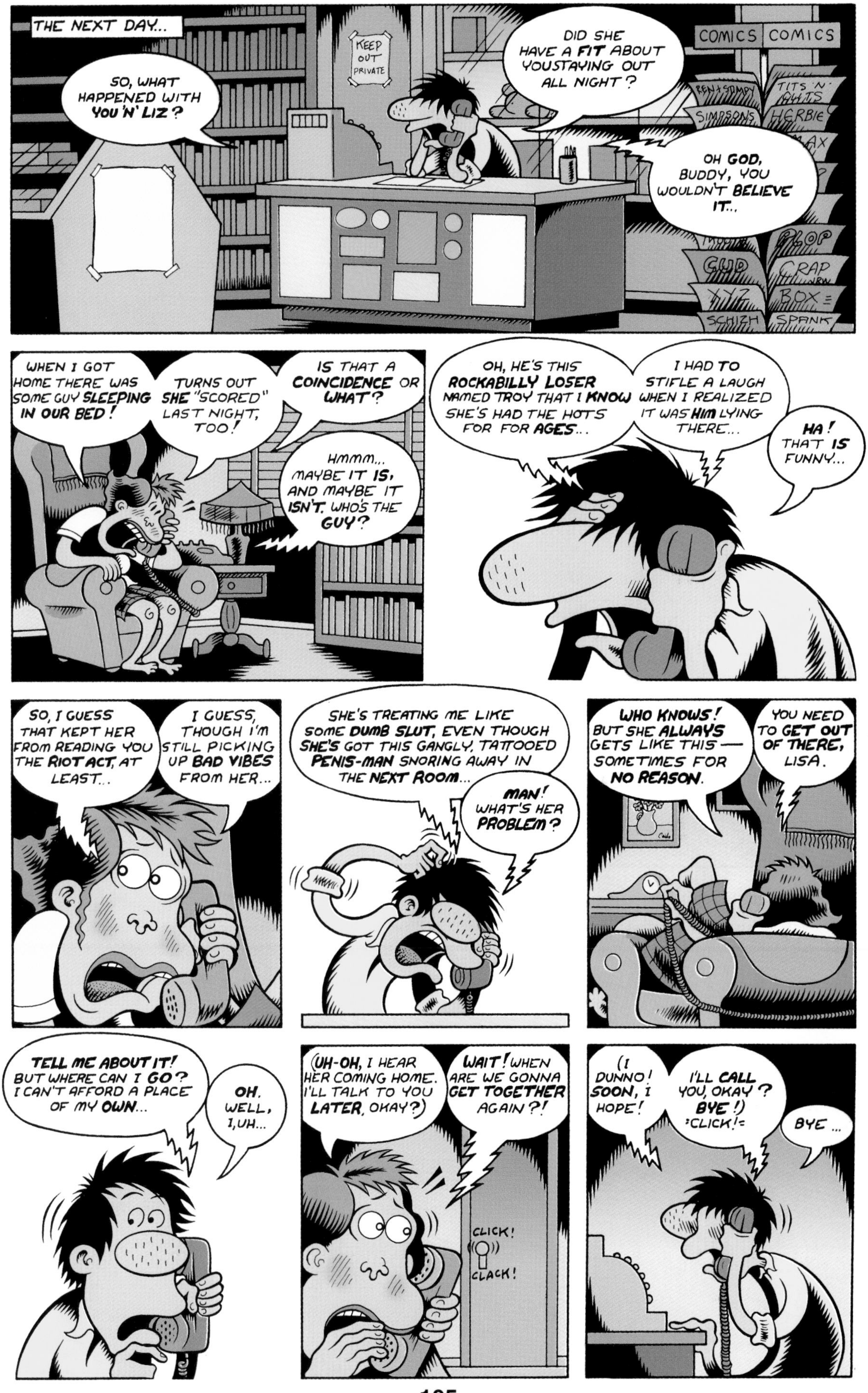
THE NEXT DAY...
SO, WHAT HAPPENED WITH YOU 'N' LIZ?
KEEP OUT PRIVATE
DID SHE HAVE A FIT ABOUT YOUSTAYING OUT ALL NIGHT?
COMICS
COMICS
SIMPSONS
HERBIE
CRAP
BOX
SPANK
OH GOD, BUDDY, YOU WOULDN'T BELIEVE IT...
WHEN I GOT HOME THERE WAS SOME GUY SLEEPING IN OUR BED!
TURNS OUT SHE "SCORED" LAST NIGHT, TOO!
IS THAT A COINCIDENCE OR WHAT?
HMMM... MAYBE IT IS, AND MAYBE IT ISN'T. WHO'S THE GUY?
OH, HE'S THIS ROCKABILLY LOSER NAMED TROY THAT I KNOW SHE'S HAD THE HOTS FOR FOR AGES...
I HAD TO STIFLE A LAUGH WHEN I REALIZED IT WAS HIM LYING THERE...
HA! THAT IS FUNNY...
SO, I GUESS THAT KEPT HER FROM READING YOU THE RIOT ACT, AT LEAST...
I GUESS, THOUGH I'M STILL PICKING UP BAD VIBES FROM HER...
SHE'S TREATING ME LIKE SOME DUMB SLUT, EVEN THOUGH SHE'S GOT THIS GANGLY, TATTOOED PENIS-MAN SNORING AWAY IN THE NEXT ROOM...
MAN! WHAT'S HER PROBLEM?
WHO KNOWS! BUT SHE ALWAYS GETS LIKE THIS — SOMETIMES FOR NO REASON.
YOU NEED TO GET OUT OF THERE, LISA.
TELL ME ABOUT IT! BUT WHERE CAN I GO? I CAN'T AFFORD A PLACE OF MY OWN...
OH. WELL, I, UH...
(UH-OH, I HEAR HER COMING HOME. I'LL TALK TO YOU LATER, OKAY?)
WAIT! WHEN ARE WE GONNA GET TOGETHER AGAIN?!
CLICK!
CLACK!
(I DUNNO! SOON, I HOPE!
I'LL CALL YOU, OKAY? BYE!)
:CLICK!:
BYE...

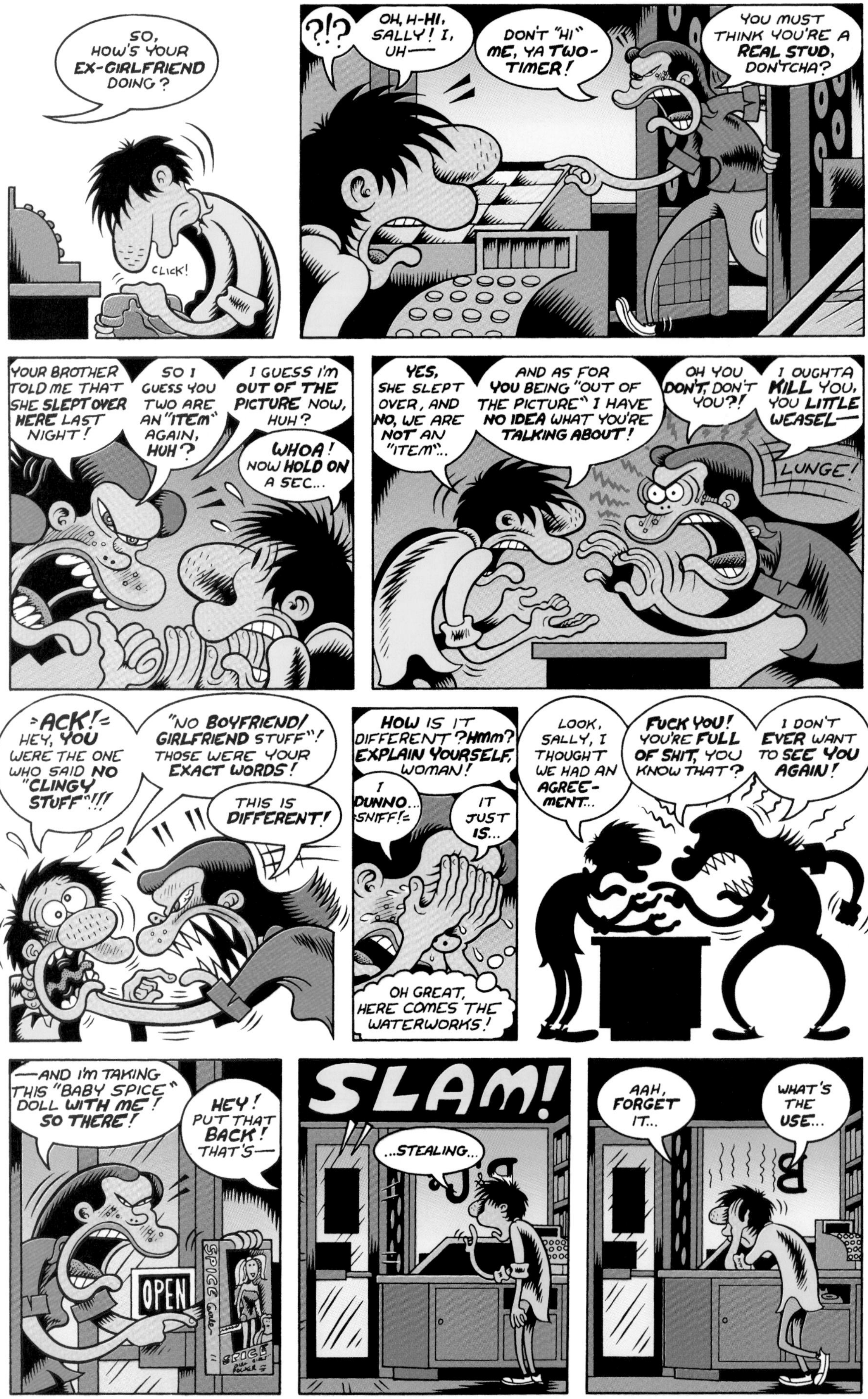
SO, HOW'S YOUR EX-GIRLFRIEND DOING?
CLICK!
?!?
OH, H-HI, SALLY! I, UH—
DON'T "HI" ME, YA TWO-TIMER!
YOU MUST THINK YOU'RE A REAL STUD, DON'TCHA?
YOUR BROTHER TOLD ME THAT SHE SLEPT OVER HERE LAST NIGHT!
SO I GUESS YOU TWO ARE AN "ITEM" AGAIN, HUH?
I GUESS I'M OUT OF THE PICTURE NOW, HUH?
WHOA! NOW HOLD ON A SEC...
YES, SHE SLEPT OVER, AND NO, WE ARE NOT AN "ITEM"...
AND AS FOR YOU BEING "OUT OF THE PICTURE" I HAVE NO IDEA WHAT YOU'RE TALKING ABOUT!
OH YOU DON'T, DON'T YOU?!
I OUGHTA KILL YOU, YOU LITTLE WEASEL—
LUNGE!
=ACK!= HEY, YOU WERE THE ONE WHO SAID NO "CLINGY STUFF"!!!
"NO BOYFRIEND/GIRLFRIEND STUFF"! THOSE WERE YOUR EXACT WORDS!
THIS IS DIFFERENT!
HOW IS IT DIFFERENT? HMM? EXPLAIN YOURSELF, WOMAN!
I DUNNO... =SNIFF!=
IT JUST IS...
OH GREAT, HERE COMES THE WATERWORKS!
LOOK, SALLY, I THOUGHT WE HAD AN AGREE-MENT...
FUCK YOU! YOU'RE FULL OF SHIT, YOU KNOW THAT?
I DON'T EVER WANT TO SEE YOU AGAIN!
—AND I'M TAKING THIS "BABY SPICE" DOLL WITH ME! SO THERE!
HEY! PUT THAT BACK! THAT'S—
OPEN
SPICE
SLAM!
...STEALING...
AAH, FORGET IT...
WHAT'S THE USE...

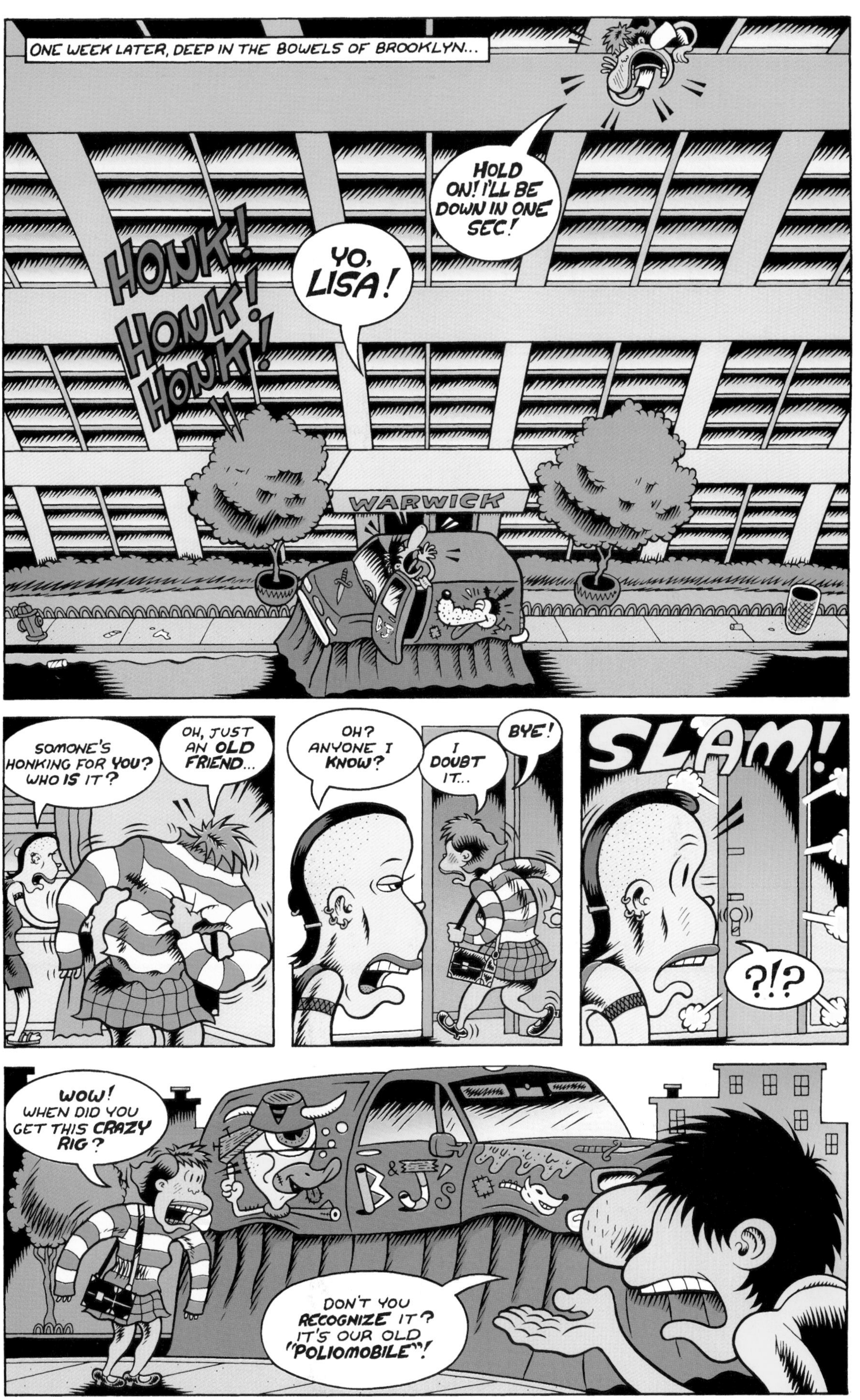
ONE WEEK LATER, DEEP IN THE BOWELS OF BROOKLYN...
HONK! HONK! HONK!
YO, LISA!
HOLD ON! I'LL BE DOWN IN ONE SEC!
WARWICK
SOMONE'S HONKING FOR YOU? WHO IS IT?
OH, JUST AN OLD FRIEND...
OH? ANYONE I KNOW?
I DOUBT IT...
BYE!
SLAM!
?!?
WOW! WHEN DID YOU GET THIS CRAZY RIG?
B & J'S
DON'T YOU RECOGNIZE IT? IT'S OUR OLD "POLIOMOBILE"!

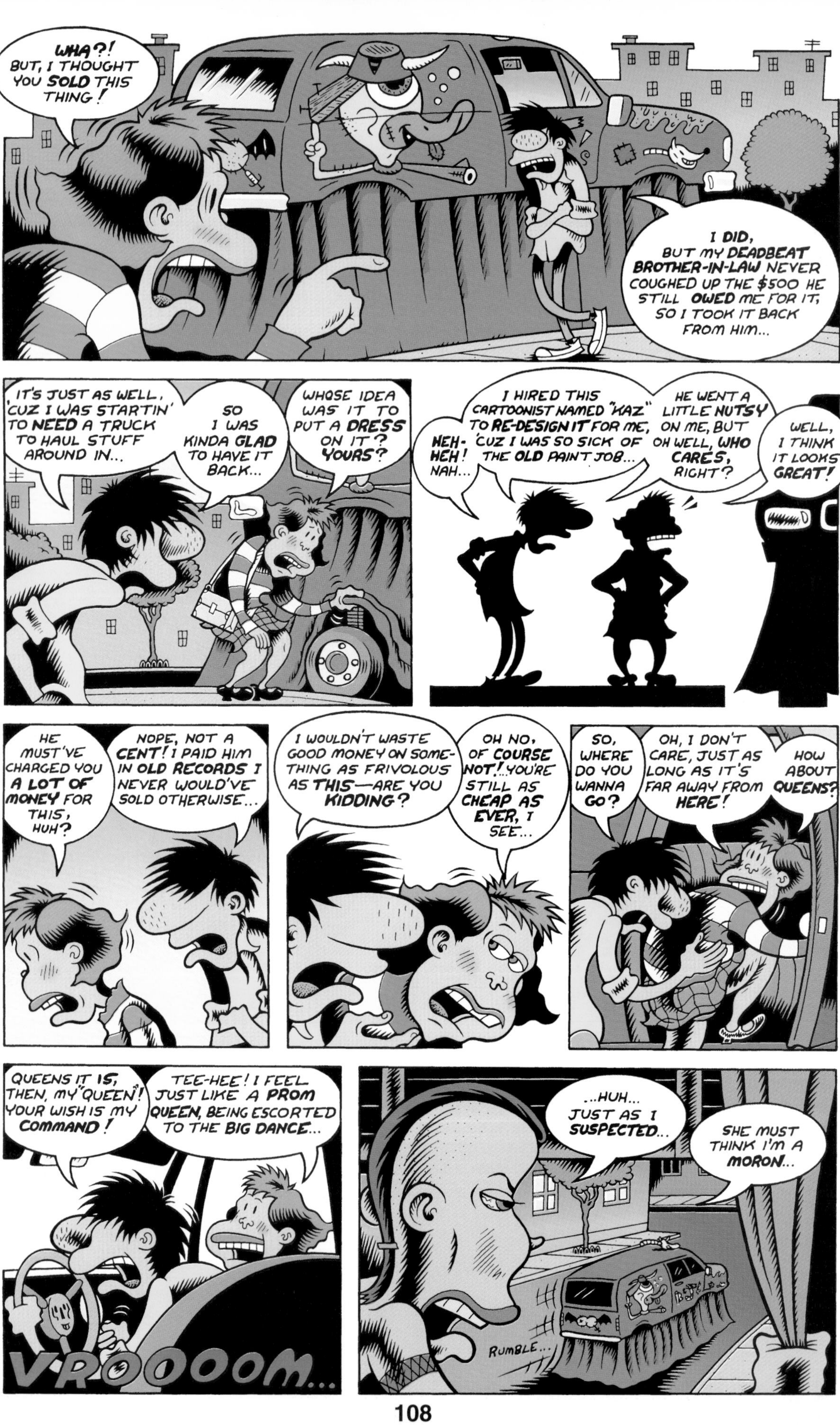
WHA?! BUT, I THOUGHT YOU SOLD THIS THING!
I DID, BUT MY DEADBEAT BROTHER-IN-LAW NEVER COUGHED UP THE $500 HE STILL OWED ME FOR IT, SO I TOOK IT BACK FROM HIM...
IT'S JUST AS WELL, 'CUZ I WAS STARTIN' TO NEED A TRUCK TO HAUL STUFF AROUND IN...
SO I WAS KINDA GLAD TO HAVE IT BACK...
WHOSE IDEA WAS IT TO PUT A DRESS ON IT? YOURS?
HEH-HEH! NAH...
I HIRED THIS CARTOONIST NAMED "KAZ" TO RE-DESIGN IT FOR ME, 'CUZ I WAS SO SICK OF THE OLD PAINT JOB...
HE WENT A LITTLE NUTSY ON ME, BUT OH WELL, WHO CARES, RIGHT?
WELL, I THINK IT LOOKS GREAT!
HE MUST'VE CHARGED YOU A LOT OF MONEY FOR THIS, HUH?
NOPE, NOT A CENT! I PAID HIM IN OLD RECORDS I NEVER WOULD'VE SOLD OTHERWISE...
I WOULDN'T WASTE GOOD MONEY ON SOMETHING AS FRIVOLOUS AS THIS—ARE YOU KIDDING?
OH NO, OF COURSE NOT!...YOU'RE STILL AS CHEAP AS EVER, I SEE...
SO, WHERE DO YOU WANNA GO?
OH, I DON'T CARE, JUST AS LONG AS IT'S FAR AWAY FROM HERE!
HOW ABOUT QUEENS?
QUEENS IT IS, THEN, MY "QUEEN"! YOUR WISH IS MY COMMAND!
TEE-HEE! I FEEL JUST LIKE A PROM QUEEN, BEING ESCORTED TO THE BIG DANCE...
VROOOOM...
...HUH... JUST AS I SUSPECTED...
SHE MUST THINK I'M A MORON...
RUMBLE...

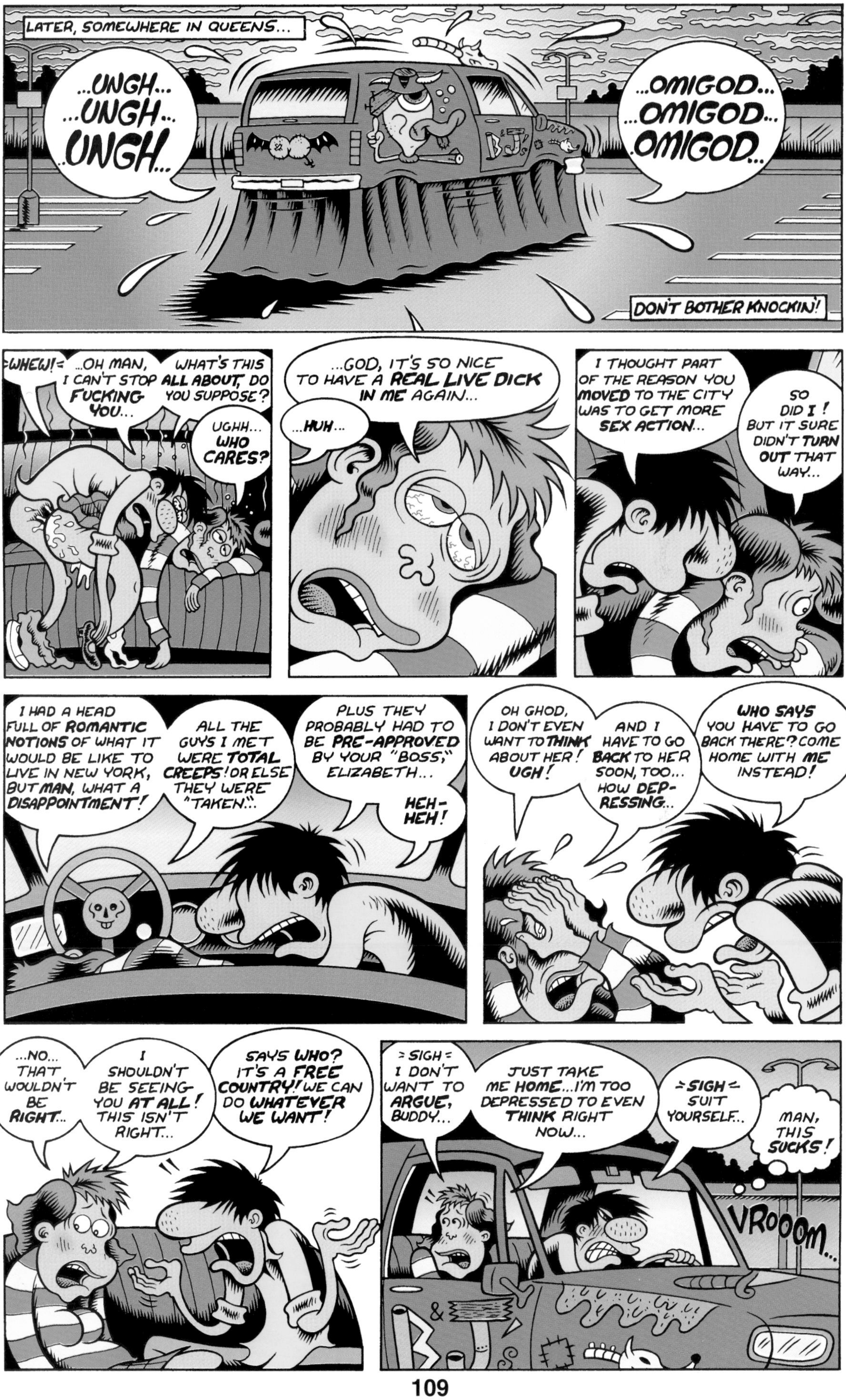
LATER, SOMEWHERE IN QUEENS...
...UNGH... ...UNGH... UNGH...
...OMIGOD... ...OMIGOD... .OMIGOD...
DON'T BOTHER KNOCKIN'!
=WHEW!=
...OH MAN, I CAN'T STOP FUCKING YOU...
WHAT'S THIS ALL ABOUT, DO YOU SUPPOSE?
UGHH... WHO CARES?
...GOD, IT'S SO NICE TO HAVE A REAL LIVE DICK IN ME AGAIN...
...HUH...
I THOUGHT PART OF THE REASON YOU MOVED TO THE CITY WAS TO GET MORE SEX ACTION...
SO DID I! BUT IT SURE DIDN'T TURN OUT THAT WAY...
I HAD A HEAD FULL OF ROMANTIC NOTIONS OF WHAT IT WOULD BE LIKE TO LIVE IN NEW YORK, BUT MAN, WHAT A DISAPPOINTMENT!
ALL THE GUYS I MET WERE TOTAL CREEPS! OR ELSE THEY WERE "TAKEN."
PLUS THEY PROBABLY HAD TO BE PRE-APPROVED BY YOUR "BOSS," ELIZABETH...
HEH-HEH!
OH GHOD, I DON'T EVEN WANT TO THINK ABOUT HER! UGH!
AND I HAVE TO GO BACK TO HER SOON, TOO... HOW DEP-RESSING...
WHO SAYS YOU HAVE TO GO BACK THERE? COME HOME WITH ME INSTEAD!
...NO... THAT WOULDN'T BE RIGHT...
I SHOULDN'T BE SEEING YOU AT ALL! THIS ISN'T RIGHT...
SAYS WHO? IT'S A FREE COUNTRY! WE CAN DO WHATEVER WE WANT!
=SIGH= I DON'T WANT TO ARGUE, BUDDY...
JUST TAKE ME HOME... I'M TOO DEPRESSED TO EVEN THINK RIGHT NOW...
=SIGH= SUIT YOURSELF...
MAN, THIS SUCKS!
VROOOM...

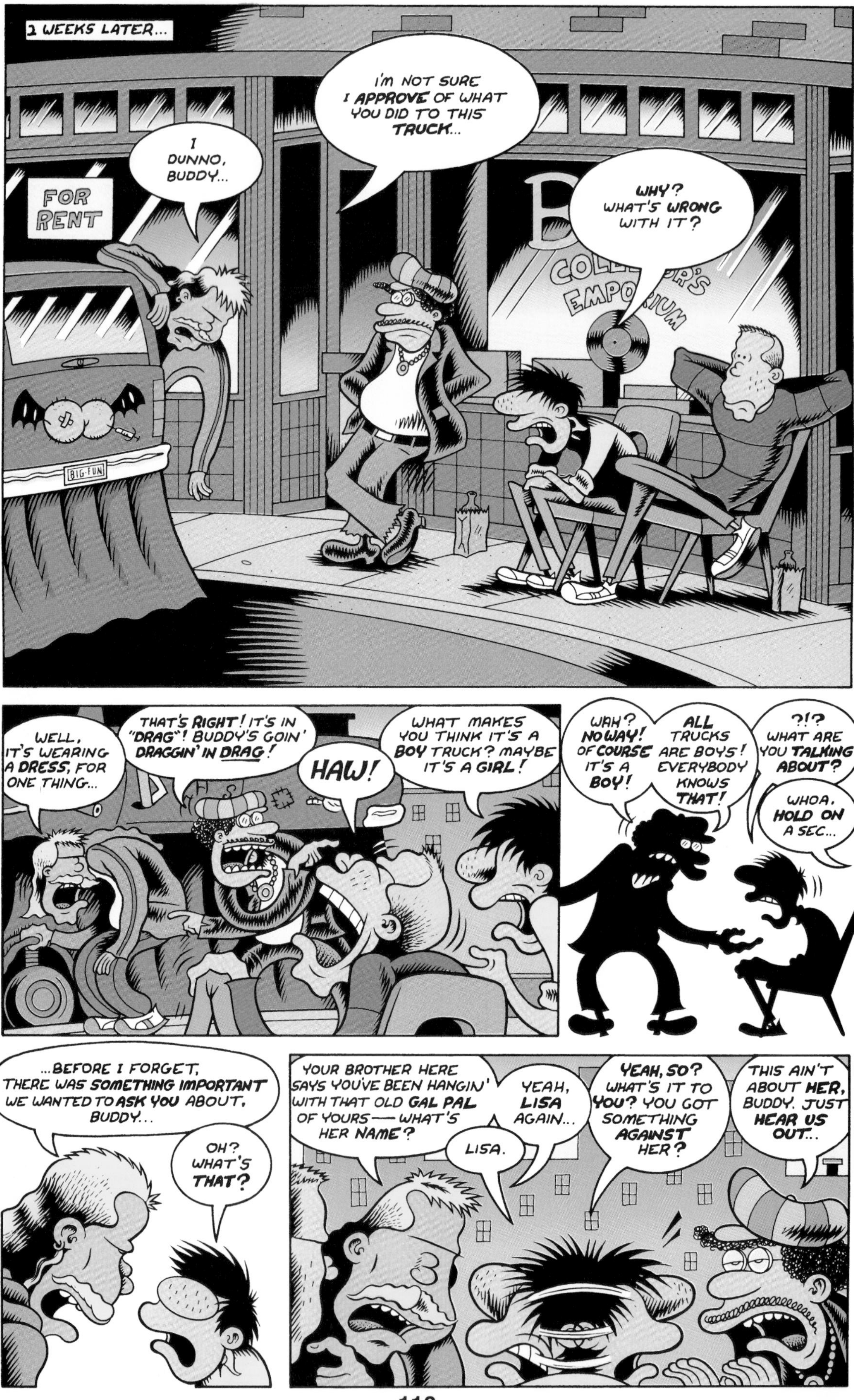
2 WEEKS LATER...
I DUNNO, BUDDY...
I'M NOT SURE I APPROVE OF WHAT YOU DID TO THIS TRUCK...
WHY? WHAT'S WRONG WITH IT?
FOR RENT
COLLECTOR'S EMPORIUM
BIG·FUN
WELL, IT'S WEARING A DRESS, FOR ONE THING...
THAT'S RIGHT! IT'S IN "DRAG"! BUDDY'S GOIN' DRAGGIN' IN DRAG!
HAW!
WHAT MAKES YOU THINK IT'S A BOY TRUCK? MAYBE IT'S A GIRL!
WAH? NO WAY! OF COURSE IT'S A BOY!
ALL TRUCKS ARE BOYS! EVERYBODY KNOWS THAT!
?!? WHAT ARE YOU TALKING ABOUT?
WHOA. HOLD ON A SEC...
...BEFORE I FORGET, THERE WAS SOMETHING IMPORTANT WE WANTED TO ASK YOU ABOUT, BUDDY...
OH? WHAT'S THAT?
YOUR BROTHER HERE SAYS YOU'VE BEEN HANGIN' WITH THAT OLD GAL PAL OF YOURS — WHAT'S HER NAME?
LISA.
YEAH, LISA AGAIN...
YEAH, SO? WHAT'S IT TO YOU? YOU GOT SOMETHING AGAINST HER?
THIS AIN'T ABOUT HER, BUDDY. JUST HEAR US OUT...

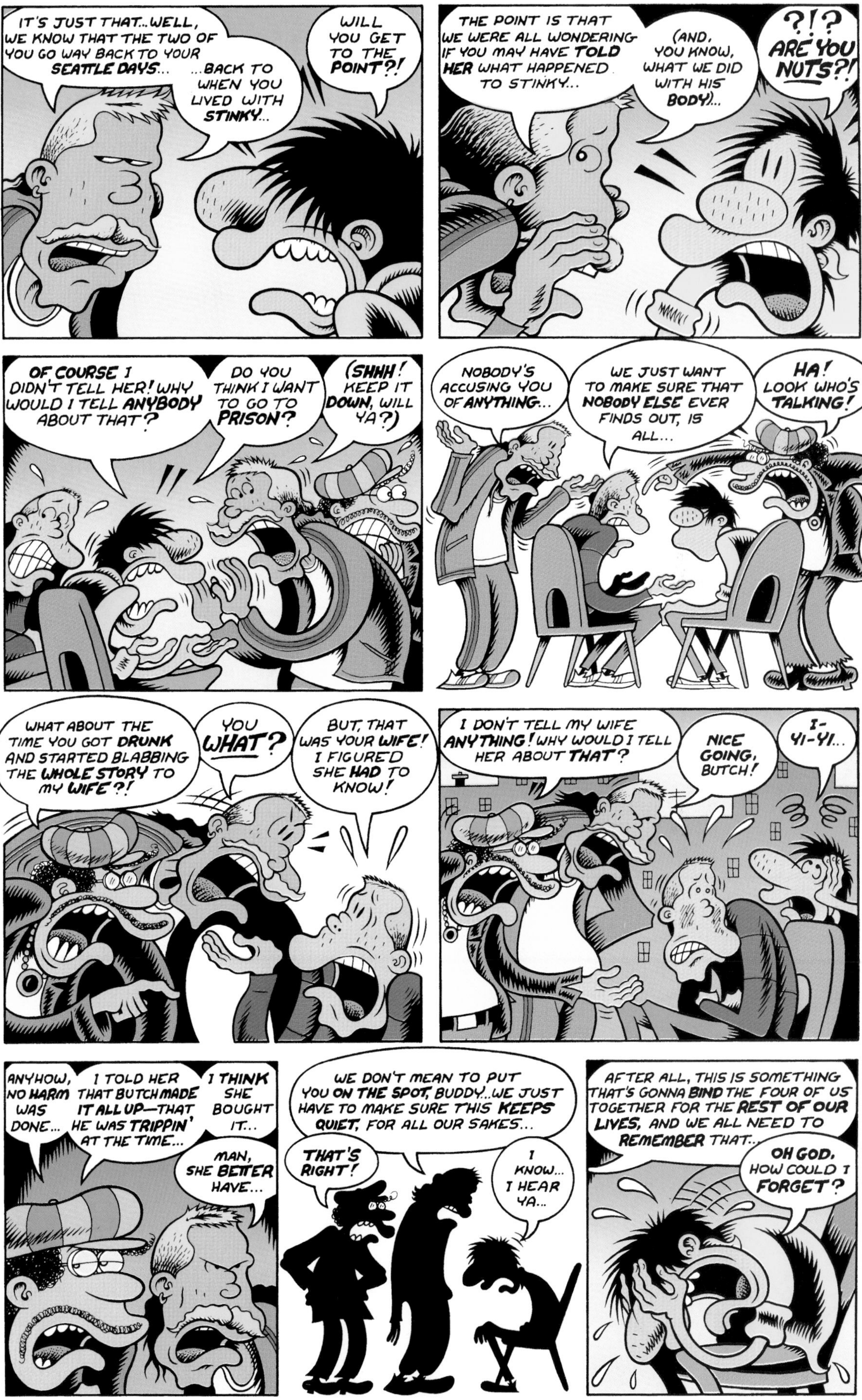
IT'S JUST THAT... WELL, WE KNOW THAT THE TWO OF YOU GO WAY BACK TO YOUR SEATTLE DAYS...
...BACK TO WHEN YOU LIVED WITH STINKY...
WILL YOU GET TO THE POINT?!
THE POINT IS THAT WE WERE ALL WONDERING IF YOU MAY HAVE TOLD HER WHAT HAPPENED TO STINKY...
(AND, YOU KNOW, WHAT WE DID WITH HIS BODY)...
?!? ARE YOU NUTS?!
OF COURSE I DIDN'T TELL HER! WHY WOULD I TELL ANYBODY ABOUT THAT?
DO YOU THINK I WANT TO GO TO PRISON?
(SHHH! KEEP IT DOWN, WILL YA?)
NOBODY'S ACCUSING YOU OF ANYTHING...
WE JUST WANT TO MAKE SURE THAT NOBODY ELSE EVER FINDS OUT, IS ALL...
HA! LOOK WHO'S TALKING!
WHAT ABOUT THE TIME YOU GOT DRUNK AND STARTED BLABBING THE WHOLE STORY TO MY WIFE?!
YOU WHAT?
BUT, THAT WAS YOUR WIFE! I FIGURED SHE HAD TO KNOW!
I DON'T TELL MY WIFE ANYTHING! WHY WOULD I TELL HER ABOUT THAT?
NICE GOING, BUTCH!
I-YI-YI...
ANYHOW, NO HARM WAS DONE...
I TOLD HER THAT BUTCH MADE IT ALL UP—THAT HE WAS TRIPPIN' AT THE TIME...
I THINK SHE BOUGHT IT...
MAN, SHE BETTER HAVE...
WE DON'T MEAN TO PUT YOU ON THE SPOT, BUDDY... WE JUST HAVE TO MAKE SURE THIS KEEPS QUIET, FOR ALL OUR SAKES...
THAT'S RIGHT!
I KNOW... I HEAR YA...
AFTER ALL, THIS IS SOMETHING THAT'S GONNA BIND THE FOUR OF US TOGETHER FOR THE REST OF OUR LIVES, AND WE ALL NEED TO REMEMBER THAT...
OH GOD, HOW COULD I FORGET?

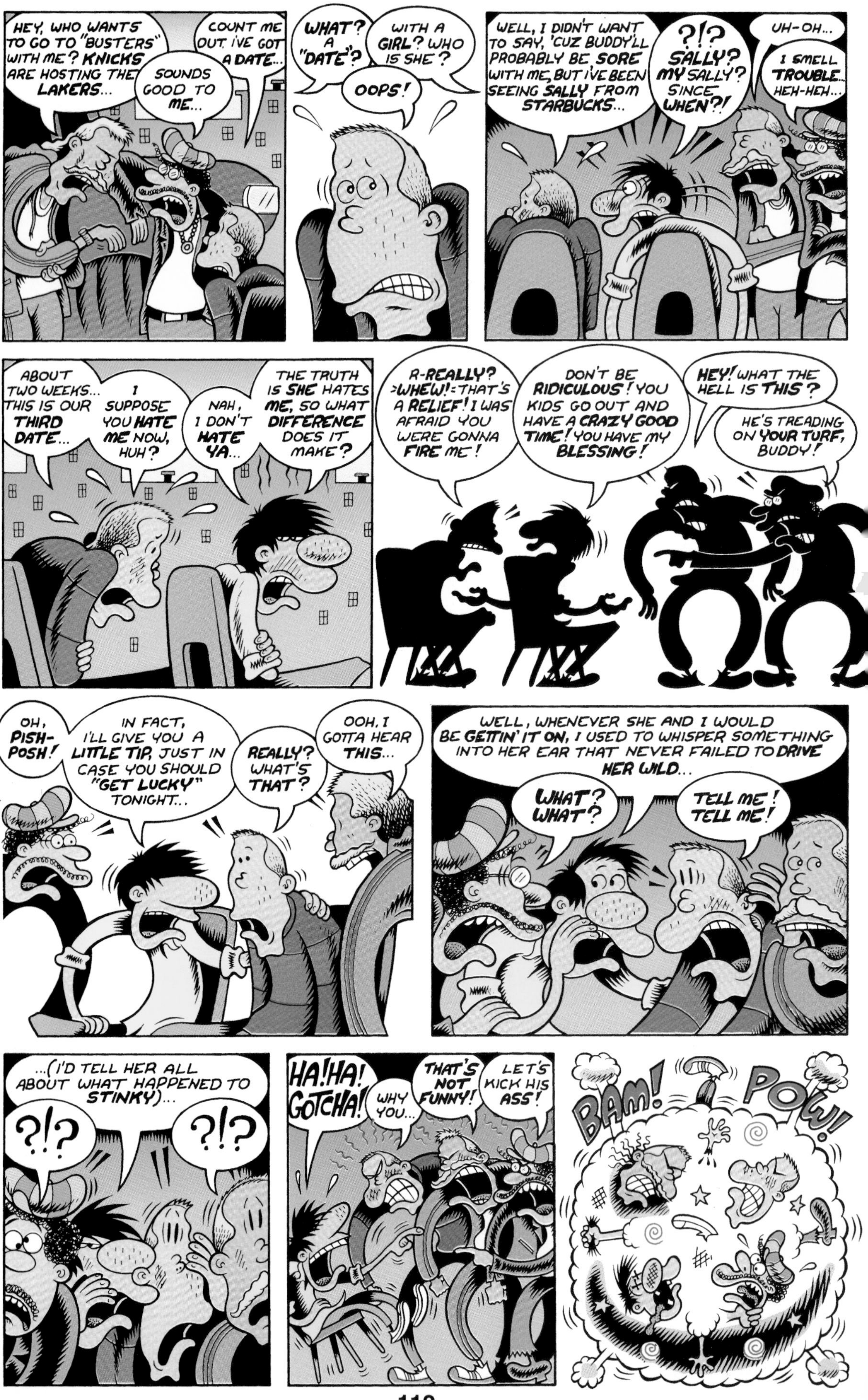
HEY, WHO WANTS TO GO TO "BUSTERS" WITH ME? KNICKS ARE HOSTING THE LAKERS...
COUNT ME OUT, I'VE GOT A DATE...
SOUNDS GOOD TO ME...
WHAT? A "DATE"?
WITH A GIRL? WHO IS SHE?
OOPS!
WELL, I DIDN'T WANT TO SAY, 'CUZ BUDDY'LL PROBABLY BE SORE WITH ME, BUT I'VE BEEN SEEING SALLY FROM STARBUCKS...
?!? SALLY? MY SALLY? SINCE WHEN?!
UH-OH...
I SMELL TROUBLE... HEH-HEH...
ABOUT TWO WEEKS... THIS IS OUR THIRD DATE...
I SUPPOSE YOU HATE ME NOW, HUH?
NAH, I DON'T HATE YA...
THE TRUTH IS SHE HATES ME, SO WHAT DIFFERENCE DOES IT MAKE?
R-REALLY? WHEW! THAT'S A RELIEF! I WAS AFRAID YOU WERE GONNA FIRE ME!
DON'T BE RIDICULOUS! YOU KIDS GO OUT AND HAVE A CRAZY GOOD TIME! YOU HAVE MY BLESSING!
HEY! WHAT THE HELL IS THIS?
HE'S TREADING ON YOUR TURF, BUDDY!
OH, PISH-POSH!
IN FACT, I'LL GIVE YOU A LITTLE TIP, JUST IN CASE YOU SHOULD "GET LUCKY" TONIGHT...
REALLY? WHAT'S THAT?
OOH, I GOTTA HEAR THIS...
WELL, WHENEVER SHE AND I WOULD BE GETTIN' IT ON, I USED TO WHISPER SOMETHING INTO HER EAR THAT NEVER FAILED TO DRIVE HER WILD...
WHAT? WHAT?
TELL ME! TELL ME!
...(I'D TELL HER ALL ABOUT WHAT HAPPENED TO STINKY)...
?!?
?!?
HA!HA! GOTCHA!
WHY YOU...
THAT'S NOT FUNNY!
LET'S KICK HIS ASS!
BAM!
POW!

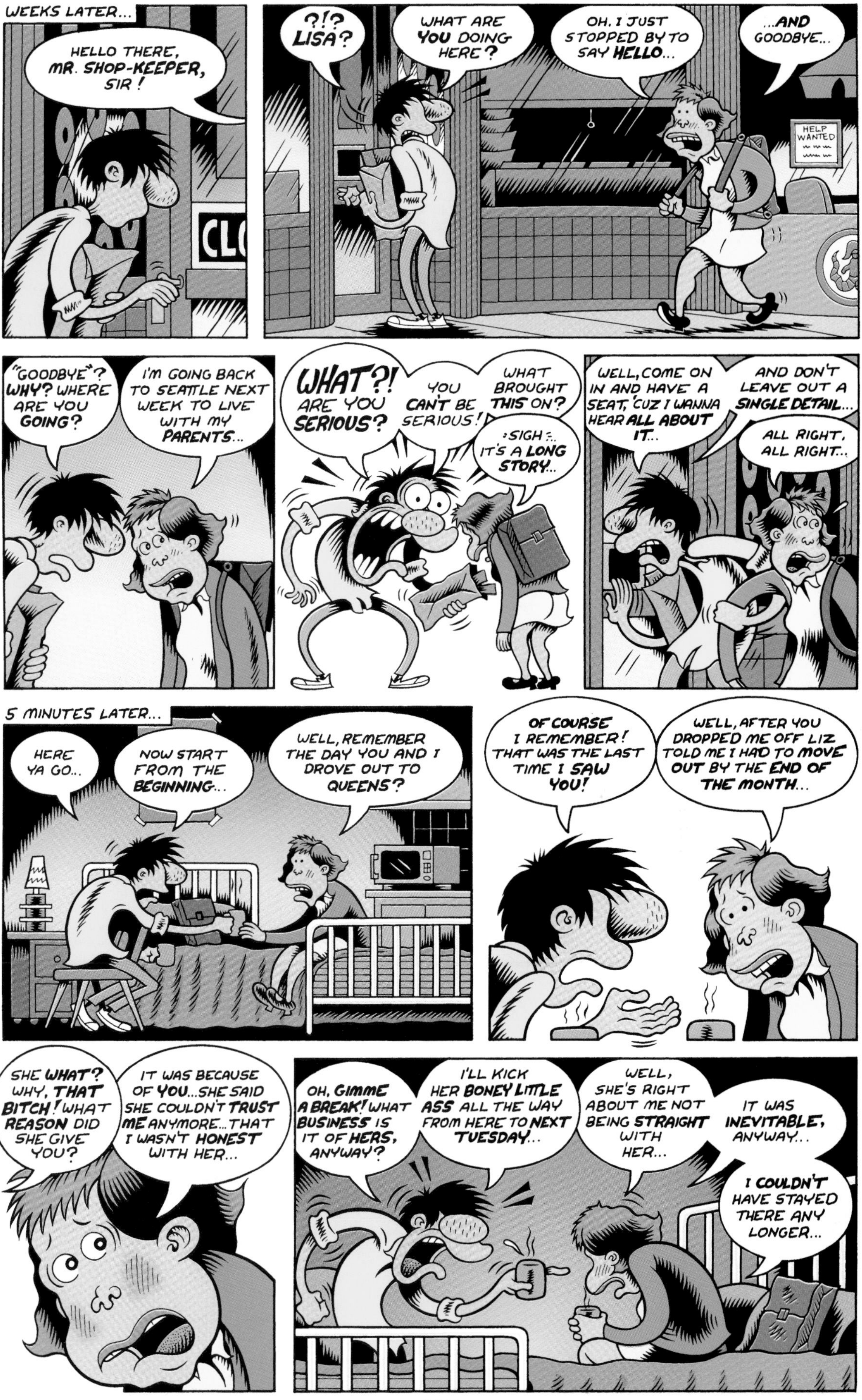
WEEKS LATER...
HELLO THERE, MR. SHOP-KEEPER, SIR!
CL
?!? LISA?
WHAT ARE YOU DOING HERE?
OH, I JUST STOPPED BY TO SAY HELLO...
...AND GOODBYE...
HELP WANTED
"GOODBYE"? WHY? WHERE ARE YOU GOING?
I'M GOING BACK TO SEATTLE NEXT WEEK TO LIVE WITH MY PARENTS...
WHAT?! ARE YOU SERIOUS?
YOU CAN'T BE SERIOUS!
WHAT BROUGHT THIS ON?
:SIGH: IT'S A LONG STORY...
WELL, COME ON IN AND HAVE A SEAT, 'CUZ I WANNA HEAR ALL ABOUT IT...
AND DON'T LEAVE OUT A SINGLE DETAIL...
ALL RIGHT, ALL RIGHT...
5 MINUTES LATER...
HERE YA GO...
NOW START FROM THE BEGINNING...
WELL, REMEMBER THE DAY YOU AND I DROVE OUT TO QUEENS?
OF COURSE I REMEMBER! THAT WAS THE LAST TIME I SAW YOU!
WELL, AFTER YOU DROPPED ME OFF LIZ TOLD ME I HAD TO MOVE OUT BY THE END OF THE MONTH...
SHE WHAT? WHY, THAT BITCH! WHAT REASON DID SHE GIVE YOU?
IT WAS BECAUSE OF YOU...SHE SAID SHE COULDN'T TRUST ME ANYMORE...THAT I WASN'T HONEST WITH HER...
OH, GIMME A BREAK! WHAT BUSINESS IS IT OF HERS, ANYWAY?
I'LL KICK HER BONEY LITTLE ASS ALL THE WAY FROM HERE TO NEXT TUESDAY...
WELL, SHE'S RIGHT ABOUT ME NOT BEING STRAIGHT WITH HER...
IT WAS INEVITABLE, ANYWAY...
I COULDN'T HAVE STAYED THERE ANY LONGER...

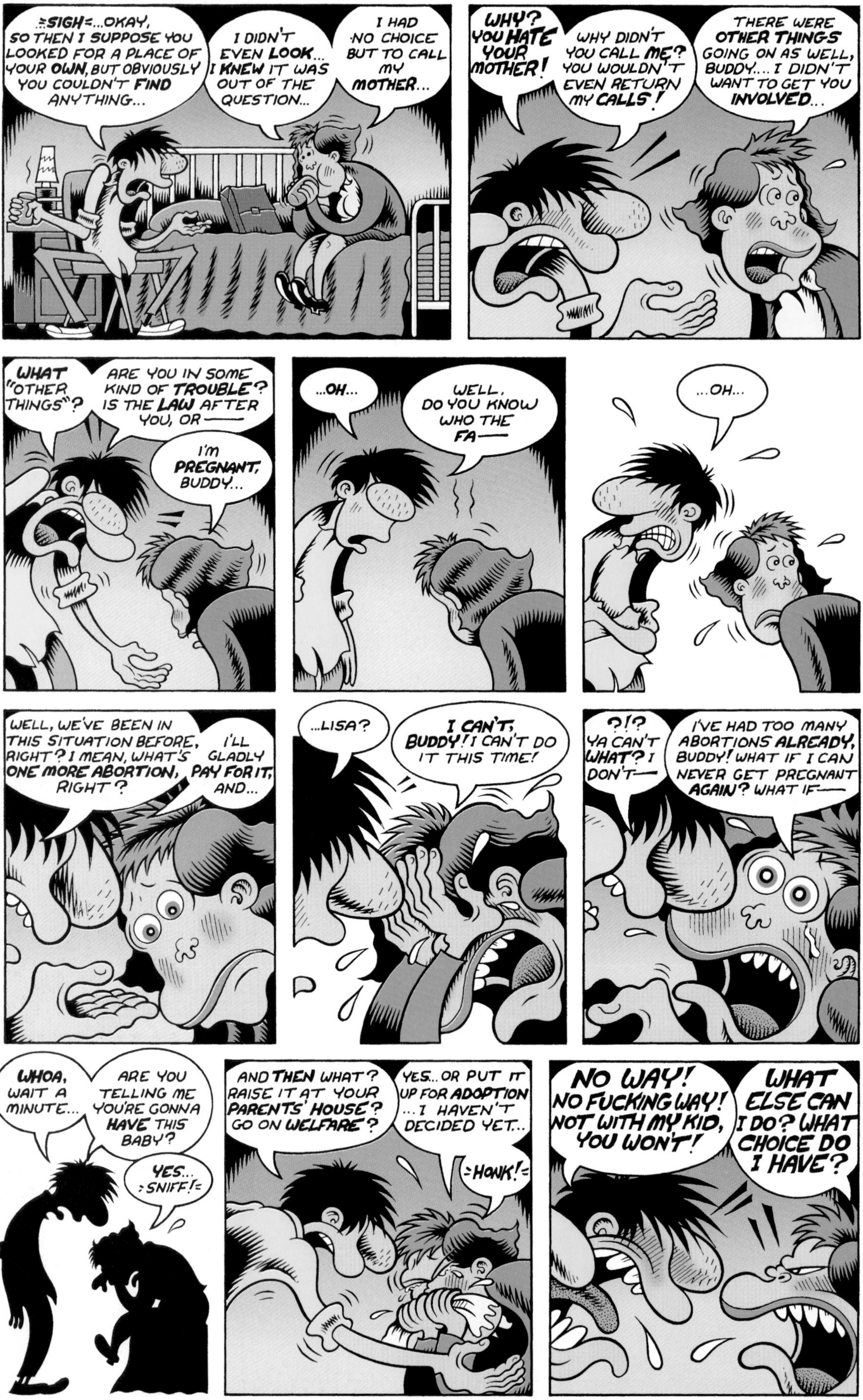

=SIGH=...OKAY, SO THEN I SUPPOSE YOU LOOKED FOR A PLACE OF YOUR OWN, BUT OBVIOUSLY YOU COULDN'T FIND ANYTHING...
I DIDN'T EVEN LOOK... I KNEW IT WAS OUT OF THE QUESTION...
I HAD NO CHOICE BUT TO CALL MY MOTHER...
WHY? YOU HATE YOUR MOTHER!
WHY DIDN'T YOU CALL ME? YOU WOULDN'T EVEN RETURN MY CALLS!
THERE WERE OTHER THINGS GOING ON AS WELL, BUDDY... I DIDN'T WANT TO GET YOU INVOLVED...
WHAT "OTHER THINGS"?
ARE YOU IN SOME KIND OF TROUBLE? IS THE LAW AFTER YOU, OR—
I'M PREGNANT, BUDDY...
...OH...
WELL, DO YOU KNOW WHO THE FA—
...OH...
WELL, WE'VE BEEN IN THIS SITUATION BEFORE, RIGHT? I MEAN, WHAT'S ONE MORE ABORTION, RIGHT?
I'LL GLADLY PAY FOR IT, AND...
...LISA?
I CAN'T, BUDDY! I CAN'T DO IT THIS TIME!
?!? YA CAN'T WHAT? I DON'T—
I'VE HAD TOO MANY ABORTIONS ALREADY, BUDDY! WHAT IF I CAN NEVER GET PREGNANT AGAIN? WHAT IF—
WHOA, WAIT A MINUTE...
ARE YOU TELLING ME YOU'RE GONNA HAVE THIS BABY?
YES... =SNIFF!=
AND THEN WHAT? RAISE IT AT YOUR PARENTS' HOUSE? GO ON WELFARE?
YES... OR PUT IT UP FOR ADOPTION ...I HAVEN'T DECIDED YET...
=HONK!=
NO WAY! NO FUCKING WAY! NOT WITH MY KID, YOU WON'T!
WHAT ELSE CAN I DO? WHAT CHOICE DO I HAVE?

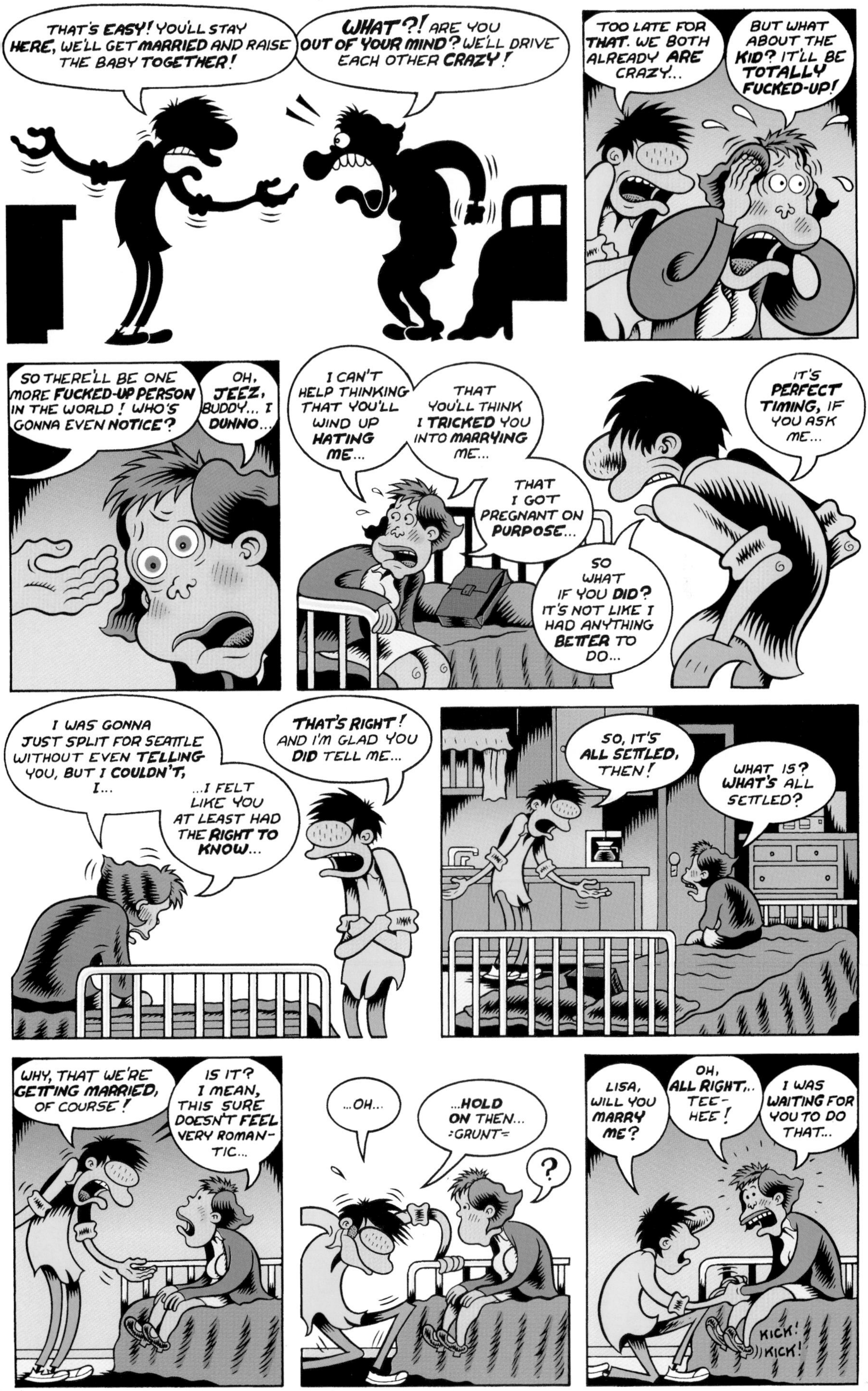
THAT'S EASY! YOU'LL STAY HERE, WE'LL GET MARRIED AND RAISE THE BABY TOGETHER!
WHAT?! ARE YOU OUT OF YOUR MIND? WE'LL DRIVE EACH OTHER CRAZY!
TOO LATE FOR THAT. WE BOTH ALREADY ARE CRAZY...
BUT WHAT ABOUT THE KID? IT'LL BE TOTALLY FUCKED-UP!
SO THERE'LL BE ONE MORE FUCKED-UP PERSON IN THE WORLD! WHO'S GONNA EVEN NOTICE?
OH, JEEZ, BUDDY... I DUNNO...
I CAN'T HELP THINKING THAT YOU'LL WIND UP HATING ME...
THAT YOU'LL THINK I TRICKED YOU INTO MARRYING ME...
THAT I GOT PREGNANT ON PURPOSE...
IT'S PERFECT TIMING, IF YOU ASK ME...
SO WHAT IF YOU DID? IT'S NOT LIKE I HAD ANYTHING BETTER TO DO...
I WAS GONNA JUST SPLIT FOR SEATTLE WITHOUT EVEN TELLING YOU, BUT I COULDN'T, I...
...I FELT LIKE YOU AT LEAST HAD THE RIGHT TO KNOW...
THAT'S RIGHT! AND I'M GLAD YOU DID TELL ME...
SO, IT'S ALL SETTLED, THEN!
WHAT IS? WHAT'S ALL SETTLED?
WHY, THAT WE'RE GETTING MARRIED, OF COURSE!
IS IT? I MEAN, THIS SURE DOESN'T FEEL VERY ROMAN-TIC...
...OH...
...HOLD ON THEN... =GRUNT=
?
LISA, WILL YOU MARRY ME?
OH, ALL RIGHT... TEE-HEE!
I WAS WAITING FOR YOU TO DO THAT...
KICK! KICK!

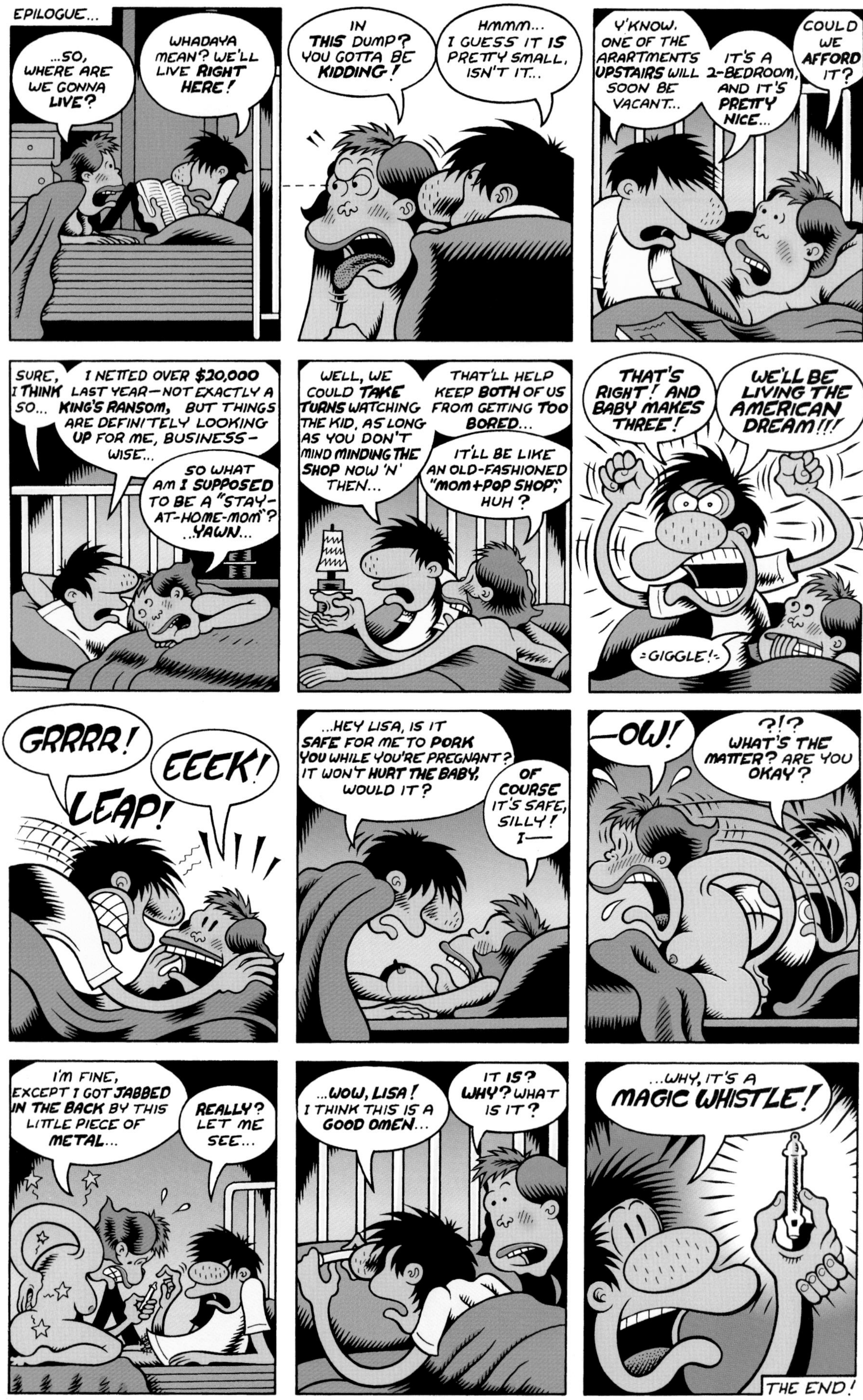
EPILOGUE...
...SO, WHERE ARE WE GONNA LIVE?
WHADAYA MEAN? WE'LL LIVE RIGHT HERE!
IN THIS DUMP? YOU GOTTA BE KIDDING!
HMMM... I GUESS IT IS PRETTY SMALL, ISN'T IT...
Y'KNOW, ONE OF THE APARTMENTS UPSTAIRS WILL SOON BE VACANT...
IT'S A 2-BEDROOM, AND IT'S PRETTY NICE...
COULD WE AFFORD IT?
SURE, I THINK SO...
I NETTED OVER $20,000 LAST YEAR—NOT EXACTLY A KING'S RANSOM, BUT THINGS ARE DEFINITELY LOOKING UP FOR ME, BUSINESS-WISE...
SO WHAT AM I SUPPOSED TO BE A "STAY-AT-HOME-MOM"? ...YAWN...
WELL, WE COULD TAKE TURNS WATCHING THE KID, AS LONG AS YOU DON'T MIND MINDING THE SHOP NOW 'N' THEN...
THAT'LL HELP KEEP BOTH OF US FROM GETTING TOO BORED...
IT'LL BE LIKE AN OLD-FASHIONED "MOM+POP SHOP," HUH?
THAT'S RIGHT! AND BABY MAKES THREE!
WE'LL BE LIVING THE AMERICAN DREAM!!!
=GIGGLE!=
GRRRR!
EEEK!
LEAP!
...HEY LISA, IS IT SAFE FOR ME TO PORK YOU WHILE YOU'RE PREGNANT? IT WON'T HURT THE BABY, WOULD IT?
OF COURSE IT'S SAFE, SILLY! I—
—OW!
?!? WHAT'S THE MATTER? ARE YOU OKAY?
I'M FINE, EXCEPT I GOT JABBED IN THE BACK BY THIS LITTLE PIECE OF METAL...
REALLY? LET ME SEE...
...WOW, LISA! I THINK THIS IS A GOOD OMEN...
IT IS? WHY? WHAT IS IT?
...WHY, IT'S A MAGIC WHISTLE!
THE END!

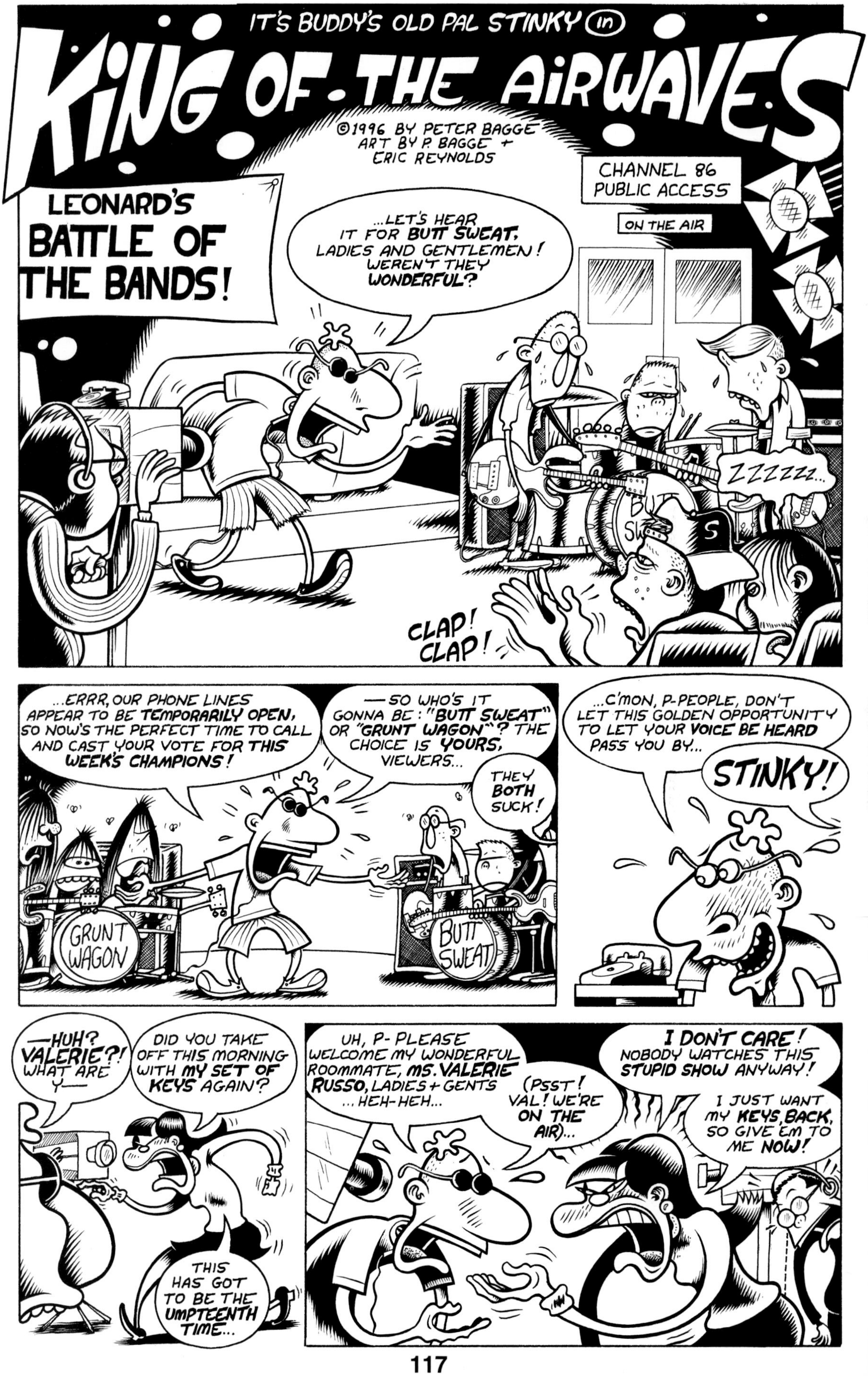
IT'S BUDDY'S OLD PAL STINKY in
KING OF THE AIRWAVES
©1996 BY PETER BAGGE
ART BY P. BAGGE + ERIC REYNOLDS
LEONARD'S BATTLE OF THE BANDS!
CHANNEL 86 PUBLIC ACCESS
ON THE AIR
...LET'S HEAR IT FOR BUTT SWEAT, LADIES AND GENTLEMEN! WEREN'T THEY WONDERFUL?
ZZZZZZ...
CLAP! CLAP!
...ERRR, OUR PHONE LINES APPEAR TO BE TEMPORARILY OPEN, SO NOW'S THE PERFECT TIME TO CALL AND CAST YOUR VOTE FOR THIS WEEK'S CHAMPIONS!
—SO WHO'S IT GONNA BE: "BUTT SWEAT" OR "GRUNT WAGON"? THE CHOICE IS YOURS, VIEWERS...
THEY BOTH SUCK!
GRUNT WAGON
BUTT SWEAT
...C'MON, P-PEOPLE, DON'T LET THIS GOLDEN OPPORTUNITY TO LET YOUR VOICE BE HEARD PASS YOU BY...
STINKY!
—HUH? VALERIE?! WHAT ARE Y—
DID YOU TAKE OFF THIS MORNING WITH MY SET OF KEYS AGAIN?
THIS HAS GOT TO BE THE UMPTEENTH TIME...
UH, P-PLEASE WELCOME MY WONDERFUL ROOMMATE, MS. VALERIE RUSSO, LADIES + GENTS ...HEH-HEH...
(PSST! VAL! WE'RE ON THE AIR)...
I DON'T CARE! NOBODY WATCHES THIS STUPID SHOW ANYWAY!
I JUST WANT MY KEYS BACK, SO GIVE 'EM TO ME NOW!

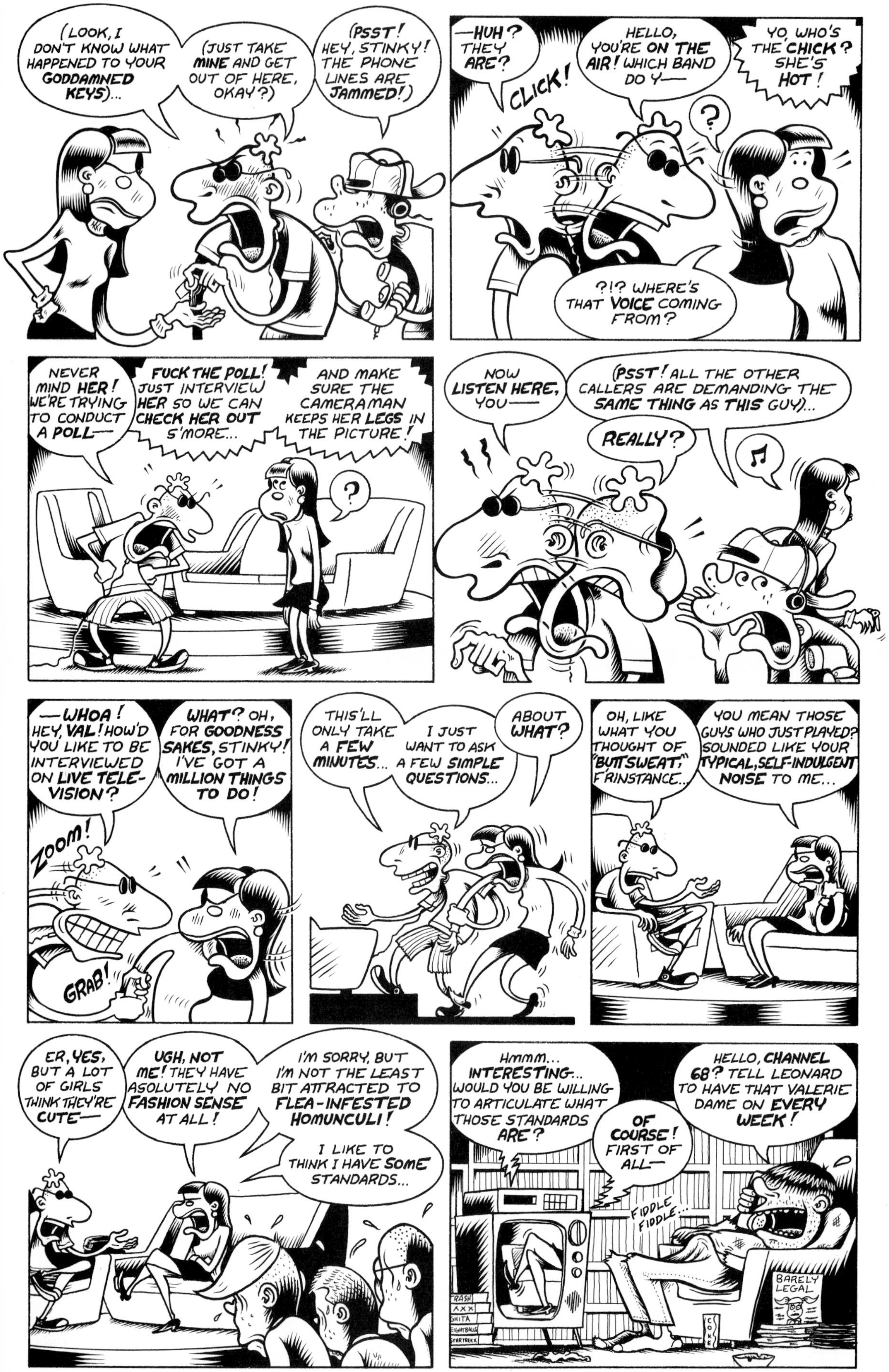
(LOOK, I DON'T KNOW WHAT HAPPENED TO YOUR GODDAMNED KEYS)...
(JUST TAKE MINE AND GET OUT OF HERE, OKAY?)
(PSST! HEY, STINKY! THE PHONE LINES ARE JAMMED!)
—HUH? THEY ARE?
CLICK!
HELLO, YOU'RE ON THE AIR! WHICH BAND DO Y—
?
YO, WHO'S THE CHICK? SHE'S HOT!
?!? WHERE'S THAT VOICE COMING FROM?
NEVER MIND HER! WE'RE TRYING TO CONDUCT A POLL—
FUCK THE POLL! JUST INTERVIEW HER SO WE CAN CHECK HER OUT S'MORE...
AND MAKE SURE THE CAMERAMAN KEEPS HER LEGS IN THE PICTURE!
?
NOW LISTEN HERE, YOU—
(PSST! ALL THE OTHER CALLERS ARE DEMANDING THE SAME THING AS THIS GUY)...
REALLY?
♪
—WHOA! HEY, VAL! HOW'D YOU LIKE TO BE INTERVIEWED ON LIVE TELE-VISION?
WHAT? OH, FOR GOODNESS SAKES, STINKY! I'VE GOT A MILLION THINGS TO DO!
ZOOM!
GRAB!
THIS'LL ONLY TAKE A FEW MINUTES...
I JUST WANT TO ASK A FEW SIMPLE QUESTIONS...
ABOUT WHAT?
OH, LIKE WHAT YOU THOUGHT OF "BUTTSWEAT," F'RINSTANCE...
YOU MEAN THOSE GUYS WHO JUST PLAYED? SOUNDED LIKE YOUR TYPICAL, SELF-INDULGENT NOISE TO ME...
ER, YES, BUT A LOT OF GIRLS THINK THEY'RE CUTE—
UGH, NOT ME! THEY HAVE ASOLUTELY NO FASHION SENSE AT ALL!
I'M SORRY, BUT I'M NOT THE LEAST BIT ATTRACTED TO FLEA-INFESTED HOMUNCULI!
I LIKE TO THINK I HAVE SOME STANDARDS...
Hmmm... INTERESTING... WOULD YOU BE WILLING TO ARTICULATE WHAT THOSE STANDARDS ARE?
OF COURSE! FIRST OF ALL—
HELLO, CHANNEL 68? TELL LEONARD TO HAVE THAT VALERIE DAME ON EVERY WEEK!
FIDDLE FIDDLE...
TRASH
XXX
SHITA
EIGHTBALLS
STARTREK
COKE
BARELY LEGAL

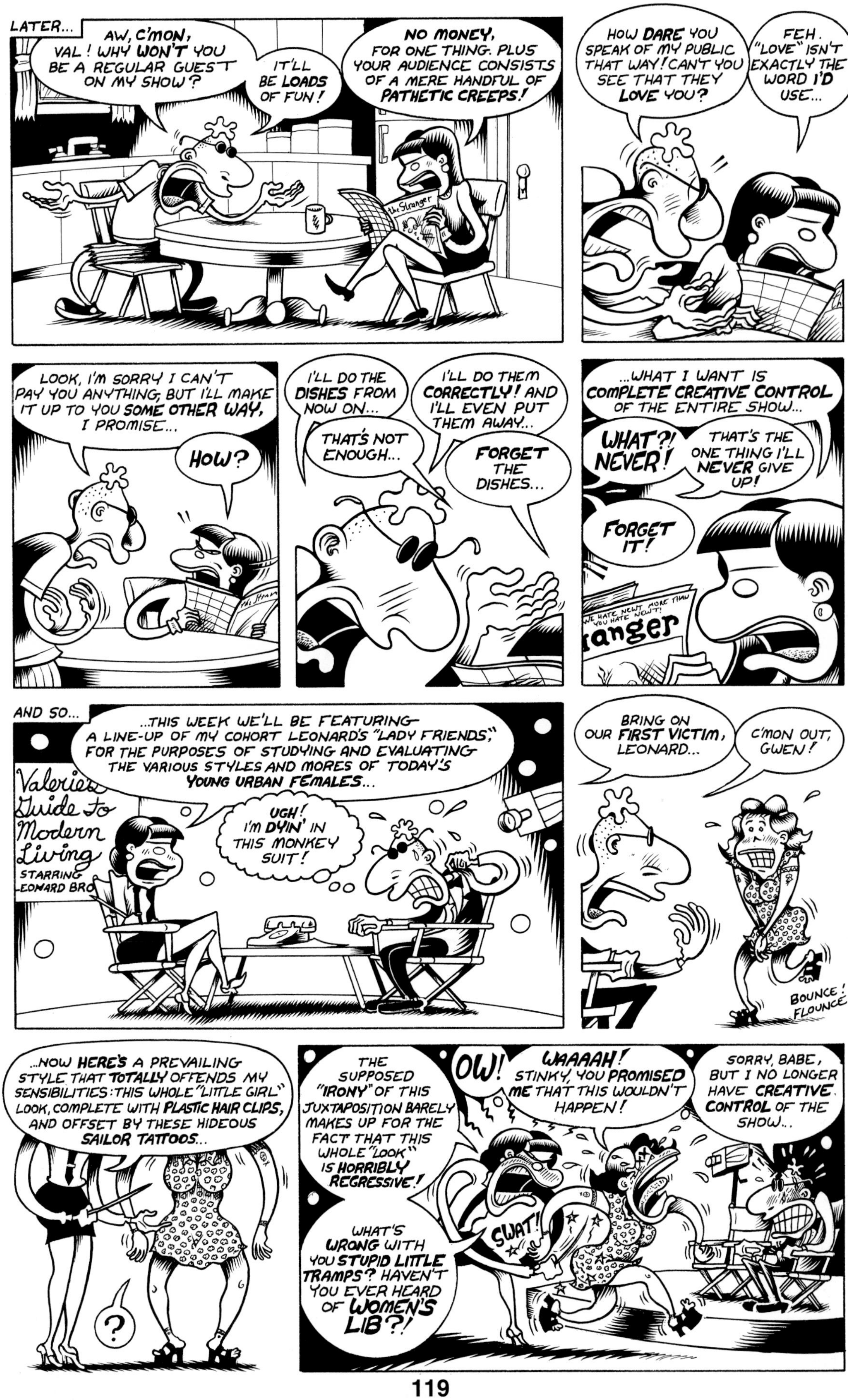
LATER...
AW, C'MON, VAL! WHY WON'T YOU BE A REGULAR GUEST ON MY SHOW?
IT'LL BE LOADS OF FUN!
NO MONEY, FOR ONE THING. PLUS YOUR AUDIENCE CONSISTS OF A MERE HANDFUL OF PATHETIC CREEPS!
the Stranger
HOW DARE YOU SPEAK OF MY PUBLIC THAT WAY! CAN'T YOU SEE THAT THEY LOVE YOU?
FEH. "LOVE" ISN'T EXACTLY THE WORD I'D USE...
LOOK, I'M SORRY I CAN'T PAY YOU ANYTHING, BUT I'LL MAKE IT UP TO YOU SOME OTHER WAY, I PROMISE...
HOW?
I'LL DO THE DISHES FROM NOW ON...
THAT'S NOT ENOUGH...
I'LL DO THEM CORRECTLY! AND I'LL EVEN PUT THEM AWAY...
FORGET THE DISHES...
...WHAT I WANT IS COMPLETE CREATIVE CONTROL OF THE ENTIRE SHOW...
WHAT?! NEVER!
THAT'S THE ONE THING I'LL NEVER GIVE UP!
FORGET IT!
WE HATE NEWT MORE THAN YOU HATE NEWT!
ranger
AND SO...
...THIS WEEK WE'LL BE FEATURING—A LINE-UP OF MY COHORT LEONARD'S "LADY FRIENDS," FOR THE PURPOSES OF STUDYING AND EVALUATING THE VARIOUS STYLES AND MORES OF TODAY'S YOUNG URBAN FEMALES...
Valerie's Guide to Modern Living
STARRING LEONARD BRO
UGH! I'M DYIN' IN THIS MONKEY SUIT!
BRING ON OUR FIRST VICTIM, LEONARD...
C'MON OUT, GWEN!
BOUNCE! FLOUNCE!
...NOW HERE'S A PREVAILING STYLE THAT TOTALLY OFFENDS MY SENSIBILITIES: THIS WHOLE "LITTLE GIRL" LOOK, COMPLETE WITH PLASTIC HAIR CLIPS, AND OFFSET BY THESE HIDEOUS SAILOR TATTOOS...
?
THE SUPPOSED "IRONY" OF THIS JUXTAPOSITION BARELY MAKES UP FOR THE FACT THAT THIS WHOLE "LOOK" IS HORRIBLY REGRESSIVE!
WHAT'S WRONG WITH YOU STUPID LITTLE TRAMPS? HAVEN'T YOU EVER HEARD OF WOMEN'S LIB?!
OW!
SWAT!
WAAAAH! STINKY, YOU PROMISED ME THAT THIS WOULDN'T HAPPEN!
SORRY, BABE, BUT I NO LONGER HAVE CREATIVE CONTROL OF THE SHOW...

LATER IN THE PROGRAM...

...NOW, CONSIDERING THIS IS YOUR *FIRST* "DATE," WHO DO YOU FEEL SHOULD BE OBLIGED TO PAY...

—LEONARD?

OH, UHHH...THE GOVERNMENT?

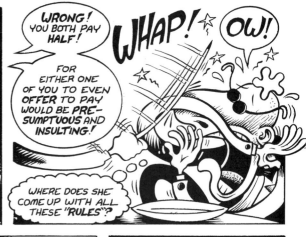

WRONG! YOU BOTH PAY HALF!

FOR EITHER ONE OF YOU TO EVEN OFFER TO PAY WOULD BE PRE-SUMPTUOUS AND INSULTING!

WHAP! OW!

WHERE DOES SHE COME UP WITH ALL THESE "RULES"?

OKAY NOW, EDNA, YOU START THE *CONVER-SATION*...

OKAY, UMMM...

"...DON'T YOU JUST LOVE THE FILMS OF QUENTIN TARANTINO?"

WRONG!

HOW UTTERLY CLICHE!

WHAP! OW!

GIMME THAT THING!

?!?

SNATCH!

NOBODY HITS ME WITH NO GOD-DAMNED POINTER, YOU *BITCH!*

AND NOBODY USES THE "B-WORD" ON MY SHOW, YOU *CUNT!*

OH BOY! CAT FIGHT!

THIS IS GONNA BE GREAT!

SOB! I QUIT!

RUB! RUB!

I CAN'T TAKE ANY MORE OF THIS *ABUSE*...

BESIDES, NO ONE'S GONNA *MISS* ME ANYWAY...

GOUGE! KICK! SCRATCH! POKE? PINCH!

WEEKS LATER...

...BEFORE WE PROCEED WITH TODAY'S *LESSON,* PERHAPS WE SHOULD TAKE A FEW CALLS...

HELLO, YOU'RE ON THE AIR!

YO, VAL, WHAT'S UP WITH THAT GET-UP YOU'RE WEARING?

Modern Living

?!? WHAT DO YOU *MEAN,* "WHAT'S UP WITH IT"? WHAT'S *WRONG* WITH IT?

YOU USED TO WEAR *SHORT SKIRTS* THAT SHOWED OFF YOUR LEGS, BUT NOW YOU'RE WEARING PANTS THAT'RE SO *BAGGY* THAT I CAN'T EVEN MAKE OUT THE SHAPE OF YOUR *ASS* ANYMORE!

120

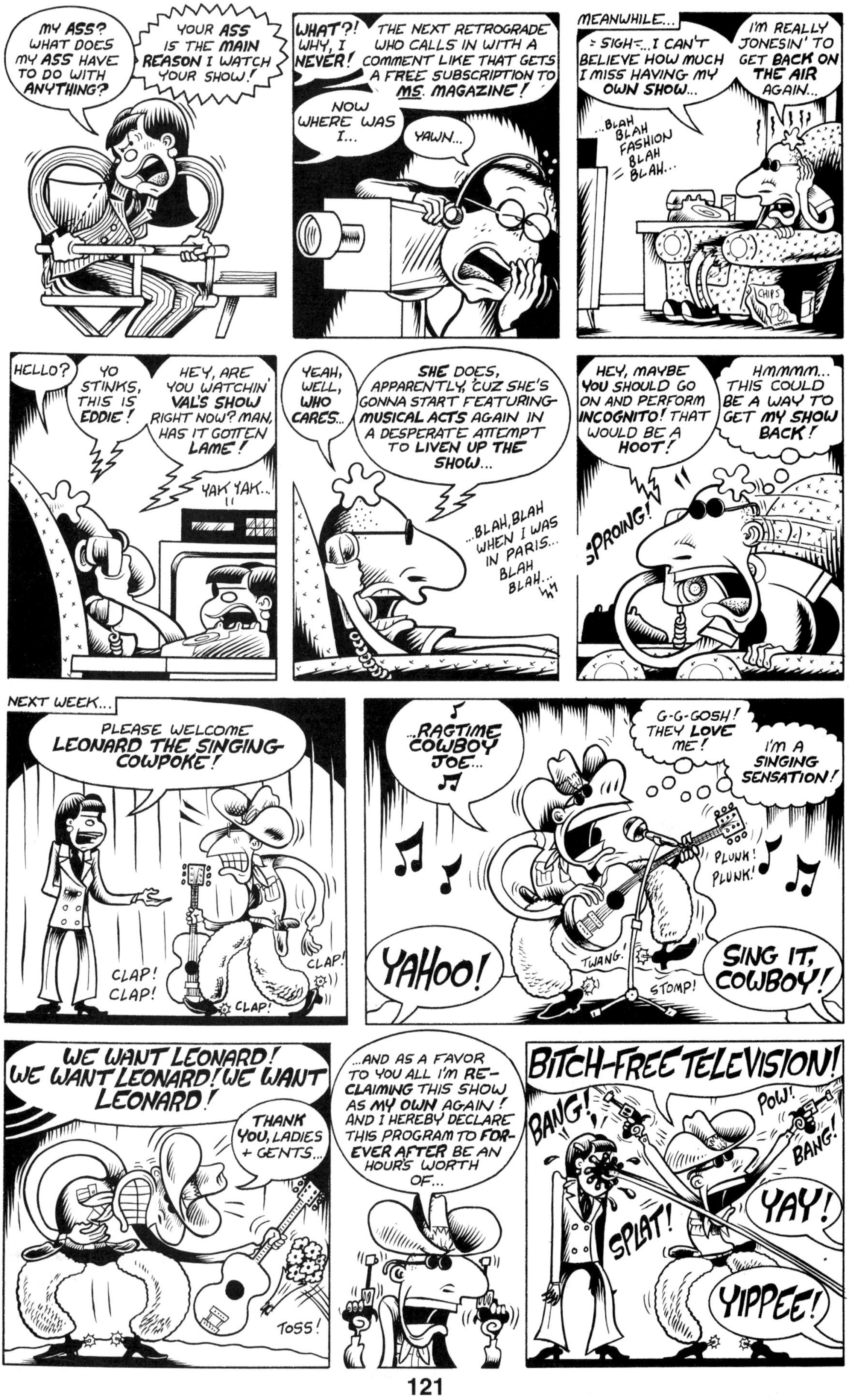

MY ASS? WHAT DOES MY ASS HAVE TO DO WITH ANYTHING?
YOUR ASS IS THE MAIN REASON I WATCH YOUR SHOW!
WHAT?! WHY, I NEVER!
THE NEXT RETROGRADE WHO CALLS IN WITH A COMMENT LIKE THAT GETS A FREE SUBSCRIPTION TO MS. MAGAZINE!
NOW WHERE WAS I...
YAWN...
MEANWHILE...
SIGH... I CAN'T BELIEVE HOW MUCH I MISS HAVING MY OWN SHOW...
I'M REALLY JONESIN' TO GET BACK ON THE AIR AGAIN...
...BLAH BLAH FASHION BLAH BLAH...
CHIPS
HELLO?
YO STINKS, THIS IS EDDIE!
HEY, ARE YOU WATCHIN' VAL'S SHOW RIGHT NOW? MAN, HAS IT GOTTEN LAME!
YAK YAK...
YEAH, WELL, WHO CARES...
SHE DOES, APPARENTLY, 'CUZ SHE'S GONNA START FEATURING MUSICAL ACTS AGAIN IN A DESPERATE ATTEMPT TO LIVEN UP THE SHOW...
...BLAH, BLAH WHEN I WAS IN PARIS... BLAH BLAH...
HEY, MAYBE YOU SHOULD GO ON AND PERFORM INCOGNITO! THAT WOULD BE A HOOT!
HMMMM... THIS COULD BE A WAY TO GET MY SHOW BACK!
SPROING!
NEXT WEEK...
PLEASE WELCOME LEONARD THE SINGING COWPOKE!
CLAP! CLAP!
CLAP!
CLAP!
...RAGTIME COWBOY JOE...
G-G-GOSH! THEY LOVE ME!
I'M A SINGING SENSATION!
PLUNK! PLUNK!
YAHOO!
TWANG!
STOMP!
SING IT, COWBOY!
WE WANT LEONARD! WE WANT LEONARD! WE WANT LEONARD!
THANK YOU, LADIES + GENTS...
TOSS!
...AND AS A FAVOR TO YOU ALL I'M RE-CLAIMING THIS SHOW AS MY OWN AGAIN! AND I HEREBY DECLARE THIS PROGRAM TO FOR-EVER AFTER BE AN HOUR'S WORTH OF...
BITCH-FREE TELEVISION!
BANG!
POW!
BANG!
SPLAT!
YAY!
YIPPEE!